WHITE SHOE

ALSO BY JOHN OLLER

The Swamp Fox:
How Francis Marion Saved the American Revolution

American Queen:
The Rise and Fall of Kate Chase Sprague—
Civil War "Belle of the North" and Gilded Age Woman of Scandal

An All-American Murder

"One Firm":
A Short History of Willkie Farr & Gallagher LLP, 1888-

Jean Arthur: The Actress Nobody Knew

JOHN OLLER

WHITE SHOE

How a New Breed of Wall Street Lawyers
Changed Big Business and
the American Century

DUTTON

DUTTON
An imprint of Penguin Random House LLC
penguinrandomhouse.com

LIBRARY OF CONGRESS CATALOGING-IN-PUBLICATION DATA
Names: Oller, John, author.
Title: White shoe: how a new breed of Wall Street lawyers changed big
business and the American century / John Oller.
Description: New York, New York: Dutton, an imprint of Penguin Random House
LLC, [2019] | Includes bibliographical references and index.
Identifiers: LCCN 2018029007 (print) | LCCN 2018032298 (ebook) |
ISBN 9781524743277 (ebook) | ISBN 9781524743253 (hc)
Subjects: LCSH: Corporate lawyers—United States—History. | Corporation
law—United States—History. | Commercial law—United States—History. |
Wall Street (New York, N.Y.) | Cravath, Paul D. (Paul Drennan), 1861–1940.
Classification: LCC KF299.15 (ebook) | LCC KF299.15 O45 2019 (print) |
DDC 346.73/066—dc23
LC record available at https://lccn.loc.gov/2018029007

Paperback ISBN: 978-1-5247-4326-0

Book design by Francesca Belanger

149061426

Again, to my family

CONTENTS

WHITE SHOE

Prologue
New High Priests for a New Century

In 1899, when Paul Cravath became a partner in the prestigious Wall Street law firm cofounded by William H. Seward, Abraham Lincoln's secretary of state, the century wasn't the only thing about to change. The standard paper clip had just been invented, and rubber bands had recently come into common use. Although that was progress in office supplies, the Seward firm, like many others, was stuck in old ways: There was no filing system, and the index was kept in an office boy's head.

For all their supposed smarts, lawyers have often lagged in adapting to technological change. After the first elevator was installed in the Seward firm in 1885, head partner Clarence Seward refused to use it. If he didn't feel like climbing the two flights of stairs to his office, he just stayed home.

When the first telephones came to New York City in 1878, lawyers considered it unprofessional to use them for business calls. Many doubted their privacy, perhaps because there was a single central exchange called "Law" for all lawyers in the boroughs. As late as 1911, recalled John Foster Dulles, who joined the prestigious Sullivan & Cromwell firm that year, "some of the older partners felt that the only dignified way of communication between members of the legal profession was for them to write each other in Spencerian script, and to have the message thus expressed delivered by hand."

Lawyers were also slow to accept the typewriter, commercialized in the 1870s. Until the mid-1880s, documents were drawn up in longhand by men who stood or sat on tall stools at high slanting desks. The best penman would write page after page and pass them down the line to scriveners, who laboriously copied them at long tables.

Stenographers who could take dictation were not used, because they were seen as intrusive. Letters circulated in their original form and were accompanied by earnest requests to return them as soon as possible. Only when the demands of the expanding legal profession finally became too much to handle in the old manner, around the turn of the century, did firms begin hiring female stenographers, secretaries, and typists to replace male copyists.

Paul Cravath, then thirty-seven and the Seward firm's newest partner, saw a need for change. The first thing he did upon joining the firm was to begin a filing system, hiring a female librarian from Columbia University to run it. But it was really the entire law office system he wanted to revamp. He realized that in the twentieth century, law firms had to become more like their most successful corporate clients: organized, efficient, and capable of expanding.

For most of the nineteenth century, the typical law office was a solo practice or a two-man partnership with a few loosely affiliated clerks. Partners shared office space and expenses but not each other's legal fees. Young men worked as clerks without pay for a few years, performing secretarial duties in exchange for a desk and access to the partners' library. Essentially free agents, they made their living by seeking out cases and clients of their own. Often they had not attended law school or taken any written bar examination before they were admitted to practice.

Law clerks received no systematic education or training at the firm; instead, their learning came from reading law books, copying papers, and observing the partners at work. Frequently the clerks were relatives or friends of the partners or the firm's clients and no one expected them to contribute materially to the actual legal work of the firm.

But to Cravath, the whole arrangement lacked discipline. It was tainted by nepotism, created divided loyalties, and produced mediocrity, not excellence. He decided there had to be a better way. He would hire the best law students, carefully train them, pay them to secure their allegiance, work them to the bone, promote them to partnership if they proved themselves, and send them on their way if they did not. As partners they would collaborate and share profits. It would become known as the "Cravath system"—a set of business management principles still in use today by law firms and consulting companies.

The system was perfectly geared to the type of lawyer Cravath had become. By the turn of the century he was one of the growing cadre of corporation or "office" lawyers who helped create the foundations of modern American business. Working hand in glove with their corporate clients, visionary lawyers such as Cravath were devising and implementing legal strategies that would drive the business world throughout the twentieth century. They headed what became known as "white shoe" firms, named for the white buck shoes worn by generations of Ivy League college men who, as members of the WASP elite, went on to run the leading law, banking, and accounting firms on Wall Street.

From the early nineteenth century to the Gilded Age, which began in the 1870s, the elite members of the bar were those charismatic lawyers whose rhetorical skills enabled them to advocate persuasively in courtrooms. The classic example was the great orator and statesman Daniel Webster, who argued more than 150 cases before the US Supreme Court and won many early landmark decisions. Another familiar image was that of the prairie lawyer Abraham Lincoln, who rode the circuit around the little towns of Illinois, making folksy appeals to juries in disputes over cows, hogs, small-time commercial transactions, and the occasional criminal case. According to legend, he almost always won.

At least through the Civil War, businessmen sought out lawyers only when they were ready to fight in court. Clients gave little thought to using lawyers as preventive measures. But the growing industrialization and urbanization of the country in the post–Civil War era, and the increasing number, complexity, and sheer size of corporations, called for a new kind of lawyer—a practical man of business whose skills were more those of a negotiator, a facilitator, and a drafter of documents than those of a trial advocate.

This new breed of high-powered corporation lawyer, originating in New York City around 1890 and flourishing there to this day, made his chief domain the conference room rather than the courtroom. The prototype was

Francis Lynde Stetson, a courtly yet steely gentleman known as the "attorney general" for the great financier J. P. Morgan. Stetson helped Morgan form the largest companies in the world—including the biggest of them all, US Steel—and tried his best to keep his famous client out of trouble, which was no easy task.

There was also William Nelson Cromwell, the silver-tongued business lawyer from Brooklyn who specialized in forming giant new corporations and resuscitating old ones when they went bust. Some critics thought he played close to the line, but none could doubt his resourcefulness. For his role in creating the Panama Canal—and the revolution that led to it—he would become the best known of all the early Wall Street lawyers.

Elihu Root, a patrician of New England stock, was the quintessential wise man who glided easily between the highest levels of government in Washington and his private legal practice in New York. An elitist, pro-corporate member of the Republican establishment, and a strong exponent of an expansionist foreign policy, Root was as responsible as anyone, save the presidents he served under, for transforming America into a world power.

Samuel Untermyer, the rare Jewish Wall Street attorney, was the anti-white shoe corporate lawyer. He became a millionaire representing large corporations, then turned on them with a vengeance to become a populist crusader for business reforms. The fresh, homegrown orchids he always wore in his lapel belied the ferociousness with which he attacked his big business antagonists.

Then there was Cravath, the youngest of the group, who launched a new model of law firm management that would be copied by nearly all major white shoe firms. Indeed, the name Cravath would become synonymous with the large Wall Street "law factory" that came into existence in the early part of the twentieth century.

<hr />

Paul Drennan Cravath was a classic small-town boy made good. He was born in July 1861, a week before the First Battle of Bull Run, in the tiny hamlet of Berlin Heights, Ohio, a few miles south of Lake Erie. Unusual for the time, both his parents were college graduates, from nearby Oberlin College, the first college in the country to admit women and blacks. Cravath's father, Erastus, was a Congregationalist minister and abolitionist who made the betterment of the African American his life's work. After the war he helped found a school for newly freed blacks in Nashville, Tennessee, that became Fisk University, where he served as president for twenty years. Accompanied by his family, including fourteen-year-old Paul, Erastus Cravath took the Fisk Jubilee Singers on a European tour to raise funds for the university.

Cravath's mother, Ruth Anna, a strong Quaker, was nearly Erastus's opposite. A no-nonsense woman, and something of a worrywart, she instilled in young Paul a sense of pragmatism to complement his father's idealism, as well as a love of books and music.

Paul Cravath received his early education at Brooklyn Polytechnic Institute while the family briefly lived in Brooklyn after the war. He attended college preparatory school in Geneva, Switzerland, during the family's European excursion and toured Germany with his father.

After graduating from the religiously oriented Oberlin in 1882 (the faculty described him as "brilliant" but a "mischief-maker"), Paul eschewed the evangelical life to pursue his ambition to become a lawyer. He studied in a law office in Minneapolis, where he intended to settle; then, after an attack of typhoid fever, he became a salesman for the Standard Oil Company in Minnesota. With the money he earned he went east to study at Columbia Law School in New York, graduating at the top of his class in 1886.

Upon graduation, Cravath took an apprentice clerkship with the Manhattan firm of Carter, Hornblower & Byrne, headed by Walter S. Carter, a leader of the New York bar. Dubbed by one legal historian as "a collector of young masters" and "the progenitor of many law firms," Carter developed a reputation for attracting the best law school graduates from Columbia and Harvard, many of whom went on to illustrious careers of their own. Among them was Charles Evans Hughes, who married Carter's daughter and would later serve as governor of New York, US secretary of state, chief justice of the US Supreme Court, and 1916 Republican candidate for president.

Carter's office was described as "a veritable nursery for young lawyers of talent." Another of Carter's "kids," as he called them, was George Wickersham, President William Howard Taft's future attorney general. Wickersham would become known as "the scourge of Wall Street" for his aggressive prosecution of antitrust cases, angering some of the same companies he had once represented.

Carter's younger partner, the elfin William Hornblower, was nominated to the Supreme Court in 1893, at age forty-two, by his friend Grover Cleveland. Opinionated and headstrong, and a voice against "political quackery," Hornblower saw his confirmation fail, a victim of private animosities. But he did frequently argue before the Supreme Court, even honeymooning in Washington, DC, so his new bride could watch his argument.

Hornblower was an irritable and difficult man, at least as Hughes remembered him many years later. Hughes never forgot how, as a young lawyer proofreading one of Hornblower's eloquent briefs, he was castigated for an egregious error. Hughes misread Hornblower's handwriting, with the result that the phrase "seven thousand dollars in CASH" came out in print as "seven thousand dollars in COAL."

Hornblower was one of the best lawyers in the city, though, and he came to believe he deserved a larger share of the Carter firm's profits. In 1887 he and Byrne broke with Carter to form their own firm. They took the Carter firm's more lucrative clients with them and asked Cravath to join them. But young Cravath chose to stay with his mentor Carter, who offered him a partnership together with Hughes.

To cement the deal, Hughes took Cravath to dinner at Martinelli's, one of the city's top Italian restaurants, and over a bottle of Chianti told him they would name the firm Carter, Hughes & Cravath. Banging his fist on the table, Cravath (who apparently had not been listening closely) exclaimed, "Make it Carter, Hughes *& Cravath*, and I'll join." On January 1, 1888, the newly christened firm opened for business at 346 Broadway in the New York Life Building, near City Hall and the courthouses.

Only a prodigy such as Cravath could have been named a partner in a respected New York law firm a mere year and a half after admission to the bar. His extroverted personality, supreme self-confidence, and imposing physical appearance all worked in his favor. At six feet four, 240 pounds, he had a huge head accentuated by small circular eyeglasses, and thick, wavy brown hair. In the words of one of his partners, he was a man of "massive elegance" and "glittering presence."

Soon enough Cravath's personal magnetism helped him land his first major client. Cravath's maternal uncle was an officer in some of George Westinghouse's companies in Pittsburgh, and he introduced his nephew to the famed inventor of the railway air brake. A few years earlier, Westinghouse had become interested in the emerging field of electrical power. Now, Westinghouse was seeking someone talented and energetic enough to represent him in his increasingly bitter legal battles with Thomas Edison. It would make Cravath's name within New York's legal and business community.

Paul Cravath, Francis Lynde Stetson, William Nelson Cromwell, Elihu Root, and a handful of other elite members of the New York bar were instrumental in forging the great capitalist enterprises that emerged in late Gilded Age America and continued their growth into the following century. Their influence was felt mainly during that period in American history, from roughly 1890 to 1916, known as the Progressive Era and encompassing the Roosevelt and Taft presidencies and Wilson's first term. During this period, and extending through World War I, the basic elements of America's liberal democratic order took root: corporate industrial capitalism, the administrative-regulatory state, and an internationalist foreign policy.

The story of the early white shoe lawyers has rarely been told, and never in assembled form. To some extent they have been dismissed or denigrated as mere tools of the oft-maligned robber barons. And there is some validity to the charge. As handmaidens to their corporate clients, these lawyers were architects of the monopolistic new corporations so despised by many. They also acted as guardians who helped the kings of industry fight off what they considered to be government overreaching. Depending on one's point of view, the original Wall Street lawyers taught their clients either how to circumvent restrictive legislation or, as Samuel Untermyer put it, how to keep "prayerfully within the law." Popular humorist Finley Peter Dunne said the corporation lawyer could take a law that looked like a stone wall to a layman and turn it into a triumphal arch.

And yet the excesses of those years tend to obscure these lawyers' achievements. They devised new, more flexible forms of borrowing and financing that provided lubrication for the growth of American business. They also made it easier for bankrupt companies to rehabilitate themselves financially and get back on their feet following the economic panics and depressions that so frequently afflicted the nation in those years. They helped create a New York City transportation system without equal in the world. As one legal scholar put it, many decades after their heyday had passed, "In a . . . Cromwell, a Cravath, or a Stetson, we shall find builders of American society as intellectually bold as a John Marshall whose molding of Constitutional interpretation and whose fashioning of the Union are familiar to all of us."

The issue that consumed the nation during the Progressive Era was the concentration of wealth and power in the hands of a small group of plutocrats who controlled such industries as oil, steel, tobacco, banking, and the railroads. And in the debates over this issue, the leading Wall Street lawyers had a major voice. Although resistant to radical reform, the most influential of them came to accept the need for more extensive market regulation to prevent the abuses of the past and to increase trust in the system. They recognized that the law had not kept pace with the nation's astoundingly rapid industrial growth and that new rules were needed so the law might catch up with economic reality.

Given their druthers, men such as J. P. Morgan and John D. Rockefeller would have preferred no rules at all constraining their business behavior. It was left to their lawyers to check their baser impulses and to navigate them through the maze of a new, more progressive legal regime. The top corporate lawyers pushed their clients away from a Wild West mentality toward greater transparency and concern for investors, and thereby served as a mediating and stabilizing force in a time of turbulent change. Having helped create the vast new impersonal corporations, the great Wall Street lawyers became part of the effort to tame them.

To help harness the growth of corporate capitalism, some of the most talented private practitioners on Wall Street took on active reform roles in government, often shuttling between private practice and public service. Who better, for example, than a Charles Evans Hughes, who had represented major life insurance companies, to expose corruption within the life insurance industry through a public investigation? And what better attorney general to prosecute big antitrust cases than George Wickersham, who had made a practice of defending large corporations before he entered Taft's cabinet?

The white shoe lawyers also exerted their influence in foreign affairs. Almost all of them strongly supported American intervention in World War I. Wall Street lawyers assisted their clients in supplying and financing the Allied war effort and pushed for American "preparedness." Paul Cravath and some of his brethren went to Europe on wartime missions and, in the course of their work, put themselves in harm's way. A number of white shoe lawyers, including a young John Foster Dulles (a protégé of Cromwell's and a future secretary of state), also helped negotiate the Treaty of Versailles, which ended the war, and actively participated in the debates over America's entry into the League of Nations.

Both at home and abroad, the white shoe lawyers were at the forefront of what has been called the "search for order" that characterized the period from 1890 to 1920 and led to the creation of a new organizational society. They began by imposing structure and efficiency on their own private law firms. They helped create the legal system that governs corporate behavior to this day. And they laid the foundations for an international order that eventually took hold.

In doing so, the white shoe lawyers helped shape the new American century.

Chapter 1

Boy Wonder

Paul Cravath was only twenty-six and barely out of law school when George Westinghouse hired him to take on the world's most famous inventor, Thomas Alva Edison.

The Pittsburgh-based Westinghouse, then in his thirties, was already well known for his invention of the railroad air brake and his innovations in railway switching and signaling. Reserved and courteous in public, charmingly blunt in private, he was driven by an idealistic desire to improve the lot of his fellow man. Although a forceful and successful entrepreneur, he disdained financiers and moneymen. He paid his employees beyond the going rate, gave them pensions and days off, and provided a safe working environment. An engineer's engineer, he pursued his work with boundless energy, imagination, and resourcefulness. By the mid-1880s Westinghouse had thrown himself fully into the burgeoning industry of electrical power and was looking forward to a free and fair contest over how best to distribute it to people.

Westinghouse's rival in that endeavor was Thomas Edison, the Wizard of Menlo Park and world-renowned inventor of the light bulb and phonograph. Just a few months younger than Westinghouse, Edison cultivated a folksy manner that belied a ruthless win-at-all-costs attitude. A garrulous man who quite enjoyed his celebrity status, Edison had a genius for self-promotion and moneymaking in addition to invention. He resented the intrusion of Westinghouse—a railway engineer—into a field that Edison had pioneered and felt belonged to him alone.

Westinghouse and Edison faced off in two separate but related disputes: One, the light bulb war, concerned Edison's claim that Westinghouse, among many other competitors, was infringing on his 1879 incandescent light bulb patent. Edison filed hundreds of patent suits against Westinghouse, and Cravath was charged with their defense. The light bulb war would drag on for years because a large part of Westinghouse's strategy, and hence Cravath's job, was to stall for time until Edison's patent expired in 1894.

But while the highly technical patent litigation brought Cravath steady business, it was the second war—the so-called War of (Electric) Currents—that first brought Cravath to public attention. This one was less a legal battle than a full-scale commercial war, fought on many fronts, that pitted Westinghouse's alternating current (AC) transmission system against Edison's direct current (DC) system. The winner would determine how electricity would be delivered to homes and businesses in the coming century—and guarantee billions for its parent company.

The Westinghouse AC system was based on the innovations of an eccentric genius, Nikola Tesla, the Serbian inventor whose patents Westinghouse licensed. Under this system, alternating current was transmitted at high voltage (1,000 to 2,000 volts) from a central generating station over very long distances for use in the bright arc lamps that lit city streets, including New York's Great White Way, starting in 1880. At the point of commercial or residential consumption, transformers reduced the current to low voltage (50 watts) to light indoor incandescent lamps and bulbs.

By contrast, the Edison DC system ran at 110 volts, which was insufficient to illuminate large outdoor spaces and could not deliver current to consumers more than a mile from each of the many generating plants Edison placed in the middle of dense population centers. But the Edison system had one major perceived advantage: safety. Edison buried his low-voltage lines underground, a costly and labor-intensive exercise that eliminated the risk of electric shock. Westinghouse's high-voltage AC lines, on the other hand, were strung up on utility poles for street lighting, intersecting with thousands of telephone and telegraph wires. In the 1880s, the skylines of New York and other major cities came to resemble a giant spiderweb. Besides their unsightliness, the suspended wires were susceptible to being blown down in a storm and, more ominously, posed a danger of electrocution.

In New York alone, dozens of people were killed by live high-voltage AC wires between 1888 and 1890—mainly electrical and other utility workers, but also unsuspecting children who touched downed wires. The outcry over this danger—known as the Electric Wire Panic—created a public relations nightmare for Westinghouse, whose AC lines were often blamed. By recent law, the AC wires were supposed to be buried underground, like Edison's. But due to neglect and lethargy on the part of the company the city hired to dig the conduits, and corruption within the Tammany-dominated board of electrical control, not enough underground conduits had been built to house the lines.

Cravath spent much of his first few years as Westinghouse's lawyer fending off attempts—many of them instigated or supported by Edison—to cripple or kill the AC system because of the safety issues. Frequently quoted in the newspapers, Cravath would dispute that Westinghouse's lines were the ones at fault, arguing that they were all safely insulated while promising to get them buried underground just as quickly as the city could complete the conduits. While Westinghouse's prior counsel had contested the city's power to compel the company to bury its wires, Cravath offered to have his clients build the conduits themselves if adequately compensated, and Westinghouse was awarded a contract to do so—at least until the courts gave the job back to the original company in a suit brought by Elihu Root.

Injunctions in the War of Currents flew back and forth; no sooner would Cravath obtain a restraining order preventing the city from arbitrarily cutting down his client's overhead wires than the injunction would be dissolved and city workers would take their axes and clippers to the lines. In October 1889, a Western Union lineman named John Feeks was ROASTED IN A NETWORK OF WIRES, as the *New York Times* headline put it, when some dead wires he was trying to cut from a telegraph pole crossed with some AC wires a mile away. As a horrified lunch crowd of pedestrians looked on from below, Feeks literally caught on fire, blue flames shooting from his mouth and nostrils and sparks flying about his feet. His body was so tangled with wires that he was suspended aloft for forty-five minutes, dangling pitiably until his coworkers managed to cut him loose and lower his charred body to the ground.

Cravath immediately agreed, on his client's behalf, to turn off the "death currents" until they could be pronounced safe by experts (this resulted in darkening the city streets, which created its own set of problems). Reacting to the crisis, Westinghouse came at once from Pittsburgh to New York and set up quarters in the Hotel Brunswick on Fifth Avenue, where Cravath moved his force of young lawyers and worked day and night and all day on Sundays.

As part of his propaganda war against Westinghouse, Edison had lobbied to have alternating current used in the first execution by electric chair in New York State—ostensibly to institute a more humane form of capital punishment than hanging, but really to associate AC with electrocution in the public's mind. He sponsored experiments in which dogs, calves, and a horse were instantly killed when zapped with as little as 300 to 750 volts of AC, less than half the voltage used in the wires strung above city streets. Although Edison had previously opposed the death penalty, he now urged the use of high-voltage AC to execute convicted murderer William Kemmler. When Bourke Cockran, a high-priced New York lawyer-politician, intervened to try to halt the execution, it was commonly assumed that Westinghouse was behind the effort, and although both he and Cravath denied it, the fact that Cravath often hired Cockran to work with him on litigated matters lent credence to the notion.

The execution did go forward in August 1890 but was bungled: Kemmler was declared dead after receiving seventeen seconds of AC charge, but as it turned out he was still alive, requiring another eight agonizing minutes of jolts at 2,000 volts that burned him to death. Cravath told the press this would surely end the electric chair as an execution method because "the mysterious character of electricity itself, about which even experts have much to learn," counseled against "further experiments at the expense of human life." Westinghouse merely quipped that "they would have done better using an axe."

Cravath, who was assisted by Charles Evans Hughes, lost almost all the Westinghouse litigation with New York City and with Edison, who was better financed and had better press. But Westinghouse ended up winning the war. As the superiority of his AC system became increasingly apparent, and the safety issues abated, the stubbornly resistant Edison was draining his company's resources by continuing the costly legal battles. In 1892 Edison was ousted from control of the Edison General Electric Company through the machinations of banker J. P. Morgan, by then a large owner of Edison stock. Morgan, represented by Francis Lynde Stetson, engineered a merger with the Thomson-Houston Electric Company, which utilized AC power in competition with Westinghouse. Managerial power of the renamed General Electric Company was transferred to the Thomson-Houston group.

After Cravath helped a financially bleeding Westinghouse raise enough new money to stave off a bankruptcy proceeding in 1891, Westinghouse went on to demonstrate the advantages of AC power by illuminating the Chicago World's Fair in 1893. Two years later he successfully ran AC power all the way to Buffalo, more than twenty miles from the new Niagara Falls hydroelectric plant, a project initiated some years earlier by Stetson. The War of Currents was over, and AC had won.

In 1896 Westinghouse and General Electric agreed to cross-license patents and share royalties to end their remaining patent disputes. Cravath became one of the two Westinghouse nominees on the private board of patent control created to supervise the agreement.

The Westinghouse experience taught Cravath that representation of a corporate client involved neither strictly law nor strictly business, but a mixture of the two. The law needed to be respected but also melded to the client's business and public relations needs. It was said of Cravath that he was "not so much a great lawyer as he was a brilliant business man and promoter endowed with a legal mind."

Cravath had left Walter Carter in 1891 to form his own two-partner firm, where he continued his legal work for Westinghouse. In 1892 he married an opera singer from Kalamazoo, Michigan, Agnes Huntington, who had first made her name on the London stage. Depending on which story one believed, she either had considered suing her ex-fiancé, a wealthy Philadelphia man, for breach of promise, or had merely asked for her letters back from him before marrying the thirty-one-year-old Cravath. With a shared love of music and theater, the Cravaths would eagerly take part in high society in Manhattan, where they owned an architect-commissioned town house on East Thirty-Ninth Street in the fashionable Murray Hill district. They were also members of the exclusive horsing set on the North Shore of Long Island—later *Great Gatsby* country—where they built a series of magnificent estates and became founding members of the legendary Piping Rock Club.

In 1899 Cravath moved to the Seward firm, then headed by a rising star of the bar named William Dameron Guthrie, a railroad litigator and specialist in constitutional law. Like almost all the white shoe lawyers, who were self-made men, Guthrie became a millionaire by earning his wealth rather than inheriting it. Suave and slender, with a black mustache and a buttoned-down look, Guthrie was born to a San Francisco port surveyor and newspaper owner and received his early education in England and France. When his father died, young Guthrie was brought to America and sent to New York City's public schools.

Guthrie began as a messenger and stenographer with the Seward firm before joining it as a lawyer out of Columbia Law School. He came to prominence by persuading the US Supreme Court to declare the 1894 federal income tax unconstitutional, one of the most important policy-making lawsuits of the era. It would take the Sixteenth Amendment to the Constitution, ratified in 1913, to overrule the Supreme Court's decision and authorize the income tax.

Guthrie was a brilliant lawyer (and workaholic) whose perfectionism caused him great nervous strain. A conservative—indeed reactionary—Republican, he longed for a political career, for which his oratorical skills suited him. Invited by William Tecumseh Sherman to give the leading address on the general's trip to Denver in 1891, Guthrie earned Sherman's approval as well as praise from the Denver papers as "the most eloquent and interesting speaker of the day . . . with commanding presence, a clear voice, and distinct enunciation."

But Guthrie, an inconsiderate and contentious man, lacked the personal warmth necessary to run for office; his overwork kept him in a constant state of irritation. A *Harper's Weekly* profile called him aggressive and "frank to the point of brusqueness." Guthrie would often butt heads with Cravath, who nonetheless was one of the few people able to work with him. In 1898 they became Long Island neighbors and on January 1, 1901, full-fledged partners in Guthrie, Cravath & Henderson. It was here that Cravath put his pioneering notions of law firm management into practice.

Eventually the Cravath name would become the most recognized one in the world of white shoe Wall Street law firms. In the meantime, two other high-powered corporate lawyers stood atop their profession as builders of the new industrialized society.

Chapter 2

"Send Your Man to My Man"

As J. P. Morgan prepared to meet with President Theodore Roosevelt on the morning of February 22, 1902, Frank Stetson had every reason to be proud of the legal work he had performed for Morgan over the past year. In early 1901 he had helped Morgan create United States Steel, the first billion-dollar corporation in world history. Later that year Stetson represented Morgan in forming the second-biggest company on the globe: the Northern Securities Company, a combination of major railroads. Both deals had helped cement Morgan's status as one of the most powerful and richest men in America, and Stetson's as its highest-paid lawyer.

But by the time Morgan arrived for his White House appointment on this particular Saturday morning, he was boiling over with anger. He was there to discuss a new antitrust lawsuit that Roosevelt's attorney general, Philander K. Knox, had just filed to stop the giant Northern Securities merger. Three days earlier, over dinner at his large brownstone on Madison Avenue in Manhattan, the sixty-four-year-old Morgan had professed shock to his guests when he received a telephone call informing him that the government was bringing the lawsuit to stop the alleged monopoly. How could this be? Morgan thought—he'd had his lawyers, including Frank Stetson, the best in the business, put the deal together to make it invulnerable to legal attack. Besides, Morgan, a loyal Republican, had been a friend of the president's father and had backed the young Roosevelt in his first run for state office twenty years earlier. As vice president, Roosevelt had even given Morgan a testimonial dinner as a means of cultivating ties with the influential classes.

The financial markets were equally stunned. During the presidency of William McKinley, whose mentor and closest advisor was the pro-business

Ohio senator Mark Hanna, Morgan and his fellow capitalist titans had faced little governmental scrutiny of their expansionist designs. This was despite passage of the groundbreaking Sherman Antitrust Act of 1890, ostensibly designed to curb the ruthlessness with which men such as Morgan and John D. Rockefeller monopolized major American industries by forming giant "trusts." The McKinley administration had been lax in enforcing that new law, giving rise to the greatest wave of industrial mergers in American history. Many of the newly formed companies controlled more than 70 percent of the market in their lines of business. As recently as 1895, the Supreme Court had declined to break up the Sugar Trust, which controlled 98 percent of the country's sugar refining capacity.

But McKinley had been assassinated in September 1901, succeeded by the forty-two-year-old reformer Roosevelt. Hanna called him a "damned cowboy" who was liable to take any unpredictable action as president, whether in the interests of American business or not. And Roosevelt's decision to file suit against the Northern Securities merger was a watershed moment, marking the passing of the McKinley era to that of Teddy the Trust Buster.

What especially galled Morgan, as he met with Roosevelt and Knox, was that the suit had been filed without warning. The government had never tried to apply the Sherman Antitrust Act to a railroad merger. Morgan complained, moreover, that he was being treated like a common criminal. Then, as Roosevelt would later recount, Morgan made a conciliatory if presumptuous gesture. "If we have done anything wrong," he told the president, "send your man [Knox] to my man and they can fix it up."

Morgan's man was Francis Lynde Stetson, the fifty-five-year-old Wall Street corporate lawyer and consummate fixer. It was perhaps not surprising, then, that despite his testy meeting with Roosevelt, the normally pugnacious J. P. Morgan—he of the bull neck, menacing eyes, and bulbous, frightening, purplish nose—suggested negotiation rather than litigation. And for that task he was turning to his longtime lawyer, and counselor, Frank Stetson.

Stetson was born near Plattsburgh in far upstate New York, the son of a prominent lawyer, judge, and Democratic officeholder from whom he learned the art of compromise and backroom deals. After graduating from

Williams College in Massachusetts in 1867 and then Columbia Law School, Stetson began his career in New York as a trial lawyer. He became active in local politics through his association with reform politician-lawyer Samuel J. Tilden, who headed the investigation of Tammany Hall, the Democratic Party machine, and its corrupt Boss Tweed.

As a staff assistant to William C. Whitney, another anti-Tweed reform Democrat, Stetson argued on Tilden's behalf in the 1876 presidential electoral dispute with Rutherford B. Hayes. As a result of this work, Whitney, the corporation counsel for the city of New York, hired Stetson as an assistant counsel, which had him constantly in the courts representing the city in various litigations, often defending against fraudulent claims. Whitney, who later served as Grover Cleveland's secretary of the navy, would also become Stetson's client in the first consolidation of New York City's horse-drawn tram system.

In 1880 Stetson went into private practice with one of the city's most eminent lawyers, Francis N. Bangs. Nearly twenty years Stetson's senior, Bangs was a physically large, combative, temperamental courtroom lawyer of the older theatrical school. He immediately recognized Stetson's abilities, commenting on a brief Stetson wrote in 1881, "I don't think I can add or subtract a word." Many lawyers go an entire career without hearing such praise from a senior partner.

One of Stetson's earliest cases at his new firm, an investigation of a New York state judge for bribery, was brought to him by Theodore Roosevelt, then a young state assemblyman. To the outrage of both Roosevelt and Stetson, the palpably corrupt judge escaped impeachment. But the episode launched Roosevelt's career as a fierce public advocate and gave him respect for Stetson, which Roosevelt would maintain in the years ahead even while they were on the opposite side of many issues.

After Bangs's death in 1885 at age fifty-seven—from too much work, too much drink, or both—Stetson became the de facto head of the firm. By this time, he was a friend and advisor to President Grover Cleveland, whom he had met in 1882 at a political event shortly after Cleveland's election as New York's governor. Stetson turned down a cabinet position as treasury secretary when Cleveland won the presidency in 1884 but became one of his most trusted counselors. After Cleveland's reelection loss in 1888, he accepted Stetson's invitation to join his law firm, where the ex-president was given the big corner office that Stetson vacated for him. Colleagues recalled the two of them often chatting together, although Cleveland mostly stayed to himself, conducted his own library research, received political visitors, and expressed irritation with the telephone. He remained at the firm until his successful campaign for a second term in 1892.

Like Cleveland, Stetson was a modest, unassuming man. Five feet seven and a half, of stocky build, he was formal and ill at ease in public but warm and congenial in private. Stetson eschewed publicity and, though versed in the art of politics, never ran for office himself.

He was known for his thoroughness. As another law partner, his nephew Allen Wardwell, said, Stetson always knew exactly what he wanted done and, meticulous in the extreme, "didn't let things go by." In college he created a spreadsheet to keep track of all his correspondence, by person and date, with some two dozen friends and family, so he would know to whom he owed letters.

Stetson's early trial experience also was useful to his later corporate practice. As Wardwell explained,

> I've always said that Stetson's great ability as a corporate lawyer came from the fact that he realized that what he drew or what he said might some day come before the court. I think what was in the back of his mind, perhaps almost unconsciously, was what was the court going to say about it? . . . His ultimate test was, "I hope this will never get to court . . . but if it does get to court, I can defend it." . . . He was so incomparably logical.

Stetson first came to J. P. Morgan's attention in 1885. Stetson was then beginning to transition out of trial work into his role as a corporate law advisor and negotiator. As a lawyer for William Vanderbilt's New York Central Railroad, for which Morgan was the banker, Stetson helped negotiate a truce between the New York Central and its archrival, the Pennsylvania Railroad, to end their encroachments into each other's territory. Morgan, who preferred cooperation to ruinous competition, was so impressed with Stetson that he hired him away from Vanderbilt. Morgan's one condition was that Stetson take Morgan's brother-in-law and less talented lawyer, Charles Tracy, into his firm. Once Tracy was ensconced in Stetson's firm, Morgan pushed him aside and began using Stetson exclusively.

Stetson's careful, analytical approach to legal problems made him so valuable to Morgan that from 1887 forward he became "our regular attorney in everything," Morgan later said. Their offices were in adjoining buildings in downtown Manhattan—Stetson in the Mills Building at 15 Broad Street and his client, the famous banker, at 23 Wall Street in the "House of Morgan." They would often put on their hats and coats for a stroll along lower Broadway to confer about Morgan's business affairs, greeting each other with a formal "Good morning, Mr. Morgan!" and "Good morning, Mr. Stetson!"

Translating Morgan's broad designs into legally enforceable documents, Stetson guided his fellow Episcopal warden on financing the creation of such iconic companies as General Electric, International Harvester, and AT&T. As Morgan once put it, he counted on Stetson to make sure "all the usual protections and loopholes" were inserted in his various deals.

In 1895 Stetson was instrumental in devising a plan for Morgan to halt a run on gold and avert a national financial crisis by arranging an emergency sale of gold to the US Treasury Department. During the key strategy meeting at the White House, Morgan and Stetson convinced Stetson's friend, President Grover Cleveland, to adopt this emergency measure. Stetson invoked an old Civil War statute as authority for the Treasury to buy gold in a private sale to replenish its reserves.

Stetson was put on a $50,000-a-year retainer with Morgan, which he received in addition to his fees for individual cases, and which did not include his profits on Morgan company stocks he was allowed to buy at insider prices. In 1901 he earned $301,997 in fees alone (about $8 million in 2019 dollars). One newspaper called Stetson "the greatest of the new school of business lawyers—men who are experts first and lawyers afterward." It was not that he wasn't a great lawyer, the paper said, but the combination of legal ability and business talent "brought him a fortune that would have been impossible to a man who was merely a lawyer."

By the turn of the century Stetson and his wife, Elizabeth ("Lizzie") Ruff, the daughter of an antebellum New Orleans US Navy surgeon, were living in a luxurious new six-story limestone mansion at 4 East Seventy-Fourth Street in New York. They also had a thousand-acre country home, Skylands, in the mountains an hour north of Manhattan, where Stetson created a botanical garden and a nine-hole golf course.

The Stetsons were part of Morgan's social circle as well, having attended the wedding of Morgan's daughter in 1900, along with President McKinley, Vice President Roosevelt, Secretary of State John Hay, and Secretary of War Elihu Root and their wives, among other luminaries. Stetson was also good friends with steel magnate Andrew Carnegie, the two of them trading visits between Stetson's Skylands estate and Carnegie's Skibo Castle in Scotland.

<hr />

It was in 1901 that Stetson helped Morgan form the Northern Securities Company to end what Morgan biographer Ron Chernow has called "perhaps the most controversial takeover fight in American history." It was between the two most dominant railroad moguls in America: E. H. Harriman, owner of the Union Pacific and Southern Pacific Railroads in the West and Southwest, and James J. Hill, head of the Great Northern Railway in the Northwest. In alliance with banker Morgan, Hill also controlled the Northern Pacific Railway that ran from Minnesota to Seattle, parallel to the Great Northern. Together Hill and Morgan outbid Harriman for control of a key Chicago railroad hub—the Chicago, Burlington & Quincy—that would connect their respective railway lines from the Great Lakes to the Pacific Ocean.

When the Hill-Morgan interests refused to allow Harriman a stake in the Chicago hub, Harriman decided to "buy the mare to get the filly." He launched a 1980s-style hostile corporate raid on the Northern Pacific itself, which had acquired the much-sought-after Chicago, Burlington. Harriman began secretly buying up large blocks of Northern Pacific stock, driving its price up from $170 to an astounding $1,000 a share in a single day, on May 9, 1901. Speculators who had shorted the Northern Pacific in the expectation its price would fall back were forced to sell other stocks to raise cash to cover their short positions, causing the market as a whole to crash. The *New York Times* called it "the greatest general panic that Wall Street has ever known."

Unable to tolerate the uncertainty, and to protect themselves from future raids, Hill and Morgan proposed a truce to their competitor. Their hand was strengthened by a bit of Stetson's legerdemain. Although the scrappy Harriman* had obtained a majority of the total stock of the Northern Pacific, it turned out that Stetson had inserted provisions in the company's bylaws and charter, enabling it to fend off unwanted suitors. In fishing parlance, as one writer explained, a minnow (the Chicago, Burlington) was swallowed by a bass (the Northern Pacific), which was swallowed by a pike (Harriman's Union Pacific), but the bass, armed with defensive fins, "compelled the pike to spew him out."

Harriman agreed to the corporate armistice. He dropped his takeover effort in exchange for a premium on his Northern Pacific shares, seats on the company board for himself and his friends, and a minority interest in a new combined company that would own all three railroads. In November 1901, the Northern Pacific, the Great Northern, and the Chicago, Burlington were placed under control of a single umbrella corporate holding company, incorporated by Stetson in New Jersey, known as the Northern Securities Company. It figured to dominate transport from the West to Chicago and possibly all the way to Morgan's New York Central. By eliminating competition, the arrangement created stability, curtailed rate-cutting, and prevented further wasteful overbuilding. Morgan, Harriman, and Hill would call it a "community of interest"; to others that was a euphemism for a monopoly.

With a market capitalization of $400 million, Northern Securities was exceeded in size only by Morgan's US Steel. Capitalized at a breathtaking $1.4 billion, the equivalent of almost $40 billion in 2019 dollars, US Steel was the largest company in world history. It was formed by merging fifteen separate steel companies and, by absorbing Andrew Carnegie's operations, it controlled two-thirds of the nation's steel production. Creating it had been a mammoth task that took all of Stetson's attention and required many late-night conferences in his office. Stetson was appointed general counsel of the new corporation, a position he held even as he remained a partner in his law firm.

---

*Fans of the movie *Butch Cassidy and the Sundance Kid* may recall "Mr. E. H. Harriman" as the owner of the railroads repeatedly robbed by Cassidy's Hole-in-the-Wall Gang.

Fresh on the heels of the US Steel conglomeration, the Northern Securities deal was announced in November 1901. The public and the press, fed up with the never-ending gigantic mergers of this sort, reacted with outrage. One politician in Minnesota, home to the Northern Pacific, declared that "the people must act with vigor to avert commercial slavery." Roosevelt was eager to establish himself as a trust buster and quietly instructed Knox to file suit to break up the railroad combination.

The government had yet to sue US Steel, but Morgan was worried that would come next. Even more than the Northern Securities Company, US Steel was Morgan's most beloved corporate child. Thus, when Morgan met with Roosevelt and Knox that Saturday in February 1902 to discuss the Northern Securities suit, it was the fear of legal action against US Steel that was uppermost in the great financier's mind.

The president and the attorney general told Morgan that, contrary to his offer to fix up the Northern Securities merger, the government wanted not to fix it but to stop it. Morgan asked Roosevelt whether he planned to attack US Steel or any of Morgan's other interests. Not "unless we find out that . . . they have done something that we regard as wrong" was Roosevelt's less than reassuring reply.

Both Northern Securities and US Steel had been created as holding companies, a corporate structure functionally the same as but different in form from the hated trusts.* Both corporate forms enabled shareholders of competing companies to pool their interests and increase their market power. The terms "holding company," "trust," and "merger" were often used interchangeably, with "trust" becoming a generic catch-all term used to describe all large business combinations. But in 1901 the holding company, for technical reasons, was viewed by many to be immune from antitrust attack. It was a legal loophole in the Sherman Antitrust Act and the brainchild of a crafty lawyer named William Nelson Cromwell.

---

*Under a corporate trust, individuals owning stock in competing corporations transfer their stock in trust to a single board of trustees, thus placing the companies under common control. The individual owners receive certificates showing their respective interests in the stocks held in trust. Hence, the Sherman "Antitrust" Act.

Chapter 3

"The Physician of Wall Street"

Another of the great new millionaire corporation lawyers to emerge at the end of the nineteenth century, William Nelson Cromwell (he preferred all three names) has been described as the lawyer "who taught the robber barons how to rob."

One look at this small, slight man with flashing blue eyes, a flowing mane of prematurely white hair, and a thick white mustache—a more dapper, less homely version of Albert Einstein—hinted at a mischievous streak. A frequenter of New York's choicest restaurants, a lover of champagne and fine sherry, Cromwell maintained "a rather theatrical look," the *New York World* observed. A glistening silk top hat habitually crowned his snowy curls. He was a quick thinker and fast, staccato talker ("no life insurance agent could beat him," the *World*'s reporter wrote), and took pride in his reputation as a clever operator. He was more a doer and a creator than an analyst or a dissector of the law, and never saw a business problem he didn't think could be solved by creative lawyering.

Born in Brooklyn in 1854, Cromwell led a hardscrabble youth, raised in Illinois by a Civil War widow whose working-class husband was killed at Vicksburg. Lacking money to attend college, he supported his family by taking jobs as an accountant, first in a railroad office and then in the Manhattan law office of Algernon Sydney Sullivan. Best known for having successfully defended a group of captured Confederate sailors on trial for their life in 1861 on a charge of piracy, Sullivan went on to become a popular anti-Tweed prosecutor and was proposed as a candidate for mayor of New York in 1873 but declined in favor of private practice.

Sullivan took an interest in his young bookkeeper and paid Cromwell's way through Columbia Law School, which he attended part-time while keeping his day job at the firm. After admission to the bar, Cromwell joined

Sullivan's law office at the corner of Wall and Broad Streets and, at age twenty-five in 1879, became a partner in the Sullivan & Cromwell firm that still bears that name today.

Sullivan, then in his fifties, was apprehensive of the growing power of corporations and trusts. Cromwell, his junior partner, had no such qualms, and when Sullivan died, in 1887, Cromwell continued building a corporate practice heavily devoted to combining railroads and other large businesses, then salvaging the wreckage when they went belly-up. He was so adept at reviving sick corporations that he was dubbed "the physician of Wall Street."

His biggest early client was Henry Villard, the Bavarian-born Civil War correspondent turned corporate chieftain. Twenty years before J. P. Morgan and James J. Hill wrested control of the Northern Pacific Railway, Villard had acquired it with Cromwell's help. Villard drove the last spike on the opening in 1883 of its transcontinental route, the nation's second, in a celebrity-filled ceremony that included former president Ulysses S. Grant.

The following year the Northern Pacific collapsed in financial ruin, a victim of cost overruns. Villard resigned as president and returned to his native Germany, leaving Cromwell to clean up the mess. Villard vacated his Madison Avenue mansion, which Cromwell saved from creditor seizure by putting the equity in Villard's wife's name, a maneuver Cromwell denied was "tricky." About repairing Villard's broken business generally, Cromwell explained, "What we needed most was a *leader* . . . through whom *alone* negotiations could be conducted. . . . I must be allowed my own way of working it out."

While Villard was in Germany plotting his return, he asked Cromwell for his "advice and guidance permanently." That was all the cue Cromwell needed to launch into a lengthy explication of his value to the financier. Cromwell had a habit of writing long-winded letters to his clients that shamelessly flattered them, convinced them of his utter fealty to them, and detailed the many ways in which his brilliant strategies had succeeded exactly as he had predicted.

"I was imbued with an abiding faith in your future," he wrote to Villard in February 1886. "I could not carry you and your affairs ever in my mind for a year, without catching fire and becoming so interested in them."

Cromwell secured a settlement and complete release of any personal claims against Villard by railroad creditors. Cromwell told his client the main creditors' lawyer was "in a very bitter and illiberal frame of mind" toward him. "It required all my tact to get this [settlement] through his hands without severe mutilation," he added. To achieve his goal, Cromwell threatened litigation he privately believed Villard would lose. And when one creditor wanted an investigation of all accounts before giving Villard a full release, Cromwell bluffed like a riverboat gambler. "I boldly assented to the suggestion. That killed it," he reported.

Only reluctantly, Cromwell said, did he bring up the issue of his fee, which he called "the only one thing in the practice of the law that I am always inclined to dodge." He said he would gladly leave it to Villard to decide how much to pay, were it not for Villard's generous spirit. Cromwell's handsome fee was paid in full.

In 1887, Villard returned from Germany in triumph to retake control of the Northern Pacific, but he lost it again in the Panic of 1893 and ensuing economic depression. After that he left the company for good. But Villard had other compensations: He acquired the *New York Post* and *The Nation* magazine and became an early financial backer of Thomas Edison. In 1889, at Cromwell's urging, Villard combined all the various Edison companies into a single Edison General Electric Company, a world cartel of which he became president and a major stockholder. J. P. Morgan, another Edison investor who participated in the huge merger—and the first person to have his residence lit by Edison's incandescent light—naturally was counseled by Frank Stetson in the deal.

Cromwell and Stetson joined forces again in the complicated and successful reorganization of the Northern Pacific that began in 1893 following Villard's exit from the company. Many railroads at the time were going bankrupt because of overbuilding and competition, and between them, Cromwell and Stetson—as well as Cravath's firm—were involved in nearly every major railroad reorganization of the era.

The dominant figure in these reorganizations may have been the banker, but as one legal study put it, "the guiding spirit is the banker's lawyer." To govern the complex proceedings, the elite Wall Street law firms wrote and rewrote the rules, developed new forms of corporate mortgages and other instruments, and controlled the reorganization process. In addition, only lawyers such as Stetson, Cromwell, and Cravath could afford to wait to be paid until the completion of the reorganization, as was customary, which helped them gain an even greater share of this lucrative work. In law as in business, the rich got richer.

In the Northern Pacific reorganization, Cromwell was appointed as counsel for the receiver (similar to a bankruptcy trustee), while Stetson again represented the Morgan interests, who by now held substantial Northern Pacific stock. Two years earlier, the thirty-seven-year-old Cromwell had shown a flair for bankruptcy work by managing to readjust the affairs of the insolvent Decker, Howell brokerage firm, which was closely tied to Villard. Despite debts of $12 million, Cromwell had it back on its feet, creditors paid off dollar for dollar, in a mere eight weeks, for which he received the unprecedented fee of $260,000.

It was an early example of what came to be known as the "Cromwell Plan," in which he would threaten creditors with a forced liquidation of a bankrupt company's assets at fire-sale prices if they did not go along with a voluntary, negotiated arrangement. The idea was that if creditors refrained from pressing all their claims in a down market, they would eventually realize a higher percentage recovery when the crisis passed. What made the plan work was Cromwell's knack for numbers, acquired during his bookkeeping days, together with his ability to analyze underlying asset values and negotiate among different hostile factions, often placing them in different rooms as he went from one to the other.

The Northern Pacific reorganization was Cromwell's biggest challenge yet—"the severest task I have ever had in [Northern Pacific] matters," he told Stetson. Shrewdly, he made sure the Northern Pacific rail properties throughout the country could not be attached, piecemeal, by impatient local creditors, a frequent problem at that time given that there was no comprehensive federal bankruptcy law to govern a bankrupt estate nationwide. A receiver had to file papers in every jurisdiction where the bankrupt's assets were located to prevent creditors from seizing them, so Cromwell hired local counsel across the country and instructed them to await a single telegraphed word from him: "File," which they did, simultaneously, at the appointed hour.

When the dust finally settled, securities holders were made whole.

Cromwell boasted he had kept "the pirates from scaling the vessel's wall." J. P. Morgan was especially pleased, as he emerged with his control of the railroad intact. One St. Louis lawyer called it "hocus-pocus legal tactics." The Northern Pacific had been, in the phrase of the day, "Morganized."

It was unsurprising, then, that when the giant US Steel corporation and Northern Securities were created in 1901, Morgan turned to Cromwell, along with Stetson, for help. For his work on US Steel, Cromwell received $2 million worth of stock, for which he paid only $250,000. Cromwell would later claim he had given Morgan the idea to buy out Andrew Carnegie and form US Steel.

Both US Steel and Northern Securities, later the same year, were incorporated as New Jersey holding companies. Shortly before passage of the Sherman Act in 1890, Cromwell had seen that the trust structure, invented in 1882 by one of John D. Rockefeller's lawyers, was becoming vulnerable to legal as well as political attack. In one celebrated case in 1889, Cromwell represented the American Cotton Oil Trust in a suit by Louisiana's attorney general seeking to bar the trust from doing business in that state. Anticipating an adverse decision, Cromwell walked into court and nonchalantly announced that the suit was moot inasmuch as all the trust assets had been transferred to a Rhode Island corporation.

The local officials were so enraged by what the New York Times called this "sharp practice" that they threatened Cromwell with personal hostilities. His tactic ended up not working, though, because the trust had already been under court order not to engage in any transactions. Cromwell devised a new stratagem: He simply had the trust dissolved and reincorporated as a New Jersey holding company.

The holding company structure had been Cromwell's invention. Until 1888, no state permitted a corporation to hold the stock of another. Working through local counsel that year, Cromwell got the New Jersey legislature to amend its corporation law to allow a corporate holding company to buy, sell, and own the stocks of any other company, just as any individual person could.

Most state courts had already held that agreements directly restraining trade, such as cartels and price-fixing, were illegal. Agreements to form corporate trusts, as a means of eliminating competition, came under similar attack. But, the argument by corporate lawyers went, creating a holding company involved no agreement in restraint of interstate trade or commerce (the words of the Sherman Act). Instead it was simply the acquisition by one corporation (the parent) of the stock of other corporations (the subsidiaries), permissible under state law.

As an added benefit, to limit their liability, holding companies were legally insulated from lawsuits against their operating subsidiaries. Like corporations themselves, holding companies were fictional entities, their creation the work of a latter-day sorcerer, Cromwell.

Beginning with the Cotton Oil Trust in 1889, and especially after the 1890 Sherman Act, a wave of trusts, many of them Sullivan & Cromwell clients, began reconstituting themselves as New Jersey holding companies to skirt the antitrust laws. For the Southern Cotton Oil Trust, Cromwell locked his firm's doors at 6:00 P.M. one evening, drew up 175 agreements overnight, and by daybreak had the trust incorporated as a New Jersey holding company. Reportedly he was paid $50,000 for a single night's work.

From 1889 to the end of the century, New Jersey became home to more than seven hundred corporations worth a total of $1 billion. Nationwide, 183 holding companies had been formed with a total capitalization of more than $4 billion—almost double the amount of money in circulation in the country.

Many corporations, especially railroads, were burdened with excessive debt and capitalized with "watered" stock—that is, stock not backed by hard assets but inflated to a face or "par" value on paper, far in excess of the actual value of the enterprise, and sold to an unsuspecting public. ("Stock watering" took its name from the practice of bloating cattle with water to increase their weight to fetch a higher price.) Watered stocks and bonds were essentially just paper certificates representing the hope of future profits and dividends.

With nearly $2 billion in new holding company paper issued by US Steel and Northern Securities in 1901, much of it watered stock, the government had finally had enough, leading to Roosevelt's decision to sue J. P. Morgan in the *Northern Securities* case. The most celebrated antitrust lawsuit in the nation's history to that point, it would be eagerly watched for the next two years as it wound its way up to the US Supreme Court.

Both Cromwell and Stetson were retained to defend the *Northern Securities* case, although Stetson with others would be more closely involved. In the meantime, Cromwell had other things to do. He threw himself into an even bigger project—one for which all his skills as a wheeler-dealer and rescuer of failed enterprises would be called upon. It concerned a path between the oceans down in Central America.

Chapter 4

"Beware of Mr. Cromwell"

Had it not been for William Nelson Cromwell, today we probably would be calling it the Nicaragua Canal.

The dream of digging a water passage across Central America dates to the 1513 crossing of the Isthmus of Panama by the Spanish explorer Vasco Núñez de Balboa, who discovered that only a narrow strip of land separated the Atlantic and Pacific Oceans. Spain proposed building a canal through Panama to allow its ships to avoid the long, hazardous Cape Horn route around the southern tip of South America but abandoned the idea as impractical. Various plans by the British and others fell through in three succeeding centuries, but the 1849 California gold rush sparked renewed interest in an interoceanic canal, this time on the part of the United States. Following a series of naval expeditions commissioned by President Ulysses S. Grant, a technical commission in 1876 recommended a Nicaragua route as the most feasible. Meanwhile, a French-backed project targeted Panama as a competing path.

For the instrumental role he played in getting the United States to switch its canal project from Nicaragua to the Isthmus of Panama, and in securing American rights to the canal zone, Cromwell's enemies would label him as "villainous," "corrupt," and guilty of conceiving and carrying out "the rape of the Isthmus." He would be accused of fomenting revolution and, in the memorable phrase of one US congressman, was called "the most dangerous man this country has produced since the days of Aaron Burr." All because, as one of his bitterest critics conceded, he had safeguarded the interests of his clients to the best of his ability. For his services he was paid $200,000 for a decade's worth of work, which, given the magnitude of his contributions, even his foes called "remarkably cheap at the price." And when his work was done, Cromwell had dramatically expanded the definition of what it meant to be an American lawyer.

Cromwell's clients were a pair of French-owned companies: the Panama Railroad Company, which operated a railroad across the narrow isthmus, and the Compagnie Nouvelle du Canal de Panama, or New Panama Canal Company, based in Paris. It was the successor to the bankrupt "Old" canal company, known as the de Lesseps firm after its inspirational promoter and head engineer, Ferdinand de Lesseps. A French national hero for having built the Suez Canal, de Lesseps had failed to finish the far more ambitious Panama project, which was abandoned in 1889. Despite almost eight years of digging, de Lesseps had managed to excavate only a third of what was required for completion. His company was hopelessly underfinanced and mired in charges of bribery, graft, and waste. French shareholders numbering two hundred thousand, mainly small investors attracted by the de Lesseps name, held worthless stock. More tragically, by some estimates, as many as twenty-two thousand laborers, including four thousand Frenchmen, died in Panama, mostly of yellow fever and malaria. The entire episode was a deep embarrassment to the proud French people.

Cromwell had no association with the old de Lesseps company. In 1893, through his American railroad connections, he had become general counsel to the Panama Railroad Company, as well as a director and stockholder. In 1896 he was hired as US counsel for France's New Panama Canal Company, which had taken over the railroad as well as the assets of the old company upon its bankruptcy. For the turnaround artist Cromwell, it would be the ultimate turnaround project.

The reorganized Compagnie Nouvelle (New Canal Company) had a fresh set of investors, although about two-thirds of them were so-called penalty shareholders—alleged illegal profiteers in the original de Lesseps venture who were forced to put up money to float the new company. The New Canal Company also acquired the old company's right, known as the Wyse Concession, which it had purchased from the Colombian government to allow it to build a canal across the Panamanian isthmus. (Panama at the time was a province of Colombia, not a separate country.) The concession, which was not transferable to a foreign power without Colombia's consent, was originally set to expire in 1893 but had twice been extended, most recently to 1904.

By the time it retained Cromwell in 1896, the New Canal Company had done some additional digging to at least maintain appearances, but there was little hope it could complete the project. Realistically its best chance of salvaging anything for its investors was to find a buyer—logically, the United States—for its assets, which included the excavations as well as assorted maps and surveys, run-down buildings, and abandoned equipment. That is where Cromwell came in. The Sullivan & Cromwell firm had influence in high places in the United States and was put in overall charge of promoting American interest in a revived Panama Canal.

It was a seemingly impossible task. At that time, in Cromwell's own words, there was "almost unanimous opinion in the United States in favor of the Nicaragua canal, which was looked upon as the American canal." Congress overwhelmingly supported a Nicaraguan route, as did the new president McKinley.

Nicaragua was a day's boat ride closer than Panama to the United States, and a Nicaragua canal was seen by influential Southern congressmen as a boon to the Gulf trading ports of Biloxi, Mobile, and New Orleans that connected to Southern railroads. Nicaragua was more than willing to grant the United States any concession it needed to build the canal there to help modernize the country. Nicaragua was less plagued by disease than the Panamanian jungle and, unlike Panama, was not subject to constant political unrest.

Above all, the Panama Canal was seen as a financial and engineering failure—"a scandalous affair of which nothing but evil was spoken," as Cromwell put it. "Public opinion demanded the Nicaraguan Canal. The only canal known, the only wanted, the only spoken of was the Nicaraguan Canal. The Panama Canal was looked upon as a vanished dream."

Given his French clients' desire to avoid adverse publicity, Cromwell stayed in the shadows at first. For the first two years of his retention he conducted a quiet lobbying operation in Washington to slow the momentum toward Nicaragua and monitor the political situation. It was mostly a negative campaign intended to emphasize problems with the Nicaragua plan.

What Cromwell needed to do, he told his clients, was to make a positive, public case for Panama.

Panama did hold several significant advantages over Nicaragua. The Panama route was less than a third the length of a canal across the isthmus of Nicaragua (50 versus 180 miles); it was a straighter line, with fewer difficult curves; and a third of the excavation had already been completed. It required fewer locks, and the average ship could pass through it in twelve hours versus thirty-three for Nicaragua. The Panama route was also more commercially developed and was paralleled by an existing railroad to facilitate the work. At the right price, the United States might buy out the French investors and finish the canal more quickly and cheaply than if it started largely from scratch in Nicaragua.

In June 1898 the New Canal Company finally accepted Cromwell's recommendation of a "different, open, audacious, aggressive" push for a Panama canal—what he called a "Napoleonic strategy" to thwart any other interocean project from taking shape. With that he launched a political lobbying campaign unprecedented for an American lawyer.

Cromwell organized a press bureau, with a $100,000 budget, to write technical and popular articles in magazines throughout the country touting the advantages of Panama over Nicaragua. The bureau was headed by former *New York World* financial reporter Roger L. Farnham, described as the head of Sullivan & Cromwell's "political department" and "one of Mr. Cromwell's henchmen and his confidential agent." Farnham, who had spent years wandering at sea and in Mexico, had a reputation for cutting corners. He also had been sued by a woman who alleged he had "accomplished her ruin" in New York's Royal Hotel (when the hotel caught fire, he jumped, leaving her to fend for herself).

Farnham sent a corps of photographers and engineers to Panama to take pictures of every inch of the canal route. They compiled scientific reports that Cromwell later turned into a detailed and illustrated pamphlet sent to each member of Congress and other high-ranking federal and state officials to introduce them to the New Panama Canal Company.

Farnham hired a team of independent press agents who, working without knowledge of one another's efforts or their connection to Cromwell, were instructed to interview congressmen to gauge their openness to a Panama route. If lobbying targets showed interest but had some doubt or question, they would find literature addressing their concerns at their office or home within twelve hours. Major newspapers, businesses, libraries, and educational institutions were also flooded with pro-Panama material. Through a "thousand and one efforts," Cromwell later recounted, persons of influence were "at last awakened and informed of the drawbacks of Nicaragua and of the advantages of the Panama route."

The leading congressional canal expert and champion of the Nicaragua route was Alabama Democratic senator John Tyler Morgan. When he saw the materials Cromwell was circulating, Morgan took to the Senate floor to denounce the sales pitch as false and misleading. Its deceptiveness, Morgan asserted, was masked only by "the veneer of its crafty diplomacy." As Cromwell's partner William Curtis would write, Senator Morgan was so unremittingly hostile toward the French canal company's American lawyers that "he would have believed us guilty of any crime or offense." Nonetheless, Morgan grudgingly acknowledged that Cromwell "took charge of the French forces as general in chief, legal counsel, diplomatic functionary, orator, and witness for the Panama Canal Co."

Still, the situation for the French forces seemed hopeless when, on January 21, 1899, a bill to build and fund a Nicaragua canal passed the Senate by 48-6. It was immediately sent to the House, where an enthusiastic majority was publicly pledged to Nicaragua. "The result of a vote in the House was absolutely certain, if a vote were taken," Cromwell wrote. "If it could not be deferred, the fate of Panama was sealed."

Cromwell then hit upon a plan for derailing a final vote in the House. Although various technical commissions had endorsed Nicaragua as a practical route, no expert panel had ever scientifically studied and compared the relative merits of Nicaragua and Panama. Cromwell proposed creating a new canal commission to investigate both routes and recommend to Congress which was superior. The Republican Speaker of the House, Thomas Reed, agreed the commission idea made sense. Reed convinced the House to postpone any final vote on Nicaragua until the expert commission could make its findings and report back to Congress.

But wily Senator Morgan, who was impatient to pass a Nicaragua bill, countered by obtaining Senate passage of a rider tacked on to a popular rivers and harbors bill, which had nothing to do with any canal. The Morgan rider irrevocably committed the United States to build a Nicaragua canal and appropriated $10 million to begin work.

There was no question the rivers and harbors bill, a pork barrel measure, was going to pass, and with Congress about to adjourn there was pressure to just pass it in the form that included Morgan's rider. "The supporters of Nicaragua were confident and even joyful," Cromwell recalled. "They were sure of favorable action by the conferees."

Cromwell needed another miracle. At the last minute he conceived a plan to enhance Panama's appeal by "Americanizing" the canal project. He got his French client to say it would be willing to reincorporate in the United States, in New Jersey, which would give the US government and American investors the opportunity to participate directly in the enterprise and to elect a number of directors, thereby broadening the base of American support for the Panama route.

Cromwell presented the proposal in writing to President McKinley on February 28, 1899. The plan was aborted months later after the French canal company's shareholders refused to ratify it, believing it contrary to their economic interests. But at this critical moment it was an effective stalling tactic. The Senate, afraid of jeopardizing the rivers and harbors bill, agreed to drop the Morgan rider and passed a law on March 3, 1899, in the final hours of the congressional session, creating the Isthmian Canal Commission with a million-dollar appropriation. The Panama cause would now enter a contest to be waged on the merits with Nicaragua—a battle of the canal routes.

The composition of the commission was critical. Cromwell argued to President McKinley that to ensure the panel's objectivity, no one who previously endorsed Nicaragua should be appointed. That included Rear Admiral John G. Walker and two other pro-Nicaragua engineers. McKinley nonetheless decided to reappoint all three men, with Walker as head, but he chose several other members from a list suggested by Cromwell and Curtis. The most important of them was George S. Morison, a close friend of Cromwell's and a onetime lawyer best known for designing several steel truss bridges across the Mississippi, Missouri, and Ohio Rivers.

Although the Walker Commission, as it became known, had intended to begin its investigation in Panama, Cromwell persuaded its members to convene in Paris, where the New Canal Company had its offices and records. On August 5, 1899, Cromwell sailed for Paris to make sure everything was ready for his guests. On August 18, the morning after their arrival, he greeted them at the Hôtel Brighton on the rue de Rivoli, overlooking the Tuileries Gardens, and accompanied them the next day to his clients' engineering offices at 91 rue des Petits Champs, a short walk from the Paris Opera House.

For the next four weeks, the nine American engineers were subjected to a daily indoctrination to the benefits of a Panama Canal. They were also given generous free time to enjoy the pleasures of Belle Époque Paris. Morison's diary records him visiting the Louvre, Notre Dame, the Palace of Versailles, and the "interesting" new Sacré-Coeur basilica then under construction. He attended a production of the opera *Faust*, which he pronounced "learned," and enjoyed much fine dining, which he only occasionally praised.

Having thoroughly educated himself in the various technical issues, Cromwell wheeled out maps, engineers' reports, geological studies, plans for dams and locks, and equipment inventories—information more detailed, extensive, and organized than that available anywhere else. It was all attractively packed in folders embossed with Sullivan & Cromwell's name on the cover and tied with dark green ribbons. Company personnel were brought in to explain the data and answer questions. The sessions were conducted in a formal, elaborate manner, almost as if the commission were sitting as a high court.

Cromwell also arranged an appearance by a group of distinguished European engineers who had previously studied the Panama route for the New Canal Company and pronounced it feasible. On August 31 they were introduced to their American counterparts over lunch (six courses, four wines) at an elegant Art Nouveau restaurant, the Pavillon Paillard, in a park along the Champs-Elysées. (The normally finicky Morison called it a "very fine lunch and pleasant occasion.") The Walker commissioners were advised that the Panama enterprise was so technically superior that if the United States did not finish the French canal then another country would. Morison, for one, was persuaded, and Admiral Walker, too, was impressed.

Cromwell was present throughout the Walker Commission's month-long stay in Paris and saw them off at a final breakfast at the Pavillon Paillard on September 11. Back in Washington, he stayed in constant and personal communication with them, supplying additional information and documents they requested, answering their questions, and overcoming their hesitations. Senator Morgan would ruefully describe Cromwell as ubiquitous and driven by his desire to defeat the Nicaragua canal movement. Cromwell, whose only professional and legal duty was to his French client—not to his native United States or anyone else—would not have disagreed.

But he did have a problem with his client. The New Canal Company was unwilling to name a price at which it would be willing to sell its canal assets to the United States. Admiral Walker specifically asked on what terms the United States could buy the French assets, but the New Canal Company's president, Maurice Hutin, would not give an answer. Hutin, a proud French engineer, stubbornly clung to the hope that France could either continue the project on its own or at least partner with the United States to finish it. But the McKinley administration—and later President Theodore Roosevelt—were not interested in partnering with anyone; they sought unqualified American control, which only Nicaragua was willing to cede.

In the meantime, Cromwell redoubled his lobbying campaign in Washington. His number one target was Ohio senator and businessman Mark Hanna, McKinley's closest advisor and a member of the same Senate Committee on Interoceanic Canals of which John Tyler Morgan was chairman. At a meeting in New York, Cromwell so impressed Hanna with the merits of the Panama route that Hanna thereafter became a dedicated supporter of Panama and a counterweight to Morgan in the Senate.

Cromwell scored another coup when, with Hanna's support, he obtained a change in the Republican Party's 1900 national platform on the canal issue. The Republican platform of 1896, like that year's Democratic platform, had endorsed a Nicaragua canal. When the Republicans met at their convention in Philadelphia in June 1900, the first draft of the platform continued the same pro-Nicaragua language as before. But Cromwell persuaded the Republican National Committee to substitute the neutral phrase "an isthmian canal" for the words "a Nicaragua Canal." Previous to this, Cromwell allegedly had donated $60,000 to the Republican Party and charged it as a business expense to his French client. It was never proved that the platform switch was a quid pro quo for the donation, but the money could not have hurt.

Still, Nicaragua's supporters held the upper hand. They argued that because Nicaragua, unlike Panama, was offering the United States a canal with no strings attached, there was no need to wait for the commission's final report. Admiral Walker also made clear to Cromwell that without a definite offering price from the French, the commission would have no choice but to recommend Nicaragua. At the same time, he privately suggested that if the French named a figure in the vicinity of $60 million for an outright sale, the commission would report in favor of Panama.

When Cromwell relayed these developments to President Hutin of the French canal company and again pressed for a firm offer, Hutin fired him. To Hutin, Cromwell was a brash American who was spending too much of the company's money on lobbying, political contributions, and press kits.

From July 1901 to January 1902 Cromwell was sidelined, reduced to watching developments from afar. During that period nothing went right for the Panama forces. Hutin took over negotiations himself but made no progress. After McKinley's assassination, in September 1901, Theodore Roosevelt confirmed he would continue the slain president's policy favoring Nicaragua.

In October, Hutin came to America and, while still refusing to name a sales price, provided an estimate that the New Canal Company's assets were worth $109 million. That was a preposterous figure to Walker, whose commission had recently valued them at $40 million. With the cost to finish construction of the Panama Canal estimated at $144 million, paying an additional $109 million to acquire the French rights would put Panama's total price tag at $253 million, well above the $189 million estimated for construction in Nicaragua. The choice was an easy one. Walker broke off negotiations with the French on November 6, 1901, and on November 16, the Walker Commission submitted its final report to Congress, unanimously recommending adoption of the Nicaragua plan.

Committees in both the House and Senate immediately reported out bills for construction and funding of a Nicaragua canal. On December 10 the United States signed a formal diplomatic convention with Nicaragua to build a canal. A week later the Senate ratified the amended Hay-Pauncefote Treaty between the United States and Great Britain, abrogating the old Clayton-Bulwer Treaty of 1850, which had prevented the United States from unilaterally building a canal across Central America. The new treaty thus removed the last legal hurdle to building a Nicaragua canal under sole US control. Panama apparently had used up its ninth life.

Having bungled his company's chance to sell its canal assets, Hutin resigned as president. His replacement was Marius Bô, a director of the prominent French bank Crédit Lyonnais, which Cromwell represented in the United States. New Canal Company shareholders, at a meeting just before Christmas, became so riotous the police had to be called in to restore order. The sentiment of the 250 shareholders, some of them women, was to get the United States to buy the canal at any price to recoup some of their investments.

On January 4, 1902, Bô cabled Washington, offering to sell the canal property, including the railroad and all concession rights, for $40 million. Panama now was actually slightly cheaper than Nicaragua, by about $5 million. But it was too late; the House ignored the offer and on January 9 voted 309-2 to approve the Nicaragua bill.

The issue seemed settled. But then Theodore Roosevelt, previously a Nicaragua man, decided the situation deserved another look. The Walker Commission report had hinted that Panama might be a better choice but for the exorbitant financial demands of the French. The new price tag had changed everything. Roosevelt called in the nine members of the Walker Commission, one at a time, to solicit their candid private views in light of the reduced French offer.

Roosevelt was mostly swayed by George Morison, the fifty-nine-year-old respected bridge designer Cromwell had brought onto the commission. A huge, walrus-mustached man, the no-nonsense Morison reiterated to Roosevelt that the engineering advantage lay decidedly with Panama.

Convinced by the technical case, Roosevelt asked the commission to submit a supplemental report switching its recommendation to Panama—

and to make it unanimous. On Morison's motion, the Walker Commission issued a new canal report on January 18, endorsed by each member, recommending Panama as the most practical and feasible route. Senator Morgan was stunned, but he vowed to proceed with a Senate vote on the same Nicaragua bill the House had already overwhelmingly passed.

At this point Hanna, leader of the Senate's pro-Panama faction, sought to bring Cromwell back in the picture as counsel to the New Canal Company. To accomplish that he chose a colorful Frenchman closely connected with the entire Panama effort, Philippe Bunau-Varilla.

The forty-two-year-old Bunau-Varilla was a graduate of the prestigious École Polytechnique engineering school, where he had been inspired by one of de Lesseps's lectures to go to Panama. He became de Lesseps's chief engineer there until the bankruptcy of the original canal company in 1889. Although he was not personally convicted of any crime, his contracting firm, in which his brother had a majority interest, was charged with improprieties and became one of the major "penalty shareholders" forced to subscribe to shares in the New Canal Company.

Back in France, Bunau-Varilla resolved to revive what he called the "Great Adventure" of Panama. His messianic goal was to see the canal finished so as to safeguard "the work of the French genius" and avenge his nation's honor.

With his cultivated manner, precise diction, and finely waxed mustache, Bunau-Varilla cut a romantic figure despite his bantam five-foot-four frame. He was bursting with energy and ideas; his later bombastic memoirs marked him as an egotist, even a fabulist, of the first order. But there is no denying that he was a zealous, indefatigable, and highly effective propagandist for the Panama cause.

Although they did not meet until January 1902, Bunau-Varilla and Cromwell had been working independently for years toward the same goal—Cromwell as a lawyer representing a private client, and Bunau-Varilla representing only his own financial interests and ideals. In January 1901 Bunau-Varilla came to tour the United States, where he lectured, proselytized, and pamphleteered. He stayed in the best hotels, with a seemingly limitless expense account, having made a fortune from his early contracting work for the de Lesseps company and his coinvestment with his brother in the French newspaper *Le Matin*. He entertained and lavished gifts—cigars, flowers, a Tiffany clock—on various people he met. He tried to convince every one of them of the superiority of the Panama route, and as one acquaintance recalled, Bunau-Varilla "never let go of an American victim . . . until he thought he had converted him."

One of his claimed converts was Mark Hanna. According to Bunau-Varilla, it was he, not Cromwell, who single-handedly turned Hanna into a Panama man. As Bunau-Varilla told it, he was on a midnight stroll outside New York's Waldorf-Astoria hotel, where he was staying, when by chance he ran into a party in evening clothes entering the hotel. One of them was Hanna, to whom he was introduced. Coincidentally, Hanna was carrying around in his tuxedo pocket a letter of Bunau-Varilla's seeking an appointment, which Hanna said he had been intending to answer when he got back to Washington. He then invited Bunau-Varilla to his Washington home to discuss Panama and, after hearing the Frenchman's pitch, declared, "Monsieur Bunau-Varilla, you have convinced me."

On the same trip, Bunau-Varilla obtained an audience with Senator Morgan, Panama's arch foe. This interview did not go as well. When Morgan insultingly rebuffed him, Bunau-Varilla raised his hand to strike his antagonist but thought better of it, settling for calling him a cruel man to his face.

At least these were the stories Bunau-Varilla spun in later years.

Much has been written of the rivalry and mutual disregard between Bunau-Varilla and Cromwell. In his book on the canal, written in 1913, Bunau-Varilla repeatedly referred to Cromwell as "the lawyer Cromwell" (intended as an expression of derision) and dismissed him as little more than a messenger with an inflated sense of his own importance. Cromwell's enemies, on the other hand, tended to portray Bunau-Varilla as Cromwell's pawn. Cromwell never publicly disparaged Bunau-Varilla in writing, but he never acknowledged his contributions, either. According to his law partner Arthur Dean, Cromwell privately made clear he "had no use for Bunau-Varilla whom he regarded as an unprincipled adventurer and meddlesome intruder."

In truth, the two men worked together cooperatively, cordially, and effectively for several critical months in 1902 when the canal question hung in the balance. It was only years later, when it came time to assign credit (or blame) for the United States' virtual seizure of the canal, that the two of them began expressing contempt for each other.

Bunau-Varilla, in particular, maintained that Cromwell had greatly exaggerated his contributions in the application for $800,000 in legal fees he submitted to a panel of French arbitrators (he would be awarded just over $200,000). There was some truth to that accusation, as Cromwell's brief to support his fee request was an advocacy piece, not a dispassionate factual recitation. What seemed to bother Bunau-Varilla most was that the lengthy brief had not so much as mentioned his name.

Many of Bunau-Varilla's disparagements came after the fact. At the time, Bunau-Varilla seemed to welcome Cromwell as a fellow evangelist of the Panama faith. They were first introduced on the night of January 22, 1902, after a meeting in Washington among Cromwell, Hanna, and powerful Republican senator John Spooner. Bunau-Varilla was impressed enough to send an urgent cable at 2:00 A.M. (his time) to his wife, in Paris, urging Cromwell's reappointment as legal counsel. Three days later Bunau-Varilla warned his influential brother, the editor of *Le Matin*, that failure to rehire Cromwell would "alienate sympathies indispensable for saving the situation."

The day after Bunau-Varilla cabled his brother, Cromwell was reinstated. Bunau-Varilla congratulated Cromwell in a telegram that read, "Your affair was settled this morning according to my recommendation which I had to renew yesterday with great force. Felicitations." Cromwell was placed on a short leash by his client, however, in terms of spending money. Cromwell telegraphed his thanks to Bunau-Varilla, saying, "Not an hour is to be lost and I will prepare to act at once. Expect important movement in our favor this morning and will give you details."

One day later the important movement anticipated by Cromwell took place. Senator Spooner introduced a bill to substitute the word "Panama" for "Nicaragua" in the canal bill then facing a Senate vote. Cromwell claimed he inspired the amendment, which is plausible given Spooner's great admiration for him. "He is wonderful in his energy, in his quickness of comprehension, his mastery of details, his power of rapid generalization, his fertility of resources," Spooner had said of Cromwell when the two of them worked together as lawyers on the Northern Pacific reorganization a decade earlier. "Full of good impulses, and altogether a lovable man . . . he can bulldoze like damnation when he wants to, and I have seen him when he wanted to."

The canal issue came down to a final floor debate in June 1902, during which Morgan made the case for Nicaragua and Hanna for Panama, now dubbed the "Hannama Canal" by some. Together, Cromwell and Bunau-Varilla supplied Hanna with the ammunition he would need. Cromwell drafted a speech for him and a minority report under Hanna's name containing all the technical, legal, and economic arguments in favor of Panama. Slickly packaged, it was stuffed with testimony, diagrams, charts, and illustrations, and Cromwell made sure it landed on the desk of every member of Congress.

The package contained one intriguing argument that Bunau-Varilla had been peddling for years but which previously had not gained any traction: The Nicaragua route ran through a volcano field. The volcanos were colorfully displayed as a series of red splotches on a huge map put up on the wall for Hanna's argument. By serendipity, one of the craters, Momotombo, a hundred miles from the canal route and thought to be largely extinct, had erupted in March. It caused some seismic activity and property damage and continued smoking and rumbling for weeks thereafter.

In mid-May, shortly before the final Senate debate, Cromwell's press bureau planted the volcano story with the *New York Sun*, which followed up with an editorial doubting "the safety of any canal constructed through this boiling, bubbling, growling and shivering section of the earth's surface." More dramatically, that same month Mount Pelée on the Caribbean island of Martinique exploded, leveling an entire town and killing thirty thousand people in the deadliest volcanic disaster of the twentieth century. A simultaneous eruption on St. Vincent Island, just south of Martinique, devastated a large chunk of that island. Although Martinique was 1,600 miles from Nicaragua, the point was driven home: A Nicaraguan canal could be wiped out in an instant.

With Cromwell and Bunau-Varilla watching from the Senate gallery, Hanna spoke in favor of Panama over two days, June 5 and 6, extended because his arthritic knees gave out the first day. Shunning bombast or oratory, the sixty-four-year-old senator was conversational, thorough, and effective. It was hailed as the greatest speech of his long career. But because Hanna had not previously shown much oratorical skill, cynical pro-Nicaragua forces alleged Cromwell had written and rehearsed the whole speech with him. A reporter for one of William Randolph Hearst's papers was also in the gallery and noticed Cromwell, "the shrewd lawyer of the corrupt Panama scheme," smiling as he watched a scene he had helped set up by his nightly visits to Hanna's home.

Although Hanna had changed several minds, the Senate vote still hung in the balance. Nicaragua's supporters had managed to blunt the volcano scare by getting the Nicaraguan president to falsely deny that any eruption had occurred on Momotombo, or any other volcano in the country, since 1835.

It was then that Bunau-Varilla had an inspiration: He recalled that one of Nicaragua's postage stamps depicted a spectacularly erupting Momotombo, with a railroad wharf in the foreground. That same wharf reportedly had been destroyed by the volcanic activity in March. What better proof of the volcano's relevance than that its own country had chosen to feature it on an official postage stamp? Bunau-Varilla bought up every Momotombo stamp he could from Washington stamp dealers, had them pasted on sheets of paper, and sent them to every senator three days before the deciding vote.

On June 19, 1902, the Senate voted in favor of Panama by 42 to 34. One week later, after initially resisting, the House changed its vote from 309 to 2 for Nicaragua to 260 to 8 for Panama. An ebullient Cromwell cabled Bunau-Varilla, "Our bill passed."

With President Roosevelt's signature on June 28, 1902, the Spooner Act, authorizing building of the Panama Canal, became the law of the land. The $40 million sale of the French property was the largest real estate deal in history to that point.

Victory has a thousand fathers, and here there were several: Hanna, Cromwell, Bunau-Varilla, Morison, and of course Roosevelt. That both Cromwell and Bunau-Varilla touted their own roles to the exclusion of the other should not obscure the fact that the contributions of each were necessary, if not sufficient, for approval of the Panama Canal.

John Tyler Morgan, who was more familiar with the intricacies of the battle of the routes than perhaps anyone, was sure he knew who was most at fault for his defeat. "I trace this man [Cromwell] back to the beginning of the whole business," he thundered on the floor of the Senate during his closing argument on the final vote. "He has not failed to appear anywhere in this whole affair. . . . Beware of Mr. Cromwell."

The battle, however, was far from over. It would continue for more than another year, although it would shift from the chambers of Congress to a world of treaty making, back-channel diplomacy, secret cables, and, finally, revolution.

In the meantime, a quieter revolution was taking place on Wall Street, where Cromwell's fellow white shoe lawyer Paul Cravath was creating a new kind of law firm.

Chapter 5

The Cravath System

Paul Cravath hated inefficiency, which is why he had hired a professional librarian to create a filing system when he arrived at the Seward firm in 1899. He also believed lawyers performed most efficiently under favorable working conditions, or at least that is how he justified his request for an extra window in the office he took on the eighth floor of 40 Wall Street. The architects refused, however, because cutting through the wall would have weakened the structure on which the penthouse rested.

To make matters worse, Cravath's office on the west side of the building was subjected to constant nitric acid fumes from the US Treasury's Assay Office next door, where gold coins and crude bullion were melted down and minted into stamped bars. Meanwhile, lawyers on the east side of the building had to endure the sewer vapors that came in from the Bank of America Building.

Cravath labored under these conditions until May 1903, when the firm of Guthrie, Cravath & Henderson moved to the sixteenth and seventeenth floors of a new building at 52 William Street, built for one of the firm's largest clients, the banking firm of Kuhn, Loeb & Co. At his new office Cravath had all the light he needed and enjoyed unobstructed views of lower Manhattan on all four sides (and no more fumes).

By the time of the move, Cravath had begun implementing the changes he considered necessary to bring law firm management into the twentieth century. His partner Guthrie had no problem with the old way of doing things; he worked mostly on his own, with a few older assistants, and had little interest in creating a new system, much less in turning the office into some sort of law factory. Yet if that is what Cravath wanted to do, Guthrie was not going to interfere. Influenced by his mentor Walter Carter, the "collector of young masters" who had first employed him in 1886, Cravath forged ahead with his innovations. In time they would be adopted by almost every other Wall Street law firm and would remain in favor for the rest of the century.

Cravath's first principle was that all new legal hires were to come straight out of law school—and only the top schools. He wanted men (and they were all men in those years) who had not acquired bad habits picked up from practicing elsewhere. He could teach new recruits the nuts and bolts of lawyering once they came to his firm; it was most important that in law school they had learned how to think like a lawyer and already had a grounding in principles of the law as taught by scholarly faculty.

Although he preferred men with good college academic records (Phi Beta Kappa if possible), he recognized that college in those days was a place many went to have a good time and earn the proverbial gentleman's C. (Cravath himself did not have a particularly distinguished record at Oberlin College.) But law school was another matter. He sought graduates who earned the highest standards of achievement there, limiting his hiring to those who had attended one of the three elite law schools at the time: Harvard, Columbia, or Yale. (A little later, an occasional graduate from such law schools as Cornell, or the Universities of Pennsylvania, Chicago, Michigan, or Virginia, would be considered.) Cravath also favored those who had been editors of the school's law review, a scholarly journal that invited only the top students to join its staff.

In subsequent decades, few students who did not meet such criteria could expect an offer to join a top Wall Street law firm. But at the time, writes Cravath's partner Robert Swaine, Cravath's hiring criteria were considered "somewhat eccentric—not to say stuffy."

Cravath did not want bland eggheads, however. He sought out those who, like himself, had strong personalities and physical stamina. Young lawyers at Wall Street firms, who became known as "associates," followed a grueling schedule, regularly working evenings and weekends. They were expected to be at their desks every Saturday morning until midafternoon, or longer if something came up. Surviving on little sleep was part of the job; it was common for associates to stay into the wee hours of the morning, and sometimes all night, proofreading documents at the printer or researching and drafting a legal memorandum that some partner wanted on his desk by 9:00 a.m. It was not manual labor, to be sure, but young lawyers did not think they were exaggerating when they came to label their law firms "sweatshops."

Associates did not share in a firm's profits (or liabilities) but were paid a salary. Cravath made sure his associates received the highest going rate of pay in the city. A starting lawyer in 1903 made about $500 a year, increasing to as much as $2,000 after five years at the firm ($50,000 in 2019 money). Although nowhere near the skyrocketing salaries associates would be paid many decades later,* it was a decent living, especially considering that clerks previously had been treated as apprentices and paid nothing. In return, associates had to devote their entire professional work to the firm; no outside business interests were permitted (the same rule applied to partners). Charitable, educational, and artistic activities, however, were not only permitted but encouraged, as Cravath believed they made for a well-rounded lawyer.

As to the training of associates, Cravath believed they should spend their first few years becoming generalists in the law before specializing in a particular area. Initially they were assigned to one partner to work exclusively on his cases and for his clients; then they were rotated to another partner to do likewise, thus giving them a look at different lawyering styles and types of transactions.

At the outset, associates were "not thrown into deep water and told to swim," Swaine explained; rather they were "taken into shallow water and carefully taught strokes." Under the Cravath system a young lawyer watched a more senior one break down a large, complex matter into its component parts and then was given one of the smaller parts to complete thoroughly and in detail. By contrast, at Sullivan & Cromwell, which, like Cravath, hired only "geniuses selected from our great law schools," as Cromwell boasted, associates were given substantial independent responsibility almost from the start.

At the core of the Cravath system was a tenure policy known as "up or

---

*By 2018 entry-level associate base salaries reached $190,000 a year at Cravath, with most of its competitors quickly following suit. Lawyers just out of law school now make almost as much as a federal judge, and senior associates earn more than the chief justice of the Supreme Court.

out." Associates were given five or six years (later eight) to prove themselves, at which point they were either promoted to partner or were expected to leave the firm. If an associate was not good enough to become a partner, Cravath thought, then keeping him around impeded the professional growth of the younger lawyers; besides which, the associate who had been passed over would lose ambition and confidence and become a drag on the system.

But the Cravath firm took care of its own by finding them positions elsewhere. Cravath-trained lawyers were highly regarded within the profession and had little difficulty finding high-paying jobs at other quality firms, which sometimes took them in directly as partners. Or with Cravath's help they might be placed within the small law department of a corporate client, where they could combine good pay and benefits with a more reasonable nine-to-five schedule. Some would start their own small law firms or gravitate to academia, or occasionally even leave the profession altogether.

Cravath partners were almost always homegrown, promoted strictly from within the firm's associate ranks. In the white shoe world no one hired a partner "laterally" from another law firm. Not only was it considered ungentlemanly to lure a lawyer away from a competitor, but also each white shoe firm sought to maintain its own unique culture, which too many laterals might dilute. The inhibition against lateral partner hiring would persist among Wall Street law firms for most of the rest of the century. (It has since become common, although not at the Cravath firm.)

If an associate did make partner at Cravath or a similar blue-chip firm (and fewer than 10 percent did), then he was virtually guaranteed job security and steadily increasing earnings until retirement or death. Partners were not fired except for extreme breaches of faith, and no one left to join another law partnership. A partner might take time off to do public service or government work but usually was welcomed back to his old firm if he wished to return. Or he might move "in house" to become a corporate client's general counsel, or even its president, which was considered good for the law firm because it helped secure its relationship with the client. Most clients were loyal, anyway, and continued to hire the same firm year after year for all important matters. It was considered bad form for one white shoe law firm to try to steal another's longtime client.

Under the old nineteenth-century model, law firm partners kept their clients and fees to themselves. Under the Cravath system, profits were pooled and shared among all the partners based on an agreed formula. Two basic formulae emerged: the lockstep system, under which compensation is tied solely to seniority, so that older partners make more than younger ones; and the origination system, under which those lawyers who bring in the most client business (so-called rainmakers) are paid the most, regardless of their age, while those who merely service the same business make less.

Both systems have their permutations; even at Cravath, which was long considered a classic lockstep firm, adjustments were made to reflect partners' relative contributions and worth. Cravath himself was paid much more than anyone else at his firm, and, according to one story, when some of his partners approached him about the possibility of moving to a pure lockstep system, he said he had no objection "as long as I get my half."

Regardless of how profits were divided, Cravath insisted that the client of one partner was the client of all and that every partner had to be willing to work on business generated by someone else. Cravath's principle of shared profits, shared work would come to be adopted by almost every other white shoe law firm.

Cravath's approach was that of a technocrat. He believed he had created a meritocracy in which talent, competence, and ambition counted more than social standing or family influence. He emphasized how many successful New York lawyers had, like himself, come from small towns and worked their way up from the bottom. Under a merit-based system such as his, factors like religious and cultural background were irrelevant.

At least that was the theory. In reality, firms such as Cravath's had a definite religious and cultural identity. Overwhelmingly the white shoe firms were, like Cravath himself, white, Anglo-Saxon, Protestant, and male. In part this was a result of real, if publicly unacknowledged, discrimination against Jewish lawyers and, to a lesser extent, Catholics. In part it was the natural outgrowth of the WASP elitist culture of the time, which led firms to select lawyers from the "right" schools and social backgrounds.

Almost all graduates of the elite law schools, from which the top law firms recruited their associates, were Protestant white males. In turn, most top law school graduates wanted to become corporate lawyers in the elite Wall Street firms, which were considered the pinnacle and best-paying of the profession. And elite corporations, most of which were run by WASPs, wanted to be represented by the white shoe law firms, which were perceived as employing the "best" men, and with whom the clients felt culturally the most comfortable. Some prejudiced clients did not want their white shoe law firm to bring a Jewish or even a Catholic lawyer, much less a woman, to a meeting.

The white shoe lawyers moved in the same social circles and, along with their clients, belonged to the same private clubs, typically one or more of the Union League, Metropolitan, Knickerbocker, or Century Association in Manhattan; Piping Rock or Maidstone on Long Island; or the Tuxedo Club upstate. They educated their children in the same Ivy League prep schools, such as Andover, Groton, Phillips Exeter, and Trinity.

The top Wall Street lawyers were generally listed in the ultimate mark of elite status, New York's *Social Register.** They supported many of the same charities and cultural and art institutions, including the Metropolitan Museum of Art and the Legal Aid Society, and were regulars on the philanthropic gala circuit. They took turns succeeding one another as presidents of New York's state, county, and city bar associations.

This mutually reinforcing system constituted a Protestant old-boy network that dominated the top Wall Street firms for years. It would remain intact from Cravath's early days until roughly the mid-1960s, when a number of large Jewish law firms attained elite status on their own and emerged as rivals for top corporate business. In time, the white shoe firms ceased discriminating against Jewish lawyers altogether and began taking them directly into their ranks. (It would take considerably longer for women and minorities to gain acceptance.)[†]

---

*The 1906 *Social Register* included Cravath, Stetson, Cromwell, Root, Guthrie, Hornblower, Wickersham, and Hughes.

[†]Women did not enter large corporate law firms in meaningful numbers until the mid- to late 1970s, and there were relatively few women partners on Wall Street before 1990 (there had been a few in the 1940s during the war). The percentage of female partners at white shoe firms would stay under 20 percent into the twenty-first century, even though by that time half of all law school graduates were women. Non-white lawyers were the last to make inroads into the white shoe world, but for years their numbers were small, and the percentage of African American partners on Wall Street remains tiny.

By modern standards the early white shoe law firms were not large. In 1906, when Cravath took over leadership of his firm, it had twenty lawyers—three partners and seventeen associates. By 1920 it had grown to eight partners and twenty-seven associates. But that was nowhere near the five hundred lawyers who were working there in 2019—and Cravath was not even among the very largest firms; about two dozen firms had more than a thousand attorneys.

But as their most prestigious corporate clients grew steadily in size and complexity, so did the elite law firms. The firms became ever more specialized as well, with separate departments for corporate law, litigation, tax, real estate, and so on. Ironically, the banes of the early lawyers—the telephone, the secretarial pool, the elevator—made possible the physical expansion of law firms to the point where they took up multiple high floors in the tallest skyscrapers in Manhattan and elsewhere.

The growth of the white shoe firms was not so much intentional as inevitable. As corporations became more industrialized, and subject to greater governmental regulation, they needed constant legal supervision. As recalled by famed lawyer and onetime presidential candidate John W. Davis, who in 1921 joined the Wall Street firm that became Davis Polk & Wardwell, the growth of law firms came about because clients demanded more services:

> You have a client who comes to you with most of his business and expects you to take care of him. One can't possibly do it all, and you find that you've got to have help. You take on another man for that purpose.... We don't try to compartmentalize consciously but it works out that way.... Little by little you find your firm growing. The main aim is not to have the largest law firm, but simply to answer the problems brought to you.... If you don't answer them they go elsewhere.

To manage their growth the white shoe firms needed effective leadership, which prompted the final element in the Cravath system: strong executive direction. Despite his emphasis on teamwork, Cravath was the dictator at his firm during its formative years. So was Cromwell at Sullivan &

Cromwell and Stetson at his firm. Most Wall Street law firms, in fact, were dominated by one or two senior partners who were more equal than others in power and pay. It was by the names of their larger-than-life, autocratic leaders that most of the great law firms came to be known.*

Cravath was legendary for the way he exercised his authority. An associate had to have been tried out by another partner before Cravath would allow him to work directly for him. And once a young lawyer failed in his first chance with Cravath he seldom got another. "In those years Cravath was imperious and given to outbursts of temper when things were not done to suit him," recalled his partner Swaine, who joined the Cravath firm as an associate in 1910 and later authored a history of the firm. Overconfident in his own conclusions, quick to criticize poor work, Cravath was intolerant of incompetence in others. He rarely complimented good work, which he said was expected.

Swaine tells a story of how one night, a tired Cravath, having taken work home, as was his custom, summoned a young associate to his house to give him the assignment of drafting some papers in a specified way by the next morning. When the associate got back to the firm's office at about 2:00 A.M., he decided, after researching some legal cases, that Cravath's instructions were wrong on a point of law, so he drafted the papers the way he thought they should be, put them in an envelope for Cravath, then went home after his all-nighter—and overslept.

When the unnamed associate (an eventual partner who, one suspects, was Swaine himself) got in late the next morning, he was told that an irate Cravath wanted to see him immediately. He went to Cravath's office and brought with him two or three law books supporting his view on the legal point in question. Cravath lashed into him, and when the young man tried to explain his thinking, Cravath cut him off, saying he didn't need some

---

*Some of the others in existence around the turn of the century, and still bearing the names of their founding partners, include Simpson Thacher & Bartlett, which represented major railroads and energy companies, including General Electric; Shearman & Sterling, counsel to banks that later became Citibank; and White & Case, which organized Bankers Trust Company and represented J. P. Morgan & Co. in the purchase of war materials by the British and French governments in World War I.

novice lawyer telling him what was right. "If you can't give me what I want, you can get out!" Cravath yelled. Then he threw across the table one of the books the associate had been trying to show him (spilling an inkwell), tore up the associate's draft, and stormed out of the room for another meeting.

When Cravath returned he found a new draft on his desk, revised in accordance with his original instructions. He called in the associate and, smiling, told him, "I knew you could do it." But when the associate tried to resume the debate on the legal point, Cravath said he didn't have time and left the room, taking with him the new draft as well as the list of cases the associate had been trying to get him to read. "That afternoon a telephone call came to the associate from Cravath's home library," Swaine recalled. Cravath said he had finally read the cases and admitted the associate was right, after all. "Send up the draft you prepared last night," Cravath told him. The incident was never mentioned again.

"Many young men were broken in will power and initiative by Cravath's forceful personality and temper," Swaine wrote, "but he had little respect for anyone who cringed before him. Those who stood up to him got along best and were the ones he advanced." Years later, in a *New Yorker* magazine profile, the writer noted that although Cravath had since mellowed, most of the young men who had worked in his office in the early years "disliked him heartily, not because of his brusqueness, but because his unfailing confidence in his own judgment demanded that everything be done his way."

Cravath could be no less intimidating to lawyers outside his firm. "I always had the feeling that he was trying physically to squelch me," said Stetson's nephew Allen Wardwell. "It took all I had to go up and see him." As Swaine similarly observed, "Seldom was he a party to a conference that he did not dominate by his driving personality, with its ruthlessness tempered by persuasiveness and patient regard for the opinions of others. He would first try to convince and argue away opposition, but he could ride roughshod over those he could not convince."

Unlike Paul Cravath, Frank Stetson was not a yeller. He was a man of politeness and social grace. While serving as a Stetson clerk in 1886, Harry

Garfield (son of the US president) heard Stetson cross-examine an elderly female plaintiff of humble condition "with as much courtesy as he would have extended to a lady in his own circle—with the result a verdict for defendants." Stetson had a perpetual calm and smiling countenance and attracted a wide circle of friends, many from Williams College, with whom he kept up a steady correspondence for decades.

Yet he ran his firm as a sole proprietorship, with himself as shopkeeper. That is, if it could even be called a firm. One of his colleagues would later label it a law firm in name only. That was because Stetson, practically alone among the top white shoe corporate lawyers, resisted the teamwork and pooling concepts pioneered by Cravath. Instead he maintained the old system in which individual lawyers worked independently, sharing office space but not clients or profits. A partner kept his own fees, bore his own personal expenses, and paid his assistants out of his own pocket. J. P. Morgan, for example, was Stetson's client, not his firm's. And when a piece of business came Stetson's way that he chose not to handle himself, he felt no obligation to refer it to one of his partners, as opposed to someone outside the firm he thought more appropriate.

Also unlike Cravath, Stetson deliberately kept his firm small and informal. Not for him was the highly structured, bureaucratized law factory others were seeking to build. The downside of Stetson's system, to the younger men in his firm, was that he had no interest in building a lasting institution in which they might continue their profitable practice. He said he would be happy to see Stetson, Jennings & Russell, as the firm was known, be dissolved after the death of the three name partners. And it would not be until after Stetson's death that his firm, which later became known as Davis Polk & Wardwell, moved to a more Cravath-like system. Eventually it would grow to more than nine hundred lawyers with ten offices around the world, from its headquarters in New York to São Paulo, Paris, and Beijing. "Little by little," as John W. Davis had put it.

———※◉※———

William Nelson Cromwell was what one today might call a control freak. He went around his office shutting off lights and picking up rubber bands and paper clips from the floor for reuse. He distrusted the mails so much that when an important paper had to be filed or delivered to other counsel, he had several copies prepared and sent by separate mailings. Often he dispatched another copy by messenger on a train or by multiple messengers on trains taking different routes. To justify his precaution, he said, "Accidents don't happen, they are permitted to happen by fools who take no thought of misadventure."

Cromwell was held in awe by the lawyers who worked for him. Once he was taking a French visitor on a tour of the office, intending to end in the library, of which he was particularly proud. Along the way he stopped to open the door of a room known as the Bullpen to show off some of his young "genius" lawyers to his visitor. Inside were six of them cooped up together working at desks that encircled the telephone switchboard and operator. Cromwell stared at them for a few moments, saying nothing, and at length "they all rose and bowed," one of them recalled. At that Cromwell shut the door and continued the tour.

Cromwell kept an impressive suite at the office for his use, but he was rarely there. He conducted much of his practice from his residence, a dark mid-Victorian mansion at 12 West Forty-Ninth Street filled with museum-quality tapestries, paintings, and objets d'art. A gold pipe organ adorned the front hallway, although to relax, Cromwell played a more modest one upstairs. It was his one hobby, which he pursued to lose himself in melody and thought.

When Cromwell did go into the office at Wall and Broad Streets, he had himself dressed by his valet and driven in by limousine. Once there he would roam the halls, quizzing associates about their work and peering inside their offices to make sure they were still at their desks. He could tell by checking their hat rack if they had left for the evening, and did not take kindly to "two hat" men who tried to fool him by leaving an extra one hanging behind.

Eustace Seligman, Cromwell's longtime tax partner, recalled him as sociable and charitable but also "conceited, arrogant, dictatorial." He conceded Cromwell was an original thinker, had a brilliant mathematical business mind, and was a great "client-getter." But Seligman regarded Cromwell's speech as overly flowery and said that in his written work Cromwell never used one word when he could say something in ten. "I never especially liked him because he wasted so much time talking," Seligman recalled.

Cromwell had done quite a bit of talking, of course, to persuade the US government to switch its canal plans to Panama. And to close the deal he would be doing a whole lot more talking, some of which, it would be charged, was downright dangerous.

Chapter 6

"The Respectable Person"

Did he or didn't he?

Whether William Nelson Cromwell incited the Panamanian revolution is the most hotly debated question about his role in the affair. Congressman Henry T. Rainey, the progressive Illinois Democrat who labeled Cromwell the most dangerous American since Aaron Burr, was sure that Cromwell was a "professional revolutionist." So were Joseph Pulitzer's *New York World* and other newspapers, as well as many historians since. Yet Philippe Bunau-Varilla—no friend of Cromwell's—would declare Cromwell innocent of the revolutionist charge, a mantle Bunau-Varilla wished to claim solely for himself.

Cromwell's longtime law partner William Curtis, who worked closely with him on the matter, insisted in his memoirs that the two of them had done nothing to foster the revolution. Curtis's testimony might be dismissed as self-serving, except that his memoirs display little genuine warmth toward Cromwell. Curtis had toiled so hard over the years at Cromwell's firm that he suffered a nervous breakdown, from which he never fully recovered.

Arthur Dean, one of Cromwell's later partners, claimed in an admiring biography written in 1957 that diligent research had "revealed nothing . . . to support the assertion that Cromwell or his associates inspired, assisted or abetted in any way the revolution." What Dean failed to mention, although he revealed it to author David McCullough twenty years later, is that Cromwell's otherwise complete business files had a huge gap: They were curiously missing anything having to do with Panama.

The Spooner Act that authorized the United States to build a Panama Canal required that a satisfactory treaty be signed with Colombia granting US control over the canal territory in perpetuity. If that condition was not met within a "reasonable time," the president was authorized to proceed instead with a Nicaragua canal.

Negotiating a treaty with Colombia would prove to be the most tortuous chapter in the entire Panama story. The ultimate failure of the whole effort would lead Theodore Roosevelt to substitute gunboat diplomacy for the more traditional kind.

The official negotiator for the United States was Secretary of State John Hay; his opposite number was Colombia's minister to the United States, Dr. José Vicente Concha. Unofficially, Cromwell served as the sole intermediary between the two governments.

A year earlier, Cromwell had played the lead role in negotiating an accord with Concha that resulted in the Hay-Concha draft treaty of April 1902. That draft, subject to ratification by both countries, provided for a $7 million up-front payment by the United States to Colombia for the canal rights, with an annual payment to be determined at a later point. The United States had the right to control the building and operation of the canal and to intervene militarily to protect it with Colombia's consent, or without its consent in case of an emergency. The agreement was to last one hundred years. The United States had wanted it in perpetuity, but Colombia had insisted on a fixed term; Cromwell broke the impasse by obtaining agreement on a hundred-year lease, renewable at the sole option of the United States for similar periods, which made it perpetual for all practical purposes.

Concha was a proud, tense man who spoke almost no English and had never ventured beyond his native country before Colombia sent him to Washington. He pressed for various changes to the April 1902 draft, all of which the Americans found objectionable. For Cromwell, the most worrisome one was Concha's request to postpone a final treaty with the United States until Colombia could negotiate with the French investors for a portion of the $40 million they were to receive from the United States. Having already lowered its price from $109 million to $40 million, the French canal company was loath to share any part of the $40 million with Colombia.

Cromwell was able to convince Hay to stand firm on the point; the United States would not yield to Colombia's request to amend the treaty. In November 1902, Hay told Concha that unless a treaty was signed the next month, before Congress adjourned, Roosevelt would switch back to Nicaragua. Colombian officials blinked and ordered Concha to sign the treaty in its current state. Concha, discouraged and at his wit's end, refused to sign and sailed back to Colombia.

His replacement, Chargé d'Affaires Tomás Herrán, was more cosmopolitan and cultured. He spoke fluent English and three other languages, had attended Georgetown University, and had spent many years living abroad. He was not a hothead like Concha. But he was no pushover, either, and the first thing he did was to increase Colombia's asking price—from $7 million to $10 million up front and $600,000 annually.

Urged by Cromwell after a long conference to raise the US bid, Hay countered by offering a $10 million initial payment and $100,000 a year after ten years. Herrán rejected it out of hand. Hay, who was now prepared to break off negotiations, advised Herrán that Roosevelt had set a final deadline of January 5, 1903, and absent agreement by then the United States would leave Panama behind in favor of Nicaragua.

Cromwell was in despair. The talks were at an impasse, and Senator Morgan was practically daily renewing his calls for Roosevelt to make a final break with Panama. On January 2, 1903, Cromwell and Curtis met with Hay in Washington, and again on January 3 at great length, pleading with him to extend the January 5 deadline. Based on their continuous conversations with Herrán, the two lawyers expressed confidence they could bring Colombia to terms if given a little more time. At this point Cromwell and Curtis were shuttling between Hay and Herrán virtually round the clock.

Late on the night of January 21, Cromwell brokered a compromise under which the United States would pay Colombia a $10 million lump sum and $250,000 annually. At 5:00 P.M. on January 22, Cromwell brought Herrán to Hay's home on Lafayette Square. After the ministers exchanged signatures, Hay turned to Cromwell, who served as the sole witness, and to show his appreciation presented him with the pen.

How was it that Cromwell, who represented a private foreign company with its own financial interests, had been entrusted with such great responsibility for the most significant commercial acquisition by the United States since the Louisiana Purchase? As a lawyer his duty was to his French client, not the United States, yet he was permitted to wield practically as much influence over the negotiations as the president and secretary of state.

No doubt his successes up to that point had impressed the White House. There is also a story, perhaps apocryphal, that Roosevelt was convinced to give Cromwell free rein on the basis of advice from Mark Hanna. "You want to be very careful, Theodore," Hanna is reported to have advised the young president. "This is a very ticklish business. You had better be guided by Cromwell; he knows all about the subject and all about those people down there." Roosevelt replied that "the trouble with Cromwell is he overestimates his relation to [the] cosmos." "Cosmos," said Hanna. "I don't know him—I don't know any of those South Americans, but Cromwell knows them all; you stick close to Cromwell."

The US Senate ratified the Hay-Herrán Treaty on March 17, 1903, by an overwhelming vote of 73 to 5. Senator Morgan did his best to try to derail the treaty by submitting some sixty amendments, which Cromwell and his partners worked successfully to defeat.

To convince senators the slightest change would jeopardize the treaty, Cromwell let them in on a little secret. It turned out that three days after Tomás Herrán signed the treaty in Hay's residence, he received the following cable from Colombia's acting president, José Manuel Marroquín:

"Do not sign canal treaty. You will receive instructions in letter of today."

⸺⬥⸺

In Colombia, strenuous opposition to the canal treaty formed almost immediately. Many Colombians thought their country was sacrificing too much of its national sovereignty to Yankee imperialism. And they wanted more money—instead of $10 million up front and a $250,000 annuity, Colombian officials considered $25 million and a $1 million annual rental to be their due. In addition, Colombia wanted a substantial cut of the $40 million the United States had agreed to pay the French canal company—anywhere from $10 million to $20 million, or a quarter to a half of the total payment.

Cromwell knew which buttons to push. To the high-minded Hay he stressed that Colombia had already pledged herself morally, and as a matter of international good faith, to ratify the treaty as signed. Roosevelt came to view the Colombians in Bogotá as "contemptible little creatures" and "bandits" whose extortionate demands were jeopardizing one of the future highways of civilization. "We may have to give a lesson to those jack rabbits," he told Hay. Even Hay, a diplomat by temperament, privately referred to the Colombians as "greedy little anthropoids." Cromwell was too careful to use any such epithets in writing, but his arguments subtly appealed to both Roosevelt's and Hay's prejudices against Latin Americans.

On June 13, 1903, at Hanna's invitation, Cromwell spent many hours in conference with Roosevelt, during which the president made clear he intended to build a canal in Panama, one way or another. Afterward Cromwell made the five-minute walk from the White House to the new Willard Hotel, where he lived when in Washington, to meet with his press agent, Roger L. Farnham. After the two men conferred, Farnham went across the street to the Washington bureau office of the *New York World*, his old employer, and gave the paper a story on the Panama Canal not for attribution. He told the *World* correspondent there would be an uprising on the isthmus, probably on November 3, Election Day in the United States, and that five or six Panamanian citizens were on their way to Washington to consult with Secretary of State Hay and other State Department officials about their plans.

The next day the *World* ran an article reporting that Roosevelt was determined to build a canal in Panama but that the Colombian Congress was likely to reject the Hay-Herrán Treaty. In that event, the report continued, Panama would secede from Colombia, Roosevelt would promptly recognize the new Panamanian government, and the United States would sign a canal treaty with Panama. The article would prove prophetic, fueling suspicions that Cromwell not only had advance knowledge of the Panamanian revolution but actively worked to bring it about.

By mid-June 1903, Cromwell was aware the treaty with Colombia was in serious trouble and was unlikely to pass. He knew this from his many operatives on the isthmus and in Bogotá, including officials of the Panama Railroad, of which he was general counsel, and from internal US State Department cables to which he was privy.

It required no special insight to foresee a Panamanian rebellion. Panama felt no strong allegiance to the rest of Colombia and had made a number of attempts at independence over the years. It was all just talk, though, until someone stepped forward to lead a takeover. And probably the best proof of Cromwell's association with the revolution is that the men who organized the movement—the junta—were the very employees of the Panama Railroad with whom he had been in constant contact.

The ringleader (El Maestro) was sixty-two-year-old senator José Agustín Arango, the railroad's attorney on the isthmus and a prominent politician. Dr. Manuel Amador Guerrero, the railroad's seventy-year-old surgeon and a man of great influence on the isthmus, enlisted in the plot as well. Short, with gray hair and a mustache, Amador had especially keen dark eyes that could flash with indignation. Amador, Arango, and other railroad employees became titular heads of the revolutionary movement.

Knowing they would need US support for their plans, the conspirators sent another railroad employee, a savvy freight agent named James Beers, to New York to meet with Cromwell. Beers's secret mission was to seek assurances from "persons of high position and influence" (meaning Cromwell) that the United States would not intervene on Colombia's behalf in the event of a Panamanian insurrection.

According to a later account, when meeting with Beers, Cromwell "promised everything to him." And when Beers returned to Panama in early August he informed the plotters that Cromwell was prepared to "go the limit" for them. They then sent Amador to meet with Cromwell in New York to arrange for money and munitions, and to obtain, if possible, direct assurance from Hay or Roosevelt that the United States would support a revolution and recognize the new government.

Under the pretense that he was going to visit his sick son in Massachusetts, Amador sailed for New York on August 26, carrying with him a cable code for his communications with the conspirators back in Panama. The code, which identified Hay as "X" and Cromwell as "W," contained thirty different numbered statements from Amador to the junta covering every conceivable contingency. Among the options Amador could communicate to his friends were:

   1. Have not been satisfied with Hay in my first conference.

     · · ·

6. Cromwell has behaved very well, and has facilitated my interviews with important men who are disposed to cooperate.

. . .

11. Delay of Cromwell in introducing me to Hay makes me suspect that all he has said is imagination and that he knows nothing.

. . .

23. Cromwell is determined to go the limit, but the means at his disposal are not sufficient to ensure success.

On his arrival in New York, Amador took an inexpensive room in the Hotel Endicott, located far uptown at Eighty-First Street and Columbus Avenue. But in meeting Cromwell he was beaten to the punch by one of his fellow passengers, José Gabriel Duque, a Cuban-born, naturalized American citizen who owned Panama City's major newspaper and a profitable import-export business.

Duque's motives in the Panama affair remain unclear and his behavior hard to explain. He had been one of the attendees at a luncheon in July 1903 at which the conspirators openly discussed revolution. Later he would assist the rebels by organizing and financing a fake volunteer "fire brigade" of 287 young men to serve as a revolutionary military force. But in between he seems to have been acting as a double agent on behalf of the Colombian government. His account of his activities—relayed only secondhand by Cromwell's bitterest critics at the *New York World*—is important, for it constitutes the most specific evidence of Cromwell's alleged involvement with the Panamanian revolution.

Duque maintained that he was on one of his regular business trips to the United States and that, despite playing poker with Amador on the voyage, he was unaware his fellow traveler was going to New York to discuss revolution with Cromwell. While Amador was uptown relaxing at his hotel, Duque dropped in at the exporting office of Andreas & Company near Battery Park, which was serving as a front for revolutionists in New York. There, as Duque rather implausibly claimed, he just happened to run into Cromwell's utility man and press agent, Roger Farnham. According to Duque, Farnham told him that Cromwell, whom Duque barely knew, wished to see him, so Duque went with Farnham to Cromwell's office at 49 Wall Street, about ten minutes away.

During their meeting, Cromwell supposedly offered Duque the presidency of the new Republic of Panama if he would bring about a revolution there. According to the testimony of the *World*'s correspondents, Cromwell also told Duque that he would furnish security for a $100,000 loan to the rebels to meet immediate expenses. (Primarily, they needed money to bribe easily corruptible Colombian soldiers on the isthmus who had been unpaid for months.)

Cromwell then called the State Department on the telephone, which he disliked using, to set up an appointment for Duque to meet Hay the next morning, September 3, and gave him a note of introduction. At Farnham's urging, Duque agreed to take a night train to Washington and to return immediately after his meeting, avoiding the need for an overnight hotel stay that would leave a record of his visit.

During his meeting with Hay in Washington, Duque revealed the revolutionists' plot and asked for the US government's support. Hay is said to have told Duque that although the Roosevelt administration could make no promise of direct assistance to the revolutionists, it was intent on building the Panama Canal and would not allow Colombia to stand in the way.

Around 1:00 P.M. Duque walked out of the State Department and made a beeline for the Colombian embassy. There Duque proceeded to disclose to legation head Tomás Herrán everything Hay had told him. He also informed Herrán that Amador was in New York intending to meet with Cromwell to plot the separatist movement.

Whether Duque was secretly in league with the Colombian government against the rebels at that point is unknown; more likely, as a strong supporter of the Hay-Herrán Treaty, Duque wanted Herrán to convey the urgency of the situation to Bogotá as a spur to ratification. In either event, he had compromised the conspirators—and Cromwell.

Herrán cabled Bogotá to alert Colombian officials to the revolutionists' plans, then wrote to Cromwell in New York, warning him that Colombia would hold him and his clients strictly accountable for any secessionist plot. As a precaution—or to create a record to protect himself—on September 10 Cromwell cabled railroad superintendent James Shaler in Panama to instruct him not to participate in any insurrectionist movements or to do anything that would provide Colombia with a pretext for canceling the French concession rights.

Meanwhile, Amador had met twice with Cromwell in New York, with radically different outcomes. In the first, extremely cordial meeting, Cromwell provided Amador with assurances akin to those he had given Beers. Cromwell made "a thousand offers in the direction of assisting" the revolution and invited Amador back for a further discussion a few days later. But in their second meeting, Cromwell's enthusiasm had vanished. By then—and unbeknownst to Amador—Cromwell had been frightened off by Herrán's stern warning. Amador also did not realize Herrán had put detectives on his trail.

When Amador showed up at Sullivan & Cromwell's offices he was falsely told that Cromwell was not in, but the old doctor camped out in the reception area until Cromwell came out and saw him. Cromwell told Amador he could not have anything more to do with him and not to come back. Dr. Amador was finally shooed out of the office.

Unable to make sense of what had happened, Amador ignored his cable code and sent his coconspirators back home a terse message: "Disappointed; await letters." He made plans to sail back to Panama, empty-handed. But then he received word from friends that if he sat tight in New York, help would come from another quarter. He cabled an equally cryptic one-word message to his friends in Panama: "Hope." Before he had a chance to explain, help did arrive, from Paris, in the form of that ardent little Frenchman Philippe Bunau-Varilla.

Bunau-Varilla would always insist that his arrival in New York on September 22, 1903, after having spent the last seven months in France, was purely fortuitous, another of the many lucky coincidences that seemed to save the Panama Canal just when hopes were flagging. He had come on a family trip, he said, deciding at the last minute to join his wife in visiting their thirteen-year-old son, who was recuperating from hay fever on a friend's estate near West Point.

Others have suspected it was no coincidence—that Cromwell, or someone at his direction, must have cabled Bunau-Varilla in Paris to say Cromwell's cover was blown and the conspirators needed some new master planner to replace him in America. Up to that point the two men were still on good terms, and in their last correspondence on file, from mid-1902, they exchanged cordial letters. Cromwell sent Bunau-Varilla a large basket of fruit to enjoy on his voyage home in July, for which the Frenchman expressed gratitude while hailing the joint efforts of "French and American genius." A month later in Paris, Cromwell expressed hope that the two of them could soon meet for a dinner to include Cromwell's wife and Bunau-Varilla's brother.

But Bunau-Varilla soon changed his tune. On September 24 he met with Dr. Amador in the Frenchman's regular hotel room at the Waldorf-Astoria, then located at Thirty-Fourth Street and Fifth Avenue. Bunau-Varilla told the doctor he had been foolish to trust Cromwell. For his part, Amador felt betrayed by Cromwell, to such an extent that, as Bunau-Varilla would later claim, Amador threatened to hunt down and kill the lawyer if the revolution failed and any of the doctor's friends were jailed and executed.

Bunau-Varilla told Amador not to worry, that he, Bunau-Varilla, would handle everything, including lending the junta $100,000 himself and verifying that the United States military would protect the new republic. Bunau-Varilla was so confident that he gave Amador a revolution kit to take home with him, including a declaration of independence, a constitution, and a national flag his wife had designed.

From the time of his arrival in New York, Bunau-Varilla said he "never saw the shadow" of Cromwell, whom he would accuse of abandoning the conspirators "cold-bloodedly to their fate." It did appear that way: Cromwell stopped answering telegrams from the isthmus and sailed for France on October 15, where he remained for three weeks. Ostensibly he went there to confer with his clients, but others would accuse him of cowardice—of escaping to Paris to disavow any connection with the potentially violent uprising he believed was coming and which he had helped set in motion. Conveniently, he did not arrive back in New York until November 17, two weeks after the revolution was over.

In what was surely one of the least unexpected insurrections of the twentieth century, the Panamanian Revolution went off mostly without a hitch on November 3—the very day Roger Farnham had predicted back in June. The US gunboat *Nashville*, carrying a few dozen marines, arrived at Colón around 5:30 P.M. on November 2. But close to midnight so did a Colombian warship, the *Cartagena*, which had some four hundred Colombian sharp-shooters on board. The *Nashville*'s commander had not yet received a cable from Washington ordering him to prevent the landing of any hostile armed forces, so the Colombian troops went ashore on the morning of November 3 unmolested. They were planning to cross on the railroad to Panama City, fifty miles away, where an uprising was rumored to be in the works.

Except there was no train—just a single luxury car and locomotive that James Shaler, the railroad superintendent, said had been set aside to escort the Colombian general and his top aides to Panama City. There was a temporary shortage of regular cars, Shaler explained, but they would arrive shortly to transport the rank-and-file soldiers. What Shaler did not say was that he had sent all the rolling stock to the Panama City end of the line so the troops would remain stuck in Colón.

The seventy-seven-year-old Shaler, a Kentuckian and Civil War veteran, was a persuasive and impressive man. He was tall, lean, and muscular ("molded like a genuine thoroughbred," as one reporter described him) and bore a distinctive, huge white mustache and bushy, pure-white hair, all of which made him stand out among the natives. His word on the isthmus had the force and effect of law. Thus, when he insisted that the Colombian general and his officers board the special car if they wanted to get to their destination, they obeyed, and when one of them became suspicious and wanted to hop off, Shaler pulled the cord himself, blew the train whistle, and sent them on their way.

When the Colombian military brass pulled into the station in Panama City, they were greeted with pomp and ceremony—all of it rehearsed and fake. They were arrested a few hours later by the garrison commander, who had agreed to support the revolution in return for $65,000 for himself and $50 for each of his men. At dusk, Duque's "fire brigade" signaled the start of the revolt by blowing their bugles. Citizens rushed to Cathedral Plaza to listen to the declaration of independence and watch the raising of the new flag. The revolution was completed without a shot having been fired.

On November 6, 1903, three days after the successful coup, the United States formally recognized the new Republic of Panama. Hay and Bunau-

Varilla proceeded to turn the Hay-Herrán Treaty with Colombia into the Hay–Bunau-Varilla Treaty with Panama, which they signed on November 18 in Washington.

Under the new treaty, Panama received the entire $10 million and $250,000 annuity previously earmarked for Colombia, which got nothing. The treaty copied many of the provisions of the Hay-Herrán Treaty that Cromwell had drafted, but Hay and Bunau-Varilla added several that were more advantageous to the United States. Most notably, the United States was given all the rights it would possess as if it were the sovereign of the territory, "to the entire exclusion of the exercise by the Republic of Panama of any such sovereign rights."

Bunau-Varilla knew that the Panamanians would not take kindly to a Frenchman signing away their sovereignty, so he had pressed Hay to conclude the treaty as quickly as possible. In fact, just as Hay and Bunau-Varilla were putting the final touches on the treaty, a delegation of three Panamanian revolutionists, headed by Amador, arrived in New York on the morning of November 17 with authority to override Bunau-Varilla on treaty matters. They planned to head immediately to Washington to oversee the negotiations, but the ubiquitous Farnham, who met them at the boat, urged them to wait for Cromwell, who was arriving from Paris in a few hours. Farnham escorted them to the Fifth Avenue Hotel, long the city's most elegant, where they spent a full day in conference with Cromwell. Much to Bunau-Varilla's later dismay, Amador forgave Cromwell for shunning him earlier, once he heard Cromwell explain that he was being ultra-cautious after being exposed by Duque.

Bunau-Varilla, who desperately wanted to be the signer of the historic Panama Canal treaty, saw the Cromwell-Amador détente as part of a nefarious effort to undermine the treaty negotiations and to satisfy Amador's "childish" desire to become the signer himself. The irony, though, is that by lingering with Cromwell until the afternoon of November 18, when they boarded the train for Washington, the Panamanian delegation arrived too late to prevent Bunau-Varilla from signing the treaty, which he did with Hay around 7:00 P.M. that evening.

The revolutionists were dumbfounded, then enraged, when Bunau-Varilla met them at the train station a couple of hours later and told them he had already signed it. One of them slapped him across the face. But eventually they became resigned to the situation and dutifully brought the treaty back with them to Panama, where the provisional government immediately ratified it on December 2. The US Senate followed with its ratification, by a comfortable 66-to-14 margin, on February 23—eight days after Mark Hanna, who had led the Senate fight for Panama, died at age sixty-six.

Bunau-Varilla's suspicion that Cromwell was plotting with the Panamanians to sabotage the treaty makes little sense. Cromwell's primary interest remained, as it had been for seven years, to accomplish the sale of his French clients' assets, and the Hay–Bunau-Varilla Treaty guaranteed just that. In fact, a couple of days after the treaty was signed on November 18, Cromwell was in Washington and offered Bunau-Varilla his compliments and congratulations. Then again in Washington on February 23, just after Senate ratification, Cromwell ran into Bunau-Varilla in the Willard Hotel and seized his hand to express his congratulations. All of which raises an intriguing question: Did Cromwell intentionally keep the Panamanian delegation occupied in New York to prevent them from putting a brake on Bunau-Varilla? Were the two of them again working independently toward the same goal?

At least some support for this theory can be found in a portion of the private memoirs of Cromwell's partner Curtis that has never made the history books. Curtis instructed those who came into possession of his story not to publish it during the lifetime of the parties, and perhaps not at all.

On November 10, 1903, while Cromwell was ending his stay in Paris, Curtis met with Roosevelt and Mark Hanna in the White House. The president asked Curtis whether he knew Bunau-Varilla, and when Curtis said yes, Roosevelt said, "I wish you would tell him to shut up and not talk so much," referring to the numerous self-aggrandizing interviews the Frenchman was giving to the newspapers at that delicate time. Rising from his chair, Roosevelt leaned over to Hanna and said, "Senator, in the language of our boyhood, I think we should be permitted to 'skin our own skunk,'" an idiom meaning to do one's own dirty work.

Later that day, Curtis sent Bunau-Varilla a confidential message relaying Roosevelt's desire for him to avoid any public statements or interviews.

The more curious part of the message, though, was Curtis's reference to the Panamanian delegation, led by Amador, that was scheduled to arrive in Washington a week later. Curtis suggested that Bunau-Varilla determine the exact credentials of the delegation to make clear there was no possible conflict of authority between him and them in the negotiation of the treaty. Then Curtis added, "We are advised that they have *full powers*. This may be a mistake—*I hope it is*."

Curtis's message shows that even at that late date, Bunau-Varilla was still communicating and coordinating strategy with the Sullivan & Cromwell firm. It also suggests that Curtis—and by extension Cromwell—was hoping the Panama delegation did *not* have the full powers that might enable them to undercut Bunau-Varilla in his negotiations with Hay.

By meeting at length with the Panamanian revolutionists on November 17, Cromwell was able to reconcile with them, ingratiate himself with them, and express sympathy with Amador's desire to sign the treaty. But in so doing he also gave time to Bunau-Varilla to push the treaty through to signing, unconstrained by superior authority. And because Cromwell's fingerprints were not on the final, one-sided treaty, he knew it would be Bunau-Varilla, if anyone, who would incur the wrath of Panama for giving away the store.

Which is exactly what happened. For all his ingenious efforts to bring the Panama Canal treaty to fruition, Bunau-Varilla would be excoriated by Panamanian nationalists for having bargained away the new nation's sovereignty. A legislative resolution years later would label him a foreign enemy of the people.

Meanwhile, Cromwell was welcomed by the Panamanians with open arms and went into their employ. On November 30 the junta entrusted him with the first flag of the new Republic of Panama, to be presented to President Roosevelt. The Panamanians had not liked Mrs. Bunau-Varilla's flag, thinking it looked too much like America's Stars and Stripes, so Amador's son, also a doctor, designed a new one.

Then, on February 23, 1904, the day Amador was inaugurated as the first president of the new republic, his son, the new consul general in New York, gave a luncheon at the Waldorf-Astoria to the local men to whom he and his father considered the new republic most indebted. Their names appeared on the menu card, with Cromwell's first, followed by those of Curtis and two other Sullivan & Cromwell lawyers, press agent Roger Farnham, and several officers or employees of the Panama Railroad.

And when it came time for Panama to invest the $10 million it was paid by the United States under the treaty, the republic chose Cromwell to oversee the fund and act as general counsel. He even became listed as one of Panama's official diplomats.

Cromwell also managed to have another client, J. P. Morgan & Co., hired as the fiscal agent to be paid a fee for disbursing the United States' $40 million to the French canal company. It was hardly a windfall for the French: Per prior agreement, 40 percent of the $40 million went to the New Canal Company, which yielded a modest 3 percent annual return for its shareholders, including Bunau-Varilla, over the ten-year course of their investment. The 60 percent that went to the old company was only enough to pay its bondholders ten cents on the dollar. Old company shareholders received nothing. Still, had there been no Panama Canal, the French investors would have been completely wiped out.

There remains the question of Cromwell's involvement in the Panamanian uprising. The charge of "professional revolutionist" is overblown, as there is no evidence he was directly communicating with the rebels in the moments leading up to the November revolution. But the claim by Cromwell's partner Dean that neither Cromwell nor any of his colleagues aided or abetted the revolution "in any way" is not sustainable, either. Cromwell certainly gave substantial encouragement to the revolutionists early on. And it is hard to believe that the key railroad employees in Panama who answered to him, particularly superintendent Shaler, would have acted without at least his tacit consent at the critical hour.

Curtis admitted that he and Cromwell were "perfectly willing and glad to have the revolution occur." They knew that if it were successful it would guarantee the success of the Panama Canal project for their French clients. But they also knew that if they were identified directly or indirectly with any of the revolutionists, Colombia would likely revoke their clients' concession and seize their railroad property.

For a time, as Theodore Roosevelt observed, Cromwell was "a typical revolutionist" who was "in it for the fun of the game." But when Duque betrayed him to Herrán, Cromwell seemed to awaken to the fact that revolution was a serious and dangerous business. He needed to pull back—or at least give himself a greater level of plausible deniability.

It is no coincidence that, in the post-revolution memoirs of Arango, the originator of the revolutionist plot, Cromwell is never identified by name, but only as *La Persona Respectable* ("the respectable person"). In their eagerness to indict Cromwell, the *World* reporters translated this as "the responsible person," implying that the junta considered Cromwell the person most responsible for the revolution. But "respectable" in Spanish translates to English as "reputable," "ethical," or "upstanding," and that is how Cromwell thought of himself. It did not fit the image of a respectable white shoe lawyer to become mixed up in a plot to violently overthrow a foreign government.

Cromwell would pridefully refer to Panama as "my canal" in later years. However, he never squarely addressed the revolutionist charge, at least publicly or in any detail, and was brusque with researchers who sought to question him about it. Dean wrote that because of Cromwell's love of the theater and flair for the dramatic, "it is quite possible that he rather enjoyed being a man of mystery."

Indeed, thought Dean, Cromwell may even have relished the "most dangerous man" moniker. According to Theodore Roosevelt, Cromwell liked to "walk around New York looking as much like a conspirator as possible and feeling ecstatic whenever the *World* accused him of being responsible for the 'Panama Infamy.'"

Famous or infamous for what he accomplished in Panama, Cromwell had become the most talked about lawyer in America.

Chapter 7

A Gordian Knot

Three weeks after the US Senate ratified the Panama Canal Treaty, the Supreme Court issued its decision in the *Northern Securities* case. By a narrow 5–4 vote, the high court ruled that the Harriman-Hill-Morgan holding company was an illegal restraint of trade in violation of the Sherman Antitrust Act and would have to be dissolved.

Although Frank Stetson had painstakingly done the paperwork on the deal to protect it from legal attack, he was pessimistic about the outcome of the lawsuit once it was filed. He believed the Supreme Court would bow to prevailing public opinion and rule against wealthy capitalists. He proved right.

The decision was a huge victory for the government—as well as a personal one for President Theodore Roosevelt—and a significant defeat for Wall Street. The court's landmark ruling put new teeth in the Sherman Act and ended the merger wave that had begun around 1890. In particular, the New Jersey holding company device—William Cromwell's great invention—was no longer the impenetrable fortress against antitrust prosecution big business had come to believe it was. The court held that to establish a Sherman Act violation the government did not have to prove that a business combination would result in a complete monopoly; it was enough to show that the combination inevitably tended to restrain trade or create a monopoly and thus deprive the public of the advantages flowing from free competition.

Newspapers hailed the decision as a great victory for the progressive movement, and the governor of Minnesota said it meant more to the people than any event since the Civil War. Roosevelt himself looked back upon it as one of the great achievements of his administration because it showed that "the most powerful men in this country were held to accountability before the law."

Stetson of course did not see it that way. He viewed the decision as reflecting a lynch mob mentality that was out to get big corporations and their lawyers simply because of their size and influence. He was joined in that view by one of the dissenting justices, Oliver Wendell Holmes Jr., who protested that the court had condemned large corporations based on bigness alone. It was this case in which Holmes issued his famous dictum, "Great cases like hard cases make bad law."

Unlike Holmes, who was widely, if not totally accurately, considered a liberal, Stetson was a Jeffersonian Democrat generally distrustful of federal power. He always considered the Sherman Act a bit of "foolishness"—a misguided attempt to legislate morality among businessmen whose natural instincts ran to their own private interest, and always would. He viewed existing state laws as sufficient protection of the public.

To nullify the *Northern Securities* decision, Stetson drafted a bill behind the scenes for US Senate consideration that would have substantially weakened the federal antitrust law. When that effort failed, he set up the Constitution Club, together with William Hornblower and other New York City bar leaders, to assail Roosevelt as an autocrat and to oppose his 1904 bid to win the presidency in his own right.

Roosevelt knew and respected Stetson and Hornblower, was always unfailingly polite, even friendly, in private correspondence with them, and occasionally sought their advice. Once, as vice president, Roosevelt had apologized to Stetson for being too busy to accept a speaking invitation, adding, "There are many reasons why I hate not to do anything you ask." But as president, Roosevelt found them to be useful public foils. He virtually welcomed opposition from "the big corporation people and lawyers, who, like Francis Stetson, are good fellows, but are incapable of taking anything but the corporation attitude."

Stetson was a realist, though, and after the *Northern Securities* decision he began cautioning his clients against forming large new business combinations. "You can't fight a community," he once said. He counseled businessmen likewise. "My client can satisfy me that this corporation is always going to be a good boy and never will do anything wrong," he explained, but that didn't mean it wouldn't be prosecuted as a monopoly. In the meantime, he devised a plan to ameliorate the adverse effects of the Supreme Court's ruling on his client Morgan that would, in effect, stick it to E. H. Harriman.

Although the Supreme Court had voided the Northern Securities Company, the court left it up to that company's board of directors as to how to dissolve the corporation. The most obvious approach was simply to return to each of the three parties—Harriman, Hill, and Morgan—the same stock they had originally contributed to form the now-invalid company. Harriman favored this method because by getting back his Northern Pacific stock, he would have the same large interest in that railroad he had acquired earlier through market purchases. With the parties restored to the status quo ante, Harriman would be free in theory to resume his prior takeover bid.

But Stetson came up with a different idea. His plan was to give each constituent party stock in each individual railroad in proportion to his Northern Securities holdings. This second, so-called pro rata distribution method would leave Harriman with a minority interest in both the Northern Pacific and the Great Northern. Harriman protested and filed suit to prevent Stetson's plan from being implemented.

Harriman's first choice to represent him was Elihu Root, the fifty-nine-year-old lion of the New York City bar who had returned to private practice just a few weeks earlier, having left his position as Roosevelt's secretary of war. Originally McKinley's war secretary, Root modernized the army, expanded West Point, and founded the US Army War College. He developed American policies for new colonial possessions, supported the American suppression of the Filipino insurrection, and favored intervention in Cuba if necessary to maintain stability there. Later, he served as Roosevelt's secretary of state, maintaining John Hay's Open Door policy with China. During his subsequent term as a US senator, Root served as the first president of the Carnegie Endowment for International Peace, helped found the Permanent Court of International Justice, and was awarded the 1912 Nobel Peace Prize.

The son of a mathematics professor, Root graduated Phi Beta Kappa from Hamilton College, in upstate New York, and obtained his law degree from New York University. He began in private practice as an old-style courtroom lawyer, then served as a federal prosecutor (appointed by his friend President Chester A. Arthur) before transitioning into one of the preeminent corporate practitioners of his day.

For someone who became respected as a pillar of rectitude, Root represented his share of robber barons. He advised the Havemeyers, owners of the despised Sugar Trust, to protect themselves by reorganizing the trust as a New Jersey holding company, a move that later enabled them to defeat the government's antitrust suit. He helped transportation magnates William C. Whitney and Thomas Fortune Ryan monopolize New York's electric streetcar system.

Root had also defended the infamous Boss Tweed, first as a junior assistant counsel in a criminal trial and later in a civil suit when Tweed was on his way to prison. Root's own mother asked him why he would aid "that wicked man. The verdict of the world is against him. The verdict of your own heart is against him." Root's answer, expressed years later in a law school commencement address, was that "no matter how vile the criminal," he was entitled to a defense based on his constitutional rights. Nonetheless, the Tweed representation would dog Root for the rest of his career, and along with Root's reputation as a corporation lawyer, it diminished his chance of ever being elected to national political office.

Root preferred to think of himself not as a corporation lawyer but as a lawyer with corporate clients. He was principally a legal technician, capable of representing any side of an issue, and adept at finding compromise solutions to seemingly intractable problems. He viewed his chief task as keeping his clients out of litigation. As he once said, "about half the practice of a decent lawyer consists in telling would-be clients that they are damned fools and should stop." A more client-friendly version of this same sentiment has been attributed to various Wall Street tycoons: that a good lawyer was one who, like Root, would tell his client not what he could not do but how to do legally what he wanted to do.

Grave and earnest in manner despite his youthful bangs, Root's calm exterior masked a vigorous fighting spirit (his only weakness was for cigars). He was also known for his witty sarcasm. When Roosevelt asked him whether he had adequately defended himself against charges of having stolen the Panama Canal, Root dryly responded, "You have shown that you were accused of seduction and you have conclusively proved that you were guilty of rape."

Unlike Roosevelt, Root was not a progressive. He never felt the same burning sense of injustice over the plight of the downtrodden that Roosevelt did. Whereas Roosevelt appealed to the common man and the oppressed classes, Root distrusted the popular will and the tyranny of the majority. He valued, above all, stability and order.

Root did recognize the need for reforms to regulate big business; as early as 1894, for example, he had urged a ban on corporate campaign contributions. But Root favored a much more gradualist approach, and he poked fun at Roosevelt's frequent bursts of righteous indignation against the corporate system. In a cover letter to him enclosing a newspaper editorial highly critical of one of Roosevelt's progressive initiatives as governor of New York, Root deadpanned, "In view of the enclosed article I must decline our further acquaintance." Roosevelt was momentarily riled until he read the editorial and realized Root was joking.

Root, who was fifty-four when he first came to Washington, always maintained he had not sought out government work. "The office of being a leading lawyer in New York City is the only one I ever cared about," he said in later years. He took the job of war secretary in 1899 only after McKinley assured him it would be mostly legal in nature. He never regretted the move, though, because he had already made more money as a Wall Street lawyer than he knew what to do with, and when he went to Washington "a thousand new interests" came into his life. He felt guilty about dragging his wife, a homebody, all over the world, but he thought she "became a happier woman than she would have been if she had stayed at home. It gave her new interests, new contacts."

By 1904 Root was perhaps the most widely respected lawyer–elder statesman in America. Two years earlier, he had played a pivotal role in the settlement of the anthracite coal strike, which threatened to create social unrest as the cold winter months approached. Because most of the coal mines were owned by railroad men, Root enlisted the help of J. P. Morgan, who held interests in major railroads.

Aboard Morgan's yacht the *Corsair*, the two men came up with a compromise—neutral arbitration. President Roosevelt virtually forced the idea down the throats of the reluctant industry men. It was the first time the federal government had intervened in a labor dispute as an impartial mediator rather than on the side of management, in stark contrast to Grover Cleveland's use of federal troops to break the 1894 Pullman railroad strike.

William Nelson Cromwell, spearheading the Northern Pacific railroad re-organization at the time of the Pullman strike, had welcomed—indeed, actively sought—military aid from the federal authorities. He insisted that "there is no such thing as a lawful strike." But Roosevelt's Square Deal was moving the country in a more progressive direction on labor as well as corporate and antitrust issues.

As a member of Roosevelt's cabinet, Root tried hard to convince businessmen like Harriman that the president, for all his rhetoric, ultimately had their best interests in mind. Now, in 1904, Harriman the railroad man wanted the eminent Root to represent him on the breakup of the Northern Securities Company. But he was too late. Just two hours before Harriman asked him to serve as his counsel, Root had accepted a $75,000 retainer to join Stetson's legal defense team. Harriman then tapped William Guthrie, Cravath's partner, to bring the lawsuit to stop Stetson's distribution plan. As Harriman's counsel, Guthrie had helped draw up the papers for the original Northern Securities merger and had defeated a private shareholder suit that tried to stop the transaction.

Ironically, a few years earlier, Root had turned down what he considered a generous offer from Guthrie to join the Seward firm. He explained that, because he was already a wealthy man, he would rather make less money elsewhere than work in the pressure-cooker atmosphere of a "large" corporate law firm (then about a dozen lawyers). As it turned out, Root chose to stay in McKinley's cabinet, and then Roosevelt's, as war secretary until January 1904, when he returned to private practice and accepted the Northern Securities retainer.

The battle over the Northern Securities dissolution method turned as bitter as the original takeover fight between the Harriman and Hill-Morgan forces. In the April 1904 hearing before the Minnesota federal court that had jurisdiction over the dispute, both parties were represented by an array of counsel seldom matched for sheer brilliance. Guthrie, whose powers of pure legal reasoning were exceeded by no one, appeared on behalf of Harriman. On the defense side were Stetson, Root, and John G. Johnson of Philadelphia, an appellate specialist the *New York Times* once called perhaps "the greatest lawyer in the English-speaking world."

The venerable sixty-three-year-old Johnson, another of J. P. Morgan's regular lawyers, had won the famous 1895 Sugar Trust case for the antitrust defendants in the Supreme Court. Like Morgan, Johnson was a prodigious art collector. Reclusive to the point of refusing to be photographed, Johnson was one of the few leading corporate lawyers in the country who practiced outside New York City. He was known for refusing pay beyond what he considered the actual value of his services. A large man, he was also famous for taking on small cases, even if they involved only a few dollars. This was not one of them.

Guthrie thus faced a formidable team. Yet, contentious as he was in his interpersonal relations, he was quietly effective in the courtroom. He was described by a local Minneapolis paper as "small of stature, boyish in face and soft of speech; he seemed like a young David going forth to meet the giant champion of the Philistines." His principal argument, which the same newspaper called "masterful," was that giving Harriman back his controlling interest in Northern Pacific stock would be better for competition than allowing Hill and Morgan to keep control of the parallel and competing Northern Pacific and Great Northern lines, as well as the Chicago, Burlington & Quincy Railroad.

But the argument that ultimately carried the day was one devised by Stetson and forcefully advanced by Root and Johnson as Stetson sat beside them in court. Because the Northern Securities merger had been declared illegal by the Supreme Court, then all the agreements that led to its formation—including Harriman's exchanges of his Northern Pacific stock for shares of Northern Securities—were also illegal. That being the case, Harriman, as a party to those illegal agreements, was not entitled, as a matter of equity, to any relief from the courts. Johnson called the Harriman interests "co-sinners" who wore the mask of public benefactors to conceal their selfish ends. The case went up to the Supreme Court, which unanimously ruled a year later in favor of Hill and Morgan.

Harriman's loss—if it can be called that, for he made more than $50 million on the deal—may have had something to do with how unsympathetic a figure he was. His genius as a modernizer and administrator of railroads—no railroad man was a greater visionary—was overshadowed by a combative disposition that caused him to make enemies easily. J. P. Morgan was feared and loathed by many, too, but he was a dealmaker who at least professed to act in the public interest when necessary to maintain order, as he and Stetson had done in the 1895 gold crisis and Morgan and Root had done in the 1902 coal strike.

Harriman, by contrast, was a Wall Street shark—an opportunist willing to blow up the system if it served his interest. Besides, he was a sniveling little man with a drooping mustache, whose meek, bespectacled appearance—that of a backroom clerk—masked an arrogant contempt for anyone who dared stand in the way of his quest for power. He once boasted he could buy any member of the legislature or judiciary he wanted, as claimed by Roosevelt, who came to despise him, a feeling Harriman heartily reciprocated.

And it would be just this bitter, disdainful attitude that would lead Harriman to bump heads with Paul Cravath in the next newsworthy public episode in Cravath's career.

On the cold Tuesday night of January 31, 1905, five weeks before his loss in the Supreme Court, Harriman attended a lavish costume ball for the cream of New York society at Sherry's, a multifloor restaurant at Fifth Avenue and Forty-Fourth Street. Although no one could have known it at the time, the event would soon lead to the first great Wall Street scandal of the early twentieth century. Harriman, Hill, and Morgan would again be involved, as would lawyers Hughes, Root, Guthrie, Cravath, Johnson, and Hornblower.

The scandal concerned The Equitable Life Assurance Society, one of three giant insurance companies that dominated an industry accounting for half of all American savings at the turn of the century. Together, the Equitable, New York Life Insurance, and the Mutual Life Insurance Company took in more money than the federal government. Their combined assets of $1.2 billion equaled almost half the deposits in the nation's savings banks. And in an age before the social safety net, life insurance was the main form of protection for individuals against death or disability; it was considered a "sacred trust" between the insurers and their policyholders.

The winter ball was thrown by James Hazen Hyde, the twenty-eight-year-old heir to the Equitable, which his father, Henry Hyde, had founded in 1859. Upon the elder Hyde's death in 1899, his son inherited majority stockholder control of the company and became its vice president and a member of the board of directors. He sat on a board that included such captains of industry as Carnegie Steel chairman Henry Clay Frick, railroad moguls James J. Hill and E. H. Harriman, financier August Belmont Jr. (of later Belmont racetrack fame), John Jacob Astor (of later *Titanic* fame), and banker Jacob Schiff, of Kuhn, Loeb & Co., which underwrote most of Harriman's ventures.

Suddenly, James Hyde was being courted by the greatest magnates of the day, who were eager to do business with an insurance company that had a huge pool of capital to invest. Harriman joined the Equitable board in 1901, at Hyde's invitation, on the same day the Equitable loaned Harriman $2.7 million that he used to finance his takeover bid for the Northern Pacific. (Harriman called the timing coincidental.) Hyde himself was invited onto the boards of more than forty other major companies, from which he drew substantial directors' fees.

But James Hyde's real interest was in the playboy social scene. He was the richest, handsomest bachelor in New York, squiring such eligible young women as first daughter Alice Roosevelt around Manhattan and the horse and coach racing tracks of Long Island. He sported a goatee, dressed in fashionable silks and satins, and ostentatiously wore yellow gloves with his blue suit—unheard of at the time.

His greatest love was for all things France—French clothing, art, theater, and opera—and for his highly publicized costume party he had Sherry's mirrored ballrooms decorated in the style of the gardens of the Palace of Versailles. Women attended in eighteenth-century dress, their hair powdered, as did some of the men, who alternatively were allowed to appear in the dress of their hunt and coaching clubs. The six hundred guests were entertained by the Metropolitan Opera's orchestra and ballet corps and a one-act comedy performed by the French actress Réjane and written specially for the occasion. After a supper of consommé, lobster, pheasant, and ice cream, followed by dancing and two more suppers, the party that had begun at the "exceptionally early" hour of 10:30 p.m. ended at seven the next morning. It was among the grandest balls the Gilded Age had ever seen.

Soon rumors started to swirl that the event had cost $200,000 and that James Hyde had charged the Equitable for it. Although the accusation was untrue, some Equitable directors became concerned that Hyde's reckless extravagance was jeopardizing the conservatism of the funds the insurance company held for the benefit of its five hundred thousand policyholders. Those concerns increased when allegations surfaced that Hyde had committed or condoned various financial improprieties involving the Equitable's assets—self-dealing and commingling of funds, insider trading, hiding of liabilities, illegal political contributions, and accounting shenanigans designed to obscure the foregoing.

Hyde and other Equitable officers were using their control of policyholder funds, together with their connections to Wall Street, to line their own pockets. The most serious questions centered on an investment syndicate, James Hazen Hyde and Associates, that acted as a middleman in buying, on the Equitable's behalf, corporate securities that Wall Street firms wished to sell. Although legal at the time, Hyde's syndicate participation created a clear conflict of interest because it enabled him to siphon off profits for himself and his associates that could have gone to the Equitable.

Before his death, the elder Hyde had placed his chief deputy, James W. Alexander, in charge of training young James in the business until he could take over management at age thirty. But now Alexander, president of the company and sixty-five years old, turned on his ward. He criticized Hyde's syndicate dealings and his "costly and ostentatious entertainments, accompanied, as they are, by continuous notoriety of a flippant, trivial, cheap description." Alexander requested that Hyde sell his majority stock interest in the Equitable and resign his positions as vice president and director.

Alexander was also pushing for the Equitable to be mutualized—that is, to give policyholders, instead of stockholders, the right to elect directors. It was a popular proposal with the Equitable's sales agents, who could tout mutualization as an added benefit to their policyholder clients and often obtain their proxies to vote. But Hyde, who stood to lose power from such a move, resisted the proposal, further alienating his mentor.

The Equitable board, which had fifty-two members, split into warring factions, with roughly half aligning with Alexander and the other half, including E. H. Harriman and his banker Schiff, siding with Hyde. Alexander hired Cravath's partner, Guthrie, as well as Hornblower and Charles Evans Hughes, to represent his interests, while Hyde retained a high-powered team that included Root and John G. Johnson, the same pair who had just won the Supreme Court case for Hill and Morgan against Harriman.

The newspapers were filled with daily front-page coverage of the board-room battle, and it was openly suspected that Harriman was angling to obtain control of the Equitable for himself. At one particularly acrimonious board meeting, Harriman, who opposed mutualization, shook his fist at Alexander and threatened to have him thrown out the window of the seven-story Equitable Building. (The city's first skyscraper, it was also the first office building equipped with an elevator.) Meanwhile, rumors also floated that J. P. Morgan, who held a major interest in New York Life, was eyeing a takeover of the competing Equitable in order to merge the two insurers.

As the crisis deepened, and with each new revelation of financial chicanery, it seemed the Equitable was headed toward bankruptcy. The Equitable board appointed a committee represented by counsel for both factions—Root, Guthrie, and Hornblower—to study the mutualization issue and seek a compromise. It went nowhere, and when Alexander, who was increasingly coming under suspicion himself for financial wrongdoing, suddenly flip-flopped and opposed mutualization, Guthrie resigned as his counsel in disgust. John G. Johnson, who had advised the mutualization committee, later refused any pay for it because there was "such a damnable scandal about everything connected with the Equitable." Root was so consumed with the Equitable mess that he asked the Supreme Court to postpone an argument he was to give in an important constitutional law case; the justices, aware of how important a healthy Equitable was to the national economy, agreed.

An internal investigation led by board member Henry Frick condemned both Hyde and Alexander for their financial self-dealings and demanded their resignations. Hyde felt betrayed by Harriman and Schiff, both of whom had endorsed the Frick report after having led Hyde to believe it would be favorable to him. Hyde dug in and refused to step down or sell his shares, for which he had received several large cash offers, including one for $5 million from Frick himself, allegedly in alliance with Harriman, though Harriman denied it.

The now rudderless company seemed on the verge of collapse. Directors were resigning by the day to distance themselves from the muck. Given its close and extensive ties with Wall Street, the Equitable's failure would threaten to bring down the nation's entire financial system.

It was at this point, in early June 1905, that Thomas Fortune Ryan, a mutual client of Root and Cravath, entered the picture. Orphaned at age five, Ryan had begun work as a dry goods clerk and stockbroker before transforming himself into a titan of American business. By dominating the American tobacco industry, public utilities, and the New York City public surface railway (streetcar) lines, he amassed a fortune as great as any of the robber barons.

Despite this, the six-foot-two Ryan was little known to the public. He kept a low profile, as his connections to New York's Democratic Tammany machine were not something he wanted publicized, and he presented himself as a charming, mild-mannered Southerner. The *New York Times* dubbed him "the sphinx of Wall Street" and asked simply, "Who is Thomas F. Ryan?" His business partner William C. Whitney, who had been Cleveland's navy secretary, called Ryan "the most adroit, suave, and noiseless man that American finance has ever known."

Root had been instrumental in the 1890s in helping Ryan gain control of New York's electric streetcar system, which replaced the old horse-drawn car companies. At the suggestion of Frank Stetson, Whitney's longtime counsel, Root created a holding company, one of the first of its kind, with the use of watered stock. Ryan later opined that 95 percent of all early railroad company and street railway stock was water, with not a dollar put in to back it.

In a short time, Ryan had parlayed a minimal original capital contribution into one of the largest transportation fortunes of the Gilded Age. By 1904, though, when the first New York City subway opened, trams and trolleys were falling behind the times and Ryan was looking to expand his transit empire underground. To represent him, Ryan chose Paul Cravath. To the Republican, Protestant Cravath, it mattered not that Ryan was a Democrat and a strong Irish-Catholic, just as Cravath had no problem frequently representing Kuhn, Loeb, the great Jewish banking firm run by Schiff that competed with the Gentile J. P. Morgan. Wall Street's white shoe law firms were almost entirely WASP, but they knew a well-paying client when they saw one.

In spring 1905—at the same time the Equitable scandal was raging—Cravath was working to obtain for Ryan's Metropolitan Securities Company various city contracts to build and operate the planned subway extensions. The advantage Ryan could offer was free transfers from his surface lines to underground rapid transit lines and vice versa. As Ryan boasted, for a nickel people in Manhattan and the Bronx could ride from their homes to their places of business at a rate of speed possible only with underground rapid transit lines operated in conjunction with surface lines, bringing "rapid transit to the door of every citizen."

Cravath appeared regularly in public hearings before the city's rapid transit commission and argued in favor of the Metropolitan group's bids over those of the rival group headed by banker August Belmont Jr., who had financed the first subway. Belmont's Interborough Rapid Transit (IRT) Company had the existing underground subway franchise and leased the city's elevated railways, but it did not control any surface lines. Representatives of the most congested parts of Manhattan and undeveloped sections of the Bronx greeted the Ryan proposals with great acclaim. The separate Brooklyn transportation system interests supported the Metropolitan over Belmont after being assured they could have lines running into their recently annexed borough. Belmont now had competition for the subway monopoly he briefly enjoyed, and Ryan appeared on his way to even greater glory.

After the death of his partner Whitney in 1904, Ryan, at age fifty-three, had begun thinking of his legacy and wanted to be remembered as someone who accomplished more in life than just making money. (He lived lavishly in a Fifth Avenue mansion with a palm court and fountain, private Catholic chapel, and three Rodin busts of himself.) Although he had no prior connection to any of the major life insurance companies, he became alarmed at the growing chaos at the Equitable and the likelihood of its bankruptcy if nothing were done. He concluded that someone needed to devise a plan for preventing "the frightful losses that would occur from the violent breaking up of the Equitable" and "the most tremendous panic that this country had ever seen." After conferring with Root and Cravath, the three of them came up with an idea they thought would appeal to the public and maybe even to James Hazen Hyde.

On the night of June 8, 1905, Ryan asked Hyde to meet him at his office at 32 Nassau Street, about a block from the Equitable Building at 120 Broadway. Hyde came with one of his lawyers, Samuel Untermyer, and upon their arrival at Ryan's inner sanctum, an office the New York Times described as a "baronial stronghold," they were greeted by Ryan and Cravath.

Ryan explained his proposal. He would buy all of Hyde's Equitable stock—502 shares, representing a majority interest—for $2.5 million, then place the shares in a blind trust to be managed by men of high integrity: his friend ex-president Grover Cleveland; Judge Morgan O'Brien, a New York state court appellate justice; and Cravath's longtime client George Westinghouse. It was Cravath who convinced Westinghouse to assume the position on top of his demanding duties at the electric company.

The three trustees would vote the stock and select twenty-four directors, while twenty-eight would be elected by Equitable's policyholders. Ryan would have no management control and his only remuneration would be modest dividends on his stock.

Although Ryan's $2.5 million was significantly less than what others had offered him, Hyde had by this time had enough of the Equitable. He would sell his stock, leave the company, and flee to his beloved Paris. To be seen as sacrificing his financial self-interest to place the company on a sound footing appealed to him as the best way out. He agreed to Ryan's terms, and Cravath was tasked with drawing up papers. Cravath was taking the lead lawyering role inasmuch as Root was conflicted—he had represented Hyde personally, and the Equitable board, and now Ryan—although he continued to maintain what one newspaper would call "a fostering eye, ever alert and ever ready to counsel and guide as the exigency may require."

The next day, June 9, the Equitable board approved the Ryan plan. Hyde, Alexander, and other high-ranking officers resigned. The press reaction was mixed but mostly positive. Some newspapers, notably Joseph Pulitzer's World, criticized Ryan as an opportunist, taking advantage of a "wolf and lamb" situation to add insurance to his business kingdom. Others, though, applauded his public-spirited rescue effort. Typical was a New York Times piece that hailed Ryan as "the man who cut the Gordian knot of the Equitable tangle."

One man who begged to differ was E. H. Harriman.

Chapter 8

"I Turned My Back on Cravath"

On Friday morning, June 9, 1905, E. H. Harriman was on his way to his Union Pacific office in the Equitable Building when he learned of the Ryan-Hyde deal. Just off the Twenty-Third Street ferry from his country home in upstate New York, he raced to his downtown office. There he telephoned Ryan to ask if the rumors he had bought the stock were true. When Ryan said they were, Harriman responded that it was "rather staggering" that Ryan, an insurance neophyte, should have control of the Equitable.

Ryan invited Harriman to come talk to him. Ten minutes later Harriman was in Ryan's office listening to him explain that he had plenty of money, that he had never done anything eye-catching, and that he thought there was now an opportunity for him to do something big. He told Harriman he hoped for his cooperation.

Harriman rather doubted the sincerity of Ryan's professed motives and told him so. According to Harriman, Ryan promised he would do nothing more to further his plan without Harriman's consent and asked where he could reach him that evening. Harriman said that normally he left town on weekends to be at his country estate but that he would stay in Manhattan that night at the Metropolitan Club and wait to hear from Ryan. Instead he was paid a late-night visit by Cravath. As Harriman would later testify:

> I went there, waited until about eleven o'clock at night, when Mr. Cravath came up to see me and then told me that Mr. Ryan had sent him; that he was sorry that he had to act without letting me know; told me what he had done, and he wanted to inform me first. I resented such treatment, and told Mr. Cravath that I was not in the habit of being trifled with in that way, being deprived of going to my home and stay-

ing in town in such a way, and that I considered that an act of bad faith and an evidence of Mr. Ryan's intentions, and said nothing more. I believe I turned my back on Cravath and walked away.

As Harriman further related, Cravath told him it was a done deal. Cravath said the three trustees had already been appointed, that "Mr. Root had insisted upon its being done at once, and announced in the New York papers, the morning papers, and that there was no time to confer with me." Cravath towered above the five-foot-four Harriman, but the wee mogul was not cowed. He told Cravath, "Mr. Ryan had a telephone on his desk and there was a telephone in the Metropolitan Club, and there would not have been five minutes lost by its announcement to me."

Harriman and Ryan agreed to talk again on Monday. And what happened between them that day led to perhaps the most dramatic, colorful exchange of public testimony in the entire sordid Equitable affair.

———◦⦿◦———

Just after the Ryan deal ended the boardroom struggle, the New York State Legislature appointed a committee to investigate the allegations of financial improprieties in the life insurance industry, including at the Equitable and the other two major life insurance companies—New York Life and Mutual Life. Cravath was retained as special counsel to advise the Equitable on the investigations, and he helped ensure that the other companies were to be thoroughly investigated as well so that the Equitable would not be scapegoated.

The lead counsel for the Armstrong Committee (named for the state senator who chaired it) was Charles Evans Hughes, Cravath's old partner from their Carter firm days. Hughes was now forty-three—a year younger than Cravath, though he had been a couple of years ahead of him at Columbia Law School, having graduated from high school at the age of thirteen.

Born in Glens Falls in upstate New York, Hughes, like Cravath, was a preacher's son and something of a prodigy. It was said that he had read all of Shakespeare's works by age eight. Despite his parents' wishes that he enter the ministry, he planned to become a college professor. After graduating from Brown University he took a position with a private boarding academy in upstate New York, where he taught Latin, Greek, and mathematics. He clerked at Carter's firm during law school and for several years after, then left to teach law at Cornell University for two years before returning to private practice in New York in 1893.

Back again with Carter, whose daughter he had married in 1888, Hughes developed a reputation as a coldly analytical, intellectual lawyer particularly skilled at investigating complex matters. A speed reader with a photographic memory, he was able to absorb huge quantities of material, then quote it all back nearly verbatim. Even Cravath, with his limitless energy, marveled at Hughes's superior work ethic. "Many nights Hughes and I sat reading law together," Cravath recalled, "but at two o'clock in the morning I was usually on the sofa, dozing, despite black coffee and wet towels, but Hughes was still reading."

Hughes was viewed by many as overly pious and austere, a perception aided by his careful grooming and long, distinguished-looking beard—dark in photos but red in person. "His was an intellectual moralism," wrote one historian. "He believed in God but believed equally that God was on the side of the facts." Later, as a Supreme Court justice, Hughes would often interrupt the lawyers before him, one of them recalling that "he cut me off in the middle of the word 'if.'"

Belying his icy exterior, Hughes was more engaging and personable in private. He was described by friends as far from unbending, a charming storyteller, and a witty conversationalist. But he was also tense and high-strung, and for years he smoked cigars to excess to relieve the stress until he gave up the habit to improve his efficiency. Hughes frequently worked himself to the point of exhaustion, and even depression, at least once receiving electroshock treatments. After an especially taxing workday he would often spend the next day in bed. He sought respite by bicycling, playing golf, and taking lengthy annual European vacations.

Hughes was a progressive Reform Republican, not beholden to the party bosses who had controlled the Albany legislature for years, and thus was seen as a good choice for the committee counsel job. He was reluctant to take it when first offered because he had recently been advising James Alexander on mutualization issues and could be seen as having a conflict of interest. But during a mountain climbing vacation in the Bavarian Alps,

Hughes was unable to concentrate on the scenery because he feared he was giving up what he told his wife would be "the most tremendous job in the United States." Thus, when Cravath on behalf of Ryan, as well as the lawyers for Alexander and Hyde, consented to Hughes's appointment, Hughes accepted the assignment and hurried home.

Beginning in September 1905, and through the Christmas holiday season, Hughes led the investigation of the "big three" life insurance companies. The hearings were held in a large chamber in New York's City Hall, packed daily with reporters and spectators. According to one study, "the scandal and investigation were the 1980s takeover wars, the junk bond boom, and the insider-trading scandals rolled into one sustained event."

Despite the sensational subject matter, Hughes soberly and methodically drew from witnesses casual admissions of financial graft and malfeasance. Many of the men who testified could not see what all the fuss was about, as it was the way everyone in the industry had been doing business for years. Hughes also produced surprising revelations about the close business ties among the supposedly staid insurers, Wall Street speculators, securities underwriters, and their industrialist partners. In search of higher returns, the life insurers were putting policyholder money into speculative, risky ventures.

Some of the most startling disclosures concerned campaign contributions to the Republican Party and its candidates in the tens and hundreds of thousands of dollars. But the real scandal was the surprising number of practices that, while ethically dubious, were technically legal, which pointed to the need for reform legislation. By sheer tenacity and clarity of mind, Hughes brought out the dramatic revelations in a way that made them understandable to the ordinary newspaper reader. He was so effective that powerful Republicans tried to pry him off the job by offering him the candidacy for mayor of New York. Feeling duty-bound to complete his investigation, Hughes declined.

Hughes was particularly adept at getting witnesses to embarrass themselves with their own words. He quizzed George W. Perkins, second in command at New York Life and a partner in J. P. Morgan's banking firm, as to how he handled the conflict of interest inherent in serving both companies simultaneously. In one particular case, Perkins hid a bad investment by

New York Life by arranging a bogus sale of $800,000 worth of the life insurance company's securities to J. P. Morgan & Co., which temporarily kept them off the insurer's books. Perkins then bought them back for the same price a few days later.

"Now," Hughes observed, "that all might have been done while you were sitting at the desk in five minutes, and when in that five minutes . . . did you cease acting as a New York Life officer and begin acting as a partner of Morgan & Company?" Perkins, widely known as Morgan's highly capable and cocksure right-hand man, said he was acting for both. Hughes followed up: "When, in your judgment, are you acting for the New York Life?" he asked. "All the time," Perkins replied. "When are you acting for J. P. Morgan & Company?" Hughes continued. "It depends on what the actual case is" was the best Perkins could offer.

Regarding a similar transaction in bonds between New York Life and Morgan & Co., Hughes asked Perkins, "When you bargained for the bonds, did you bargain with any person other than yourself?" Perkins answered, "I can't recollect, but I think I did it myself, probably." Hughes later got Perkins to admit to disguising a $50,000 New York Life contribution to Roosevelt's 1904 presidential campaign by writing the check in his own name and then obtaining reimbursement from the insurance company. Although an indictment against Perkins was eventually thrown out on the grounds that he lacked criminal intent, he ended up paying back New York Life the $50,000, with interest, out of his own pocket.

The climax to the Armstrong hearings came on December 8, when Thomas Ryan was called to testify about his purchase of James Hyde's stock. He was now represented solely by Cravath, as Root had rejoined Roosevelt's cabinet, this time as secretary of state, after John Hay died in July. The hearing room was heavy with anticipation as the savior of the Equitable finally took the stand.

Ryan began by calmly explaining his purpose in buying the stock: to prevent a panic, and to place voting control of the Equitable in the hands of men of such high character that their motives could not be questioned. He regarded the purchase as a great public service but admitted he was motivated in part by the desire to protect his own financial interests.

Then, toward the end of his testimony, Ryan was asked whether anyone had wanted to share ownership with him. He hesitated and asked whether he really had to answer. When Hughes told him yes, Ryan revealed, "Mr. E. H. Harriman desired to share the purchase with me, and I refused." Ryan had made up his mind that he did not want a partner, he told Harriman, and he did not want anyone interfering with his plan for trustees. Nor did he think anyone previously connected with the Equitable as a director, such as Harriman, should have an interest in the company going forward. His relations with Harriman became quite strained for several days, he added.

But when Hughes pressed for details as to what Harriman had said, Cravath, representing Ryan, objected. This was, Cravath asserted, an "unofficial" and "private" conversation between Ryan and Harriman that Ryan was not required to disclose. Undeterred, Hughes and the committee chairman directed Ryan to answer. "My advice is that you are not required to answer," Cravath said aloud to Ryan, who responded to Hughes, in turn, "I refuse to answer on counsel's advice." Hughes pressed several times more. "Do you still refuse to answer?" he asked Ryan. "I do under advice of counsel" was the response. In all, Ryan declined more than a dozen times, on advice of counsel, to say what Harriman had said to him.

RYAN WON'T TELL screamed the headline in the *New York Times* the next day. In the meantime Hughes and the committee asked the county district attorney to prosecute Ryan for refusing to answer a legislative inquiry, a crime punishable by up to one year in jail and a $500 fine. Cravath told Root the committee was probably concerned that if it did not press for Ryan's testimony it would be accused "of having shielded Harriman or being influenced by the occult political influence which Mr. Harriman is popularly supposed to wield."

Cravath was too good a lawyer not to realize that his objection to Hughes's questioning of Ryan was groundless. The conversation between Ryan and Harriman was not an attorney-client communication, nor was there any exception allowing someone to withhold private conversations from legitimate legislative inquiry. ("There is nothing confidential about the insurance business now," the *New York Times* uttered.) Furthermore, having testified about his own side of the conversation, as well as part of what Harriman had told him, Ryan was in no position to claim confidentiality as to the rest of it.

Then why did Cravath advise him not to answer? Possibly Ryan thought that as a Southern gentleman he shouldn't air someone else's dirty laundry in public. Cravath may not have tried too hard to talk Ryan out of that position, as Cravath would have had no desire, either, to unduly embarrass Harriman, a longtime client of Cravath's law partner Guthrie.

In any event, Cravath had to know his objection would not stick, and it didn't. When District Attorney William Travers Jerome concluded that Ryan was required to answer the questions, he called Cravath in for a private conversation to tell him so. After gaining assurances from Cravath, Jerome told the committee that Ryan would answer their questions when they recalled him to testify. Cravath had wisely backed down.

Ryan took the stand again on December 12. Well coached by Cravath, he opened by saying he had meant the committee no disrespect; he had merely wished to preserve the confidence of his conversations with Harriman until he became satisfied he was legally required to answer, which he was now prepared to do. Then, when asked what Harriman had said to him about sharing in the purchase, Ryan testified about a meeting the two of them had on Monday, June 12, in Ryan's office, at which both Root and Cravath were present. What he said startled the committee and those in attendance.

As Ryan recounted, Harriman said that because he had devoted a large amount of time and work to the Equitable's woes, Ryan should not have come into the situation without consulting him. According to Ryan, Harriman then demanded to be let in on one half of the stock purchase for himself. He also wanted an equal voice in management and the ability to name two trustees in addition to the three Ryan had chosen.

As Ryan further testified, Harriman said that he didn't think Ryan's plan could be approved without his help and that if Ryan went forward without sharing in the purchase, Harriman's "entire influence, whether political, financial or otherwise, would be against me." But Ryan made clear to Harriman that he was going forward with his plan the way he and his lawyers had constructed it, even if Harriman opposed it.

HARRIMAN WANTED HALF was the large headline in the next day's *New-York Tribune*. Other newspapers blared, HARRIMAN HOLD-UP DESCRIBED BY RYAN and HARRIMAN THREATENED TO RUIN ME—RYAN. Cravath privately told

Root that, if anything, Ryan had erred on the side of mildness in describing Harriman's threats. It now became inevitable that Harriman would be recalled to testify about the same conversations.

Three days after Ryan's testimony, Harriman again took the stand and tried to make light of the situation. "I want you and this committee, and everybody else, to understand that I have something else to do besides devoting my time to life insurance," he told Hughes at the outset. "And when a man has some sixteen thousand miles of railroad and thirty-five or forty steamships . . . he has not much time to think about life insurance, and I should not think Mr. Ryan would, either."

But as the questioning continued, Harriman was forced to admit that in substance much of what Ryan said about their Monday meeting with Root and Cravath was true. "Of course, I was incensed at the treatment I had received," Harriman testified, "which led me to further doubt the sincerity of Mr. Ryan's purpose, and I opened, I think, with a remark something like this: 'You want my co-operation?' He said, 'Yes.' I said, 'Well, I will tell you what I will do. I will take half your stock. I don't know what it cost and do not care—provided you will agree to the appointment of two additional trustees who will be absolutely independent.'"

Asked about his threats of using his influence against Ryan, Harriman conceded, "I may have said what they say, as to using my influence in every way. I don't know whether I said politically or not. I may have done so." Hughes asked Harriman if he had exercised his influence against Ryan, to which he replied, "Not yet."

The Armstrong Committee concluded its hearings two weeks later. Hughes, now a public hero and rising political star, issued a report recommending legislative changes. Cravath praised it as fair and impartial, even if, as he wrote to Hughes, "some of the recommendations seem rather drastic."

As a result of the investigation, the legislature passed tightened regulations to protect policyholders by requiring mutualization and ending speculation with insurance funds. Life insurers were prohibited from owning common stock, engaging in commercial banking, or underwriting securities. Political contributions were banned. Under the new law, officers and directors would be held personally accountable for their actions, and several of the former officers and directors, including Hyde, were sued by their companies for recovery of ill-gotten gains. District Attorney Jerome obtained fifty-six indictments, including of many of the top insurance executives, although no one ended up going to jail.

The ultimate legislation was also softened, based on a number of changes proposed by Cravath behind the scenes. In a letter to ex-president Cleveland, Cravath explained he sought "to meet the suggestions which have been made by the practical men of the life insurance companies." And in response to agitation on the part of some insurance companies to seek federal regulation rather than a multitude of conflicting state regulations, Cravath convinced the Equitable it would be unwise to support proposed legislation in Congress for a federal insurance law.

Guthrie had given Cravath his opinion that such a bill was likely unconstitutional as beyond the power of Congress to regulate interstate commerce. Frank Stetson favored federal insurance regulation for the sake of uniformity, but he, too, thought a constitutional amendment was necessary to give Congress jurisdiction. The Equitable and most of the insurance companies ended up taking that view, which would prevail in the courts for another forty years.

The reforms coming out of the Armstrong investigation were, as the Equitable historian John Rousmaniere has written, "the first pervasive, rigorous regulatory system in American finance." The Armstrong report's approach to state regulation would remain the industry's working bible for decades, and even in the 1990s one senior insurance company executive said he kept it handy as a reminder of why insurance companies should avoid aggressive investment practices.

By the conclusion of the Armstrong investigation, Cravath was Thomas Ryan's trusted personal counsel. Then on Christmas Eve 1905, just as the Armstrong Committee was winding down, the public was treated to another Ryan thunderbolt. His Metropolitan streetcar transit group, which had been trying all year to muscle its way into the subway construction business, announced it was merging with rival August Belmont Jr.'s subway company. As a result, all competition between the two transportation companies ended.

"The community gasped," wrote one early chronicler of the city's rapid transit history. "It seemed impossible that the rival traction interests which had been at each other's throats in competition for the new rapid transit lines should come together." Belmont would later explain that he'd been driven to merge by Ryan's proposal to build subways and offer free transfers to surface lines. "We couldn't stand that kind of competition, and so we combined with them," he said.

In fact, this had been Ryan's and Cravath's plan all along. They knew the Metropolitan's surface lines would lose business once the subways opened, so they bid for subway franchises to position Metropolitan either to sell out to Belmont or to force him to merge.

The merger was bitterly attacked in the press, particularly by the Hearst papers and Pulitzer's *World*. William Randolph Hearst was running for governor of New York in 1906 on the Democratic ticket as a populist/progressive champion of the working man, and at a boisterous rally in Brooklyn on October 1 he singled out Cravath as one of the "corporation attorneys and paid political agents" of corrupt interests. "Paul D. Cravath is the general utility man for Thomas Fortune Ryan, puts on the black mask, hoists the black flag, and boldly enters the domain of law or politics at the demand of that political pirate and financial freebooter," Hearst thundered. He noted that Cravath was the former law partner of Charles Evans Hughes, the Republican candidate for governor who was running against Hearst. "I wish publicly to thank Mr. Paul D. Cravath for his opposition to me," Hearst concluded.

Cravath worked hard for Hughes's election, drawing thanks from President Roosevelt for being one of the few Wall Street lawyers willing to support an avowed reform candidate. "It has been disheartening to have as many of the men of large means sullenly refusing to aid in the Hughes campaign, apparently because they regard the Republican Party with me at the head as bad as Hearstism," Roosevelt confided in a letter to Cravath on October 31, 1906, a week before the election. According to Roosevelt, business kingpins viewed any government efforts to rein them in as an appeal to class hatred and incitement of "the mob to plunder the rich." Such an attitude, Roosevelt wrote, "seems to me is as unpatriotic as it is foolish."

Roosevelt sensed in Cravath a kindred spirit—a conservative protector of the system who recognized changes were needed to guard against a revolution from below. In 1900, then New York governor Roosevelt named Cravath vice chairman of a state commission to draft landmark legislation to ensure minimum standards of light, air, and cleanliness in New York City multifamily dwellings. By 1906 Cravath was chairman of the Tenement House Committee of the Charity Organization Society of the City of New York, one of whose members was Jacob Riis, whose book *How the Other Half Lives* had launched the housing reform movement.

By the time of his October 1906 letter, Roosevelt had not only come to value Cravath's advice but to enjoy his company. As the president wrote to him, "After I come back from Panama won't you come on here and take lunch or dinner with me? I should like to go over a number of matters with you."

After Hughes narrowly defeated Hearst, Cravath congratulated Roosevelt and offered his own political views, which dovetailed with the president's. "The adjustment of the misunderstandings between the rich and the poor which have made Hearstism possible will, it seems to me, be the important political work for the next few years," Cravath wrote. "It is only because of the policy which you have pursued and the confidence which you have inspired among workingmen . . . that we still have the opportunity of working out the adjustment between labor and capital under a conservative administration of public affairs, instead of under an administration dominated by the influences which Hearst represents."

Cravath went on to chide the very type of men he represented:

> The men who stand for the great corporations and other aggregations of capital will be very dull if they do not soon realize that in national affairs they must look to you for protection against injustice and in receiving that protection must be content to accept justice uncomplainingly. . . . As a lawyer for corporations I propose to do what I can in the direction of bringing about a change for the better in the attitude of my friends towards the unsolved problems in which they are so deeply connected.

Cravath closed his letter with what amounted to a remarkable apology to the president, on behalf of himself and his white shoe brethren. "I am moved to write this letter," he explained, "because I confess that at times I have shared some of the prejudices against your policy, and some of the doubts as to its fairness and wisdom with which a Wall Street lawyer is surrounded."

"I wonder if you realize what an awfully nice letter yours to me of November 7th was," Roosevelt replied. "It pleases me so much that I am going to show it to Root tomorrow. Now I am going to inflict a wrong on you in return for your kindness. I want you to read my exchange when it comes out and frankly tell me its defects and shortcomings from the standpoint that you and I both occupy—that is, the adjustment of the misunderstandings between rich and poor which have made Hearstism possible. Would you mind doing this?"

As Cravath and Roosevelt hoped, Hughes ended up pursuing a reform agenda during his two terms in Albany as governor. One of his signature accomplishments was passage of the Moreland Act, which allowed the governor, in person or through others appointed by him, to investigate any department, board, or bureau in the state, to bring charges, and to recommend remedial legislation. He also expanded the powers of the state's public service commissions and gained passage of child labor laws. Hughes's success as a reform governor would eventually propel him to the Supreme Court and nearly to the White House.

Cravath, too, was now a public figure. He was featured in an article that ran in many newspapers that year, titled SOME MODERN MILLIONAIRE CORPORATION LAWYERS. It carried profiles of Stetson, Cromwell, Hornblower, and other exemplars of New York's powerful white shoe bar. The writer cited Cravath and his partner Guthrie as among the "clever law partners under 50." Cravath "carries himself in a 'stately' manner, and his size and carriage combined make him a marked man in a crowd," the article read. "He has been termed 'ponderous and irresistible'; he never shows surprise or exasperation; his gestures are deliberate and his elocution effective. He is a first-class cross-examiner, his profile is classic, and he dresses impressively."

Although the newspaper writer did not yet know it, Guthrie had withdrawn from his partnership with Cravath on April 30, 1906. Guthrie's nervous energy, which, as Robert Swaine, the firm's historian wrote, "made everyone about him jumpy," had begun to take its toll. He was becoming increasingly inconsiderate and impossible to work with; on one occasion, upon reaching his office dripping with sweat from his walk downtown, and finding his secretary, who usually rubbed him down, away, he enlisted one of the law associates to perform the honors.

Cravath, too, was full of energy, but his "was that of unbounded physical strength," wrote Swaine, "and while he, too, exhausted many of his associates, their exhaustion came from sheer inability to keep up with his pace." Guthrie came to resent Cravath's capacity for work and his growing reputation as a corporate lawyer, and the two began to get on each other's nerves. Guthrie decided to leave the firm to concentrate on trials and other matters.

Guthrie's departure left Cravath, now the lead partner in the firm of Cravath, Henderson & de Gersdorff, free to develop his "Cravath system" of law firm management. It was a system Guthrie had never much cared for, even though he did not actively interfere with it. With Cravath now in charge, he would make his firm into the model for all large white shoe firms to follow.

Chapter 9

"Nothing but a Paid Attorney"

Following his Panama Canal adventure, William Nelson Cromwell seemed to generate controversy wherever he turned. In fact, he reveled in it.

CROMWELL AND MORGAN IN TEMPER OVER CANAL read the headline in the February 27, 1906, *New York Times*, which reported on an examination—or inquisition—of Cromwell before the Senate Committee on Interoceanic Canals, which had subpoenaed him to testify about his role in the canal project. The lead examiner was John Tyler Morgan, the Alabama senator who had championed a canal through Nicaragua only to be thwarted by the choice of the Panama route, for which he held Cromwell responsible.

Morgan was now pushing the notion of buyer's remorse. After the heady days of 1903–4, when America had taken the canal and signed a treaty, the digging had become stalled because of accidents, disease, inadequate machinery, personnel changes, bureaucratic red tape, and disagreements over the design (sea-level versus lock system). Although the Panama deal was irreversible—there was no going back to Nicaragua—Morgan was intent on making his chief nemesis Cromwell the whipping boy for everything going wrong with the canal venture.

The two men could not stand each other. Although both were lawyers, and both had championed an interocean American canal, they had almost nothing else in common: Cromwell, a rock-ribbed Republican, was a self-made Brooklyn boy whose father had given his life to the Union cause, while Morgan, a Southern Democrat, was an ex-Confederate general, former slaveholder, and fervent segregationist. The Civil War had left him bitter toward the Republican Party and the North in general, and his disdain for the smooth-talking New York lawyer was palpable.

Morgan started in with the prior year's resignation of the project's highly valued chief engineer, John Findley Wallace. The previous June (in 1905) had marked a low point for the project when Wallace abruptly resigned to take a higher-paying job in private industry. Secretary of War William Howard Taft, to whom Roosevelt had delegated the task of overseeing the excavation, was enraged that Wallace left the government in the lurch.

At the hearings before Morgan's committee eight months later, Wallace testified that a major reason he quit was Cromwell's interference with his work. Wallace testified, to Morgan's obvious glee, that he considered Cromwell a "dangerous man."

It was not that Cromwell was belligerent, Wallace said; for all he knew, Cromwell's motives may have been pure and patriotic. The problem was Cromwell wore so many hats when it came to Panama: fiscal agent for the Panamanian government, director of the Panama Railroad, stockholder in the electric light utility company on the isthmus, and advisor to Taft. Indeed, when Taft was out of town, Cromwell, who had taken up temporary residence in Washington, practically ran the War Department as far as the canal was concerned. As Wallace explained, "Here was a man [Cromwell] who occupied no official position, but who had the ear of the Administration, and a word from him could upset my plans or my policy or cause instructions to be given me that I might not be willing to carry out."

When Cromwell came before the committee on February 26, 1906, he was ready to pounce. Wallace, Cromwell said, had given the committee a radically different explanation for his resignation than the one he had given Taft at the time he quit. Back then, in a meeting with Cromwell and Taft, Wallace had cited only his better job offer and health concerns. Cromwell then produced a letter Wallace had written to him just three weeks before he resigned, in which he praised the handling of the canal by Roosevelt and Taft and "the wisdom of their 'privy counsel' [Cromwell]." In the same letter, Wallace referred to Cromwell as a "skilled and polished diplomat" and closed with, "permit me, my dear Cromwell, 'to lift my hat to you.'"

This was more than Morgan could bear. Making no effort to hide his animosity, he badgered Cromwell for the details and exact words used in conversations with Wallace and Taft. Cromwell responded that he could recall only the substance and that he was not in the habit of "recording pho-

nographically the exact words of every conversation." It then became a series of verbal jousts:

MORGAN: In other words, you like to put your own construction on
            language rather than to recite it as it occurred?

CROMWELL: I do not, sir; and I will not accept your construction of it,
            either.

                        . . .

MORGAN: So that you are presenting us with the essence instead of
            the facts?

CROMWELL: I have presented you with the facts, which are the es-
            sence.

                        . . .

MORGAN: There are some subjects you seem to treat very lightly.

CROMWELL: Some subjects are worth treating lightly.

Cromwell went on to relate how, in a meeting with Taft the previous
June, he and Wallace grasped each other's hands, both of them with tears
in their eyes. Cromwell called it a painful moment, as it was clear that Wallace was giving up the chance for immortal fame and that everything they
had worked for was about to be for naught. On hearing this testimony, Morgan accused Cromwell of sermonizing and sentimentality.

Cromwell testified that luckily, almost immediately after Wallace resigned, a replacement engineer had appeared on the scene—John F. Stevens,
who had built the Great Northern Railway for James J. Hill. Stevens was
about to leave for the Philippines with Taft to advise on railroad construction in that country when Roosevelt, through Taft, offered him the Panama
job. His inclination was to say no, but Cromwell talked him into accepting.
David McCullough, in his book on the canal, calls it "probably the most
valuable service yet rendered by the clever, 'silver-tongued' attorney."

When Cromwell testified he was performing his investment services for the Republic of Panama for free because he considered it "an honor," Morgan seemed incredulous. Another senator asked why Cromwell had served Panama in this capacity without compensation, to which he responded: "Because of the broad instinct of good nature, which has prompted me to do so much for that cause, Senator, and for the other consideration that I have more money than I need, unfortunately." Cromwell placed his net worth above a hundred million dollars.

Morgan continued probing various aspects of Cromwell's connection to the canal interests, and Cromwell repeatedly refused to answer based on attorney-client privilege, leading Morgan to assert that he was dodging questions. "Senator, you must change your terms with me. I have not dodged anything," Cromwell responded indignantly, to which Morgan replied, "Well, you have dodged, and have done very little else." Morgan threatened to have the Senate hold him in contempt for not answering. Privately, Cromwell and his partner William Curtis had fully expected Cromwell's refusals to answer would result in his being held in contempt, and they sought out Philadelphia's John G. Johnson for advice in the matter. When no contempt proceedings were brought, they tried to compensate Johnson for his service, but he refused any pay for helping out his brother lawyers.

The press felt that there was no point in further scolding Cromwell and that the clever lawyer, not the elderly senator, had gotten the better of the sparring. The *New York Times* asked rhetorically, "How will the torturing of Cromwell aid Congress and the President in the great undertaking before them?" The *New-York Tribune* similarly editorialized, "Let the dead past bury its dead."

In the meantime, Cromwell had acquired a new foil who sported a dark mustache, to Cromwell's white, but who would claim the hero's mantle of the white hat to Cromwell's black.

———◦◦◦———

At the beginning of the twentieth century almost no Wall Street corporate lawyers, and none of the prominent New York law firms, were Jewish. Although a substantial percentage of the city's lawyers were Jewish, they mostly practiced as members of what was snobbishly referred to as the "lower bar." Elite lawyers tended to view the lower bar as excessively commercialized and full of ambulance chasers. To Elihu Root, for example, they were in "the lower grade as to attainment and cultivation."

A recognized exception was Samuel Untermyer, an active Zionist who became the most well-known legal gadfly and liberal activist among the Wall Street lawyers of his day. Something of a paradox, he attained immense wealth by forming, representing, and investing personally in large corporations and other businesses. Yet he was a crusading, vitriolic critic of what was commonly referred to as "high finance."

Untermyer was a relative rarity—a Southern Jew, the son of a German-Jewish merchant who had immigrated to Virginia and produced military uniforms for the Confederacy during the Civil War. "Hurrah for Jeff Davis," Untermyer had shouted, as a boy, when Union troops entered his Lynchburg birthplace.

After the elder Untermyer died bankrupt in 1866, Samuel and his widowed mother moved to New York, where he was educated in the public schools and took a job as an office boy in a law firm at age fifteen. Upon graduation from Columbia Law School in 1878 he went into a law partnership with two of his brothers. It was the only Jewish corporate law firm on Wall Street. Unlike the doyens of the white shoe firms, Untermyer aligned himself with New York's Democratic Tammany Hall machine, which led to many business introductions. Despite Tammany's reputation for political corruption, Untermyer reasoned, "Between the Irish leaders of Tammany and the high-toned Jew-hating Presbyterians on the other side I consider Tammany the lesser evil for men of our race."

By the time he was twenty-eight, Untermyer was earning $100,000 a year and had built his mother a large house on East Ninety-Second Street. He was a millionaire before age thirty, largely from forming successful German American breweries with the aid of British capital. As he related the story, the London bankers he went to meet would not give him an appointment at first, so he entered their directors' meeting unannounced and convinced them of the merit of his proposal.

Untermyer's specialty was trial work, for which he prepared by rising each day at 4:00 A.M. and reading long documents for hours before breakfast. A brilliant cross-examiner, he conceded a draw to only one man who ever faced him on the witness stand—John D. Rockefeller Sr., who saw five or six questions ahead all the time and whose expression, a glint of recognition, meant he anticipated where Untermyer was heading.

But Untermyer also proved adept at corporate law, helping organize industrial trusts and holding companies during the great merger wave that preceded the *Northern Securities* case. The most important of these, the International Steam Pump Company, was financed by the Lehman Brothers family, close friends of the Untermyers'.

As early as 1900, one white shoe lawyer remarked that "Mr. Untermyer's firm, though composed of Hebrews, has the reputation of being quite strong and influential." The firm's clients included theater owners David Belasco and the Shubert Brothers, the New York Giants baseball team, William Randolph Hearst, and mining tycoon Daniel Guggenheim and his brothers, one of whom later founded the New York City art museum of the same name.

Untermyer cultivated his celebrity status and aggressively marketed his firm's name, using newspaper advertising and public relations in a manner disdained by elite lawyers at the time (and later prohibited by bar association rules). In one case he was paid $775,000 to arrange a merger of rival copper companies; asked to comment, Paul Cravath merely exclaimed, "Whew," adding he did not think he ever received a fee as large.

Untermyer did not, however, rate a listing in the *Social Register*, which was reserved for members of WASP families and "polite" society. Nor was he welcome at certain clubs, resorts, and hotels. He contented himself with growing rare orchids and breeding championship dogs on his 113-acre estate, Greystone, overlooking the Hudson River in Yonkers, New York. It featured an English castle and tower, and its Indo-Persian paradise gardens were so impressive that Untermyer opened them to the public once a week.

Some of Untermyer's early ventures were of dubious legality. In one case, a New Jersey court concluded he had been the "managing genius" behind a fraudulently formed, monopolistic straw paper company—which made paper from grains, not wood—and which dumped its worthless stock on the public before going bankrupt. The court found that Untermyer, who was serving as a principal and promoter as well as a lawyer for the deal, had drafted a misleading public prospectus. It valued the stock on the explicit assumption that the company, as a monopoly, would be able to suppress competition.

Perhaps the court's censure, or a guilty conscience, contributed to Untermyer's later zeal as an anti-Wall Street proselytizer. Or his wealth gave him the freedom to become a cause-oriented "people's lawyer." Untermyer maintained that a young attorney starting out in practice needed to make $5 million to secure his independence.

Untermyer's first major attack on Wall Street came in 1903 in connection with the failure of the United States Shipbuilding Company. The year before, as part of a merger of large shipbuilding companies, US Shipbuilding had acquired all the stock of Bethlehem Steel Company, in which steel magnate Charles M. Schwab (no relation to the famous stockbroker) held the controlling interest. Schwab, a former protégé of Andrew Carnegie's, had gone on to become president of the giant US Steel holding company formed by J. P. Morgan. Schwab has usually been credited with planting the idea for the controversial US Steel deal in Morgan's head after a dinner at Manhattan's University Club (although Cromwell claimed it was he who gave Morgan the notion). In any event, after completion of the deal, Schwab bought Bethlehem Steel as a private investment and decided to swap it out for stocks and bonds in the new shipbuilding company.

Schwab enjoyed gambling: He had reportedly broken the bank at the roulette tables in Monte Carlo before losing most of his winnings. But in structuring the US Shipbuilding deal he stacked the deck in his favor. In exchange for his Bethlehem Steel stock he received $20 million in stock in the new shipbuilding company, plus $10 million in bonds secured by Bethlehem's plant and properties in Pennsylvania as collateral. As a result, if the new company proved successful his stock would give him a huge profit, but if the company defaulted on his bonds he would reacquire Bethlehem's assets. His bonds were further protected by a second mortgage on the shipbuilding company's other properties.

Bethlehem Steel, now a subsidiary of US Shipbuilding, performed well after the merger, but the overall shipbuilding company was a total failure. When its financial difficulties became apparent, a reorganization committee was formed with Cromwell as its counsel. The committee proposed a reorganization plan that US Shipbuilding's stockholders and creditors believed favored Schwab at their expense. Under the plan Schwab put up $2 million in desperately needed new working capital, in exchange for which his second-mortgage bonds were to be replaced by new first-mortgage bonds, giving him a priority lien on all the shipbuilding company's assets. A group of the company's creditors hired Untermyer to sue to stop the reorganization plan; on their behalf, he obtained appointment of a receiver to handle the shipbuilding company's affairs until a fairer deal could be worked out.

Although Untermyer and Cromwell were on opposing sides in the controversy, the real fireworks took place between Untermyer, Schwab, and Schwab's counsel, William Guthrie. Untermyer kept the newspapers filled with accusations of fraud and conspiracy against Schwab, a tactic white shoe lawyers regarded as unseemly. "It is almost ludicrous to read his [Untermyer's] performance in the press," Guthrie wrote to Cromwell. Again complaining about Untermyer, Guthrie wrote to another lawyer, "Unfortunately, men who have none of the instincts of gentlemen are now in the ranks of our profession, which once was filled with men of honor."

Untermyer ended up subjecting Schwab to a blistering, four-hour cross-examination during a hearing in January 1904. Guthrie accused Untermyer of harassing the witness and asked that the proceedings be suspended. To Guthrie's frustration, the garrulous, amiable Schwab kept ignoring his instructions that many of Untermyer's acerbic questions need not be answered. Schwab repeatedly decided for himself what questions to answer, reducing Guthrie to plaintive cries of "Please, Mr. Schwab."

Schwab had looked foolish at times, but because of his personal charm he managed to come across as a prudent, hard-bargaining businessman rather than a common criminal, as Untermyer sought to portray him. Nonetheless, the public pressure Untermyer created—and a report by the receiver highly critical of Schwab—led to a negotiated settlement a month later. Schwab accepted a reduced interest in a newly organized company to be run by him as president and chairman. It would be known throughout most of the twentieth century as Bethlehem Steel.

Ironically, among those who had faith in Schwab's ability to turn the company around was Samuel Untermyer. Convinced of the fundamental value of the Bethlehem Steel plant, Untermyer himself bought fifteen thousand shares of the new company, which turned out to be wildly successful under Schwab's leadership. When the stock skyrocketed in value during World War I, Untermyer made millions on it. He would then call Schwab a resourceful, farsighted steel manufacturer and promoter.

There was another prominent Wall Street lawyer who benefited greatly from the corporate reorganization that created Bethlehem Steel. When it came time for Schwab to choose a corporate law firm to handle the company's affairs, he tapped Guthrie's partner, Paul Cravath. Bethlehem Steel would remain an important client of the Cravath firm for years to come. When giant corporations fall apart, and the pieces are put back together, there are always winners and losers. The lawyers can generally be counted among the winners.

—————•◎•—————

Although Cromwell and Untermyer avoided direct confrontation during the US Shipbuilding battle, they would square off at least twice more in 1906, starting just after Cromwell finished testifying before the Senate committee. The first of these clashes concerned Wells Fargo, the famous express company, which had recently come under the control of the railroad titan E. H. Harriman.

The Wells Fargo controversy generated headlines in New York during the hot summer of 1906. The company's minority shareholders were complaining that Wells Fargo, though earning a return of 30 to 40 percent a year, was paying only an 8 percent dividend. It is hard to overstate the importance of dividends to stockholders in those years, as many small investors depended on them as a source of consistent income. As a result, a group of Wells Fargo shareholders filed suit to compel payment of a dividend of at least 16 percent and to obtain access to the company's books and records, which Harriman had been keeping from the public.

To represent them in the New York state court, the shareholders hired Untermyer, who had been burnishing his reputation as a champion of minority shareholder rights and had attained public notice representing James Hazen Hyde in the Equitable fight the year before. To defend the suit, Harriman chose Cromwell.

Cromwell convinced Harriman to allow a financial statement of Wells

Fargo's assets, liabilities, and earnings to be issued, but otherwise he opposed opening the company's books to shareholders. Cromwell's partner
Curtis convinced the New York judge to deny the shareholders' request to
see the books on a technicality: Wells Fargo was incorporated in Colorado,
so even though the books were physically in New York, the court there had
no jurisdiction to grant access to them.

The battle then shifted to the company's annual meeting scheduled in
August, at which the minority shareholders represented by Untermyer
hoped to elect a new, sympathetic slate of directors committed to paying
higher dividends. The outcome of the election depended on which side
gathered more shareholder proxies to vote for its director slate.

Cromwell decided the best way to obtain the necessary votes was to buy
them. He sent a team of purchasing agents armed with cash throughout
New England, where most of the stock was held, to solicit proxies and to
offer a premium to shareholders who declined to give their proxies but might
be willing to sell their shares. They were offered as much as $325 for shares
trading at $275 in the market, and which had been trading at $175 when
the fight began.

The annual Wells Fargo meeting was held on August 9, 1906, in the
company's building at 51 Broadway. Normally a sparsely attended affair, the
meeting this time drew dozens of stockholders, lawyers, and reporters. Despite the summer heat, they had to close the windows because the noise
from the trolleys and elevated trains was so deafening that those in attendance couldn't hear the proceedings.

It was a typical Cromwell production. He insisted that each of numerous
motions be subjected to an actual ballot count rather than a voice vote, so
the meeting, which had begun at 10:00 A.M., was still going on well past
6:00 P.M., when the first returns on any question were announced. The participants had to take up new business ignorant of the outcome of prior votes;
because one of the motions was for an adjournment, they kept going not
even knowing whether the meeting had been legally adjourned. Most of the
motions by shareholders were to compel the paying of higher dividends;
Cromwell opposed all of them and moved to leave all dividend decisions to
the discretion of the board of directors.

Those present were treated to what the *New York Times* described as "a rapid-fire contest of wit between Samuel Untermyer for the minority and William Nelson Cromwell as the Harriman champion." In the end, as the *Times* reported in a front-page story headlined HARRIMAN SMOTHERS WELLS FARGO MINORITY, the Harriman ticket was elected by an overwhelming vote. All motions to force higher dividends were defeated.

Whether Cromwell's flowery speeches during the meeting made any difference is hard to say, but one of them was widely quoted in the next day's press. Wells Fargo's express business, he argued, owed its success entirely to Harriman's railroad connections and "executive genius." Harriman "cannot be replaced," Cromwell said, "for he moves in a higher world into which we may not enter." Cromwell's "higher world" comment would be derisively thrown back at him and Harriman in months to follow.

Not long after the Wells Fargo battle ended, Cromwell and Untermyer were back at each other in a similar contest. This time it concerned the election of directors of New York Life. Unlike the Equitable, a stock company, New York Life was a mutual company, which meant that policyholders chose the directors. Again Cromwell represented the company and its director slate, while Untermyer was retained by an insurgent group known as the International Policyholders' Committee.

This was the first election to be carried out under New York State's new insurance law passed in the wake of the Armstrong Committee investigation and under the supervision of the state's Department of Insurance. It was closely watched, for it had been New York Life that had borne the brunt of criticism, and criminal indictments of its officers, stemming from the insurance investigation conducted by Charles Evans Hughes.

Knowing that the New York Life election would be under a microscope, Cromwell proceeded cautiously and pragmatically at first. He recommended New York Life post policyholder lists with the state insurance department, to be made available to the insurgents. He pointed out this would make a favorable impression on the press and the state insurance superintendent.

But the contest would not remain genteel for long. After he was hired by the policyholders' committee, Untermyer hurled allegations of a rigged election. He contended New York Life was carrying on a campaign to defeat the insurgents by using company funds to pay employees and agents to distribute marked or mutilated ballots. That is, the policyholders entitled to vote were being given ballots already marked in favor of the administration ticket, with the names of the insurgent slate crossed out. Untermyer brought suit in New York state court for an injunction to prevent New York Life from continuing that effort. This led to what the *New York Times* called A LIVELY COURT DAY IN THE INSURANCE FIGHT, featuring many spirited exchanges between Cromwell and Untermyer.

"My learned friend, with his vivid imagination, should be writing novelettes," Cromwell said in response to Untermyer's charges. In his brisk, nervous manner, Cromwell insisted that irregularities, if any, were committed by independent insurance agents working on a commission basis who sent out ballots at their own initiative and expense. He produced multiple affidavits from company officials stating that no company money or employee time had been spent in favor of the administration ticket.

Cromwell declared that the company was going to protect itself against Untermyer's assaults and was not going to "stand here helpless like the statue of Nathan Hale in City Hall Park with our hands tied while we are shot in the back—or rather while assassins of reputations stab us in the back." Addressing his adversary directly, Cromwell asserted Untermyer had "made the greatest mistake of [his] professional career by coming into court with this suit," then amended his statement only slightly to say it was Untermyer's clients who had made the mistake.

Untermyer gave as good as he got, saying that "anybody who attempts to oppose these financial pirates is subjected to vituperation and abuse in the interest of men who six months ago were doing their best to keep out of prison." He suggested the whole case be submitted to a referee to determine the facts, and when Cromwell objected that such an inquiry would constitute a fishing expedition, Untermyer responded, "And I would catch some good fish, too."

The court ruled in favor of New York Life, finding insufficient evidence to support Untermyer's allegations. ANOTHER CHARGE DISPROVED— UNTERMYER LOSES OUT AGAIN, gloated one pro-insurance industry trade publication. With no injunction in place, the election went forward, amid allegations of fraud on both sides, and ended in an overwhelming victory for the administration ticket after months of counting disputed ballots. A simultaneous election held for trustees of Mutual Life, in which Untermyer made similar allegations of fraud on behalf of the policyholders' committee, also produced an administration victory.

Untermyer received some partial vindication a few years later when a report by the new state superintendent of insurance concluded the Mutual had spent substantial policyholder money in 1906 to elect its administration slate. The report found that during the election period the Mutual had doubled the amount of its advances to agents, in effect buying their allegiance to support the company ticket. It was not the same grossly fraudulent conduct Untermyer had charged against New York Life, but it was enough to prompt him to call the life insurer elections a "farce."

To Cromwell, though, the New York Life election, like the Wells Fargo fight, and his survival of the canal hearings, had been a win. He might have said of himself what he said of Harriman—that he moved "in a higher world." And in the midst of those battles he would become embroiled in another, equally bitter one, again on behalf of the man who dwelled with him in that same lofty realm.

―――――――《●》―――――――

E. H. Harriman owed much of his career as a master railroader to Stuyvesant Fish, the president of the Illinois Central Railroad. Harriman had started out as an office boy and Wall Street stockbroker before getting his feet wet in the railroad business in 1879. Harriman, together with his friend Fish, became a director of a small upstate New York railroad that ran to Lake Champlain. Four years later, Fish, by then a vice president and board member of the Illinois Central, got Harriman a seat on that board. By 1887 Harriman was chairman of the finance committee and vice president of the Illinois Central, Fish having ascended to the presidency. Together they worked to modernize and expand a railroad line that at the turn of the century ran from the Great Lakes to New Orleans.

By that time, Harriman had far outpaced Fish as a railroad titan. Harriman controlled the Union Pacific, which he merged with the Southern Pacific in 1901 to form the largest railroad company in the world (not to mention a target for outlaws like Butch and Sundance). Then came the bold raid on the Northern Pacific, resulting in the ill-fated Northern Securities

Company held illegal by the Supreme Court in 1904. Significant Harriman interests in the Baltimore & Ohio, the Atchison, Topeka & Santa Fe, and other lines would follow. But Harriman always wanted more: The diminutive plutocrat had a Napoleonic dream of running one giant, harmonious railroad system. And that had gotten him thinking about taking control of the Illinois Central, which would require ousting his friend Stuyvesant Fish from his position as president.

Fish, then in his midfifties, prided himself as an old-style railroad man who kept his line under independent, local, conservative management, in contrast to men like Harriman and Hill, who sought to build empires. He enjoyed the loyalty of a large number of small, widely scattered stockholders, including the proverbial widows and orphans, who received their regular dividend payments from the company. For years they had willingly given him their proxies to vote for the election of directors, including himself, at the annual meeting.

The son of Hamilton Fish, the former New York governor, US senator, and Grant's secretary of state, the tall, stately Fish was popularly viewed in the press as an "Abe Lincoln type"—a plainspoken man of the people who ran his railroad for the benefit of its shareholders, not outside financial interests. Still, the Illinois Central had made him fabulously wealthy and a leader of Gilded Age society, with three grand residences: an immense town house on Madison Avenue in New York, a country estate on the Hudson River upstate, and an oceanside mansion in Newport, Rhode Island. Although Fish himself had little interest in the social scene, his wife, Mamie, entertained lavishly and eccentrically: She had her own personal court jester concoct outrageous theme parties; for one of them, she kept her dinner guests guessing at the identity of the mysterious European prince she had invited—which turned out to be a monkey dressed in white tie and tails.

Along with his bankers, Jacob Schiff's Kuhn, Loeb & Co., Harriman and his allies began buying up blocks of Illinois Central stock in 1905 and into early 1906. Rumors abounded that Harriman was out to add the Illinois Central to his vast railroad empire. By February 1906 it was no secret that Harriman and Fish were feuding and that the former protégé was intent on dislodging his mentor from office.

Exactly what had caused the falling-out remains unclear. The commonly accepted story posited that the Illinois Central fight was mixed up with an ongoing battle within Mutual Life Insurance. Stuyvesant Fish was a trustee of the Mutual and in late 1905 began agitating for a full-scale independent investigation of the company's management by a special committee. But Mutual Life's new president, business lawyer Charles A. Peabody, preferred a go-slow approach and resisted the committee's efforts to obtain information. Fish angrily resigned both from the special committee and as a Mutual trustee. He then launched the International Policyholders' Committee to challenge the Mutual's administration slate in the upcoming election, retaining Untermyer to represent the insurgent group.

Peabody was also a director of the Illinois Central as well as Harriman's Union Pacific, and he was increasingly friendly with Harriman. The story went that Peabody, to punish Fish for his meddling in the Mutual's affairs, enlisted Harriman in a plan to expel Fish from his beloved Illinois Central.

Others suggest a different reason Harriman turned on Fish. Harriman learned that Fish was using Illinois Central funds to engage in some dubious self-dealing transactions, ostensibly to pay for the extravagances of his socialite wife. Although Harriman tried to keep it secret at first to protect his old friend, when Fish could not or would not stop the unethical dealings Harriman decided he had to go. Still another theory, of questionable validity, holds that Harriman was upset that Mamie Fish had snubbed his wife by not inviting her to a society tea party in Newport because she thought her too dull.

The simplest explanation, though, is that Harriman wanted the Illinois Central and was not the sort of man who let personal friendships stand in the way of his grand designs. He had once betrayed a close confidant by using confidential information he had promised to keep secret. When the friend protested, Harriman responded, "I must be the judge of what is right and wrong in these things."

For his fight against Fish, Harriman needed someone just as hard-nosed. So he turned again to William Nelson Cromwell.

Harriman could force Fish from the presidency if he could gain the votes of seven of the thirteen Illinois Central directors. Harriman had the support of six, including himself; six others favored Fish or were undeclared. There was one vacancy, so control turned on whoever was appointed to fill it.

In a peace agreement signed by Fish, Harriman, and Peabody in July, Fish committed to let a majority of the rest of the directors fill the vacancy, in exchange for which Harriman agreed Fish could vote the shares held by Harriman and his associates at the annual meeting. But when the directors nominated one of Harriman's fellow Southern Pacific directors, Henry W. de Forest, to fill the vacant slot, Fish reneged on the deal. He said de Forest was a tool of Harriman and would turn over control of the Illinois Central to Harriman's Union Pacific. Fish proclaimed his intention to keep the Illinois Central independent at all costs, further endearing himself to the press.

At the explosive annual meeting on October 17, Fish nominated his own slate and a different man for the vacancy, prompting Cromwell to accuse Fish of bad faith. "I request that you fulfill your agreement," Cromwell said, glaring at Fish. "I will never cast a single vote for Mr. de Forest," Fish responded. At that point a stockholder who had seconded most of Fish's motions at the meeting declared that Cromwell was "nothing but a paid attorney." Cromwell rejoined, "And who are you? Aren't you an attorney?" When the man said he was there as a stockholder, not a paid attorney, Cromwell said, "You are a mighty convenient stockholder, bobbing up every time Mr. Fish pulls a string, seconding motions and asking questions." The stockholder told Cromwell he had tried to treat him with courtesy, to which Cromwell replied that courtesy was wasted on him.

When the proxies were counted, Fish had won a victory for his slate, but it was short-lived. The directors were put off by Fish's refusal to honor his prior agreement and began switching their allegiance to Harriman. On November 7 the board voted 8–4 to replace Fish as president.

Harriman had won the fight, again with Cromwell's help, but he had lost points for deposing the popular Fish. "Mr. E. H. Harriman has again hoisted the black flag of piratical high finance," declared the *Richmond Times-Dispatch*. To the *Philadelphia Press*, Harriman's victory was "one of those ruthless exercises of the power of sheer millions which diminish public confidence in railroad investments and make the small investor feel that he has no security, no adequate defense for his rights, and no efficient way to exercise his voting power."

The *Wall Street Journal* dubbed Harriman the "Colossus of Roads" but begged to remind him that "the Colossus of Rhodes was destroyed by an earthquake." He was advised to remember that as much as the American people admired superior leadership, they were "aroused to the point of revolt against excessive financial concentration."

No one understood that progressive sentiment better than President Theodore Roosevelt. And he was about to wage a major war against E. H. Harriman to drive that point home. Curiously, this time one of Harriman's legal defenders would be Paul Cravath, a man Harriman had once literally turned his back on.

Chapter 10

"High Finance"

By the end of 1906 Paul Cravath had arrived. With a year as the head of his firm behind him, Cravath was among the top half dozen best-known and wealthiest corporate lawyers practicing in New York. He had also entered the higher echelons of polite society.

Earlier in the year he had been a cofounder of the New Theatre, a non-profit repertory house dedicated to advancing American dramatic art. He and his wife were now receiving invitations to weddings attended by the likes of President and Mrs. Roosevelt, and to exclusive events such as a Long Island steeplechase. Although Guthrie had left the firm, Cravath and he were still Long Island neighbors in posh Locust Valley, and in January 1907 they bought a two-hundred-acre farm adjoining their country estates. Cravath became a major booster of Locust Valley, helping create not only the Piping Rock Club but also the local fire district, the region's largest horse show, and hundreds of miles of preserved equestrian trails. He also advanced the incorporated village movement to give estate owners zoning powers to protect their suburban enclaves.

As part of their white shoe ethos, the leading lawyers of New York, Cravath included, were typically active in charitable and social causes. Stetson's charities, for example, were his beloved Williams College alma mater and Alpha Delta Phi fraternity, the Episcopal Church, the Metropolitan Museum of Art, and the New York Botanical Garden in the Bronx. Cromwell supported the relief of Romanian children, local bar associations, and programs for the blind (Helen Keller was a personal friend).

Cravath would become active in the Metropolitan Opera, but his earliest civic efforts were directed toward improving New York City's deplorable tenement housing conditions. When New York's landmark housing law was enacted in 1901, based on the bill drafted by the commission of which Cravath was vice chairman, a group of the city's real estate owners attacked it as a socialistic infringement of their private property rights. They chided Cravath for speaking to tenement issues when he lived comfortably on East Thirty-Ninth Street near Park Avenue.

But Cravath would prove a dogged advocate of better tenement housing. In late 1906, after the Charity Organization Society committee found that 357,000 New York rooms had no windows, in violation of law, he complained publicly that "three generations will sleep in the smother of these unventilated boxes." Citing "unspeakably bad conditions," he asked the mayor to hire more inspectors for the city's tenement housing department. Cravath would remain active in the housing reform movement for many years, during which conditions in the tenements were significantly improved.

In mid-1906 Cravath had also added a feather to his professional cap by representing Kuhn, Loeb in an unprecedented placement of a $50 million French bank loan to the Pennsylvania Railroad. The railroad needed financing for an ambitious program of expansion that included building its tunnels under the Hudson and East Rivers into Manhattan. With the Pennsylvania having exhausted available American capital, the parties looked to the French.

The deal was touted as the first major issue of American securities placed wholly in the French market and as a harbinger of further heavy French investment in American companies. Due to the complexities of French law, it took several weeks of negotiation and paperwork to get the transaction completed. (Cromwell, well versed in French law and business, represented the Paris lending banks.) Importantly for Cravath, this was his first major taste of international finance, and it helped spark an interest in foreign affairs that would grow in years to come.

For all these reasons, as the year 1907 opened, everything seemed to be going Paul Cravath's way. But he was about to enter the most difficult and controversial chapter in his career.

<hr />

Cravath previously had not been associated with a capitalist as unpopular as E. H. Harriman. He was the lawyer for George Westinghouse and Thomas

Fortune Ryan—both highly successful businessmen—but they were different: Westinghouse had taken on Edison and brought light to millions, and Ryan had brought order to the Equitable chaos while maintaining a low profile. Harriman, though, was considered to be, in Theodore Roosevelt's words, one of the "malefactors of great wealth" seeking to "enjoy the fruits of their evil-doing."

In November 1906, just one week after the news that Harriman had ousted Stuyvesant Fish as president of the Illinois Central, the Interstate Commerce Commission announced it was launching an investigation into railroad consolidations. Established in 1887 as an independent agency under the Interstate Commerce Act, which made railroads the first industry subject to federal regulation, the ICC was charged with ensuring that railroad rates were just, reasonable, and nondiscriminatory. But early court decisions had emasculated the agency's power and rendered it all but toothless.

It was not until Roosevelt took office and made the strengthening of railroad regulation his number one domestic legislative priority that new laws breathed life back into the ICC. The 1903 Elkins Act ended the common practice of the railroads granting, or being extorted to grant, rebates to their most loyal and powerful customers, such as John D. Rockefeller's Standard Oil trust. Next came the Hepburn Act, enacted in 1906 with Roosevelt's strong support. The most important piece of federal railroad legislation since the Civil War, the Hepburn Act gave the ICC power to establish maximum railroad rates (subject to limited court review), to require a uniform system of railroad accounting, and to view the railroads' financial records.

Under its expanded authority, the ICC in late 1906 decided to examine more closely the consolidation and combination of railroads, including their rates, facilities, and practices. It sounded, on the surface, like a general investigation of the entire industry. But it quickly became apparent that—despite his later denials—it was a one-man hunt targeted by Theodore Roosevelt against E. H. Harriman.

The two men had recently had a major falling-out. In the past, and despite Roosevelt's attack on the Northern Securities merger, the president and Harriman had enjoyed cordial relations. Harriman, a solid Republican, had at Roosevelt's request raised $200,000 for the New York State Republican Party in 1904, including $50,000 of his own money. But Harriman felt betrayed by Roosevelt's failure to keep a promise to appoint Harriman's friend, New York senator Chauncey Depew, as ambassador to France. Thus, when in 1906 the party came calling for money for Roosevelt's hand-picked reform candidate for New York governor—Charles Evans Hughes—Harriman said he would not give a single dollar to the campaign.

Then, to Roosevelt's chagrin, Harriman, along with other railroad men, had strenuously opposed the Hepburn bill with a propaganda campaign of their own. With Harriman's public reputation tarnished by the Equitable scandal and his unseating of the popular Fish from the Illinois Central, Roosevelt decided it was a politically opportune time to sic the ICC on the Colossus of Roads. The main subjects of the ICC inquiry were to be Harriman's 1901 merger of the Union Pacific and Southern Pacific, and the Union Pacific's acquisition of other railroad stocks, some of which were re-sold at large profits.

When the ICC hearings opened in January 1907, Harriman was represented by his regular in-house railroad counsel, Robert Lovett, and by John G. Milburn, a prominent Buffalo attorney who had recently joined the New York City law firm of Carter & Ledyard, where a young Franklin Roosevelt began a clerkship the same year. Cravath appeared at the hearings as counsel for Kuhn, Loeb, which had acted as Harriman's bankers in all his major deals.

Cravath did not technically represent Harriman, but as the hearings went on his role expanded to the point where he came to be referred to as Harriman's attorney. Ironically, this was a result of the ICC's inordinate focus on one of Harriman's smaller, less consequential deals: his acquisition of the Chicago & Alton Railroad. It was to become one of the most publicly reviled transactions of the entire Progressive Era.

When Harriman bought the Alton in 1899 it was an apparently sound, conservatively run railroad, but it was suffering from years of neglect of its physical operations. It had not added a mile of road in seventeen years nor made many improvements to existing properties. Through a syndicate organized by Kuhn, Loeb, Harriman bought the Alton for about $40 million in cash and pumped in another $50 million to $60 million by issuing debt.

Harriman admitted the railroad had been overcapitalized, with its stock inflated to a par, or face, value exceeding the demonstrated value of the underlying property. But he said that with the improvements he planned, business would increase sufficiently to support the new capital structure and meet all interest and reasonable dividend obligations. In this Harriman proved right, for he had gone on to run the railroad successfully for a number of years, doubling profits while increasing traffic, improving facilities, and reducing passenger and freight rates. Over the course of 1904 to 1907 he gradually ceded control to another railroad, the Rock Island, after which the Alton's financial condition began a steep decline.

What turned the Alton deal into a cause célèbre in 1907 was its original financing. By rejiggering the bookkeeping after their purchase of the railroad, Harriman and the syndicate members managed to pay themselves a large early dividend. And by selling bonds to themselves at a price of $65, then reselling them for more than $90, they had profited handsomely. All told, Harriman said, the syndicate had made $24 million on the Alton reorganization. In effect, he and the syndicate members recouped some of their investment early rather than leave more money in the company as a cushion against future downturns.

At the time of the acquisition in 1899 these features of the transaction had attracted little if any criticism. The Alton was hardly a major railroad. But by 1907, when it was encountering financial difficulties under new management, the public mood had shifted. In the ICC hearings the original financing was attacked as "indefensible"; the syndicate was accused of "crippling," "looting," and "scuttling" the railroad through Harriman's machinations. The Alton was being held up as a classic example of the sins of the past in railroad financing—the worst kind of avaricious behavior that men such as Harriman had blithely engaged in before Roosevelt took office.

Although Cravath was not personally involved with the original Alton deal, he took on the mantle of defending it before the ICC. In part this was because his former partner Guthrie had done the legal work on the transaction, and because Kuhn, Loeb, a regular Cravath client, was so heavily involved with it. In addition, Cravath made a better spokesman than the combative Harriman, who sometimes had trouble explaining the deal himself. More than once, when confronted by the ICC's counsel with some anomalous accounting aspect of the transaction, Harriman responded that there must have been some sort of mistake.

Cravath, better than anyone else, including Harriman's personal attorneys, was able to elucidate the details of the deal and to put it in perspective. It was true, Cravath admitted, that the Alton illustrated how easy it was to overload companies with watered stock. When abused, the practice operated as a fraud on unsuspecting investors and creditors who had relied on the stated par value (generally $100 a share) as an indicator of actual value. In fact, par value was a fictitious, artificial number bearing no relation to the actual market value of the stock.

But as Cravath pointed out, stock watering was a common practice before and around the turn of the century. To raise needed capital, promoters of companies routinely placed artificially inflated values on the common stock they sold to the public, sometimes calling it "goodwill" or "services." They believed that through innovation and hard work they could increase the earning power of their properties over time, sufficient to carry the debts and pay dividends on the stocks.

Cravath ventured to say that despite many abuses, the watering of stock had been helpful in the past, when the country was still growing, by "providing the incentive to able, courageous men, having faith in the future, to develop the properties which they purchased and which they then sought to make more valuable." Even the anti-Wall Street crusader Samuel Untermyer, who had made millions forming companies with watered stock early in his career, defended the practice as necessary. Without stock watering, he said, "you never would have had a railroad built."

Although questionable in hindsight, the Alton financing was no different from the financing of hundreds of other companies, Cravath said—done in accordance with the methods in vogue at the time. Moreover, the deal was open and aboveboard, with nothing hidden or concealed from investors. The transaction was neither illegal nor fraudulent; the only thing that had changed was public opinion and a heightened scrutiny of the moral aspects of high finance.

All of that said, Cravath then made an extraordinary series of statements that may have reflected the private thinking of many of his corporate lawyer peers, but which were rarely if ever uttered publicly by any of them. Expressing

what he called "my own individual judgment and not speaking for my clients," Cravath said he agreed there should be greater restrictions on the issue of new securities than in the past, including federal regulation if
necessary. And if it was the ICC's view that the types of transactions exem-
plified by the Alton transaction should be banned, or allowed only under the
ICC's supervision, then he would have no quarrel. He went on to say,

> Perhaps a lawyer arguing a case has no right to express his views on
> questions of economic policy, but I quite agree that the time has come
> in the development of our country, when, in balancing advantages and
> evils, the advantage would be in favor of a much stricter regulation of
> the issue of stocks and bonds, a much greater conservatism enforced
> by law than has prevailed in the past.... And yet we must not forget
> the conditions which existed when these securities were issued.

Cravath provided his analysis of the Alton situation in a brief submitted
directly to President Roosevelt. Cravath's opinions ended up being mirrored
by the ICC in its final report on its investigation. It concluded that some
reasonable regulation should be imposed on the issuance of securities by
railroads engaged in interstate commerce, both to make them safer and
more secure investments and to boost public confidence in them. It also
recommended that competing railways be prohibited from having common
directors or officers. Although highly critical of the Alton financing and
Harriman's railroad consolidations, the ICC said it had discovered no violation of law by Harriman or others in connection with the Alton or with
Harriman's other railroad stock dealings.

By aggressively protecting his clients while still managing to sound reasonable, Cravath had helped achieve a favorable outcome. He would continue to echo the same theme in public hearings on possible federal railroad
regulation a couple of years later, arguing that in the past "corporations were
too free to do what they chose" and that federal laws were needed requiring
"the complete disclosure as to what stocks represent." He also thought that
publicity would cure much of the evil of corporate insiders buying stocks at
a low price and selling them to their own corporations at a higher price.
Cromwell, too, urged his corporate clients to make fuller disclosure in their

annual reports, mainly to inspire greater investor interest and confidence in the securities they were trying to sell.

Cravath's advocacy of federal securities regulation was ahead of its time. It would not be until 1920, when the railroads nationalized during World War I were returned to private operation, that Congress adopted federal regulation of the issuance of securities by railroads. The regulation of securities issues by companies generally engaged in interstate commerce would not come until 1933, as part of the New Deal legislation passed in the wake of the 1929 stock market crash.

In the meantime, the best corporate lawyers recognized that some sort of solution to the problem of watered stock needed to be found, at least at the state level. The idea they pursued, originated and forcefully advocated by Frank Stetson, was the issuance of "no-par" stock. It dispensed with the fiction that par value represented the actual value of stock, so that unsophisticated investors would no longer be misled into thinking a share of stock bought at $100 par value was actually worth $100; it was merely a fractional interest in the total net assets and earnings of the corporation.

Prompted by Stetson, the New York State Bar Association drafted a bill in 1907 to allow New York corporations to issue no-par or nominal par value ($.01) stock. The bill would eventually become law in 1912, making New York the first state to permit no-par common stock. Soon almost every other state followed suit. The wide use of no-par stock did not eliminate the possibility of fraud by corporate insiders in issuing securities, but it ameliorated the problems caused by stock watering.

Although the ICC had found no illegality in the Alton transaction, it would haunt E. H. Harriman to the end of his days. In addition, Theodore Roosevelt was not about to let the little fellow off the hook. Before leaving the presidency, Roosevelt directed his attorney general to file an antitrust suit to dissolve the combination between Harriman's Union Pacific and Southern Pacific. It was a move driven more by politics and animus than by logic or public policy, as the two railroads did not serve the same territory.

Harriman, who made enemies easily, was sometimes his own worst one. He did not endear himself to the government when in his ICC testimony he was asked whether, if he could, he would add the Santa Fe, the Northern Pacific, and the Great Northern to his Union Pacific–Southern Pacific empire. "If you would let me" was his tart reply.

The Supreme Court eventually ruled in the government's favor in the antitrust suit, ordering the breakup of the Union Pacific and Southern Pacific. Cravath, who had represented Kuhn, Loeb partners Jacob Schiff and Otto Kahn in the antitrust case, was then retained by the Union Pacific to develop the plan of dissolution to comply with the Supreme Court's ruling.

By the time of the Supreme Court's ruling against him in 1912, Harriman was three years in his grave, a victim of stomach cancer. His survivors included his son, Averell, who made his name as a politician and a diplomat, two things no one would have accused E. H. Harriman of being. Upon Harriman's death his longtime banker Schiff said, "When we laid the little man into the grave near the quiet village church, a power was buried which it will hardly be possible to replace."

The contents of Harriman's $60 million estate revealed an ironic postscript to the Equitable scandal. Harriman had tried but failed, via none-too-subtle threats, to obtain half of the stock that Thomas Ryan had bought from James Hazen Hyde. But it turned out that sometime after the dust had cleared in the Equitable matter, Harriman did manage to persuade Ryan to sell him half of his Equitable stock. Ryan later sold out his remaining half interest to J. P. Morgan, who ended up buying Harriman's Equitable shares from his widow. Morgan thus gained control of the Equitable, which he had been rumored to be seeking at the time of the scandal in 1905.

———⊷⊶———

Just as the ICC's investigation of Harriman was winding down, another investigation that would involve Cravath was gearing up. This one concerned the New York City transit system in which Cravath had played an integral role, first in helping Thomas Fortune Ryan expand his streetcar empire into subway construction, then in merging his interests with August Belmont Jr.'s subway company. But unlike the ICC investigation, which if anything had enhanced Cravath's reputation, the transit probe would expose him to accusations of personal malfeasance. Accused of looting in conspiracy with

Ryan, Cravath for a time would become "a symbol of rapacious capital," as the *New Yorker* would later put it. The entire experience would leave Cravath bitter and disillusioned.

Despite the initial uproar over the merger between Ryan's Metropolitan and Belmont's IRT, and rancorous attacks on Ryan and Cravath by the Hearst papers, a public railroad board investigation in 1906 had found nothing illegal in any of the transactions. The New York courts had likewise rejected several stockholder suits challenging the transactions as fraudulent. But in July 1907 the new Public Service Commission in New York launched a fresh investigation of its own. The impetus was widespread public dissatisfaction with city transit service, but the PSC soon began to focus on the financial side of the merger.

The financial aspects assumed even greater significance when the Metropolitan—the surface transportation half of the combined company—collapsed in October 1907 and went into receivership. As it turned out, rather than increasing the surface lines' business, as the Ryan group had hoped, the subways had cut deeply into the Metropolitan's revenues. Belmont's IRT, the subway portion of the company, was able to stand on its own and avoid bankruptcy.

With the collapse of the Metropolitan system the PSC turned its attention to the complicated corporate structure that Cravath and Guthrie, working with the Kuhn, Loeb bankers, had put in place for Ryan back in 1902. They had created a tangled web of subsidiary surface transit companies, leases, and operating agreements, all placed under the umbrella of the Metropolitan Securities holding company. Because Guthrie had left the firm in 1906, it now fell to Cravath to defend the Metropolitan structure, along with numerous intercompany transactions Cravath had overseen as counsel for Kuhn, Loeb and Metropolitan Securities, of which he became a director.

The PSC counsel and lead investigator was William M. Ivins, a reform politician who had lost a run for New York mayor in 1905. Described by the *New York Times* as second only to Charles Evans Hughes as an investigator, Ivins proceeded to unearth a series of facts highly embarrassing not only to the Metropolitan but to Cravath.

First came the revelation that ten years' worth of the Metropolitan's books and records Ivins was seeking, covering the period leading to the formation of the company in 1902, had been destroyed in 1905. As the company's secretary-treasurer, a Mr. Moorhead, admitted, he had sold the books to a junkman for $117. Because the destruction occurred while Cravath was counsel to the company, he was sensitive to any suggestion that he had condoned or known about it at the time. Indeed, few things are more petrifying to a lawyer—or more career-threatening—than being accused of destroying evidence.

Cravath's sensitivity became apparent when, later in the hearings, Ivins charged that "these gentlemen deliberately destroyed their own books." When Cravath objected to Ivins's statement, Ivins reminded him of Moorhead's prior testimony about junking the records. Cravath begged to correct him. "You say 'these gentlemen,'" Cravath interjected. "He [Moorhead] is a gentleman, not 'these gentlemen.'" Ivins retorted that Moorhead was a "very subordinate subordinate" who never would have destroyed the books without the authority of someone superior to him. That led to the following exchange:

CRAVATH: That is your assertion.

IVINS: That is the result of my study of the minutes of all these companies.

CRAVATH: That is not in the evidence.

IVINS: Well, I will put it into evidence and swear to it if you wish it.

CRAVATH: I do not put lawyers on the stand.

IVINS: Well, I do.

The records-destruction issue was soon overtaken by a more serious charge. In 1902 Metropolitan Securities had bought the franchise rights for an as-yet-unbuilt railroad—to connect the Wall and Cortlandt Street ferries in lower Manhattan—from one Anthony Brady for $965,000. The Cravath firm had conducted a corporate records search and pronounced the validity of the transaction.

Then, during the 1907 PSC investigation, Ivins elicited testimony from Brady that he had previously sold the same railroad rights to William C. Whitney, Ryan's longtime business partner, for $250,000. That sale was canceled, and when Brady in turn sold the rights to the Metropolitan, Whitney instructed him to add almost $700,000 to the purchase price. After receiving the $965,000, Brady kept $250,000 for himself and, again on Whitney's instruction, gave the rest to Whitney, Ryan, and some other prominent cofinanciers of the Metropolitan to be divided among themselves. These payments went to reimburse them, as it turned out, for secret political contributions they had made on Metropolitan's behalf to the Republican Party in the 1900 campaigns and to local Democratic Tammany politicians. The net effect of the transactions was that Brady made his $250,000; Ryan, Whitney, and their associates were made whole on their unauthorized campaign contributions; and the Metropolitan overpaid by $700,000 for the unbuilt railroad. It was viewed as a plain mulcting of the Metropolitan transit company's assets.

There was nothing to indicate that Cravath had known any of these facts at the time. He had no choice but to advise the other Metropolitan directors they were duty-bound to file suit on behalf of the company to recover the illicit payments from the individuals who had received them, including Cravath's important client Ryan. The suit was eventually settled out of court for the full amount of the claim, with Metropolitan Securities receiving back the $700,000 it had overpaid Brady.

Ryan denied knowing the money that reimbursed him had come from the Brady sale. Whitney obviously knew, but he was dead. District Attorney William Travers Jerome, who had convened a grand jury investigation, cited Cravath for contempt when he refused to testify to his conversations with Ryan on the ground of attorney-client privilege. Jerome was known for personally leading police raids on city gambling houses, using axes to break in. Jerome was also the prosecutor in the "trial of the century" concerning the

1906 murder of socialite architect Stanford White by millionaire Harry Thaw over Thaw's showgirl wife, Evelyn Nesbit.

Jerome was the same man who in 1905 had persuaded Cravath to allow Ryan to testify in the Equitable matter, despite a claim of privilege, after Ryan was threatened with contempt by the Armstrong Committee. This time, however, Cravath did not back down and fought the contempt charge. Fellow members of the bar came to his defense, including American Bar Association president Alton B. Parker, the Democratic candidate for president against Roosevelt in 1904. Bolstered by their arguments that Cravath's invocation of the privilege was proper, a New York state court sustained Cravath's refusal to testify and heavily rebuked Jerome.

Undaunted, Jerome continued investigating and brought Cravath before another grand jury to ask him to provide a factual overview of the history of the Metropolitan up to its formation in 1902. This time Cravath did not refuse to answer any questions, and Jerome later concluded no crimes had been committed either in connection with the Brady sale or in any other Metropolitan transactions. Jerome was pilloried in the press for his inaction and timidity and was accused of being too cozy with business interests. A stockholder committee of the Metropolitan then petitioned Governor Charles Evans Hughes to remove Jerome as district attorney, but after a lengthy independent investigation Hughes declined to do so. Jerome argued that although many of the transactions he looked into were ethically suspect, they were not provable crimes.

Despite the absence of any criminal indictments, Cravath's name had been sullied through constant close association with transactions viewed by many as immoral if not illegal. New York's daily socialist paper, in a story on October 17, 1907, headlined HERE THEY ARE: TABLOID SKETCHES OF MEN IN THE LIMELIGHT, listed Cravath among the "Who's Who?" in the local transit "swindle." He was identified as a corporation lawyer of previous high reputation and as personal counsel to the king of the swindlers, Thomas Fortune Ryan, whose halo from his beneficial role in the Equitable matter had since worn off. That very day, Ryan, who had been making noises for months about severing his various Wall Street ties, announced he was retiring from all interest in the IRT-Metropolitan transit system.

For Cravath, the worst of the Metropolitan saga was yet to come. In the meantime, a new crisis was brewing. This one concerned another long-time client, George Westinghouse, and it would end with their acrimonious parting.

In many ways Americans in October 1907 had every reason to be optimistic about the future. Technology seemed to offer limitless opportunities for human advancement. On October 11 the British ocean liner *Lusitania* arrived in New York four days and twenty hours after leaving the coast of Ireland, breaking all speed records for transatlantic crossings. On October 14 the *New York Times* reported that a French surgeon believed he had discovered a cure for cancer. And on October 17 the first wireless press message was sent across the Atlantic, from London to New York, via the Marconi system, which was opening a transatlantic wire system to the public.

By contrast, the nation's financial system remained archaic. Plagued by the lack of a central monetary authority, the country was fated to suffer through periodic episodes of boom, bust, and panic, followed by severe economic depressions such as those that commenced in 1873 and 1893. By mid-October 1907 the United States was in another downturn, with unemployment rising and stocks having declined by 50 percent from their peak the previous year. Then on October 22 the bottom fell out completely when the Knickerbocker Trust Company, New York City's third largest, had to shutter its doors to stop a run on its deposits. The collapse of the Knickerbocker (whose president, Charles Barney, committed suicide) led to a run on other banks in New York and across the country. It was to be known as the Panic of 1907.

With no central bank to inject liquidity into the system, the job of stemming the panic fell again to one man: J. P. Morgan. Even such financial giants as E. H. Harriman and Thomas Fortune Ryan looked to Morgan to provide a solution. Morgan famously summoned the leading bankers in New York to his private library on Madison Avenue and locked them inside overnight until they agreed to contribute to a $25 million rescue plan. At 1:00 p.m. the next day, the Trust Company of America (TCA), another key financial institution, told Morgan it would have to fold if it did not receive an emergency loan before its 3:00 p.m. closing time. A pair of bankers who had been up all night studying TCA's accounts reported to Morgan that although the TCA was teetering, it was still solvent and savable. Morgan turned to his fellow bankers and said, "This is the place to stop the trouble, then." With a $3 million loan the TCA survived the immediate crisis.

It was not all altruism on Morgan's part: As part of the rescue plan, he offered to buy the ailing Tennessee Coal, Iron & Railroad Company (Tennessee Coal), a major competitor of Morgan's US Steel. Because the purchase raised serious antitrust concerns, Morgan sought clearance from President Roosevelt, who had told Morgan he would not sue to break up US Steel unless he discovered it had done something wrong. Despite his well-publicized opposition to large trusts, Roosevelt (supported by Root) agreed not to object to Morgan's purchase of the Tennessee Coal. Roosevelt would be accused of hypocrisy, and the episode would later play a key role in the rift between him and his successor, William Howard Taft.

Thanks to Morgan's private money-raising efforts—and matching US Treasury loans placed at his disposal—the bank crisis passed. With Stetson's legal advice, Morgan also crafted a plan to prevent New York City from defaulting on its payroll and borrowing obligations and going into bankruptcy. Morgan drove himself nearly to exhaustion during the crisis, working nineteen-hour days while popping lozenges for a bad cold and chomping on twenty cigars a day.

The stock market soon recovered, although many industrial companies were forced into receivership by the financial squeeze and continuing depression. The Metropolitan surface transportation system was a victim of the panic, as were many railroads, whose owners blamed Roosevelt's rate-regulation legislation for depreciating the value of their properties. But perhaps the biggest casualty of the panic was George Westinghouse.

The day after the run on the Knickerbocker in New York, several of the Pittsburgh-based Westinghouse companies, including Westinghouse Electric, were placed in temporary receiverships. They were not insolvent or losing money; as the New York Times wrote, the situation "does not involve a failure—it seems a contradiction of terms to use the word in connection with George Westinghouse." But the massive debt burdens necessitated a reorganization of the company. The crisis worsened when jittery Pittsburgh banks and Morgan's New York bank group were either unable or unwilling to bail out the main competitor of the Morgan-controlled General Electric.

Cravath raced to Pittsburgh to oversee the situation personally. He told the press that creditors would be paid in full if they were patient and showed forbearance. Working with banks, creditors, bondholders, and the reorganization committee, Cravath managed to help steady the ship. Negotiating behind the scenes, at one point he noted that in the draft minutes of one of the committee meetings "the name Cravath appears entirely too often. I have crossed it off wherever possible."

It would take roughly a year to lift the receiverships. Cravath wrote to one of his partners that the events had so unsettled his nerves that he was going to spend the next morning looking at paintings and architecture at Pittsburgh's Carnegie Institute to regain his normal state of mind. Years later he would say the Westinghouse restructuring was in many ways "the most remarkable voluntary readjustment of capital with which I am familiar."

But the resolution ended up costing Westinghouse control of his company, and with it his close friendship with Cravath. As part of the rearrangement, Westinghouse agreed to let a directors' committee elect a chairman of the board, a new position, with Westinghouse remaining as president. But when the board named a chairman and amended the by-laws to make him chief executive officer as well, Westinghouse attacked him as incompetent and launched a campaign to regain control. Westinghouse's attempted coup, which Cravath opposed, ended in failure.

Their break came when Cravath wrote Westinghouse the following letter: "My obligation is to the Westinghouse Company and I think you have gone back on the arrangement you have agreed to. I think my duty is to the Board of Directors and to the company and to the plan of reorganization to which you assented and which I was instrumental in carrying through."

Westinghouse continued in a diminished presidency for several years, then went into physical decline and died in 1914. At a Westinghouse Electric Company dinner ten years later, Cravath lauded him as a genius, saying, "No man I have known combined so many of the qualities that make for greatness as George Westinghouse." Because of his courage and boldness he had suffered and weathered financial setbacks, Cravath said, but never financial defeat. "Today all the enterprises that he founded are sound and prosperous, and their financial structures . . . rest upon the sound foundations that he laid." Cravath might have added that it was his early days as a lawyer, representing Westinghouse in the wars with Edison over light bulbs and currents, that laid the foundation for his own remarkable career. It was, however, a career that was coming under increasingly hostile attack.

Chapter 11

"I Hope I Am a Wiser Man"

N
ot even Frank Stetson could save Paul Cravath from further grief in the Metropolitan transit affair.

In January 1908 Cravath was sued for fraud on one of the Metropolitan intercompany transactions he had supervised. The $3 million suit, filed by the federal receivers for the New York City Railway, a failed subsidiary of the Metropolitan Securities Company, named Metropolitan and several of its directors, including Cravath, as defendants. Cravath had not been personally sued in his professional career before, and the fact that Stetson, who rarely appeared in court anymore, agreed to serve as trial counsel for the defense indicated the suit was a serious matter.

In substance, the suit charged that back in 1902, Cravath and the other directors had caused New York City Railway to take out a roughly $6 million loan from its parent holding company, Metropolitan Securities, which then forced the railway company subsidiary to pay back $9 million to retire the loan only a month or two later. That produced an exorbitant profit for Metropolitan Securities of $3 million, or 30 percent, on a very short-term loan.* The suit alleged that the transaction deprived New York City Railway's creditors of $3 million in assets to pay their claims—assets taken from New York Railway by its parent company for no consideration.

As usual in such matters, the truth was more complex. As Cravath testified, when Stetson put him on the witness stand, the transaction had been structured for tax reasons and for settling intercompany accounts, not for any fraudulent purpose. And because all the various Metropolitan subsidi-

---

*In technical terms New York City Railway issued roughly $9 million in debentures, with a par value of $100, to Metropolitan Securities at a discounted price of $70, which Metropolitan redeemed at par, or 30 points over the issue price.

ary companies, including New York City Railway, were part of a single corporate enterprise with no conflicts of interest, it made no difference how the
assets of the companies may have been shuffled among one another.

That was true as far as it went, but the plaintiff-receivers in the lawsuit
did have a point. They represented creditors of the New York City Railway,
who were entitled to satisfy their claims from that company's assets, separate
and apart from the assets of the other Metropolitan entities. If New York
City Railway had in fact been insolvent in 1902, when the loan repayment
took place, then the $3 million profit made by Metropolitan Securities was
illegal and would have to be returned to the city railway. And that could be
the case even if, as Stetson maintained, and as Cravath testified, the directors had acted innocently and without knowledge of the city railway's insol-
vency at the time of the loan repayment, five years before the company went
into receivership.

But all these nuances became lost amid lurid allegations that the New
York City Railway coffers had been "looted" by the defendants' scheme and
conspiracy to transfer company assets beyond the reach of the creditors for
the benefit of themselves. These rhetorical flourishes were largely the ema-
nations of the plaintiffs' attorney, a giant of the legal profession—Joseph
Hodges Choate.

The seventy-six-year-old Choate was from that earlier generation of trial
lawyers known more for their courtroom eloquence and wit than for their
legal arguments. "His method goes right to the human heart," the *New-York
Tribune* once said, observing that he often spoke with his hands in his pockets. He was sly about taking liberties in court, as in one case, bearing upon
the honesty of the transactions of a fur trader whom Choate repeatedly referred to as a "skin merchant." Back when Stetson was still doing trial work,
Choate once upbraided him for interrupting; Choate explained to the judge
that it was the winter solstice, the shortest day of the year, and he needed all
the time he could get.

A past president of the American Bar Association and New York's state
and city bar associations, Choate ran for and lost the Republican US sena-
torial nomination for New York in 1897. In 1899 President William McKinley appointed him US ambassador to the United Kingdom, a position he
held until 1905. "There are people who think that if Choate had been the

slightest bit politic about his public statements he might well have been President of the United States," recalled Allen Wardwell, one of Stetson's law partners.

Choate's greatest skill was in cross-examining witnesses. "He was charming, very affable and very genial," Wardwell said, but "when he was going to hit, you couldn't know." Even at age seventy-six he retained much of the old spark, and he would take direct aim at Paul Cravath.

In a related $5 million lawsuit, Choate compared the Metropolitan situation to the Chicago & Alton Railroad reorganization done by E. H. Harriman. These were fighting words given the infamy the Alton recapitalization had attained. Everyone would remember, Choate told the court, how "a band of capitalists broke into the [Alton] and helped themselves to $10 million or $15 million." The Metropolitan looting, he said, was of the same school of theft, as when a Dutch master's painting is done after the school of Rembrandt.

Cravath, who was representing the Metropolitan, angrily protested Choate's "mudslinging" at the persons involved with the Alton deal. He pointed out that he had represented them in the ICC investigation of the Alton and was duty bound to defend their honor because they were not present to defend themselves. Cravath was so upset that after the court adjourned he would not let the matter drop, instead buttonholing Choate for an extended sidebar conversation on the subject. Choate was overheard to say that when he excoriated the Alton reorganization he hadn't known that Cravath had defended it before the ICC. Regardless, Choate maintained that his characterization of the Alton deal was amply justified by the facts.

In the suit against Cravath and others over the $3 million loan repayment, Choate was more pointed in his accusations. On cross-examination, after Cravath had testified to the reasons for the transaction, Choate asked, "Mr. Cravath, can you give no better excuse than that which you have now given for the act of yourself and your associates?" When Cravath tried to elaborate, Choate said again, "You can give no other or different excuse or explanation? . . . Nothing else?"

In his closing argument Choate said his clients were widows and orphans whose claims against the New York City Railway remained unsatisfied. It was, he said, the greatest financial fraud ever committed in New

York. His oratory took even higher flight: "I think it was Mme. Roland who said, on her way to the guillotine, 'Oh, Liberty, what crimes have been committed in thy name!' Well might these unhappy creditors have exclaimed when the *debacle*—as Mr. Stetson has so well called it—came: 'Oh, high finance, what crimes have been committed in thy name!'"

Turning and gesturing toward Cravath, who sat next to Stetson at the defense counsel table, Choate continued:

> The question still remains: Why did you do it? Mr. Cravath here has made many explanations, but they are worse than none. He's very gallant about it, and comes bravely into the lists [medieval combat arena] with rueful countenance but in the true spirit of chivalry; with visor down and spear at rest, he rushes upon us for the protection of his associates who don't care or don't dare to appear. He insists that there was nothing but the most honest intention. . . . And Mr. Stetson also says it was done in good faith. . . . Now, I don't dispute Mr. Cravath's good intentions . . . but we all know that very gloomy places are paved with good intentions.

The *New York Times* thought Choate had argued "with the force of a man many years his junior." In a curious scene after he concluded, all the lawyers in the room—except for Cravath—crowded around Choate to congratulate him on his spirited performance. Stetson, although one of the opposing counsel, was the first to shake his hand. White shoe lawyers were nothing if not collegial.

The $3 million suit was eventually settled, together with the earlier related $5 million suit, for a total of $5.5 million. Without admitting any wrongdoing, the individual defendants put up $1.5 million of the total, with the other $4 million to come from the combined Interborough-Metropolitan group. Although Jacob Schiff of Kuhn, Loeb objected to Cravath's contributing anything to the settlement, Cravath reportedly paid $100,000 in cash into the pot.

Having to settle a suit he believed to be meritless was bad enough, but the lowest blow, for Cravath, came when his ex-partner Guthrie sided with his accusers. In 1902 Guthrie had been at least as involved as Cravath was in setting up the Metropolitan's complex intercompany structure that later came under attack as Alton-like. Yet Guthrie implausibly denied, against much evidence, that he had known anything about the controversial $3 million loan transaction. He suggested that had he been consulted in 1902 he would not have agreed with Cravath that the transaction was permissible. Cravath wrote to Guthrie, "I think your memory is at fault in believing that you were not informed of the transactions."

Their dispute did not end there. Two years later Cravath was subjected to every lawyer's nightmare—the filing of an ethics complaint with a bar association's grievance committee. The complaint came from a retired lawyer and railroad investor who alleged that the wrecking of the Metropolitan had hindered city and subway development.

Quoting from Choate's closing argument, the complaint charged Cravath, as counsel and director of the Metropolitan, with having actively participated in and personally profited from the "flotation and inflation" of the Metropolitan's assets. Although this charge related more directly to the original formation of the company, for which Guthrie bore equal responsibility, than to the $3 million loan repayment, Guthrie continued to attack Cravath in letters to the grievance committee and bar association. Guthrie then filed the letters in the bar association's library so they would be made public.

The grievance committee determined that no action against Cravath was warranted, and even Choate said publicly there was no basis for any discipline. Choate jokingly told reporters he ought not to be held responsible for things he might have said about Cravath in court. William M. Ivins, who had crossed swords with Cravath during the PSC investigation in 1907, also sent Cravath a sympathetic letter. But the damage to Cravath's relationship with Guthrie was permanent. Some years later Guthrie told Cravath's partner Robert Swaine that he fondly recalled the old days and thought he and Cravath should patch up their differences. "But to Cravath," Swaine wrote, "Guthrie's 'treachery' was 'beyond forgiveness.'"

Just what motivated Guthrie to turn on Cravath remains elusive. Swaine speculates that Guthrie felt that Cravath had not been aggressive enough in his defense of their legal fees for their Metropolitan work. As Ivins had brought out in the PSC investigation, those fees had totaled $435,000. In testifying before the PSC, Cravath chose not to go into great detail about the nature and extent of the legal services for which he and Guthrie had been paid. Guthrie then wrote Cravath a lengthy letter saying Cravath owed a better explanation "to the public and to the profession and to ourselves." But because Ivins had stated for the record that he thought the fees were not only reasonable but moderate in light of the complexity of the services rendered, it is hard to see why this issue should have spurred such animus on Guthrie's part toward Cravath.

After withdrawing from his partnership with Cravath in 1906, Guthrie maintained a successful law practice of his own. But Guthrie had always been jealous of Cravath's greater commercial success, so that may have played a part in Guthrie's decision to attack him. The one realm in which Guthrie managed to outdo Cravath was in real estate: Cravath's Long Island English country mansion, Veraton, named for his daughter, Vera (his only child), was luxurious but not as grand as his neighbor Guthrie's Meudon, an awe-inspiring eighty-room estate in the image of a château built by King Louis XIV outside Paris.

Then, too, political differences may have soured the Cravath-Guthrie relationship. Guthrie detested the progressive movement and opposed all forms of federal regulation of business and much state regulation as well. He fought against the income tax, the inheritance tax, the antitrust laws, maximum work hours laws, even federal child labor laws—all of which he regarded as class warfare against property owners or violations of freedom of contract. Later, as president of the New York State Bar Association, he argued against membership for "immigrants and their progeny" who posed a "difficult and grave problem and menace" to "the elite of the Bar, the best of the Bar." This despite the fact that Guthrie was a devout Catholic, a disfavored religion at the time and almost as much a rarity among the highest echelons of white shoe law firms as were Jews.*

---

*Such nativist sentiments were not uncommon among elite members of the bar, especially after the great wave of immigration to the United States in the first decade of the twentieth century. Elihu Root, for example, said in 1916 that the legal profession needed to reduce the influence of the huge number of immigrants from countries "which differ so widely in their fundamental conceptions of law and personal freedom from ourselves." George Wickersham warned the bar association against allowing membership to hordes of immigrants who did not speak English. At that time the term "immigrant" was a code word for Eastern Euro-

Guthrie would not have welcomed Cravath's evolving views on the need for stricter federal regulation of the securities market. To Guthrie, any such talk marked one as soft on socialism and a traitor to his class. Cravath was hardly a socialist; he was a moderately conservative Republican and was never associated with the progressive movement. He did not hesitate to criticize proposed reforms when he thought they went too far.

But Cravath's experience with such publicly vilified transactions as the Alton reorganization and the Metropolitan transit system implosion had chastened him. He no longer believed, if he ever had, that corporations and their chieftains should be given the run of the house. Guthrie never did relinquish that view.

The Metropolitan experience left Cravath somewhat cynical, aloof, and disillusioned as to personal loyalties. The public allegations even caused some of the Cravath firm's idealistic young associates to question the firm's integrity. "When I came in there, I naturally had my eyes open to whether the office was honorable, and whether the ends that they were serving in helping their clients were good ends," recalled Nicholas Kelley, who arrived at the firm in 1909. He came to the view that the office "was extraordinarily honorable" and that what they were doing—taking companies in financial difficulty and making them better, so they could operate and be productive—was "a useful thing." Kelley, who had joined the Socialist Party in college, stayed at Cravath for six years before leaving for a smaller firm. He later worked in the Treasury Department, became the main lawyer for Chrysler Corporation, negotiated for the construction of the Chrysler Building, and went on to become the lead partner in the firm of Kelley Drye & Warren, one of New York's oldest and most prestigious.

One lesson Cravath drew from the Metropolitan saga was that it was a mistake for a lawyer to sit on the board of directors of a corporate client. It placed too great a strain on the objectivity a lawyer was required to maintain. Henceforth the Cravath system would mandate that none of the firm's partners or associates would serve as a director of a client company, hold stock

---

pean Jews, who were making up an increasing percentage of large-city lawyers, practicing as part of what was considered to be the "lower bar."

in any client company, or have a financial interest in any transaction in which the firm was acting as counsel.*

"Your criticism of my 'error of judgment in being both counsel and director' is much milder than the circumstances merit," Cravath told Ivins in response to a kindly worded letter. "I hope I am a wiser man than I was ten years ago."

---

*The "no client directorship" rule would routinely be subject to exceptions, though, both at the Cravath firm and elsewhere. Increasingly over time, when a large law firm became the regular outside counsel to a corporation, a senior partner would go on its board of directors, either at the client's request or because the lawyer wanted to cement the relationship. Cravath, who gave up most of his corporate client directorships after the unhappy Metropolitan experience, stayed on the boards of various Westinghouse companies, even becoming acting chairman of the Westinghouse Electric Board from 1927 to 1929.

Chapter 12

Conscience of a Conservative Lawyer

While he was preparing Cravath's trial defense in the Metropolitan case, Frank Stetson found time, as always, to devote to his greatest passion in life outside his wife and legal practice: his Williams College alma mater. With their legal training and business skills, many Wall Street lawyers donated their time to volunteer organizations that welcomed them onto their boards for their judgment and expertise, and Stetson was a good example.

Being childless, Stetson treated Williams as he would a favorite son or daughter. A trustee of the college since 1899, Stetson involved himself deeply in every aspect of the school's administration—its finances, curriculum, faculty hiring, dormitories, and physical plant—and carried on a voluminous, nearly daily correspondence with school officials for many years. He went back for trustee meetings and annual commencement exercises, accompanied by his Japanese valet in the absence of his often-bedridden wife.

No Williams College matter was too small for Stetson's attention. He weighed in on such minutiae as the desired frequency of chimes during commencement season and the measurements for a new dining table for his old fraternity. In the middle of the Panic of 1907, though busy advising J. P. Morgan, he wrote to the school's general contractor to point out that the dead elms on campus needed replacing and suggested where to plant the new ones.

For a new alumni house on campus Stetson wrote to the college treasurer, "I am more and more impressed with the possible advantage of employing, as waiters in the commons, Japanese, whom I have employed for a number of years and who are very competent and docile and especially anxious to extend their educational facilities." Japanese students, he thought, were "so accustomed to mingling aristocracy with domestic service that they would feel no loss of caste with fellow students."

Because he consistently provided sound advice—and gave hundreds of thousands of dollars to the school—Stetson's views were accepted as authoritative. When, in 1908, the college became concerned about an undue emphasis on athletics, it turned to Stetson to draft a revision to the school's policy on intercollegiate sports. Stetson's proposal—to limit athletic contests to schools within New England, and not more than two hundred miles from Williams, with a maximum of two contests per season in any one sport—was unanimously adopted. He allowed as how college athletics fostered traits such as manhood, fortitude, cooperation, "good-humored persistence [and] equanimity under defeat." But limits were necessary at Williams, as everywhere, he explained, because "there is in our national temperament much which tends to excess, if not to riotous exuberance."

As Williams College regularly looked to Stetson for guidance, so, too, did his colleagues within the bar. Among other efforts, he was instrumental in helping the American Bar Association draft the first nationwide code of ethics for lawyers (eleven states had their own codes). Through a select committee on which Stetson served, the ABA produced a code of thirty-two ethical canons approved at the ABA's convention in 1908 and later adopted by nearly every state bar association.

The new Canons of Ethics, it was reported, were mainly designed to drive "shysters" out of the legal profession, the "unworthy men who have found their way into its ranks" (a veiled reference to Jewish and Catholic immigrant lawyers). One of the canons prohibited lawyer advertising, a lifeblood of Samuel Untermyer's practice, as beneath the profession.* But the canons also came at a time when the public, and even some members of the corporate bar, viewed elite corporate lawyers like Stetson as tools of the great corporations who had lost their moral compass.

In 1907 fellow corporate attorney John R. Dos Passos (father of the novelist), wrote that the modern lawyer was "a mere commercial agent—a flexible and convenient go-between." He worked "in his office, away from the

---

*In 1977, overturning many state legal ethics rules, the Supreme Court held that lawyers had a first amendment right to advertise their services.

public gaze—his machinations are in the dark, and are insidious and secret."
Legendary Harvard law professor and future Supreme Court justice Louis
D. Brandeis thought corporate attorneys had shirked their obligation to use
their powers for "the protection of the people." Like Samuel Untermyer,
Brandeis was the Southern-born son of European Jewish immigrants and
was active in the Zionist movement. Like Untermyer, he made millions
early in his career as a corporate lawyer. And like Untermyer, Brandeis
became an idealistic crusader against Wall Street and the men who represented it.

Brandeis, a Bostonian, criticized Wall Street lawyers for failing to distin-
guish between their ethical obligations when representing one private client
against another versus when they lobbied or testified on behalf of their corporate clients in opposition to legislation intended to curb corporate behavior. In the former case, Brandeis wrote, lawyers were entitled to take every
proper legal advantage they could to secure a favorable result for their client.
But Brandeis maintained that when seeking to secure or oppose legislation,
lawyers had a duty to consider the public interest. He found it disturbing that
corporations and their lawyers so often vociferously opposed passing laws
designed to solve social and economic problems, and challenged the same
laws, once enacted, in court. Brandeis summed up his views in a succinct
phrase: "We hear much of the 'corporation lawyer,' and far too little of the
'people's lawyer.'"

Similar concerns were voiced by legal scholars such as Roscoe Pound,
who served as dean of Harvard Law School for thirty years, and Princeton
University president Woodrow Wilson. And the great Supreme Court justice Felix Frankfurter related the story of how he soured on corporate law
practice when, as a young lawyer, he attended the ICC hearings on E. H.
Harriman's railroad interests. Frankfurter recalled how, when asked difficult
questions, Harriman would turn to his lawyers and ask them a question or
two. "The way Mr. Harriman spoke to his lawyers, and the boot-licking deference they paid to him . . . led me to say to myself, 'If it means that you
should be that kind of subservient creature to have the most desirable clients, the biggest clients in the country, if that's what it means to be a leader
of the bar, I never want to be a leader of the bar. The price of admission is
too high.'"

Stetson, however, made no apologies for his work. He regarded corporate law practice as a noble calling and its leading counselors a necessary bulwark against the tyranny of the majority, as expressed in overreaching legislation. In Stetson's view, a lawyer's only duty was to defend the interests of his client—whether a corporation or an individual—to the fullest possible extent, except as specifically prohibited by law or the lawyer's own moral conscience. Thus, he maintained, a lawyer had no obligation to advise a client to honor the spirit, rather than the letter, of the law; if something was not expressly prohibited, it was permitted. And in rejoinder to Brandeis's invocation of the public interest, Stetson asserted that lawyers must discharge their duty to their clients "undeterred by clamor of the public or the press."

Stetson's views were echoed by John W. Davis, the man who succeeded him as head of Stetson's firm before running for president. "I never conceived at that time that it was my duty to reform the law," Davis would recall of his turn-of-the-century lawyering days. "It was my duty to find out what the law was, and tell my client what rule of life he had to follow. That was my job. If the rules changed, well and good."

Consistent with these sentiments, Stetson pushed for adoption of a canon making clear that until a new statute was definitively upheld and construed by a judge, a corporate lawyer was free to challenge its validity in court and advance his own interpretation of what it meant. Stetson's proposed Canon 32, codifying this view, was unique among legal ethics codes at the time. It was included in the 1908 national ABA code and remained there for nearly sixty years. The 1908 Canons were eventually superseded by newer sets of rules, but to this day the lawyer's principal ethical duty remains to defend her client zealously, within the bounds of the law. Brandeis's notion that a lawyer representing a private party has an equal duty to the public has never been codified.

Still, it would be wrong to think that the public distrust of big corporations and their lawyers in the early part of the twentieth century had no impact on the way lawyers approached their practice. Cravath spoke of the need to educate clients to the moral responsibility as well as the legal responsibility not to mislead the public in stock transactions. Elihu Root conceded that lawyers, by instinct conservative and opposed to change, were often oblivious to the fact that the laws they were helping to enforce had become unjust. "I am conscious that I have myself argued cases and drawn papers and given advice in strict accordance with laws whose wisdom it had never occurred to me to question, but which I should now, after many years of thinking what the law ought to be, condemn," he said in a 1906 address.

Stetson maintained that most businessmen had no desire to violate the moral law. Nevertheless, he thought that "the judicious and helpful advice of the corporation lawyers" could nudge their clients in the direction of socially desirable behavior. "If in the discharge of this conscientious duty we shall be tactful and persistent," he said, "we may help to establish for our corporations a higher standard of methods and morals, so that in operation they shall meet at least the popular conception of beings with souls and consciences." Slowly, the white shoe bar was mellowing into a more benevolent lubricant of corporate America.

———◉———

Stetson's other major project in 1908 placed him in a national effort to revise the federal antitrust laws. By that time nobody was particularly happy with the Sherman Antitrust Act, which had been in effect for two decades. Businessmen and their lawyers, including Stetson, thought it an irksome encroachment on free enterprise; more than this they despaired of the uncertainty it created. Never knowing when a corporate expansion or acquisition would lead to an antitrust suit, entrepreneurs found it hard to raise new capital, and many blamed the Sherman Act and Roosevelt's anti-business legislation for creating the Panic of 1907. "So long as the baiting of corporations and anti-capitalistic talk of our political leaders continues," wrote Cravath's client Jacob Schiff, "we shall have no general revival of industrial affairs."

The public and the muckraking press criticized what they considered to be selective, arbitrary enforcement of the antitrust laws. Why, for example, did the government sue the Northern Securities Company and Standard Oil but not the even bigger US Steel?* Likewise, the Supreme Court's

---

*The same type of question would continue to be raised as long as companies grew to become enormous: Why did the government sue Bill Gates's Microsoft in the late 1990s but

antitrust decisions, although trending strongly in favor of the government, lacked uniformity and predictability.

Among the biggest critics of the Sherman Act were farmers and trade unions. Agricultural cooperatives that limited the supply of crops and kept farm prices high could run afoul of the antitrust laws. As for organized labor, although most courts had upheld the right of workers to bargain collectively and even to strike against their employers ("peaceful" activities), unions remained subject to prosecution for illegal practices such as boycotts of third parties. This became painfully evident when, in February 1908, the US Supreme Court held that a hatters' union in Danbury, Connecticut, violated the Sherman Act by organizing a nationwide boycott of a fur hat manufacturer that declared itself an open shop (i.e., did not require union membership to work there). The leaders of the hatters' union were later held personally liable for more than $200,000 in damages, an unheard-of sum in those days.

Finally, even Theodore Roosevelt came to conclude that the Sherman Act needed amending. For all his bravado about the evils of big business, much of which was for show, Roosevelt had never believed that big meant bad. In the new industrialized world bigness was inevitable. Roosevelt wanted to punish bad conduct, not size alone.

To be sure, some large corporate combinations were deserving of censure—those that deliberately destroyed competition, raised prices, and reduced the quality of service. But there were others that, although restraining trade to some degree, served the public interest.* Whether a trust was

---

not, at least as of 2019, Mark Zuckerberg's Facebook, or tech giants Google or Amazon, which dominate the internet search engine and e-book industries, respectively? As an April 22, 2017, *New York Times* opinion piece asked, "Is it time to break up Google?" See also Elizabeth Kolbert, "The Content of No Content: Is Big Tech Too Powerful?," *New Yorker*, August 28, 2017.

*For example, large companies enjoy economies of scale and create efficiencies whose benefits can be passed on to consumers. They are in a better position than small companies to invest in research and development that produce technological innovation. Again, with reference to modern companies, is Amazon a good thing because consumers find it reliable and easy to use, or does its dominance keep e-book prices artificially high? Is Facebook's undisputed monopoly of social media (it also owns Instagram, WhatsApp, and Messenger) good

"good" or "bad" needed to be determined in each case—not by judges who had little understanding of business and economics but by experts in the field who, as Roosevelt envisioned it, would be part of the federal executive branch.

The problem with the Sherman Act, in the opinion of Roosevelt and others, lay in the Supreme Court's all-or-nothing approach. Under the common law predating the Sherman Act—that is, judge-made as opposed to statutory law—only "unreasonable" restraints of trade were illegal. But the prevailing Supreme Court rule, as set forth in the *Northern Securities* case, was that all direct restraints of trade, reasonable or not, violated the law. *Northern Securities* was a great symbolic victory for Roosevelt at the time, but it left the government in the position of either failing to enforce the law (a policy that would prove disastrous a decade later under Prohibition), or prosecuting large swaths of the business, labor, and farm communities as criminals.

Also, given the Justice Department's limited resources, bringing intermittent individual lawsuits was ineffective. There were too many big corporations to go after, even if the government were inclined to do so. And the court process was slow. It was more important to nip bad combinations in the bud by regulating them in the national interest under a new federal incorporation law. More specifically, Roosevelt wanted the federal government to license corporations, to publish and review their proposed deals in advance, and either bless them if they were found to be reasonable or prosecute them if they were not.

The task of formulating a new law to accomplish these goals fell initially to the National Civic Federation, a private, nonpartisan group consisting of prominent representatives of business, labor, and the public. The group also included religious and educational leaders, journalists, farmers, and government officials. The NCF was considered a moderate progressive organization (labor leader Samuel Gompers and social reformer Jane Addams were members), but it was mostly controlled by its business and financial representatives and their lawyers. As evidence of this, the NCF looked to two

---

because it connects everyone for free, or bad because it can dictate privacy terms and advertising rates?

eminent corporation lawyers, both of whom had counseled J. P. Morgan in the formation of US Steel, to draft a bill to send to Congress.

One was Victor Morawetz, a petite, sociable, highly literate bachelor at the time and former partner in the Seward firm, the predecessor to the Guthrie and Cravath firms. Born in Baltimore to an Austrian immigrant doctor, Morawetz was one of the few Jewish members of the elite corporate bar. He was educated in Europe, where he learned several languages, and studied medicine at the Sorbonne. At age sixteen he traveled to the Spanish Pyrenees to serve as an aide-de-camp for the Carlist forces in their war against the Spanish monarchy. While there, he covered the war for the *Baltimore Gazette*. Morawetz later became an expert violinist and an ardent foxhunter.

Morawetz made his professional mark as a young man, writing the first modern authoritative treatise on corporate law. His reputation led Andrew Carnegie to hire him as his personal attorney for several years. Morawetz joined the Seward firm in 1887 and became a name partner there, with Guthrie, three years later. While at the firm, Morawetz often associated with Stetson to help J. P. Morgan reorganize insolvent railroads in which Morgan held large interests.

As a result of his successful reorganization of the Atchison, Topeka & Santa Fe Railway, Morawetz left the Seward firm in 1896 to become Morgan's handpicked general counsel of that railroad in New York, and later chairman of its board's executive committee. As a reform-minded expert in railroad law, he was influential in helping shape both the 1903 Elkins and 1906 Hepburn Acts championed by Roosevelt to enhance federal regulation of the railroads. On the side, he helped Stetson and Guthrie in drafting many of the documents to form US Steel. Stetson called him "perhaps the most accurate mind with which I have ever come into contact."

In early 1908 Morawetz gained the distinction, along with Cravath, of being named by progressive Wisconsin senator Robert La Follette as one of the hundred men who allegedly controlled the industrial and financial life of the country (it was not meant as a compliment). His appearance on the list, though, would be short-lived. By that time, Morawetz had made enough money in the stocks of the Atchison, Topeka railway and other companies he had helped reorganize that he was able to retire from both the railroad and from active private legal practice. He wanted to devote more time to his outside interests: academic legal writing, political science, and boys' clubs and schools. A few years later, at age fifty-two, he would marry a women's suffragist twenty years his junior, after first falling in love with a painting of her.

As a legal theoretician with practical experience, Morawetz was just the sort of man the NCF was looking for. Known for his objectivity, he was viewed as sensibly moderate—someone who had created and profited from great corporations, and believed in the capitalist system, but who recognized the public's desire to restrain corporations through expanded government regulation. Originally a Democrat, but increasingly aligned with the Republican business elites, Morawetz was among those corporate men seeking a middle way between laissez-faire capitalists and socialists who wanted to upend the system.

The other corporate lawyer the NCF turned to was Frank Stetson. He and Morawetz worked well together and, although Stetson was not associated with the reform movement, the two of them were not far apart philosophically.

Stetson and Morawetz produced a draft bill in February 1908 that reflected Roosevelt's thinking, albeit in milder form. It would have amended the Sherman Act to prohibit only unreasonable restraints of trade. Although that was a vague term, corporations could obtain government guidance to provide them with greater certainty. They could voluntarily choose to register with and become licensed by a federal corporations agency, publicly file detailed information about their finances and stock issues, and submit their contracts to the relevant government agency for advance approval.

If approved as fair and reasonable, the agreements would be exempt from lawsuits under the Sherman Act; otherwise the government or private parties could sue to invalidate them. Corporations that chose not to register could also be sued for antitrust violations, although they could defeat the suit by proving the fairness and reasonableness of their contracts. Meanwhile, labor gained some additional protections under the draft bill, although not a total exemption from the Sherman Act.

For Jeffersonians such as Stetson, these were fairly significant allowances for government involvement in the private sector. But Roosevelt was not satisfied with the Stetson-Morawetz draft because he thought its regulation of business was too light. Rather than a flat, unconditional amendment of the Sherman Act to allow reasonable restraints of trade, coupled with voluntary licensing, he insisted that corporations submit to the registration and licensing provisions as a condition of obtaining the more lenient reasonableness standard. Otherwise too many corporations might forgo registration altogether, with its requirement of extensive publicity, and take their chances in court, armed with a new "reasonableness" defense they did not enjoy under the Supreme Court's existing rulings.

A select group of NCF members, including Stetson and Morawetz, attended a series of White House meetings designed to iron out these differences. Roosevelt's secretary of state, Elihu Root, sat in on some of the meetings, while the president himself maintained a close watch over them. Roosevelt thought that properly amending the Sherman Act would be a political advantage to the Republican Party in the upcoming presidential election.

As revision after revision was made to the draft bill, Stetson and Morawetz continually attempted to water it down while Roosevelt pressed to strengthen it. He said he would veto any bill that did not make protection for reasonable restraints of trade strictly contingent on federal licensing and executive branch approval. "The more I think it over," he said, "the more I believe that to pass the bill on the Stetson–Morawetz line would be worse than passing nothing." The public would view it as a corporate lawyers' creation and a cave-in to the power of their large clients.

Roosevelt's view prevailed. In the final version of the bill submitted to Congress in late March, known as the Hepburn amendments to the Sherman Act,* the legislation was made even stronger. It placed in the hands of the president, rather than executive agency heads, the power to prescribe the information to be furnished publicly by companies that registered, and to change the requirements whenever he saw fit. Court review of executive branch decisions was to be significantly limited. It practically made the president of the United States a corporations czar, with the validity of every ma-

---

*Named for the House chairman who introduced it, and not to be confused with the earlier-enacted Hepburn Act on railroad rates named for the same man.

jor business combination subject to his approval. Described by business historian Martin Sklar as a "statist" solution that would effectively turn large private corporations into public utilities and capitalists into public servants, it was a more radical attempt at corporate regulation than anything another Roosevelt, Theodore's cousin Franklin, would propose under the New Deal a generation later.

As hearings moved forward in Congress on the bill, Stetson and Morawetz distanced themselves from it. They considered the Roosevelt version too great an expansion of federal executive authority and possibly unconstitutional. Stetson lobbied against it in private letters to Roosevelt confidant James R. Garfield, son of the late president and a Williams College alumnus who had clerked in Stetson's office twenty years earlier.

Despite calls by legislators to have Stetson and Morawetz appear and testify, they never did. Probably, the bill's sponsors knew their testimony would not be helpful. Roosevelt viewed them as "lukewarm" on the bill.

The irony is that even though the original Stetson-Morawetz draft had become a much more radical Roosevelt bill when submitted to Congress, and bore little of their mark, congressional opponents used the two corporate lawyers' "authorship"—especially their ties to J. P. Morgan's US Steel—to cast aspersions on the entire product. So as not to risk a humiliating political defeat for the president when the bill drew major opposition, Roosevelt's allies did little to correct the misimpression that Stetson and Morawetz had a large hand in writing the final bill.

The Hepburn amendments died in committee. In addition to objections by capitalist leaders that the bill was too extreme, small manufacturers opposed it because they did not want to weaken the Sherman Act prohibition against union boycotts, which were a greater threat to them than to large corporations. Labor, in turn, had pressed unsuccessfully for total immunity under the antitrust laws and thus gave only qualified support. Farm leaders were divided and either stayed silent or voiced opposition. And because Roosevelt was a lame-duck president, having announced his intention not to run for another term, he lacked the political clout to ram the bill through in an election year. He ended up keeping his administration's public identification with the bill to a minimum.

In the end, the various NCF constituencies could not come together on any one bill, and the Sherman Act was not changed. That left the law as it stood, to be interpreted case by case by the Supreme Court. Enforcement would be up to the next president and his attorney general. Monopolists would take their chances that they would not be sued or that they could win in court. And what was known as the "Trust Question"—the proper relation of large business organizations to popular government—would remain the dominant issue in American law and politics for the foreseeable future.

The Roosevelt presidency was coming to a close. His chosen successor was his good friend, and secretary of war, William Howard Taft. A former government lawyer and federal judge, Taft had strong ties to the business and legal world. But if Stetson and his fellow corporate lawyers thought the new administration would go easier on their clients under the antitrust laws than had Teddy the Trust Buster, they would end up badly mistaken.

Chapter 13

"The Scourge of Wall Street"

The first sign that William Howard Taft might in some ways turn out to be even more progressive than Roosevelt came when he refused to take William Nelson Cromwell's money for the 1908 presidential election campaign. After his nomination by the Republican convention in June, Taft announced he would not accept corporate contributions. But when his friend Cromwell offered him his personal check for $50,000, Taft turned it down as well. Taft said he was sure Cromwell had the purest of motives but that the gift would be subject to misinterpretation when publicly disclosed, as Taft had pledged to do.

As Taft explained to Cromwell, he feared being tainted by Cromwell's relations with corporate interests, and specifically his highly publicized defense of E. H. Harriman in various cases. Taft asked Cromwell to withdraw the contribution and then, if he wished, make a much more modest one.

Roosevelt, who had gladly taken large political contributions from Harriman and other businessmen in his own presidential campaign in 1904, told Taft he was being overly sensitive. In the end, Taft's campaign accepted $15,000 from Cromwell, who was among the top half-dozen individual contributors. Cromwell also served on Taft's public advisory committee during the campaign—raising money, preparing position papers, and mediating among bickering campaign officials. Cromwell called the campaign work his "'vacation,' and a most enjoyable one, too." He was rumored to want the secretary of state job (which he denied), but Taft made clear in private that Cromwell's corporate connections made it politically impossible for him to join the administration in any official capacity.

Taft consulted with Roosevelt and Root on his nomination acceptance speech, then reviewed it with Cromwell, making a few changes suggested by each. Read today, it is remarkable for showing just how far in the progressive direction the Republican Party had moved since the days of McKinley. Taft is often thought of as the conservative who disappointed Roosevelt by failing to fulfill his reform agenda, but Taft's rhetoric was downright Rooseveltian. He decried corporate "breaches of trust," "rebates and discriminations by railways," "violation of the antitrust laws," and "the overuse of stocks and bonds on interstate railways for the unlawful enriching of directors," all of which, he said, had "quickened the conscience of the people and brought on a moral awakening among them."

He was determined to ensure "equality of all before the law" and "to save the country from the dangers of a plutocratic government." He wanted to limit the influence of money in politics and promised to continue Roosevelt's progressive and regulatory approach to business abuses. He advocated the corporate licensing and publicity provisions of the Hepburn antitrust amendments that Roosevelt had pushed without success. Taft even supported exempting industrial union strikes from the antitrust laws by legislation if the courts were not inclined to do so.

Although none of this could have sounded good to America's corporate titans, they were gradually moving in the same direction, in part because of the subtle prodding by the likes of Cromwell, Cravath, and other Wall Street lawyers. "The lawyers in New York dealing with businessmen sympathize with their clients, but I think they're less conservative than their business clients as a rule," observed Frank Stetson's law partner Allen Wardwell.

To the corporate and legal establishment, Taft was acceptable enough. Although he wanted to punish lawbreakers he had no desire to interfere with legitimate business or to attack bigness for its own sake. By contrast, the alternatives were anathema to corporation men: William Jennings Bryan, Taft's Democratic opponent, was seen as radical and destructive of business, and industrial tycoons certainly had no use for the third-party candidate, socialist Eugene V. Debs.

It is hardly surprising then—if slightly ironic—that one of Taft's biggest contributors (at $20,000) was J. P. Morgan, who had been so enraged by Roosevelt's Northern Securities suit. Other Taft donors included Republican lawyers Cravath ($5,000 given under his wife's name), Elihu Root,

George Wickersham, and Joseph Choate; political independent Victor Morawetz; and Cromwell's partner William Curtis, a conservative, anti-Bryan Democrat. Businessmen Thomas Edison, John Jacob Astor, Cornelius Vanderbilt, and Jacob Schiff and Otto Kahn of Kuhn, Loeb gave to Taft as well.

Stetson and Hornblower, as loyal Democrats, did not donate money to Taft. But unlike in 1904, when they actively campaigned against Roosevelt in favor of Democrat Alton B. Parker, they could not bring themselves to support Bryan in 1908. After Taft easily defeated Bryan in the November election, Stetson privately called the results "gratifying."

That fall also saw Root elected as New York's US senator and Hughes reelected as the state's governor. National domestic politics was now dominated by Republican leaders who, though conservative by instinct, supported some degree of business regulation. Wall Street men and their white shoe lawyers were moving in sync with this new political center, a sort of "conservative progressivism."

———◦◉◦———

Having spent much of the past several years in Washington advising Taft on the Panama Canal construction and helping in his campaign, Cromwell returned to New York full-time after the election to resume his legal practice. On December 29, 1908, he hosted a dinner for his partners, former associates, and new recruits at his favorite high-society restaurant, Delmonico's. (It was the first dining establishment in the United States to take the French name "restaurant" and to have printed menus, a separate wine list, and white tablecloths.) The twenty lawyers who gathered in an upstairs private dining room had their caricatures drawn, which Cromwell had hung on the office wall. The dinner turned into an annual event funded by Cromwell's donation of $10,000 to establish the Sullivan & Cromwell Society.

———◦◉◦———

To succeed Root as secretary of state, Taft chose Philander K. Knox, Roosevelt's former attorney general. Knox, a onetime corporate lawyer for Andrew Carnegie, had helped carry out Roosevelt's trust-busting agenda; it had been Knox who filed the celebrated suit against the Northern Securities

Company. For Taft's attorney general he would follow a similar route, reaching into the private corporate legal world for his chief law enforcement officer. But the man he chose would turn out to be a far more aggressive prosecutor of antitrust cases than anyone before him, or since. Indeed, George Wickersham was to become known as "the scourge of Wall Street."

Born in Pittsburgh in 1858, George Woodward Wickersham supported himself through work as a telegraph operator and zookeeper's clerk. He started out at Lehigh University in Pennsylvania intending to become a civil engineer. The 1870s were a time of interest in practical science and technology, and the great tendency of the age, as he later recalled, was toward "pure materialism." But a literature professor who spotted in Wickersham a taste for letters persuaded him to "give up the study of calculus for that of Blackstone." He obtained his law degree from the University of Pennsylvania in 1880 and after a brief stint working for a Pennsylvania judge moved to New York City in 1882 to take a clerkship with Chamberlain, Carter & Hornblower. Later renamed Carter, Hornblower & Byrne, it was the same firm where Paul Cravath and Charles Evans Hughes began their careers as protégés of Walter Carter.

At Carter's firm, Wickersham befriended fellow clerk Henry W. Taft, brother of the future president, beginning a long association between the two men. Wickersham shortly left to take a position with Strong & Cadwalader, the oldest law firm in New York City, founded in 1792. Henry Taft soon followed Wickersham to Strong & Cadwalader, where they both became name partners.

Of the two lawyers, it was actually Henry Taft who specialized in antitrust work at Strong & Cadwalader. Wickersham's practice focused on banks, railroads, and transportation companies, including August Belmont Jr.'s Interborough Rapid Transit Company, which had built the first New York City subway. But Wickersham developed a reputation as one of the most talented lawyers in the city and, given his connection through the brother of President Taft, he was offered the job of attorney general. As Taft would say of his choice of Wickersham, "He is a corporation lawyer, but why the United States should not have the benefit of as good a lawyer as the corporations, I don't know."

Wickersham was widely considered the strongest member of the president's cabinet on domestic affairs. His appearance conveyed a sense of quiet dignity: a large mustache; small, round spectacles; thin, graying hair; and conservative, well-tailored suits. But it was his charming, amiable personality that endeared Wickersham to his friends and colleagues.

Born to a Quaker family before turning Episcopalian, Wickersham had a lofty conception of law as the "expression of the will of God working through his people." He brought a broadly humanistic, intellectual mind-set to public service, based on his deep understanding of history and literature. Perhaps the most learned of all the white shoe lawyers, he was a student of ancient Greece and Rome, the Renaissance, the French Revolution, and Anglo-American institutions and traditions. He could quote the historians Herodotus, Thomas Carlyle, and Lord Acton at will, as well as Homer, Cervantes, and Emerson. He was particularly knowledgeable about English legal history and the popular resentment of monopolies, the evils of which England had sought to curb by statute as early as 1436.

Wickersham believed that during America's industrial development period, lawyers had met the needs of the hour by devising the legal machinery that allowed corporations to expand. But he thought the law had gone too far in allowing the accumulation of great wealth. The law, he said, had failed to consider the interests of those "who had but a humble share" of the overall pie. Corporations had been given great power but were left with little accountability for their actions. Lawyers had suffered in reputation by becoming too closely associated with their business clients and interests, and had gained material success at the expense of public criticism.

On the positive side, Wickersham pointed out, it was lawyers who suggested remedies for the evils created by giant corporations and got legislation enacted to curb their abuses. By providing such solutions, he said, lawyers could "redeem the profession from the reproach of being merely the trained experts of selfish forces."

Wickersham sought redemption and then some. During Taft's presidency, Wickersham instituted twice the number of antitrust actions, in half the time, as the Roosevelt administration had brought during its tenure— some eighty-nine in four years under Taft versus forty-four in the eight years of Roosevelt's presidency. (McKinley, by contrast, had instituted just three.) Wickersham hired capable assistants regardless of their political affiliations and ran the Justice Department as he would a large metropolitan law office.

The sheer breadth of the list of products and industries targeted by Wickersham is astonishing: paper and cardboard; plumbing supplies; meat, butter, and eggs; magazines and posters; New England milk; motion picture patents; lumber and kindled wood; coffee; shoe machinery; fertilizer; cash registers and adding machines; flour; thread; cotton; tar; sugar and candy; window glass; watches; horseshoes; oil and turpentine; copper wire; wallpaper; aluminum; stone; freight railways; and Kellogg's Corn Flakes. Not all the lawsuits were successful, but most ended up with either a government-compelled breakup, a criminal guilty plea or verdict, or a consent decree—a form of negotiated settlement pioneered by Wickersham, later commonplace, that allowed defendants to agree to cease their anticompetitive behavior without facing a court trial.

Wickersham did not particularly care whose feathers he ruffled. Although Westinghouse and General Electric still competed in the manufacture and sale of incandescent lamps, Wickersham accused them of price-fixing and monopolistic behavior in connection with the patent cross-licensing agreement that Westinghouse's friend Paul Cravath had been supervising. The two electric companies entered into a consent decree to end their arrangement.

A year into his office, Wickersham faced accusations that he was too close to the hated Sugar Trust, which his partner Henry Taft had defended in a lawsuit while they were together at the Cadwalader firm. Wickersham had not worked on the case but shared in the fees afterward. Wickersham's response, which finally silenced his critics, was to file a massive antitrust suit against the Sugar Trust and thirty-nine associated individuals.

"Wickersham has out-radicaled the radicals," observed Frank Vanderlip, the president of National City Bank. Vanderlip noted "great disgust" on Wall Street with Wickersham's torrent of antitrust suits and speculated he might harbor political ambitions. Washington, DC, had produced "an absolute mental change" in Wickersham, who had become "really the most feared member of the Administration," Vanderlip thought.

Despite Vanderlip's speculation about his motives, Wickersham never sought elective office. Nor had he changed his mental outlook; he just had acquired a chance to implement his long-standing views. He was a committed capitalist who believed the best way to protect the system was by spreading the wealth a bit. "A man who owns a little house worth twenty-five hundred dollars, on which he has paid five hundred dollars, and the balance of which he is gradually paying off through his savings, is the most potent bulwark against socialism that can be devised," he once wrote.

Privately, Wickersham was stung by the accusations by businessmen such as Vanderlip. Replying to a sympathetic letter from his old friend Frank Stetson, Wickersham confessed that although he had expected criticism and opposition, he had not anticipated "the willful misrepresentation, the willingly accepted lies, which a portion of the press and of the community has treated me to." He recognized that as a representative of corporate interests Stetson was now on the other side, but Wickersham hoped that would not affect their relations. "I have looked up to you for so many years . . . have turned to you so often for counsel and help . . . that it would indeed be a bitter blow were I to forfeit your friendship now when I need it more than ever before," he wrote. "Surely we may differ on economic questions without abating in any degree a friendship of many years."

For all the charges leveled at him by Wall Street—for all the sacrifices he had made in leaving private practice for the attorney generalship—Wickersham did not regret taking the job. "I felt," he explained to Stetson, "that the opportunity to devote oneself to the service of one's country does not always come to a man, and that when it does, he would be guilty of what Dante calls 'the great refusal' should he refuse to answer the call."

The attacks continued. The popular magazine *Puck* put on its front cover an illustration showing a huge red flying insectlike creature labeled "Wickersham," wielding a pitchfork as he descended on a fleeing crowd of Wall Street men. Publicly, Taft supported Wickersham's aggressive antitrust policy, but the president became so concerned with the political fallout that he privately assured businessmen that if reelected he would not include Wickersham in his new cabinet.

In the meantime, Wickersham's two most important antitrust cases were holdovers from the Roosevelt administration. Both involved giant trusts that had been reconstituted as New Jersey holding companies. The first was a suit to break up John D. Rockefeller's Standard Oil of New Jersey, which by 1900, through various cutthroat business practices, had grown to control 90 percent of the nation's refined oil.

The second lawsuit was to dissolve the American Tobacco Company, which had been formed in 1890 by the brothers Duke, then merged in 1898 with Thomas Fortune Ryan's tobacco interests in transactions handled by Guthrie and Morawetz. The tobacco representation was a profitable one for them, but distasteful nonetheless. Morawetz considered the American Tobacco people impossible to get along with, and Guthrie hated tobacco so much that he once hung a NO SMOKING sign in the Seward firm's library, a rarity at the time. He resigned as counsel, but not before the firm earned $100,000 in fees for putting together the merger.

With further consolidations, American Tobacco, which included the companies R. J. Reynolds and Bull Durham, came to control 95 percent of cigarette manufacturing in the United States. It also dominated the chewing tobacco and snuff industries and had a significant position in cigar making. Elihu Root, who had long represented Ryan, tried to convince the Roosevelt administration to negotiate a settlement with the tobacco company, but he was overruled, and Roosevelt's attorney general, Charles Bonaparte, brought suit under the Sherman Act.

While Roosevelt was still in office, the lead prosecutor in the tobacco case was Bonaparte's special assistant, James C. McReynolds. A former law professor at Vanderbilt, McReynolds had joined the Cravath firm in 1907 as a senior associate. Cravath expected to make him a partner to help compensate for the loss of Guthrie, who had withdrawn from the firm the previous year. But one month after entering the firm, McReynolds left to join the Justice Department and was put in charge of the prosecution of American Tobacco. After Wickersham became Taft's attorney general in 1909, he and McReynolds worked together on the case.

In early 1910, the Standard Oil and American Tobacco cases made their way to the Supreme Court, where Wickersham argued for the government, along with McReynolds in the tobacco case. The defense attorneys were some of the most prominent lawyers of the time: Philadelphia's John G. Johnson, who had helped J. P. Morgan defeat E. H. Harriman in the *Northern Securities* case; John G. Milburn, Harriman's attorney during Roosevelt's ICC war on Harriman; William Hornblower, the onetime failed Supreme Court nominee who frequently argued before the court; and William Ivins, the aggressive investigator of the Metropolitan transit system and Cravath from a few years earlier.

As a result of court vacancies created by death and retirement, and because the cases were so controversial and complex, the Supreme Court heard them twice—the second time together, in January 1911, before a full court. The cases generated more anxiety and suspense on the part of the nation than any previously taken up by the high court. It was not just that the fate of two giant corporations was at stake. Even greater interest lay in the probability that the Supreme Court would decide—this time definitively—the momentous question of whether the Sherman Antitrust Act prohibited all restraints of trade or only unreasonable ones. A closely related question was whether the mere existence of a corporation's power to control the market with, say, more than a 50 percent share, made it an illegal monopoly whether it had acquired such power fairly or not. That is, in the law's eyes, was big by definition bad?

If the Supreme Court's answer to that question was yes, then as a practical matter it would put an end to virtually all large aggregations of capital. Businessmen would no longer be able to form gigantic business combinations, whether trusts, mergers, or holding companies. The likes of US Steel and General Electric would not be seen again, and emerging behemoths such as General Motors would be stopped dead in their tracks.

This was, in fact, what many populists hoped for: a return to the days when small producers; independent, self-employed proprietors; and farmers dominated the nation's economy. The legal questions to be decided in the oil and tobacco cases were thus not mere abstractions but would determine what kind of economic system—what kind of society—the United States would be in the twentieth century.

Associate Justice John Marshall Harlan was the leader of the court's anti-corporate, pro-small producer wing. A Kentuckian by birth, he had gone from slaveholder to civil rights supporter and was the lone dissenter in the infamous *Plessy v. Ferguson* case in 1896, which upheld racial discrimination laws under the "separate but equal" doctrine. Harlan believed the Sherman Act had been enacted to rid the country of a new form of slavery resulting from aggregations of capital in the hands of a few individuals and corporations. Only by returning to a state of vigorous competition among small business owners could the United States, in his judgment, become a truly good society.

Harlan's attitude was evident during the oral argument in the American Tobacco case. When Hornblower stood to speak in defense of one of the tobacco companies, the seventy-seven-year-old Harlan, then in his last year of life, interjected to complain of the poor quality of chewing tobacco. "It is rotten. We cannot get any good chewing tobacco anymore," he said, implicitly blaming the tobacco monopoly. Hornblower responded that he wasn't a chewer and wouldn't know. It is not recorded whether Harlan was chewing as he spoke, or using one of the many spittoons available in the courtroom at the time.

The conservative, pro-business leader of the court was another Southerner, Edward Douglass White, described by one court observer as having the appearance of a "jovial monk." In December 1910, just a month before the reargument in the oil and tobacco cases, the sixty-five-year-old White was elevated from associate to chief justice by President Taft following the death of the sitting chief justice, the conservative Melville Fuller.

The press had widely expected Taft to name New York governor Charles Evans Hughes, then only forty-eight, to the chief justice position. The business community viewed Hughes with suspicion based on his aggressive investigation of the Equitable in 1905 and his progressive record as governor. But Stetson vouched for him, and business opposition faded away. By contrast, William Jennings Bryan castigated Hughes, a white shoe lawyer, as a captive of corporate interests. Bryan conceded Hughes was honest— someone "who personally opposes vice, and is a punisher of small crimes, but shows no indignation at the larger forms of legalized robbery."

Taft did appoint Hughes to the Supreme Court, but only as associate justice, not chief. It was speculated that Taft chose White instead because White was old and overweight and would not long serve in the position, and Taft—who wanted to be a Supreme Court justice even more than president— hoped to succeed White someday. (If that was Taft's thinking, it worked out, for after White's death in 1921, Taft was appointed chief justice by Warren Harding.)

At the oral argument in January 1911, Hughes, being a new justice, said nothing to tip his hand as to where he was leaning. John G. Johnson, for the defense, pressed the point that large business combinations are not unlawful, per se, and that the government had no power to prevent a law-abiding company from acquiring another. He asked rhetorically how the court could "safely substitute for the herculean work of the financial giants the puny efforts of the pygmies that will be left in trade?"

For the government, Wickersham conceded that mere power or size did not constitute an illegal monopoly, but he said the defendant companies were hardly idyllic enterprises. He entertained the courtroom by reading correspondence from the tobacco companies' top officers to local managers instructing them to sell below cost in certain localities to wipe out their competition, but not to spend a dollar more than necessary to accomplish that result. He ridiculed the testimony of the tobacco men who maintained they never had any idea of restraining trade. "With solemn visage and pious mien they would sugar the devil himself," Wickersham said.

Throughout the early months of 1911, tension mounted in anticipation of release of the court's decisions in the oil and tobacco cases. On every Monday, the court's typical decision day, the business world held its collective breath. And on every Monday that passed without a ruling the stock market shot up or down based on speculation as to the outcome.

On May 13 the *New York Times* reported that one stock brokerage house had sent a letter to the justices pleading for a quick decision because "the business of the whole country is at a standstill." It reached the point where, as the *New-York Tribune* put it, "Nobody seemed to care particularly what the decision would be. What was wanted was an ending of the uncertainty that for so many weary weeks had oppressed business in the Street."

On Monday, May 15, 1911, the Supreme Court chamber, then located in the Capitol building, was crowded with reporters and spectators, with a line stretching out the courtroom through the corridors all the way across the rotunda. When the large clock above the justices ticked past 4:00 P.M., the court's normal quitting time, the crowd began to disperse. Then Chief Justice White suddenly and matter-of-factly announced he had the opinion and judgment in Case No. 398, and everyone instantly recognized the Standard Oil decision was coming. Word quickly spread, and those who had left scurried back to be present for the historic occasion, with even senators struggling to gain admission. White then proceeded for almost an hour to synopsize the opinion.

The *New York Times* headline the following day summed up the ruling: STANDARD OIL COMPANY MUST DISSOLVE IN 6 MONTHS; ONLY UNREASONABLE RESTRAINT OF TRADE FORBIDDEN. It had been a victory for the government in the specific case, but a relief for commercial interests in general. The court ruled against Standard Oil, ordering that as an antitrust violator it had to be broken up into multiple pieces (some thirty-four separate companies would eventually emerge, including Exxon, Mobil, Amoco, and Chevron). That part of the decision pleased progressives. But the near-unanimous decision, from which only the aged Justice Harlan dissented, also reassured the business world by holding that only "unreasonable" or "undue" restraints of trade were forbidden by the Sherman Act. Rockefeller's Standard Oil had driven out all competition by cutting prices, forcing railroad rebates, and buying up rivals, which made it easy to conclude it had unduly restrained trade.

Two weeks later the court reaffirmed its Standard Oil ruling in the tobacco case. The court found American Tobacco guilty of anticompetitive conduct and ordered it to be broken up in six months as well. Out of it came R. J. Reynolds (makers of Camel and Winston cigarettes), Liggett & Myers (L&M and Chesterfields), and Lorillard (Newport and Kent), among others. The court condemned the tobacco trust not because it was big but because it had acted flagrantly, with the object of crushing competitors. Henceforth the "rule of reason" would become the guiding principle for court review under the Sherman Act. For better or worse, large corporations were here to stay.

Despite the mixed result, Wickersham called the Supreme Court decisions a sweeping win for the government. Taft was more circumspect at first but soon heartily endorsed the high court's rule of reason approach. In fact, as a federal appeals court judge, Taft had adopted a similar approach in an influential earlier case known as *Addyston Pipe*. There he stated that restraints merely "ancillary" to the main purpose of a lawful contract should be allowed.

A lawyer who had previously sued Standard Oil for the state of Missouri said the Supreme Court's rule of reason decisions were a victory for those companies that "had led clean lives" and grown in size through fair competition, a superior product, and more efficient business methods. "Those corporations, however large they may be, whose methods have been fair and square and manly and have fought an open and above board fight with their competitors, using no poisoned arrows, have nothing to fear from the Sherman law," he concluded.

Others reacted less favorably. Senator Robert La Follette thought the court had let big business off the hook by declaring that only unreasonable restraints of trade were to be forbidden. To progressives such as La Follette and Louis Brandeis, there was no such thing as a "good" trust.

Some corporate lawyers criticized the decisions from a different angle. Testifying before Congress, Frank Stetson said the rule of reason, although an improvement over prior, stricter interpretations of the Sherman Act, still created too much uncertainty for business because it was such a vague standard. "As an important business man once said to me," Stetson recounted (probably referencing J. P. Morgan), "'I do not so much care what the law is, as to know what it is; when I know what it is, I will conform to it.'"

Stetson resurrected the idea that corporations should be able to seek a license from a federal corporation commission that could provide them some form of advance clearance for their business combinations and contracts. He had not changed his view that the country would have been better off without any federal antitrust law. "The law never does anything concretely; it never makes any money for anybody; it never provides anything except a punishment," he told Congress. But in light of public opinion ("you can't fight a community"), he saw no realistic possibility of eliminating the Sherman Act or further amending it. Limited regulation by persons conversant in business and economics was preferable to leaving everything in the hands of unelected, nonexpert judges. In the meantime, he said, businessmen were "stopping; they are not going on. The reason is that they could not get from their trusted counsel advice that it is wise or prudent to go on."

Some newspapers ridiculed the view that the best corporate lawyers would not or could not counsel their clients on how to behave under the antitrust laws. "Will Samuel Untermyer turn away saying he cannot answer?" asked the *New York World*. "Will John G. Johnson, of Philadelphia, throw up his hands? . . . or William D. Guthrie, or Francis Lynde Stetson? Is any big business or the attorney therefor incapable of knowing when it is combining with the intent and effect of monopoly? Or when it is blackjacking competitors out of existence through local price manipulations, exclusive agreements, rebates and otherwise?"

A year after the oil and tobacco cases, Wickersham won another big victory when the Supreme Court ruled that the late E. H. Harriman's merger of the Union Pacific and Southern Pacific Railroads in 1901 was an illegal combination under the Sherman Act and had to be broken up. In later cases the court would provide additional clarity by holding that certain categories of business conduct, such as price-fixing, bid rigging, and geographic division of markets, were unreasonable per se, eliminating the need for extensive judicial inquiry.

Theodore Roosevelt, eager to reenter the political arena, conceded the Supreme Court's oil and tobacco decisions had accomplished a certain amount of good by breaking up those trusts. But what was urgently needed, he said, was enactment of drastic and far-reaching legislation to put the giant trusts under the same kind of tight controls the government exercised over the railroads and other common carriers under the Interstate Commerce Act. Taft and Wickersham could bring all the antitrust suits they wanted, he said, but only a federal corporation agency—similar to the Interstate Commerce Commission—could provide the kind of ongoing supervision and speedy enforcement that was needed.

Roosevelt added that in the end, government control of large industrial corporations might even have to go much further than existing government control over the railroads. Because the ICC, per Roosevelt's prior legislation, already had significant control over the setting of railroad rates, Roosevelt was hinting that the government—maybe even the president himself—might need to set prices on commodities manufactured and sold by regular businesses. This was a bridge too far for people like Stetson, and for Taft. Although Wickersham thought the idea of federal price controls worth considering, he ventured that such a novel, radical idea likely would be impossible to implement. He believed that government lawsuits under the Sherman Act were an effective means of policing bad business behavior.

It was one such lawsuit that brought about the final rift between Roosevelt and Taft. For some time after his return from his African big-game safari the previous year, the former president had been increasingly critical of Taft for not pushing more boldly for the progressive reforms Roosevelt had begun. Taft had promised to "complete and perfect the machinery" of government and law that the Roosevelt administration had put in place, and he had achieved some notable successes. These included a new railroad law, the Mann-Elkins Act, drafted substantially by Wickersham, which strengthened the ICC's powers and extended its jurisdiction to telephones, telegraphs, cable, and wireless communications. But in the view of Roosevelt and other progressives, Taft had not gone far or fast enough and had surrounded himself with big business owners, special interests, and corporate lawyers such as Cromwell, Wickersham, and Taft's own brother Henry.

Ironically, it was a decidedly anti-corporate action that caused Roosevelt to erupt. In late October 1911, with Taft's approval, Wickersham brought an antitrust suit against US Steel, as Roosevelt had once threatened to do. Frank Stetson was immediately retained to defend the world's largest company in what one newspaper described as a "financial Armageddon."

In part, what incensed Roosevelt was that the suit was filed at all. Roosevelt had told J. P. Morgan in 1902 the government would not prosecute his US Steel Company unless it had done something illegal. Because Roosevelt had taken no action against Morgan's company in the succeeding seven years, Taft's lawsuit could be read as implicitly charging that Roosevelt had been lax in enforcing the antitrust laws.

But what enraged Roosevelt even more was what the lawsuit said. The government's petition reminded everyone that during the Panic of 1907 Roosevelt had allowed US Steel to acquire its rival, the Tennessee Coal, Iron & Railroad Company, as part of Morgan's plan to rescue the nation's economy. Wickersham's pleadings alleged Morgan had been motivated not only to stop the panic but also to acquire control of a major competitor, which now needed to be stripped from the steel giant. The implication, which the press readily endorsed, was that Roosevelt had either been hood-winked by Morgan or, worse, had actively facilitated an unlawful acquisition.

Taft did not read the petition before it was filed and afterward said it was too late to do anything about it. Roosevelt regarded it as an act of betrayal, or at least evidence of Taft's incompetence and Wickersham's malice. Most historians believe that Wickersham did not deliberately seek to embarrass the ex-president but instead displayed a careless lack of political tact. But there is also evidence that Wickersham, loyal to Taft and upset by Roo-sevelt's attacks on him, knew exactly what he was doing.

Elihu Root called the snafu a "minor source of annoyance" that Roo-sevelt blew out of proportion. Overreaction or not, it fed Roosevelt's growing desire to challenge the incumbent Taft for the 1912 Republican nomination.

Wickersham played a key role in another incident that prompted Roo-sevelt to renounce his successor. While Roosevelt was in Africa, what be-came known as the Ballinger-Pinchot affair erupted into a major controversy. A government land official named Louis Glavis accused Taft's interior sec-retary, Richard Ballinger, of improperly giving away valuable protected Alaskan coal lands to a private syndicate led by J. P. Morgan and the Gug-genheim family. After conferring with Wickersham and reviewing the evi-dence with him, Taft fired Glavis, who then took his allegations to the press. When US Forestry chief Gifford Pinchot, a progressive environmentalist originally appointed by Roosevelt, publicly sided with Glavis, Taft fired Pin-chot, too, for going outside the chain of command.

Louis Brandeis then became involved as a lawyer for Glavis and Pin-chot. Brandeis uncovered the fact that Wickersham's formal report on the matter had been backdated to make it appear Taft had the report before him when he made the decision to fire Glavis. Although Taft had the benefit of Wickersham's thinking and notes, and statements from Interior Depart-ment officials exonerating Ballinger, the attorney general's final report was not completed until some weeks later.

Wickersham belatedly admitted he had backdated the report, and Taft admitted to Congress that he had directed Wickersham to do so. Even though Ballinger was cleared of any wrongdoing, and the misdating did not affect the outcome, the incident was embarrassing for both the president and his attorney general. More significantly, the entire affair drove a wedge between conservationists and anti-conservationists, between progressives and conservatives, and ultimately between Roosevelt and Taft.

By late 1911 it was apparent that Roosevelt was eager to challenge Taft for the Republican nomination. After keeping his intentions secret for several months Roosevelt finally declared in February 1912: "My hat is in the ring."

Two months later, Taft, increasingly estranged from Roosevelt, had Wickersham launch another antitrust suit that angered the ex-president. This time the target was International Harvester, which Guthrie and Cravath (for Harvester) and Stetson (for J. P. Morgan) had helped form in 1902. The megamerger, which combined Cyrus H. McCormick's Harvesting Machine Company with the Deering family's Harvester Company, gave the new Morgan-controlled corporation 85 percent of the agricultural equipment market. It had been a tense, delicate negotiation between the rival factions, and the McCormick family, although represented in the deal by Cravath, consulted William Nelson Cromwell to make sure they were not getting "euchred," as Cromwell put it. With typical immodesty Cromwell told them they would have been better off had they come to him in the first place.

The Harvester merger was completed shortly after Roosevelt's decision to sue the Northern Securities Company. Stetson told the merger parties it was two years too late for organizing big trusts and cautioned that the amalgamation would make an inviting target for a populist president seeking to court the farmers' vote. The merger indeed came under government investigation, but Roosevelt, believing Harvester was one of the so-called good trusts, decided not to prosecute. Paul Cravath persuasively argued to Roosevelt's attorney general, Charles Bonaparte, that Harvester was conducting its business fairly and honestly and that an attack on any legitimate business enterprise would have serious adverse consequences.

When Wickersham finally brought suit against Harvester in April 1912, Taft made public several letters indicating that in 1907 Roosevelt had quashed a planned lawsuit by Bonaparte. The embarrassing correspondence suggested Roosevelt had acted so as not to antagonize the Morgan interests, which had been largely friendly to his administration. Roosevelt countered that Taft, as a member of his cabinet, had not protested at the time and was only releasing the letters then, on the eve of the Massachu-setts Republican presidential primary, for political advantage.

The 1912 presidential election would be among the bitterest and most consequential in US history. It would be dominated by the Trust Question, with Taft taking the moderately conservative position; Roosevelt the most radical, progressive one; and a Democratic governor and former university president seeking a middle ground between the two. The Democratic can-didate was a lawyer himself, but as he often told the public, he didn't think too highly of the profession.

Paul Cravath, one of the new breed of Wall Street corporate lawyers who built American big business, c. 1899. A man of "massive elegance" and "glittering presence," he developed the "Cravath system" of law firm management, which remains commonplace today.

Cravath's earliest major client, George Westinghouse, was blamed for many of the electrocutions that took place in New York between 1888 and 1890, including this one of Western Union lineman John Feeks. Cravath represented Westinghouse in the War of Currents that pitted Westinghouse's high voltage AC system against Thomas Edison's DC system.

Cravath's law partner, the brilliant, ultraconservative William Guthrie, was an unyielding opponent of the income tax and other progressive reform legislation. Nearly impossible to work with— he "made everyone about him jumpy"— Guthrie eventually broke with the more moderate Cravath, who refused to speak to him in later years.

Francis Lynde Stetson was the most respected member of Wall Street's white shoe corporate bar. He is pictured here in 1882, a few years before becoming the "attorney general" for J. P. Morgan, for whom Stetson organized giant companies such as US Steel and International Harvester.

J. P. Morgan, the great financier, in 1902. Morgan bankrolled many of the most hated, monopolistic corporations, known as the "trusts," that were the bane of the Progressive Era from 1890 to 1914.

E. H. Harriman (left), the piratical owner of the Union Pacific and Southern Pacific Railroads, was dubbed the "Colossus of Roads." Harriman's 1901 attempted hostile takeover of the Northern Pacific Railway, controlled by J. P. Morgan, ended in a truce to form a combined railroad conglomerate—the Northern Securities Company—organized by Stetson. The alleged monopoly sparked a public furor and drew a landmark antitrust lawsuit from President Theodore Roosevelt in 1902, giving rise to his nickname "Teddy the Trust Buster" (right).

This cartoon, entitled "Jiu-Jitsued," shows Roosevelt disabling the Northern Securities Company railroad trust with a martial arts hold.

" JIU-JITSUED "

William Nelson Cromwell, another millionaire corporate lawyer, was known as "the physician of Wall Street" for salvaging the wreckage from railroads and other large companies when they went bankrupt. His greatest turnaround project was the Panama Canal, representing French investors who sold the canal rights to the United States. Cromwell was instrumental in convincing Congress to build in Panama over opposition from supporters of a Nicaragua Canal, and he was later accused of fomenting the Panamanian revolution that led the United States to take over the canal territory.

Philippe Bunau-Varilla, the flamboyant French engineer and investor who, together with Cromwell, lobbied relentlessly in favor of the Panama Canal. The two men came to denigrate each other's contributions—Cromwell called the Frenchman "an unprincipled adventurer and meddlesome intruder," and Bunau-Varilla proudly claimed the title of revolutionist solely for himself.

Cromwell and Bunau-Varilla used this postage stamp to illustrate the danger of active volcanoes in Nicaragua, thereby swaying congressional opinion in favor of Panama.

James Hazen Hyde, the playboy heir to the Equitable Life Assurance Society. Hyde's reckless extravagance with policyholder funds led to the first great Wall Street scandal of the early twentieth century and a public investigation in which most of the leading white shoe lawyers played a role.

The notorious 1905 costume party thrown by Hyde at Sherry's in New York, decorated in the style of the gardens of the Palace of Versailles. Among the grandest balls of the Gilded Age, it was rumored that Hyde charged the Equitable $200,000 for it, leading to calls for his ouster from management.

Throughout 1905, the Equitable scandal made for front-page headlines. Many believed the Equitable fight was really one for control of the giant life insurance company by financial magnates E. H. Harriman and J. P. Morgan.

Charles Evans Hughes, who began his career as a corporate lawyer in partnership with Cravath, rose to national prominence as lead investigator of the life insurance industry for the New York State Legislature in the wake of the Equitable scandal. The public acclaim for his handling of the investigation catapulted Hughes to the governorship of New York, followed by his appointment to the Supreme Court and nomination as the 1916 Republican presidential candidate.

Hughes and his wife, Antoinette, the daughter of Hughes's original senior law partner. Antoinette (Carter) Hughes campaigned heavily for her husband in the 1916 presidential election, as did the "Hughesettes," supporters of women's suffrage.

Thomas Fortune Ryan, one of Cravath's business tycoon clients, was known as "the sphinx of Wall Street" for his noiseless, unobtrusive manner. Ryan ended the Equitable crisis by buying control from James Hazen Hyde, to the consternation of E. H. Harriman, who had demanded half of Hyde's stock for himself.

Elihu Root, who also represented Ryan in the Equitable matter, began his career as a Wall Street lawyer and later served as secretary of war for McKinley and Roosevelt. He also served as Roosevelt's secretary of state and as a US senator. The quintessential foreign policy wise man, Root was the most widely respected lawyer-elder statesman in America in the early twentieth century and the intellectual leader of the Republican Party.

Root's support of William Howard Taft (left) for the 1912 Republican presidential nomination led to a nearly permanent rift with Theodore Roosevelt, who mounted a third-party candidacy after losing the nomination to Taft. Root and Roosevelt partially reconciled in 1915 to support American military preparedness for World War I, a movement favored by nearly all of Wall Street's white shoe lawyers. After the war, Root played a leading role in the debate over America's entry into the League of Nations.

How the millionaire white shoe lawyers lived: An aerial view of Meudon, William Guthrie's eighty-room estate on Long Island, built in the image of a King Louis XIV French château.

Guthrie taught constitutional law at Columbia University for many years. The writer Upton Sinclair called him "a corporation lawyer, rich, smooth, hard, and ignorant."

Cravath, Guthrie's Long Island neighbor, had his own country estate, Veraton, named for his daughter, Vera. Cravath and his wife, the former opera star Agnes Huntington, were founding members of the legendary Piping Rock Club in nearby Locust Valley, New York.

Cravath, a regular participant in Long Island horse shows, is pictured here (left) with financier August Belmont Jr., for whom the famous thoroughbred racetrack is named. The occasion was a 1912 saddle-horse show at Belmont Park, in which both Cravath and his daughter posted entries.

The Francis Lynde Stetson home at 4 East Seventy-Fourth Street in Manhattan. Stetson also had a thousand-acre summer home in the mountains north of Manhattan, where he created a botanical garden and a nine-hole golf course. By 1901, Stetson was earning $300,000 a year in legal fees (about $8 million in 2019 dollars), not counting his profits from the J. P. Morgan & Co. stocks he was allowed to buy at insider prices.

Francis Lynde Stetson, around the time he became president of the New York City Bar Association in 1910. "Incomparably logical," according to one of his law partners, Stetson was meticulous in the extreme and "didn't let things go by."

George Wickersham, another Wall Street corporate lawyer who gained fame through public service. Wickersham served as Taft's attorney general and brought some eighty-nine antitrust suits in four years—double the number brought by Teddy the Trust Buster in eight years. For his aggressive enforcement of the antitrust laws, Wickersham became known as "the scourge of Wall Street."

THE WICKERSHAM WILL GIT YER IF YER DON'T — WATCH — OUT!

This 1911 *Puck* magazine cover shows a flying creature labeled "Wickersham" holding a large webbed fork in one hand and papers labeled "Trust," "Dissolution," "Disintegration," and "Sherman Law" in the other, descending on a fleeing crowd of Wall Street men. The caption reads, "The Wickersham will git yer if yer don't—watch—out!"

The masthead reads:

New-York **Tribune.**

STANDARD OIL COMPANY ORDERED DISSOLVED; REASONABLE RESTRAINT OF TRADE NOT UNLAWFUL

The May 16, 1911, *New-York Tribune* announcement of the Supreme Court ruling ordering the breakup of John D. Rockefeller's Standard Oil trust, a case handled by Wickersham. Although a victory for the government, the watershed decision also established the "rule of reason," meaning that large corporations would be prosecuted under the antitrust laws only for unfair behavior to restrain competition, not for bigness itself. The principle remains in place today.

The elfin William Hornblower, one of the leading corporate lawyers to advocate for the rule of reason, began his career as a senior lawyer to Paul Cravath and Charles Evans Hughes before leaving to form his own successful Wall Street firm. Hornblower was nominated to the Supreme Court at age forty-two by his friend Grover Cleveland, but saw his confirmation defeated over private political animosities. He did, however, frequently argue before the Supreme Court, once arranging to honeymoon in Washington, DC, so his new bride could watch him in action.

Samuel Untermyer, the anti-white shoe lawyer, was one of the few Jewish attorneys to develop an influential Wall Street corporate law practice in the early twentieth century. A liberal gadfly and antagonist of J. P. Morgan, Untermyer is best remembered as counsel for the 1912 Pujo Committee's investigation of an alleged "money trust" controlled by Morgan and other top Wall Street bankers. The homegrown orchids Untermyer always wore in his lapel (as in this picture) belied the ferociousness with which he attacked his big business adversaries.

Under a blistering cross-examination by Untermyer, seventy-five-year-old J. P. Morgan (right) denied the existence of a money trust and insisted that character, not money, counted most on Wall Street. Some people blamed Morgan's death three months later on the strain of testifying, but the real legacy of the Pujo hearings was their spurring of the passage of the Federal Reserve Act of 1913. It created the Federal Reserve System to control the nation's money supply.

David Lamar, "the Wolf of Wall Street," created a sensation in 1913 when he impersonated US congressmen over the telephone in a bizarre blackmail plot. Among those he tried to trick with his admitted "pure fabrication" were Cravath and Stetson. The Lamar episode exposed a seedy underbelly of Wall Street that white shoe lawyers preferred to avoid, but which they had to deal with from time to time because the tremendous amounts of money at stake inevitably attracted bottom-feeders.

Louis Brandeis, the "people's lawyer," was a millionaire corporate attorney before becoming a well-known Harvard Law School professor and frequent critic of large corporations. Brandeis's influential writings about "the curse of bigness" and Wall Street bankers' use of "other people's money" made him anathema to businessmen such as J. P. Morgan. In 1916, Brandeis became the first Jewish justice on the US Supreme Court following one of the most contentious confirmation battles in the nation's history.

Brandeis's main target was J. P. Morgan's New Haven Railroad, which monopolized transportation in New England and spent itself into ruin. In a 1914 government investigation fomented by Brandeis, New Haven's directors were pilloried for blindly following Morgan's expansionist dictates, as parodied in this editorial cartoon. Most of Wall Street's top white shoe lawyers were involved in the hearings on the New Haven Railroad scandal, which gave impetus to the final business reform legislation of the Progressive Era.

Almost all of Wall Street's white shoe lawyers strongly supported American intervention in World War I, and several of them, including Paul Cravath, put themselves in harm's way during wartime missions in Europe. While touring the Allied trenches during the Battle of Verdun in 1916, Cravath came within three hundred yards of German fire. He is shown here (center) at an Allied camp on the Western Front in Reims, France, in 1917.

Later in life, William Nelson Cromwell, who boasted a net worth of more than $100 million, sought ways to give his money away. He contributed heavily to charities for French victims and veterans of World War I and to various causes for the blind. He is pictured here (left) in 1937 with Helen Keller and philanthropist M. C. Migel, head of the American Foundation for the Blind, during the presentation of an award to Cromwell from that organization.

John Foster Dulles succeeded Cromwell as head of the influential Sullivan & Cromwell firm, and for three decades he was the world's leading international business lawyer until his appointment as US secretary of state by President Eisenhower in 1953. Dulles is shown here, at age thirty, at the time of the Paris Peace Conference in 1919, which he attended as a member of the US delegation. Dulles played a key role in the negotiation of Germany's reparations obligation to the victorious Allied nations as part of the Treaty of Versailles.

Chapter 14

"A Civilization Which Is Called Christian"

Not every case a Wall Street lawyer works on is big and important; fewer still present issues of national significance such as *Standard Oil* and *American Tobacco*. And although Wall Street lawyers seldom deign to handle cases involving petty domestic disputes, bitter divorces, or small-time criminals, occasionally they do so as a favor to some important corporate client. One such case for Paul Cravath was the attack on banker Mortimer Schiff, son of Kuhn, Loeb client Jacob Schiff, by the younger Schiff's butler.

In 1912, when Cravath became involved in the Schiff case, the phrase "the butler did it" had not yet entered the lexicon. It did not become a cliché until sometime after mystery writer Mary Roberts Rinehart's 1930 novel, *The Door*, in which the butler was the murderer.

But there was precedent. In 1900, James Byrne, a partner in the white shoe firm headed by William Hornblower and a former "Carter kid," was the lead lawyer in the sensational case of William M. Rice, who was murdered by his butler. An eighty-four-year-old Texas millionaire who had moved to New York, Rice was found dead in his apartment on Madison Avenue, where he lived alone with his valet. With the help of Byrne, who represented one of Rice's suspicious executors, it was proven that Rice's personal lawyer had forged the old man's will, named himself as inheritor of the bulk of the estate, then enlisted the valet to kill Rice with chloroform. The case turned Byrne into a legal star.

The Rice litigation was a high-stakes one involving an estate that went to establish Rice University in Houston. The Schiff case that Cravath worked on was a more trifling matter, although it created nearly as many headlines.

The case began, without Cravath's involvement, in 1907, when Schiff fired his twenty-one-year-old Swedish butler, Foulke E. Brandt (a.k.a. Laurence de Foulke). Brandt's transgression was writing a crude letter to Schiff's wife telling her of his noble birth and declaring his love for her. A month later, when the Schiffs returned to their Fifth Avenue home after a night out, Schiff discovered Brandt in his bedroom, wearing Schiff's dressing gown and slippers. Brandt hit his former employer on the forehead with a bowling pin and displayed a large carving knife he had taken from the kitchen (for self-protection, Brandt later claimed, in case Schiff or one of the servants set upon him).

Brandt said he was destitute and had come to Schiff for help. Thinking he was dealing with a madman, Schiff parlayed with Brandt for a few minutes to calm him down, gave him $50, escorted him out of his home, and told him to come to his office three days later to discuss the matter further. When Brandt arrived, Schiff had a pair of detectives arrest him. The charges were burglary, assault, and larceny (Brandt had stolen a pair of diamond pins worth $200). Brandt pleaded guilty to burglary and was sentenced to thirty years in state prison.

The incident attracted only brief press attention at the time. But it erupted onto the front pages in January 1912 when Brandt, then in the fifth year of his prison term, applied to New York's governor for a pardon. The newspapers, the state attorney general, and other prominent citizens took up his cause. Brandt was hailed as a hero of sorts—a member of the servant class unjustly and excessively punished for infringing on the rights of the privileged few. His supporters argued the burglary charge to which he had pleaded was legally defective because Brandt had not entered Schiff's home forcibly (Brandt variously claimed he came in through an open door, or used a key given to him by another servant, or crawled through an ash chute in the basement).

Schiff hired Cravath, along with several other lawyers, to oppose the pardon application. Schiff did not object to clemency until he learned that Brandt, in his application, changed his story to say he had gone to the Schiffs' home to keep an illicit rendezvous with Mrs. Schiff. According to Brandt, he had lied about his presence there in order to save her honor. On Schiff's behalf Cravath argued clemency was unwarranted in light of Brandt's scandalous insinuations about Mrs. Schiff. The crusading local district attorney tried to turn the tables by threatening to indict Schiff and others, including his original attorney in the matter, for a criminal conspiracy to railroad Brandt into a long prison sentence.

Schiff testified before the grand jury, after waiving immunity, and was represented by Cravath. The grand jury cleared the thirty-four-year-old banker of any wrongdoing. The jurors volunteered their view that Brandt, while technically not guilty of burglary because of the lack of forced entry, had committed assault and grand larceny. Cravath issued a statement afterward saying Schiff had been exonerated and Brandt found to be a lying criminal. The grand jury investigation ended just in time for the Schiffs to board the White Star passenger liner *Olympic* bound for England; during the voyage the *Olympic* received a distress call from its sister ship *Titanic* but was too far away to provide rescue.

As for Brandt, his pardon request was initially rejected but later granted—not because he was innocent but because the sentence was excessive. As a condition of his release from prison Brandt expressed regret, admitted lying about Mrs. Schiff, and promised not to profit from any books, stage plays, or other notoriety about the case. Brandt moved to Minnesota, where he found lumber work, but, in violation of his parole terms and hounded by detectives, he returned to New York. After a chorus girl turned down his marriage proposal when she learned of his criminal record, he left the country for good to return to his native Sweden.

In his voluminous history of the Cravath firm, author Robert Swaine does not mention the Brandt case. Perhaps he considered it too insignificant, but his book includes references to thousands of other minor, mundane matters, none of which received the kind of publicity this one did. More likely, Swaine did not want to highlight one of those rare cases in which an elite Wall Street lawyer had to muddy his white shoes.

———◈———

Theodore Roosevelt believed that of all the men serving in his cabinet, only Elihu Root had the qualities to succeed him as president. The two men's friendship dated back more than thirty years, from when Root, as an influential New York lawyer, supported the young reformer Roosevelt in his first race for state assemblyman. When Roosevelt successfully ran for governor of New York in 1898, Root made the legal case for Roosevelt's eligibility over objections that he had previously claimed residency in Washington, DC, to avoid paying New York City taxes. Roosevelt was caught in an inconsistency in the affidavit he submitted on his taxes because, as Root later recalled, Roosevelt "was a youngster" who "didn't know much about business or business affairs." Root helped save Roosevelt's candidacy with a hairsplitting argument about the meaning of the word "residence" and with an emotional speech at the Republican state convention. From that point on, Root had Roosevelt's implicit trust.

Not that their relationship was always smooth. Roosevelt's most pronounced quality was his combativeness, and "he was often so with me," Root later recalled. But Roosevelt was intelligent, open to receiving advice, and quick to make up after a spat. Roosevelt's frequent passionate outbursts were short-lived and carefully calculated; "he knew just what he was going to say," Root recounted.

Having served as Roosevelt's secretary of state, war secretary, and overall reliable advisor, Root might have secured the Republican presidential nomination for himself in 1908 had he wanted it. But he declined to run. Roosevelt thought him unelectable because of his corporation connections, and Root agreed, believing that "a New York lawyer for a lot of rich men would not make an effective candidate." Instead, Root fully supported Roosevelt's choice of Taft to succeed him. Root became a Taft loyalist in the US Senate, to such an extent that he joined Old Guard Republicans in siding with President Taft for renomination in 1912—against the challenge of Theodore Roosevelt and the progressive wing of the party.

Root was bothered by Roosevelt's effort to create a split between Republican regulars and the progressive insurgents. To Root, Roosevelt was like the old minister who "never thinks the new one preaches as well as he did." Root also thought Roosevelt petty for breaking with Taft because he was "so darn mad" over the Tennessee Coal issue in Wickersham's US Steel lawsuit.

For his part, Roosevelt continued to attack Wickersham, saying his breakup of Standard Oil and American Tobacco had been a "make-believe strangle" that accomplished less than nothing. Like many progressives, Roosevelt thought the plans of dissolution approved by Wickersham were too lenient and still allowed the new, separate companies too much power. (Asked for his reaction to the Supreme Court's 1911 decision, John D. Rockefeller had said, "Buy Standard Oil," which proved to be good advice, as the new companies' share prices skyrocketed.) What was needed now, Roosevelt continued to believe, was a federal commission with authority to regulate general industrial corporations—including their pricing—similar to the ICC and its power over railroads.

Elihu Root's conservativism was more in line with Taft's political philosophy than with Roosevelt's increasingly radical vision, known as the New Nationalism. New Nationalists sought both greater power for "the people" through such pure democracy mechanisms as the direct primary, the initiative, and the referendum, and at the same time, greater national administrative power for the federal government to advance social justice.

Because of his distrust of the uneducated masses, Root opposed most proposals for direct democracy. And there was one particular issue that made it impossible for him to support the former president. During the primary campaign Roosevelt proposed that the voters in each state be given the power to recall certain judicial decisions by the state's highest court. Courts in a number of states, based on their own constitutions, had been striking down social welfare legislation on subjects such as employee safety and child labor. Adopting the reasoning of lawyers such as William Guthrie, the courts concluded that such laws infringed upon the freedom of contract and property rights of employers. For example, New York's highest court ruled that the state's new workers' compensation law, applicable to certain hazardous industries, violated the due process rights of employers by imposing liability on them without fault.

Roosevelt's proposal would have permitted the people of the state to override that and similar rulings by popular referendum. He did not propose to subject decisions by the US Supreme Court, or interpretations of the US Constitution, to popular referenda, nor did he propose that individual judges could be recalled. But to Taft and the more conservative-minded, Roosevelt's proposal was a dangerously radical idea that violated separation of powers between the judicial and legislative branches of government.

Root viewed Roosevelt's proposal as daft—"a perfectly wild program," he told a friend. "I could not have been for Roosevelt in the face of that,"

Root explained, adding that Roosevelt "didn't care much for rules of law." But Root did. Root admired Taft's judicial mind; "he wanted to hear both sides and then reflect," Root observed, whereas Roosevelt "wanted to hear and then jump." On the other hand, Root found that Taft—a slow, plodding thinker—was difficult to budge once he reached a decision, in contrast to Roosevelt, who made up his mind quickly but was easily influenced to change it.

At the opening of the Republican National Convention in Chicago in June 1912, the delegates were fairly evenly split between the incumbent Taft, who controlled the party machinery, and Roosevelt, who had won almost all the elective primaries, a new feature of the nomination process that year, but not yet the way most delegates were chosen. Because about 250 state delegation seats were in dispute over claims of fraud and irregularities, mostly lodged by the Roosevelt forces, selection of the convention chairman—who would have the power to make procedural rulings—was crucial.

Taft's managers put forward Root for the chairmanship, a choice bitterly opposed by Roosevelt because Root was a confirmed Taft supporter by then. In a key test vote on the power of the rival factions, Root was narrowly chosen as chairman by a vote of 558-502. When the result was announced, a series of fistfights broke out that required police intervention. Hundreds of Root's fellow Republicans, supporters of Roosevelt, glared at the distinguished former cabinet member with hate in their eyes. Roosevelt claimed that Root had won by fraud and that 70 to 80 of the votes in his favor had been stolen. He labeled his old friend Root as someone who was now controlled by bosses and special interests and favored reactionary policies.

Aided by Root's rulings from the chair, the Taft forces beat back Roosevelt's delegate challenges. The proceedings were marked by scenes of turbulence bordering on a riot, with the police called in again to stop dozens of brawls. Because Roosevelt's delegates, in accordance with his instructions, refused to take part in the vote, the convention easily nominated Taft on the first ballot. Charging fraud against Root and others, Roosevelt bolted the convention and led his supporters to form a third party—formally the Progressive Party but affectionately nicknamed the Bull Moose Party after Roosevelt boasted shortly afterward that he felt "fit as a bull moose."

Roosevelt later said he could never forgive Root because he "took part in as downright a bit of theft and swindling as ever perpetrated by any Tammany ballot box stuffer." But Root felt justified in his rulings and assured Taft that his claim to the nomination was entirely valid.

The Republican split gave Democrats an excellent chance to recapture the White House by nominating the progressive New Jersey governor and former Princeton University president Woodrow Wilson. The Trust Question became the major issue in the campaign, with Wilson "triangulating" to occupy a position to the left of Taft and to Roosevelt's right.

Taft's policy was to continue to rely on the judiciary, and ultimately the Supreme Court, to interpret and enforce the Sherman Antitrust Act based on the rule of reason. Roosevelt wanted greater federal administrative regulation—a corporations or trade commission, federal licensing, price controls—under executive branch control with reduced reliance on the courts. He had come to believe that giant corporations were inevitable and that it was more important to regulate them than to try to break them up. Except for extreme cases, he saw them as efficient rather than pernicious.

Wilson took a middle position between Taft and Roosevelt. "I am for big business, and I am against the trusts," he declared. He would handle business through a combination of a mild-mannered federal commission—he favored a fact-finding agency without licensing or pricing authority—and aggressive federal antitrust enforcement subject to judicial review. Following his advisor Louis Brandeis, Wilson asserted that large businesses needed to be sued if they threatened to become monopolies. And if a corporation was monopolistic it needed to be broken up, not merely regulated. Wilson derided the Progressive Party's desire for central federal planning with the phrase "Ours is a program of liberty; theirs a program of regulation."

Wilson also suggested the states themselves should increase their level of antitrust action. As governor of New Jersey, for example, he had pushed through legislation ending the state's favorable treatment of holding companies—the same law Cromwell had succeeded in getting passed a quarter century earlier.

Frank Stetson would have preferred a more conservative, pro-business Democrat than Wilson. For one thing, Wilson, a lawyer himself (though he had practiced for only a year), had been harshly critical of Wall Street lawyers. In a 1910 address, while president of Princeton, Wilson said corporate lawyers had been "sucked into the maelstrom of the new business system of the country." Echoing Brandeis, the professorial Wilson urged lawyers to become more like public servants and less like specialized technicians who focus on minute examination of particular aspects of the law in the service of their private corporate clients. Wilson might well have been describing Frank Stetson himself.

Nonetheless, unlike in 1908, when white shoe Democratic lawyers such as Stetson, Hornblower, and William Curtis could not stomach William Jennings Bryan, in 1912 they supported and gave money to Wilson. They preferred him to the Republican Taft and the ultraprogressive Roosevelt. Stetson, a self-described "radical free trader," also found favor with Wilson's low tariff policy.

Wall Street's Republican lawyers, meanwhile, lined up almost unanimously behind Taft. Cromwell was again one of his biggest money contributors, and Guthrie, in a widely publicized speech, called Roosevelt "a socialist at heart" who had done more than anyone to stir up class warfare. Roosevelt in turn assailed Guthrie and Root as "corporation lawyers" acting "as counsel against the people."

Two decisions by New York's Court of Appeals (the state's highest court) illustrated the philosophical divide between Roosevelt and the corporation lawyers. The first, in 1885, was the "tenement house tobacco case," in which a New York City man was criminally prosecuted for attempting to carry on a cigar-making trade in his tenement house apartment. The court ruled the criminal statute an unconstitutional violation of the man's liberty, noting that the manufacture took place in apartment rooms wholly separate from the cooking and sleeping quarters and no tobacco odor pervaded those quarters. During the 1912 campaign, Root and Guthrie defended the court's ruling, arguing that the statute infringed on the tenant's freedom to support himself and his family and was passed at the request of big tobacco factory owners to prevent legitimate competition from home manufacturers. Roosevelt contended the court was thwarting legislative attempts to ensure more sanitary tenement housing conditions.

In a second case, decided in 1896, a twenty-one-year-old woman working in a hardware factory in Buffalo had her arm crushed in a machine with uncovered cog wheels in violation of a safety regulation. The court held that because the danger was visible and plainly known to her, the woman had assumed the risk and could not recover in a lawsuit against her employer. Roosevelt mocked the decision as holding that "the Legislature could not interfere with the liberty of that girl in losing her arm." Root and Guthrie responded that nothing in the court's decision prevented the legislature from changing the law to make the employer liable in such circumstances.

Frank Stetson almost certainly would have agreed with those court decisions, as well, at the time they were rendered. A conservative libertarian, he had disdained the Sherman Antitrust Act and helped William Guthrie oppose the federal income tax as unconstitutional in 1894. When Congress passed the Sixteenth Amendment in 1909 to authorize an income tax and sent it to the states for ratification, Stetson, along with Guthrie and other leading lawyers such as Joseph Choate, Victor Morawetz, and then governor Charles Evans Hughes, urged the New York legislature not to ratify it. Eventually both New York and the necessary three-fourths of the states ratified the amendment, with support from President Taft, Attorney General Wickersham, and, surprisingly, the conservative New York senator Elihu Root.

But in the election year of 1912, as he reached the age of sixty-six, Stetson's views were evolving. Unlike Guthrie, Stetson had never been a doctrinaire reactionary; for example, he supported prison reform and workers' compensation, and defended freedom of speech for radical professors and students at Williams College. For a new political science professor, he objected to the selection of "a statistician, a demagogue, or a reactionary," and instead wanted someone who could "stimulate an interest in the knowledge of the literature of Political Economy." Stetson's philosophy was that of a classic liberal who favored limited government in all realms.

But Stetson's hands-off attitude toward business had softened over the years. He had come to believe that federal regulation of business could serve as a buffer to absorb "the shocks between the corporations and an impatient or critical public." In an influential *Atlantic Monthly* article in July 1912 titled "The Government and the Corporations," Stetson allowed that some government supervision and regulation of corporations—a federal commission, even—was necessary to prevent public injury. He received some fan mail for the piece, including from one journalist who called it "clear, frank, convincing, and above all, needed in order to clear the air of economic and political cant."

Stetson admitted his position on a federal commission "would have been abhorrent" to the previous generation of businessmen and their lawyers, himself included. As his client J. P. Morgan was once famously quoted as saying, "I owe the public nothing." But Stetson, like Morgan, a deeply religious man, now opined that "a civilization which is called Christian" owed its citizens protection against the worst corporate degradations. And through such oversight he hoped corporations would discover within themselves "at least the similitude of a soul." He had become nearly a Wilsonian Democrat. For Francis Lynde Stetson, an Episcopalian warden and the most respected and influential member of the corporate legal bar, it had been a spiritual journey indeed.

Like most of their robber baron clients, almost all the top white shoe lawyers were religiously devout. And despite their reputations as millionaire, heartless technocrats, they were frequently given to private acts of charity. During the 1912 election campaign, for example, after the death of John Marshall Harlan, the anti-corporate dissenter in the Supreme Court's rule of reason decisions the year before, a group of Wall Street lawyers organized a $40,000 fund to help Harlan's impoverished widow and daughters. The leaders of the effort included Stetson, Cromwell, Root, Morawetz, John G. Johnson, and that committed foe of public welfare William Guthrie. "Although we did not always agree with Justice Harlan's decisions," their fundraising letter read, "there is no doubt of his earnest and patriotic desire to discharge the great duties of his office according to his best lights." They could only hope that one day the public would view their own labors in the same sympathetic light.

———————

Paul Cravath was perhaps the least overtly political of the leading white shoe lawyers. In his private legal practice, he never believed political influence and connections were as important as legal skill, diligence, and quality of work. He thought too many lawyers oversold their political influence to attract business from gullible clients, and thus he never claimed to have special influence with judges or, as his partner Swaine put it, the "ability to produce a magic result."

Cravath's campaign contribution to Taft in 1908 had been given under his wife's name, and in 1912 neither he nor Mrs. Cravath was listed as having contributed money to any of the three major candidates. Nor did he make any public statements for or against any of them. He may have felt conflicted: As a lifelong Republican he likely voted for Taft, but Roosevelt was an old friend and political confidant. And Cravath's most important client, Jacob Schiff, supported Wilson and contributed heavily to his campaign.

When Wilson handily won the presidency in November as a result of the Republican split, Cravath was probably relieved that the bitter contest was finally over. A week after the election he, his wife, and his seventeen-year-old daughter, Vera, attended the opening night of the Metropolitan Opera season. Held at "the old Met," then located at West Thirty-Ninth Street, not far from Cravath's residence, the performance featured Enrico Caruso in Puccini's *Manon Lescaut*. It was a glittering, brilliant occasion, also attended by Mr. and Mrs. August Belmont Jr., several Vanderbilts, and Eleanor Butler Alexander-Roosevelt, daughter-in-law of the former president. The only vacant box was the one normally reserved for the family of John Jacob Astor, who had gone down in the *Titanic* in April of that year.

J. P. Morgan was in attendance that night, too, as was the noted Wall Street attorney Samuel Untermyer. It is not recorded whether they saw or spoke to each other at the opera house. But a month later they would confront each other in perhaps the most famous lawyer–witness exchange of the entire Progressive Era.

Chapter 15

"Money Cannot Buy It"

I congratulate our country on its great opportunity to destroy Wall Street government and accomplish lasting economic reform." So wrote Samuel Untermyer to Woodrow Wilson by telegram in July 1912 upon Wilson's nomination as the Democratic candidate for president. Untermyer, a Democratic Party regular, added that he was "unreservedly enlisted" in Wilson's campaign provided the candidate turned down all Wall Street financial contributions.

Writing from aboard the Cunard Line's RMS *Caronia*, which had issued the first ice warning to the *Titanic* three months earlier, Untermyer was headed to Baden-Baden to take his annual spa cure. But he told Wilson he would gladly return earlier if needed to help win the election. In the meantime he sent Wilson's campaign a check for $10,000.

With a Democrat headed to the White House for the first time since Grover Cleveland, and the Democrats in control of Congress for the first time in two decades, Untermyer was in a heady mood. Earlier in the year, he had been selected as chief counsel to a US House of Representatives subcommittee formed to investigate the so-called Money Trust. Untermyer had been agitating for such an investigation for some time. The main focus of the Pujo Committee, named for its chairman, Louisiana Democrat Arsène Pujo, was the concentration and control of the nation's money and credit by a small number of Wall Street men, especially J. P. Morgan and his associates.

Untermyer was the perfect choice to serve as Morgan's antagonist. He claimed that a "money oligarchy" headed by Morgan was a dangerous and vicious system that in the previous five years had concentrated a money power greater than any known in the preceding fifty years. Untermyer was a champion dog breeder at his Yonkers estate, and his collies had bested

Morgan's at the 1906 Philadelphia Dog Show, embarrassing the man who had popularized the collie breed in America. And being Jewish, Untermyer triggered a visceral antipathy on the part of Morgan, whose anti-Semitism was well established.

When Untermyer was announced as the Pujo Committee's lawyer in April 1912, Morgan's son cabled his father in Venice to say the investigation was likely to be most unpleasant. Morgan's librarian, who generally reflected her boss's views, said he was dreading facing Untermyer, whom she described as "underbred, disgusting and scoundrelly . . . like a nasty little Italian flea attacking a mountain lion."

Untermyer was suave and shrewd and capable of turning on the charm as needed. He had many celebrity and entertainment industry clients and friends. But his anti-business rhetoric, coupled with an insinuating and often abrasive manner, made him anathema to establishment figures. In 1911, President William Howard Taft expressed his disgust with Untermyer's character and said he had no sympathy with "the so-called 'Money Trust' Investigation," which he considered a harassment by inquisitors. Taft confided this to Roger L. Farnham, who had left his job as William Nelson Cromwell's press agent to join the National City Bank of New York, one of the targets of the Pujo Committee investigation.

The socially exclusive William Guthrie considered Untermyer "ungentlemanly," and Paul Cravath had sparred with him in a 1910 court case in which he and Untermyer represented rival factions in a meatpacking company. UNTERMYER AND CRAVATH GET PERSONAL OVER DRESSED BEEF read the headline in the *New York Sun*, which reported that Untermyer accused Cravath of a "diabolical" plot to thwart Untermyer's client. Cravath responded that Untermyer was guilty of unprofessional conduct. A year later, Cravath criticized Untermyer for proposing certain corporate law reforms, such as abolishing holding companies, that Cravath considered too radical.

Untermyer accepted the Pujo Committee retainer only on the assurance that the investigation would have wide latitude and that he be given complete charge of it. He proceeded cautiously at first, insisting the main branch of the inquiry be postponed until after the 1912 election so as not to appear overly partisan. He also set the bar low, making clear he did not believe there was any such thing as a "money trust" in the sense of a definite, fixed agreement among financial men in violation of law, such as had been found in the oil and tobacco industries.

Rather, Untermyer said, the money trust was simply a dangerous concentration of financial power in the hands of a few individuals in New York. In addition to Morgan, they included such men as George F. Baker, chairman of the First National Bank of the City of New York, and James Stillman, chairman of the National City Bank of New York (the two institutions would eventually merge to form what became Citibank). Morgan, Baker, and Stillman were commonly referred to as the "Trio," especially after they came together under Morgan's leadership to help stem the Panic of 1907.

Although Morgan was credited at the time for having saved the nation's financial system, the Panic of 1907 had exposed a fundamental weakness in the system: the absence of any central banking authority to supply a ready reserve of liquid assets in a crisis. Even if private bankers could be trusted to act out of high-minded motives—and Untermyer did not think they could be—it was unwise for the government to give so much power to a few giants of finance. The country needed new legislation allowing it to cope with inevitable disruptions in the business cycle and to establish an official lender of last resort. The Pujo Committee's task was to provide the factual groundwork for federal banking and currency reform, and proving some sort of "money trust," even an informal one, was central to that aim.

Untermyer had another, more personal, goal in mind. He badly wanted an ambassador post in the Wilson administration—preferably to Germany, the land of his forebears, or France. Alternatively, he was reputed to covet a cabinet position, especially as attorney general.

Frank Vanderlip, National City's president, charged that Untermyer's whole ambition was to "get a whitewash for his character." Presumably this was a reference to the trouble Untermyer had early in his career when a New Jersey court accused him of fraudulently forming the straw paper monopoly. Or perhaps Untermyer was seeking a measure of respect his white shoe peers denied him on account of his religion. In the end Wilson declined to give him an ambassadorship on the basis of concerns about Untermyer's previous work as a trust lawyer. Wilson had been president of Princeton when Untermyer was censured in the New Jersey straw paper case, and although he respected him, memory of the scandal dissuaded the president-elect from rewarding the liberal activist lawyer with any official post.

Back from Europe in the fall of 1912, Untermyer began gearing up for the main part of the money trust investigation. A significant obstacle was his inability to compel certain information—particularly confidential client records—from the banks he had targeted. He had hoped for an amendment to the national banking acts to give him the powers he needed, but although the House passed such an amendment, the legislation died in the Senate.

The comptroller of the currency had some of the information he wanted, so Untermyer appealed to President Taft to direct the comptroller to release it. Attorney General Wickersham advised Taft it was discretionary with the president whether to order the comptroller to supply any information. Taft eventually instructed the comptroller to provide the committee with limited information that Untermyer called the least important among the records he sought.

Untermyer had even less ability to require his primary target, J. P. Morgan, to supply his bank's books and records. Unlike First National and National City, both of which were federally chartered, J. P. Morgan & Company was a private bank. Accordingly, Frank Stetson advised Morgan he could refuse to cooperate if he so chose. Not wanting to appear obstructive, Morgan voluntarily accepted the committee's subpoena to testify. He also allowed Stetson to provide Untermyer almost all the information he sought, other than that relating to the confidential affairs of the bank's clients. In return Stetson obtained Untermyer's agreement to complete Morgan's testimony as quickly as possible because Morgan was planning to go abroad.

Apart from being wealthy corporate lawyers and avid horticulturalists, Stetson and Untermyer had little in common. Their correspondence, mostly polite and formal on the surface, revealed the fundamental antagonism between them. Stetson was quick to point out that his clients' willingness to cooperate did not imply their agreement with the premise of the Pujo Committee—that is, "there are many abuses in the existing financial system and that the entire system is sadly in need of a 'thorough overhauling,' presumably by legislation." To the contrary, private-sector businessmen such as Morgan believed that, if left alone, they were more capable of wise national financial management than any government bureaucrat might be. They considered the system fine as is.

For his part, Untermyer did not accede to Stetson's request that Morgan's lawyers be allowed to question the bank witnesses they represented in the hearings. Untermyer called the suggestion unusual and impractical, insisting that he alone would question the witnesses. Stetson responded testily, telling Untermyer, "Your unwillingness to concede this was and is the basis of our feeling that the desire to cooperate is not altogether reciprocal." It was largely gamesmanship on Stetson's part, as witnesses before Congress are rarely allowed to be questioned by their own counsel.

Stetson understood that Untermyer, being hostile to Wall Street, was not looking for ways to give Morgan and other financial men a platform to offer their personal views. Untermyer assured Stetson that his banking clients would have an opportunity to explain or expand upon their answers after being interrogated by counsel for the committee. But as both of them knew, belated attempts by witnesses to explain what they really meant are rarely as convincing as the initial testimony. It was to be Untermyer's show. But the main actor was the seventy-five-year-old Morgan. As Frederick Lewis Allen, the best-known chronicler of the Progressive Era, wrote, "It was as if—through the agency of the Pujo Committee—the American public were asking this man, at the close of his extraordinary life, 'Tell us, before it is too late, have you really controlled American business?'"

———※———

Samuel Untermyer was caught off guard when J. P. Morgan entered the Pujo Committee hearing room at 2:00 p.m. on Wednesday, December 18, 1912, creating a stir among the spectators gathered there. The previous day, Untermyer had telephoned one of Morgan's lawyers to say that although Morgan had originally been scheduled to begin his testimony on Wednesday, the committee now would not be ready to hear from him until the following day.

But Morgan had decided to take a private train from New York to Washington anyway, arriving around 6:30 p.m. on Tuesday with an entourage of some fifteen persons, including a stellar cast of lawyers. Frank Stetson was with him, of course, as were eighty-year-old Joseph Choate, the veteran trial lawyer, and former US senator John Spooner, sponsor of the Panama Canal bill and now back in private practice. None of Morgan's lawyers would be able to help him as he testified, but they were there for last-minute strategizing and to provide moral support.

Untermyer was as surprised as anyone when Morgan strode into the hearing chamber on Wednesday afternoon, accompanied by his lawyers, business partners, son, and daughter, and made his way with them to some open seats. Wearing a Chesterfield overcoat, he walked with aid of a mahogany cane, his iconic top hat in hand.

In order to put Morgan on the witness stand that afternoon, Untermyer hurried through the remainder of his questioning of an accountant who had compiled some statistical information about the alleged money trust. It was a dry but enlightening presentation. For another hour, the witness provided charts and tables illustrating how connected the nation's major financial and industrial companies were through interlocking directorates—that is, the practice whereby members of a corporate board of directors serve on the boards of multiple corporations. Morgan heard his own name frequently invoked.

Probably the most telling statistic concerned the Morgan-Stillman-Baker Trio. Just a few firms controlled by them had 341 interlocking directorates in 112 companies with total resources of more than $22 billion, an amount equal to almost 60 percent of the nation's gross domestic product. Their influence extended not only to banks and trust companies but also to insurance companies, railroads and transportation systems, public utility companies, and other industrial corporations. By becoming directors of the corporations they controlled, the major banks could then make the investment decisions for those other companies—including whether to issue and sell securities, the price at which to sell them, and to whom they would sell them, including, if the banks so chose, to the banks themselves. The banks also became the place where their controlled industrial corporations deposited their money, further increasing their power.

The relationship among the three big banks headed by the Trio was also incestuous. Morgan was the largest outside investor in Baker's First National and held a large block of the stock of Stillman's National City, on whose board Morgan's son sat. The Trio effectively controlled the nation's second largest bank, National Bank of Commerce, as well as Chase National Bank. And with Morgan's purchase of a controlling interest in the Equitable from Thomas Fortune Ryan and E. H. Harriman's estate in 1909, the Trio now held sway over all three major life insurers (the Equitable, Mutual Life, and New York Life). Baker and Stillman further agreed that anytime Morgan wished, they would together take half the Equitable stock off his hands.

Morgan seemed weary when he first took the witness chair at 3:00 P.M. on Wednesday. The night before he had been suffering from a bad cold, and after growing tired of listening to his lawyers had retired to smoke a Cuban cigar and play his favorite game of solitaire into the early-morning hours. His testimony was mercifully brief and uneventful, limited to confirming some basic information about his bank's organization and operations. After half an hour of questioning by Untermyer, Chairman Pujo adjourned the hearing until the next morning.

When the hearing resumed on Thursday the room was packed to standing-room capacity. As always, Untermyer wore a lapel boutonnière of fresh orchids grown on his Yonkers estate. Morgan again showed up with a retinue of lawyers and family. One newspaper reported seeing Paul Cravath, Jacob Schiff's lawyer, hovering nearby.

Alert and refreshed after a night's rest, Morgan riveted the attention of everyone in the chamber. The drama began when Untermyer asked Morgan about the power he wielded in the financial world. Morgan surprisingly denied the premise. "When a man has got a vast power, such as you have—you admit you have, do you not?" Untermyer inquired. "I do not know it, sir," Morgan responded.

UNTERMYER: You admit you have, do you not?

MORGAN: I do not think I have.

UNTERMYER: You do not feel it at all?

MORGAN: No; I do not feel it at all.

Even more startling was Morgan's denial of his control of his own bank.

UNTERMYER: Your firm is run by you, is it not?

MORGAN: No, sir.

                    . . .

UNTERMYER: You are the final authority, are you not?

MORGAN: No, sir.

UNTERMYER: You are not?

MORGAN: No, sir.

UNTERMYER: You never have been?

MORGAN: Never have.

Morgan explained that his bank ultimately was controlled by its board of directors, not him alone, but his curt denials flew in the face of accepted wisdom. As did the following exchange:

UNTERMYER: You do not think you have any power in any department of industry in this country, do you?

MORGAN: I do not.

UNTERMYER: Not the slightest?

MORGAN: Not the slightest.

Morgan could not dispute the facts and figures being thrown at him, but he could and did challenge Untermyer's interpretation of them. Much of what he was peddling was nonsensical, but the frankness, simplicity, and consistency with which he delivered his testimony gave it an authoritative ring.

The financier waffled a bit on whether he welcomed competition. He said he favored cooperation over competition but that he didn't mind "a little competition." Then he quickly switched the subject to offer his views on the main question before the committee: whether a money trust existed in the country. Morgan insisted no such monopoly was possible, that there was no way a man could create a trust on money. "You can get a combination that can control business," Morgan conceded, "but you cannot control money."

But, Untermyer asked, did not Morgan himself vigorously seek money, in the form of deposits, for his bank? Did he not compete for money to increase his control? "I should doubt it," Morgan replied. "I have been in business for a great many years in New York and I do not compete for any deposits. I do not care whether they ever come. They come."

Morgan was warming to the process. He waved off any assistance from others except for an occasional throat lozenge from his daughter seated behind him. Untermyer bore in on Morgan with rapid-fire questions, asking if he was going too fast. Morgan assured the lawyer he could keep up. He dismissed Untermyer's suggestion that he might be tired and said he did not need to break for lunch (they did anyway).

Morgan would occasionally bang the table or stomp his cane for emphasis, then swivel in his chair to look at his son, daughter, and attorneys to gauge their approval. He even chuckled along with the audience when they broke into laughter, as when Untermyer asked him to confirm that he had a very large interest in the National Bank of Commerce, to which Morgan replied no, not much, only about a million dollars' worth. Above all he was firm, not defensive, even when denying the seemingly obvious.

Would Morgan at least agree that concentrating power and control in the hands of a few men was bad for the country? "No, sir," he replied to Untermyer. Was it not dangerous to have the same directors running banks and other institutions that were supposed to be competing with one another? "I do not see any danger in it at all" was Morgan's retort.

Untermyer asked why Morgan had bought the Equitable shares from Thomas Ryan in 1910. "Because I thought it was a desirable thing for the situation to do that," Morgan answered. Untermyer followed up: Was the stock not safe in Ryan's hands? Morgan replied that he supposed it was; he just thought it was better off with him owning it. Untermyer asked why, to which Morgan responded, "That is the way it struck me."

"Is that all you have to say about it?" Untermyer continued. "That is all I have to say about it," Morgan confirmed.

It would not have occurred to Morgan that anyone would require an explanation of his business judgment. "If it is good business for the interests of the country to do it, I do it," Morgan testified. And when Untermyer asked Morgan whether it was possible that his judgment was sometimes mistaken—that perhaps he subconsciously equated his own selfish interests with the best interests of the country, Morgan said he doubted that was ever the case.

The most dramatic moment in the testimony came when Untermyer tried another tack to force Morgan to admit the overriding importance of money. "Is not commercial credit based primarily upon money or property?" he demanded to know. "No, sir," Morgan replied, "the first thing is character." Untermyer, short and thin, had moved within arm's length of the six-foot-tall, corpulent witness. The questions now came quickly:

UNTERMYER: Before money or property?

MORGAN: Before money or anything else. Money cannot buy it.

. . .

UNTERMYER: If that is the rule of business, Mr. Morgan, why do the banks demand, the first thing they ask, a statement of what the man has got, before they extend him credit?

MORGAN: That is what they go into; but the first thing they say is, "We want to see your record."

UNTERMYER: Yes; and if his record is a blank, the next thing is how much has he got?

MORGAN: People do not care, then.

       . . .

UNTERMYER: He does not get it [credit] on his face or his character,
       does he?

MORGAN: Yes; he gets it on his character. . . . Because a man I do
       not trust could not get money from me on all the bonds
       in Christendom.

Morgan's emphasis on "character" was, in the heat of the moment, his escape hatch for implausibly denying the critical importance of money to the business of banking. But it also reflected the fundamental difference in thinking between financial barons such as Morgan and reformers like Untermyer. To Morgan, the wealth that he and other plutocrats had accumulated—even while widening the gap between rich and poor—was self-evidently proof of their moral superiority. He trusted himself and his fellow bankers to do the right thing, while Untermyer was looking for mechanisms more certain and reliable than the professed good faith of the banking oligarchs to ensure the public good.

The Progressive Era had seen many critical moments: Roosevelt's decision to sue the Northern Securities Company as an antitrust violator; the ICC assault on Harriman's railroad financings; the Supreme Court's landmark decisions in the oil and tobacco trust cases. But nothing had so personified the clash of ideas—new and old—as these exchanges between a wily corporate lawyer turned social activist and an aging, unapologetic defender of the financial status quo.

At the end of his five hours of testimony Morgan rose from his witness chair and shook hands with each member of the Pujo Committee, and with Untermyer, too, and thanked them for their courtesy. Untermyer later told the press that whatever one's opinion of the concentration of the control of the nation's money and credit, "Mr. Morgan was animated by high purpose and . . . never knowingly abused his almost incredible power."

Back in New York, congratulatory telegrams poured into Morgan's office and home from all over the world. They praised Morgan for what they called his straightforward, plainspoken answers. "I don't see how you kept your temper under Mr. Untermyer's almost insolent persistence," wrote one admirer.

A Minneapolis magazine opined, "When all is said and done, and sifted and reported on, the matter resolves itself into just this: which is more worthy of public confidence, the lawyer retained by a committee to find a money trust, or the man who has spent a lifetime studying the finances of the world?" The *New York Times* expressed a consensus view that Morgan had "lost no prestige through his appearance. . . . On the contrary, his willingness as a witness and his evident sincerity and frankness seems to have created a distinctly favorable impression."

Although Stillman was conveniently in Europe throughout the hearings, Baker of First National testified near the end and grudgingly gave Untermyer a little more of what he was looking for. The mutton-chopped Baker was insouciant for most of his testimony, as when Untermyer asked him what he understood a money trust to be. "I give . . . up. I don't know," he replied with a chuckle. "You think everything is all right as it is in this world, do you not?" Untermyer goaded him. "Pretty nearly," Baker answered.

But Untermyer pressed forward. Baker said he did not think the concentration of control of credit was then dangerous, because it was in "good hands." Unscrupulous men, he thought, would never be able to retain enough deposits or securities to wreck the country. Then Untermyer asked whether it would be dangerous if control became even more concentrated than it presently was. Baker pondered the question for a moment and then answered, to the surprise of everyone, including his lawyers, "I think it has gone about far enough."

Untermyer sensed a breakthrough. "You see a peril in that, do you not?" he asked. "Yes," Baker conceded.

UNTERMYER: So that the safety, if you think there is safety in the situation, really lies in the personnel of the men?

BAKER: Very much.

UNTERMYER: Do you think that is a comfortable situation for a great
                    country to be in?

Baker answered very slowly, "Not entirely." Untermyer, satisfied to close
on that note, said, "I think that is all" and excused Baker from the stand.

According to *The Bellman* magazine in Minneapolis, the Pujo hearings
were "a complete fiasco" that had "accomplished nothing good, unless the
remunerative employment of Mr. Samuel Untermyer may be so considered." But although Untermyer's investigation had not proved any formal
conspiratorial agreement (just as he predicted it would not), the Pujo Committee concluded there was "an established and well defined community of
interest between a few leaders of finance . . . which has resulted in great and
rapidly growing concentration of the control of money and credit in the
hands of these few men."

As the committee reported, "What may be virtually the power of life
and death over our banking institutions rests uncontrolled in private hands."
These were hardly surprising conclusions, but they were significant for the
fact that a congressional committee had officially pronounced them. As
popular journalist Mark Sullivan wrote, they validated the feeling of many
an average American who felt that "he was being 'put upon' by something
he couldn't quite see or get his fingers on; that somebody was 'riding' him;
that some force or other was 'crowding' him."

Although the Pujo Committee report recommended various remedial
legislation aimed at investor protection, including proposals relating to the
stock exchanges, none of the proposed bills was passed into law. Untermyer
was particularly disappointed in the failure of a securities regulation bill that
died because of Wall Street opposition and a lack of support from the Wilson administration, which feared harming a sluggish economy.

But the money trust investigation did have a significant impact on the
national debate over progressive reform. The Pujo Committee's findings
inspired support for the Federal Reserve Act, which Wilson made a priority
of his legislative agenda and was passed in 1913. It created the Federal Reserve System, with a central bank and twelve regional reserve banks, to control the nation's money supply. (The regional structure had been Victor
Morawetz's brainchild.) As a further indication of the impact of the Pujo

hearings, one portion of the Clayton Antitrust Act, enacted in 1914 to supplement the Sherman Act, prohibited interlocking directorates among competing companies.

The Pujo hearings had another important legacy, at least in the minds of some. Within three weeks of finishing his testimony Morgan sailed for Egypt with his family. He suffered a physical and mental breakdown while traveling along the Nile and went to Rome, where his condition deteriorated. Art dealers crowded the lobby of Rome's Grand Hotel, hoping to sell their wares to the great collector, who was lodging upstairs, before it was too late. On March 31, 1913, in the hotel's eight-bedroom royal suite, Morgan died in his sleep. Flags on Wall Street flew at half-mast. When John D. Rockefeller heard it reported that Morgan's fortune was "only" $80 million, he said, "And to think he wasn't even a rich man."

Morgan's partners and many other people were sure the strain from the Pujo hearings had brought on the great financier's demise, for which they placed the blame squarely on Untermyer. One fellow banker said that "the Pujo Committee Investigation killed Morgan. Morgan was a very sensitive, shrinking man and all his exterior bluff was simply a protecting coating."

Perhaps the hearings had hastened Morgan's death, but the reality was that Morgan was already a very sick man. Morgan's son Jack, who would inherit the business, discounted the Pujo theory, noting that his father had performed well in Washington and that he was too big a man to have been annoyed by "miserable little things like that." The junior Morgan maintained, "There is no use in letting that little rascal Untermyer smile a happy face and say, 'I brought it off after all.'" Still, Jack Morgan never forgave Untermyer, whom he referred to privately as "the beast."

The face of Wall Street for three decades, Morgan was now gone in body. But his name, and spirit, would infuse the final great Wall Street scandals of the Progressive Era, in which Paul Cravath, Frank Stetson, and William Nelson Cromwell would all have visible roles.

Chapter 16

"The Wolf of Wall Street"

To Paul Cravath, the mysterious telephone caller was "the man with the mellifluous voice." Before long the man would be unmasked as a Wall Street wolf in false garb, and the bizarre ensuing scandal would make front-page headlines for months. It exposed a seedy underbelly of Wall Street that respectable, white shoe lawyers preferred to avoid, but which they had to deal with from time to time because the tremendous amounts of money at stake inevitably attracted bottom-feeders. Most of all the scandal would demonstrate that for Wall Street corporate men who came under attack by predators, their first line of defense, and strongest buffer, was their favorite lawyer.

In mid-April 1913, while in his office in New York, Cravath received an anonymous phone call asking if he was counsel for the Union Pacific Railroad in the dissolution proceedings arising from the Supreme Court's recent antitrust ruling ordering the breakup of the Union Pacific and Southern Pacific. When Cravath confirmed that he was, the caller went on to identify himself as a person of importance in the Democratic Party in Washington and say that the Union Pacific was handling the case very badly. Instead of sending a corporate man to Washington to negotiate a consent decree with the US attorney general, the caller said, the company needed to send a politician skilled at diplomacy.

Responding to the mysterious caller, Cravath said he would not talk any further with someone who would not give his name. The caller replied that he would not give his name, but that he would give Cravath the name of a man Cravath knew well who *would* give him his name as well as further information.

The man Cravath needed to speak with, the caller said, was Edward

Lauterbach, a sixty-eight-year-old warhorse lawyer long active in New York City politics. A product of the Republican machine boss system, he was nicknamed "Smooth Ed." Cravath knew Lauterbach from the electricity battles of the late 1880s, when they were involved in litigation over burying electrical wires in underground conduits.

Lauterbach, a railroad and transit system lawyer who once had done work for J. P. Morgan, was now long past his prime. But the caller implied that Lauterbach (despite being a Republican) was the man the Union Pacific needed to plead its case to the new Wilson administration and the Democratic-controlled Congress. Cravath ignored the call and took the train to Washington to resume negotiations with Wilson's attorney general, James C. McReynolds, who had briefly been Cravath's senior associate in 1907.

After several more calls from the same anonymous man, who still refused to give his name, Cravath happened to run into Lauterbach, whose office was just down the street from Cravath's. "I said to him somewhat jocularly, 'Lauterbach, who is the man with the mellifluous voice who has been telephoning me about the Union Pacific, and who tells me you that you will give his name if I apply to you?'" Cravath later recalled in testimony before Congress. Lauterbach would say only that he thought no good would come from his revealing the name.

At the same time the anonymous man was calling Cravath to suggest using Lauterbach in the Union Pacific negotiations, he was making similar calls to other top lawyers, including Frank Stetson and Lewis Cass Ledyard, a personal advisor to J. P. Morgan. To each of them, the caller said Lauterbach was the man they needed to accomplish what they wanted in Washington. In these conversations, though, the caller falsely identified himself using the names of various prominent Democratic politicians. In some calls he impersonated New York congressman Daniel J. Riordan, in others he said he was Pennsylvania's A. Mitchell Palmer. Because none of the men receiving the phone calls knew or had ever spoken with Riordan or Palmer, they were unaware the calls were not really from those congressmen.

But who *was* the caller? It turned out that the man's name was David Lamar—or Lewis, or Levy, or Simon Wolf, or Isaac Frankenstein, or any other of the many pseudonyms he was said to have used. Lamar was better known, though, as "the Wolf of Wall Street."

Largely forgotten today, David Lamar was one of the most colorful and enigmatic figures in America in the early twentieth century. No one knew his real name, or where he was born, or when (it was sometime between 1858 and 1877). Near the turn of the century Lamar had come east from Omaha to work as a gumshoe for powerful Wall Street brokers, then launched his own business as a stock speculator and con man.

He became known as a "plunger"—someone who bet against stocks, selling them short, while creating rumors of trouble for the targeted corporations to drive their share prices down. He also instigated strike suits—that is, actions brought by small stockholders to embarrass giant corporations in hopes of being bought off by them.

In particular, Lamar had earned the enmity of J. P. Morgan by seeking to block, first, the Northern Securities merger in 1901, and then a major bond issuance by Morgan's US Steel in 1902 to retire $200 million of preferred stock. In the latter case, Lamar told Morgan's deputy, George W. Perkins, that he could stop all the litigation against the bond deal if Morgan gave him an option on forty thousand shares of US Steel stock. Perkins, who considered Lamar part of the "nest of rascals" who habitually brought blackmailing lawsuits against the Morgan interests, immediately told him to leave his office and not come back.

The bond deal lawsuits, in which Stetson and Guthrie represented Morgan, were eventually defeated or settled for nuisance value. Guthrie, who reluctantly went along with paying one of the plaintiffs $100,000 for his common stock to end the matter, found dealing with the blackmailers "extremely disagreeable." He added in a letter to Stetson, "I have never in my life listened to meaner or more puerile argument than we got from the other side."

Although he obtained little to nothing from Morgan, Lamar had better success against a gullible John D. Rockefeller Jr. Lamar tricked him into buying millions of dollars' worth of United States Leather, using money borrowed from his father, while Lamar was selling the stock. Lamar made a bundle on the deal while young Rockefeller squandered his liberal allowance.

Stocky and squarely built, Lamar was known for his suave manners and expensive clothing, including a diamond-studded cane. He radiated optimism and confidence, once explaining his methodology as follows: "Put up a bluff. Make 'em think you've got far more than you really have, and they will have all kinds of respect for you. The rest will be easy."

He frequented Broadway nightclubs and high-class restaurants, where he ran up huge unpaid food and wine bills. After he left his wife in 1909 to marry a chorus girl one-third his age, the first Mrs. Lamar nonetheless spoke admiringly of his skills. "He can just make a stock do anything," she marveled. "He can make it go up or down just as he wants to. He is wonderful." He changed offices constantly, preferring to occupy desk space at points around the city to avoid being pinned down. The *New York Times* described him as "more of an eagle than a wolf. He swooped down, left an imprint of his talons and was gone."

Lamar made and lost several small fortunes during his career and was in and out of jail for minor swindles and for other, more serious charges. In 1903 he hired the gangster Monk Eastman and his thugs to beat up a coachman who had disobeyed Mrs. Lamar's order to fetch her runaway dog. Just as the coachman was about to give his evidence against Lamar in police court on an assault charge, Eastman's gang knifed him and knocked him unconscious. A jury that later acquitted Eastman and Lamar was hooted by the spectators as it left the courtroom.

During World War I Lamar was convicted for impeding arms shipments to the Allies in conspiracy with a German naval intelligence agent. The German operative paid Lamar $300,000 to foment strikes at munitions factories, but Lamar kept most of the money for himself. He jumped bail and fled to Mexico before being apprehended by government authorities to serve his one-year sentence.

Lamar's most famous encounter with the law, however, came with his 1913 impersonations of Democratic politicians. He was called to testify as part of a congressional investigation into what President Wilson labeled insidious efforts by lobbyists to influence legislation, particularly the tariff reduction bill that Wilson had made his top priority. Lamar testified at length, as did Lauterbach, Cravath, Ledyard, and the indignant impersonated congressmen, Riordan and Palmer. Stetson did not end up being called, but his name frequently came up as one of the targets of Lamar's plot.

Although Lamar refused to give his real name to the congressional committee, he frankly admitted to his fraud. "It was a pure fabrication from beginning to end," he testified. "Do not take it seriously. It is all a perfect farce." Besides the congressmen, Lamar also admitted to impersonating the Democratic national chairman in a phone call to his Republican counterpart. Lamar dismissed it as "nothing but malicious mischief."

Lamar testified that his main object had been to restore his friend Lauterbach to the good graces of J. P. Morgan & Co. and the bankers at Kuhn, Loeb & Co., all of whom had allegedly blackballed Lauterbach. Although Lauterbach had once enjoyed good relations with them, these leading bankers no longer employed him because of his close association with the disreputable Wolf of Wall Street. Lamar explained that in impersonating the politicians, he was just trying to gain Lauterbach an audience with the financiers so that Lauterbach might rehabilitate himself in their eyes and obtain their business again.

As "Congressman Palmer," Lamar called Morgan's friend Ledyard, a corporate lawyer and prominent figure in New York society. Ledyard was president of the New York City Bar Association, a founder of the New York Public Library, and a past commodore of the New York Yacht Club. He drafted Morgan's will, became an executor of his estate, and was so adroit in his dealings that it was said he could "kiss six hands at one time."

"Palmer"—that is, Lamar—told Ledyard that if the Morgan interests hired Lauterbach, the old lawyer would be able to favorably influence Congress in various ways, including by controlling the Pujo Committee's money trust report then being drafted.

As "Congressman Riordan," Lamar told Frank Stetson that Lauterbach could convince the government to drop its prosecution of US Steel. Stetson was representing Morgan in the US Steel litigation and was concerned that the Supreme Court's rulings in the oil and tobacco trust cases portended defeat for the steel corporation. But he refused to bite on "Riordan's" offer. "Mr. Stetson began to talk to me about some church," a frustrated Lamar said, adding that in his opinion Stetson was "not human."

Cravath's client Otto Kahn of Kuhn, Loeb & Co., the bankers for the Union Pacific, received a call directly from Lauterbach offering his lobbying services. Lauterbach told Kahn he could help ward off radical elements in Congress who sought to block the Union Pacific's dissolution plan. These same elements, Lauterbach said, wanted to reopen the investigation of the Chicago & Alton reorganization that had caused Harriman so much trouble before he died. Lauterbach said he was confident he could prevent that from happening. Kahn, too, took a pass.

Lamar insisted that his friend Lauterbach was unaware of his impersonations, a claim Lauterbach echoed. Lauterbach did admit he had discussed with Lamar his desire to ingratiate himself with the Morgan group and Kuhn, Loeb, and that in speaking to Ledyard and others he had exaggerated his Washington connections and influence. Lauterbach also resented the fact that Ledyard, after correctly guessing that Lamar was the man impersonating Palmer, had allowed Lauterbach to continue pitching his services so Ledyard could gain information to uncover the scheme. Lauterbach felt Ledyard had entrapped him and was out to crush him for his affiliation with Lamar.

Lauterbach and Lamar claimed their efforts in relation to the Union Pacific were public-spirited. They said they genuinely opposed, on policy grounds, the dissolution plan Cravath was negotiating with Attorney General McReynolds. In reality, the two schemers hoped to create congressional hostility to the dissolution plan, then put forward Lauterbach as someone who could calm the waters.

Lamar also fed the papers a story that back in 1901, Harriman and Kuhn, Loeb had falsified the Union Pacific's books to inflate its assets by $82 million to finance Harriman's takeover of the Northern Pacific. After Lamar testified to the alleged manipulation, Cravath took the stand to denounce him as a liar who was trying to depress the Union Pacific's stock price for speculative purposes (the word "liar" was stricken from the record as too inflammatory). The accountant whose work Lamar cited as the basis for his charge later admitted he'd been in error and that there had been no improper accounting.

No one at the hearings believed Lamar had gone to all these lengths just to help his friend Lauterbach land some business. They suspected a blackmail scheme—that Lamar's intention, and possibly Lauterbach's as well, was to persuade one or more of the respected Morgan and Union Pacific business-men, or their eminent lawyers, to go along with the plan to exert improper influence over elected officials. If any of these men of assumed integrity and honor acceded to the underground plot, they would then be subject to ex-tortion. As Ledyard put it, Lamar and Lauterbach "would own them for all time and could bleed them to any extent."

That is how the prosecuting authorities viewed it. Lamar was indicted for impersonating a federal officer, and Lauterbach for conspiring with him to blackmail Morgan and others. Lamar was convicted and sentenced to two years in a federal penitentiary in Atlanta. He challenged his conviction all the way to the US Supreme Court, which ruled that a US congressman was an officer of the United States for purposes of the impersonation statute, an issue that had been unclear.

The criminal charges against Lauterbach were dropped, but he was se-verely censured by the New York courts. The episode would mar his legacy, which otherwise included his active involvement in local charities, in par-ticular as a trustee of the Hebrew Orphan Asylum.

For Lauterbach, who probably knew more than could be proven in court, the reasons for his actions were simple enough. As he testified, "I had had domestic difficulties; my wife had divorced me, and I had lost social and professional standing, and an affiliation with their [Kuhn, Loeb's] interests and the Morgan interests would have done me great good." He had a law office with thirty-two employees and no business to sustain them. There was "nothing else left for me," he testified.

Lamar's motives were more complicated. Undoubtedly he was driven by a desire for money, but he also craved attention. He had delusions of gran-deur, testifying, for example, that he had inspired J. P. Morgan's formation of US Steel and had given Morgan the idea for how to settle the anthracite coal strike in 1902. He also took credit for initiating the congressional inves-tigation of US Steel that led to the government's antitrust lawsuit. In fact, Lamar had merely drafted a resolution urging the investigation and used it to try to blackmail the House of Morgan.

Lamar clearly relished his role as a foe of the moneyed interests. He had a visceral hatred of business titans and their "respectable" white shoe lawyers, and he asserted that by engaging in lies and impersonations he was just fighting Wall Street using its own methods. "I was sick of the persecution," he said. "Sick of these rumors about my being a scoundrel, a liar, a thief, a blackmailer; sick of having Kuhn, Loeb & Co. and J. P. Morgan tell my friends that if they did any more business with me all their loans would be cut off; that they could never borrow another dollar. That was the thing that set me in motion."

He asserted that by disguising his identity he was only trying to draw his enemies into the open to expose the baselessness of their ostracism of Lauterbach and himself. "If these gentlemen would mend all their ways, would recant all their heresies, would begin all over again, de novo . . . if they would be good instead of bad," Lamar testified, then he and Lauterbach, "the men who had evidence of their wickedness would be inclined to forgive them."

His reasoning was convoluted, and Lamar was hardly the best messenger for attacking Wall Street. But his attitude was not unusual among the body politic. The Morgans and Harrimans of the world were still commonly reviled, even in death. One US congressman took to the floor to say that Lamar's frauds paled in comparison with those committed by Morgan.

The moguls' lawyers were not far behind them in unpopularity. "Who are the lawyers who are making the large sums of money today?" asked one newspaper at the time, noting that in recent years lawyers had increased their incomes by taking as their pay the stock of corporations they organized. Among those singled out for mention were William Nelson Cromwell, Francis Lynde Stetson, Elihu Root, and William Guthrie.

More lively than consequential, the Lamar scandal nonetheless illustrated the stark, bitterly personal divide between the attackers and defenders of the Wall Street status quo—in particular, between the outcasts and the white shoes. Lawyers such as Cravath, Guthrie, and Ledyard may have found dealing with the likes of David Lamar to be distasteful, but it was part of their job, and they did it well. The Lamar scandal had one tangible legacy, too: passage of a federal statute making it a felony to impersonate a congressperson.

The next great Wall Street scandal, and the last of the Progressive Era, would be of unquestioned significance. Once again it would embroil the ghost of J. P. Morgan, while involving his most trusted lawyers.

Chapter 17

"The Curse of Bigness"

The New Haven Railroad scandal would nearly land Lewis Cass Ledyard, who had helped put David Lamar in jail, behind bars himself. For one of the rare times in his career, Frank Stetson's judgment would be publicly questioned during the government's investigation into the New Haven's affairs. William Nelson Cromwell would make a typically flamboyant entrance in the sensational inquiry. And Paul Cravath's firm, appearing for the first time as the New Haven's counsel, would do what it did best: serve a high-profile, well-paying client.

The downfall of the New Haven (formally, the New York, New Haven & Hartford Railroad) marked the end of an era. It was the finale to the struggle that characterized the period from 1890, when the Sherman Antitrust Act became law, to 1914, when the last of the business reform legislation of the Progressive Era was enacted. Nearly every major character from the period was involved or had his name invoked in the New Haven scandal, and many of the controversial business episodes of the era were recalled. The issue of monopolization, which had been hotly debated over the previous quarter century, was front and center. And when it was over, and the last business reform measures became law, the Trust Question was resolved, for better or worse, allowing the nation to move on to other matters.

At the beginning of the twentieth century, few corporations were more powerful, or venerated, than the New Haven Railroad. It was the lifeblood of transportation in New England and a safe blue-chip stock that for three decades had been paying a steady 8 percent dividend to widows, orphans, and trust estates. Its debt was low and, unlike many of the nation's major railroads, it was not overcapitalized with watered stock. But to the man who controlled the New Haven, J. P. Morgan, it was not enough. The New Haven held a special place in Morgan's heart, as he was born in Hartford and rode the New Haven trains as a boy. He was rumored to have more of his personal fortune invested in the New Haven than in anything else. In 1903 Morgan brought in a new president, Charles S. Mellen, and the two of them went on a buying spree that all but wrecked the company and damaged the reputations of both men and many others.

Mellen worked his way up through various railroad positions in New England, where he came to the attention of Morgan, who sent him west in 1896 to run the reorganized Northern Pacific Railway. Mellen chafed under the leadership of Morgan's ally, James J. Hill, and in 1903 readily accepted Morgan's offer to come back east to run the New Haven.

Mellen, fifty and balding by then, was known as the "last of the railway czars." He was whip-smart, detail-oriented, and strong-willed, but given to flippancy and sarcasm. Theodore Roosevelt, a personal friend, called Mellen a "first class fellow," no doubt influenced by Mellen's contribution of $50,000 of New Haven money to Roosevelt's 1904 campaign.

When it was expedient for Mellen to say so, he would claim that he was completely under Morgan's yoke. "I took orders from J. P. Morgan, Sr.," he told financial journalist Clarence Barron. "I did as I was told, and when Morgan, Sr., who always sat at my left hand in the meetings of the board, desired the approval of his directors, he got it, and don't you think he didn't!" As Mellen explained, it was Morgan's way, when he wanted to cut off discussion or opposition, to pound his fist and thunder, "Call a vote. Let's see where these gentlemen stand." And "we always stood where he expected us to stand," Mellen said. "We stood in awe of him."

In reality, Morgan and Mellen both dominated the New Haven board of directors, who routinely deferred to their superior expertise. Unwieldy in number, the board included a collection of elderly, non-railroad men from Connecticut and Massachusetts, as well as directors from the Morgan-controlled New York Central Railroad and the Mutual Life Insurance Company. With additional representatives from Standard Oil, American Express, and the Pennsylvania Railroad, the New Haven board was the epitome of the practice of interlocking directorates castigated by the Pujo Committee.

As a result of its aggressive acquisition program, the New Haven gained a virtual monopoly over all transportation in New England. It not only bought up almost all the other railroads in the region but also all the trolley systems, steamship lines, and, for good measure, electric, gas, and water utilities. When directors asked whether the growing monopoly might violate the antitrust laws, they were assured by the railroad's general counsel, Edward Robbins, and later by Ledyard as well, that the New Haven was safe from federal prosecution under the Sherman Act because of its Connecticut state charter. It was bad advice but the directors accepted it without question.

In 1907, the New Haven sought to buy a controlling block of stock in the Boston & Maine Railroad, the most significant line in Massachusetts. Initially, Mellen and Morgan convinced Roosevelt to let the New Haven acquire the Boston & Maine, despite antitrust concerns, in part to keep it away from Roosevelt's bête noire, E. H. Harriman, who was also interested in the line. Roosevelt said he could give no guarantees of legality but that he was disinclined to bring a prosecution.

Afterward, though, the Massachusetts Supreme Court ruled the purchase illegal under Massachusetts law. In response, Mellen had the New Haven "sell" the Boston & Maine shares to one of his cronies, John Billard, to keep it in friendly hands. Billard put up no cash in the deal, instead using money borrowed from the New Haven. The New Haven then successfully lobbied the Massachusetts legislature to change the law to allow it to buy the Boston & Maine. At that point Billard gave his shares back to the New Haven in return for a hefty $2.7 million profit for himself, despite having taken no risk when he "bought" the stock. By using Billard as a stalking horse the New Haven gained control of the Boston & Maine.

That was a defeat, at least temporarily, for Louis Brandeis, who had made the New Haven's purchase of the Boston & Maine exhibit A in his escalating public crusade against the trusts. Brandeis condemned monopolies on the dual grounds that they wielded too much power and were too large to be capably and efficiently managed. He especially attacked the investment bankers, like Morgan, who controlled railroads and large industrial corporations and used other people's money to finance risky, speculative expansions of the business—while reaping huge commissions and underwriting fees for themselves. Brandeis decried the "financial recklessness" that inevitably followed investment banker control.

Undeterred by the capitulation of the Massachusetts legislature, Brandeis carried on a seven-year publicity war against the New Haven, which he was convinced was a financial ticking time bomb disguised by accounting trickery. In fact, in the decade from 1903, when Mellen became president, to 1913, the New Haven's capitalization more than quadrupled, from $93 million to $417 million, and its bonded indebtedness rose nearly twentyfold, from $14 million to $242 million.

The New Haven wildly overpaid to expand its monopoly, per Morgan's custom of offering large, round numbers for desired properties without haggling over price. Morgan liberally watered the stock of companies he bought or formed, on the assumption the business would grow to service the debt and pay the dividends—especially if he could eliminate competition. As William Nelson Cromwell once observed, Morgan "had an instinct for discovering popular feeling toward investments," but he was "only a banker" and prone to the reckless inflation of securities to enhance his own profits. Most of the time it worked out, as in the case of International Harvester and US Steel. In the case of the New Haven it did not.

The New Haven's debt burden came to be a millstone around its neck, to the point where the railroad was unable to fund the maintenance and repairs necessary to ensure public safety. That became painfully obvious when the New Haven suffered a series of gruesome, deadly accidents. One of them, in September 1913, killed twenty-one vacationing New England passengers and injured scores of others.

The public outrage over dangerous service, coupled with Brandeis's relentless media campaign against the New Haven monopoly, demanded the government take legal action. Adding financial insult to physical injury, in December 1913 the New Haven skipped its dividend payment for the first time in forty years, leaving thousands of New Englanders without Christmas money.

J. P. Morgan had been spared that indignity, as by then he was nine months in his grave. His son, Jack Jr., promised to cooperate with government investigators and, as a good faith gesture, resigned his interlocking directorates on thirty corporate boards, including the New Haven's.

To replace Mellen, who resigned in 1913, Jack Morgan brought in a new president and chairman, Howard Elliott, who had succeeded Mellen as president of the Northern Pacific in 1903. Hoping to improve the railroad's public image, Elliott hired the Cravath firm to work out an antitrust settlement with Attorney General James C. McReynolds, who was preparing a civil and criminal case against the New Haven and its directors.

Paul Cravath was already busy negotiating consent decrees with McReynolds in the Union Pacific and International Harvester antitrust cases. As a result, Cravath's partner Walker D. Hines was put in charge of presenting a plan of dissolution to the Justice Department for the New Haven. A mild-mannered, scholarly expert in railroad law, as well as general counsel to the Atchison, Topeka & Santa Fe Railroad, Hines had joined the Cravath firm in 1906 as a replacement for the departing William Guthrie.

It seemed that under new management the New Haven might be able to make a graceful exit from its legal difficulties. But Brandeis pushed for further investigation. He had recently excoriated the New Haven in a series of *Harper's Weekly* articles that he turned into an influential book called *Other People's Money, and How the Bankers Use It*. Building on the Pujo Committee's findings, Brandeis held up the New Haven as the exemplar of what he called "the Curse of Bigness." Now, Brandeis wanted public, Pujo-like hearings to expose the financial chicanery and malfeasance of the old New Haven regime and to embarrass his deceased and longtime nemesis J. P. Morgan.

Brandeis was perhaps the only man the Morgans hated more than Samuel Untermyer. Ironically, earlier in his career as a corporate lawyer, Brandeis had played a part (he would claim unwittingly) in helping the New Haven gain its railroad monopoly by filing a series of crippling lawsuits against a New Haven competitor. A year before launching his attack on the Boston & Maine, Brandeis lobbied against Massachusetts legislation to rein in the monopoly enjoyed by one of his clients, United Shoe Machinery Corporation, in which he was a director and an investor.

But by 1907, having earned millions to secure his independence, Brandeis was a committed anti-monopolist, at least for large corporations. A champion of small business, Brandeis defended the right of small firms to engage in price-fixing and other restrictive practices, such as trade associations, to enable them to better compete with larger concerns. Perhaps not coincidentally, most of Brandeis's Massachusetts clients were small merchants or medium-size manufacturers, not giant conglomerates.

Many of Brandeis's Boston legal colleagues viewed him as ruthless, devious, and two-faced. As with Untermyer, anti-Semitism was always lurking behind such sniping. Mellen, for example, had a New Haven–friendly magazine accuse Brandeis of waging his campaign against the railroad as part of the "age-long struggle between Jew and Gentile." But Brandeis was undeterred. As he wrote to his brother, "The man with the hatchet is the only one who has a chance of winning in the end."

In pressing for additional public hearings on the New Haven, Brandeis also earned the enmity of Attorney General McReynolds, who was afraid witnesses forced to testify under oath would obtain immunity from prosecution, thereby complicating his planned criminal lawsuit. But to Brandeis, educating the public on the evils of monopoly and scandalizing the New Haven were more important. The bitterness McReynolds felt toward Brandeis would carry over to when both men served on the US Supreme Court.

Brandeis got his wish for a renewed investigation. The Senate directed the Interstate Commerce Commission to conduct a full public inquiry into the New Haven. The ICC hired an aggressive, ambitious, headline-hungry special counsel, former governor Joseph Folk of Missouri, to run the hearings. Hines of the Cravath firm appeared for the New Haven and its new management and promised complete cooperation. Stetson, representing J. P. Morgan & Co., made the banking firm's documents relating to the New Haven available to Folk.

One man pleased by these developments was David Lamar, the Wolf of Wall Street, who had been pressing the Senate to investigate the Justice Department's dissolution plan for the New Haven. Lamar, in Washington to avoid arrest in New York following his indictment for impersonating congressmen, was seen watching the debate from the Senate gallery in February 1914.

The ICC investigators faced a formidable task in that the New Haven had a bewildering tangle of 336 subsidiaries created to disguise its financial operations. Many were corporations that did nothing and were headed by dummy directors, such as clerks and secretaries, who were told to sign official documents they neither read nor understood.

One of the early witnesses in the ICC hearings was the gregarious, enormous James Buchanan "Diamond Jim" Brady, consort of the actress Lillian Russell, and a close friend of Mellen's. Brady freely admitted to having served as a dummy stockholder for one of Mellen's companies. Brady, a manufacturer of steel cars and railway supplies, sold millions' worth to the New Haven without the railroad asking for competitive bids. He considered his gifts of a few hundred dollars' worth of diamonds to Mrs. Mellen and the wives of New Haven purchasing agents to be insignificant, and downplayed his own extravagance. "I don't spend much money, but I wear a few jewels," he testified. Both were considerable understatements, and the rest of his testimony shed little light on the railway's financial structure.

By the time Mellen took the stand on May 14, 1914, he was testifying with immunity, just as McReynolds feared. This angered the attorney general so much that he practically tossed Folk out of his office when he learned of his intention to put Mellen under oath. Asked by Folk, seconds after being sworn in, to state his occupation, a smiling Mellen replied, "Helping the Interstate Commerce Commission."

Mellen was taken through the major acquisitions the New Haven had made over the years and, as the *New York Times* reported, "his story of high finance in that railroad filled his hearers with wonderment." He was peppered with questions about the temporary sale of Boston & Maine stock to his friend Billard, which the other directors thought entitled Billard to, at most, his reasonable expenses in the deal, not a $2.7 million profit. But both Mellen and Billard insisted the sale was legitimate.

The transaction that captured the most attention during the hearings, though, concerned an odd little suburban railroad line linking Westchester County and New York City. The ill-fated road was the New York, Westchester & Boston Railway, or Westchester for short.

In 1906 Mellen had been approached with a new railroad proposal by a banker named Oakleigh Thorne, president of the Trust Company of America (TCA). Thorne and his business partner, Marsden Perry, a shady expawnbroker, were investors in a promotional company that held a New York City franchise for construction of a commuter railroad running from Port

Chester, New York, near the Connecticut line, to 133rd Street in the Bronx at the Harlem River. There passengers could detrain and catch the Third Avenue El for downtown.

The Westchester company was floundering financially, mainly because it was embroiled in protracted litigation with a rival company, known as the Port Chester, that claimed a franchise over essentially the same route. Both franchises were of questionable validity, and between them the two companies owned little beyond their rights-of-way and some real estate. But Thorne told Mellen that if the New Haven supplied the funds, he and Perry could buy out their rival, clear up the franchise issues, build the new railroad, and turn it over to the New Haven.

Mellen had no interest in the idea. The New Haven already had a commuter line running from Port Chester to Manhattan's Grand Central Terminal, paralleling the proposed new Westchester route. Mellen saw little point to the New Haven spending millions to build a brand-new railroad that would largely be competing with the New Haven itself.

But at Thorne's insistence, Mellen agreed to take the idea to the New Haven board. To Mellen's surprise, J. P. Morgan immediately embraced the proposal and had a three-man special committee appointed, with himself and Mellen as members, to pursue the plan.

Frank Stetson, appointed as special counsel to the committee, was tasked with drawing up a contract with Thorne and Perry. Under the unusual agreement, the New Haven authorized the two promoters to spend whatever was necessary to acquire for the New Haven two-thirds of the stock of the Westchester and Port Chester companies. They were to be paid a 7.5 percent commission on anything they spent, with no limits. Mellen was instructed to advance the New Haven's money, to be placed in a "Special Account No. 2" at J. P. Morgan & Company, from which Thorne and Perry could draw from time to time. They basically had a blank check.

The whole arrangement was kept secret from the public, from New Haven's stockholders, and even from the rest of the New Haven board. To limit the number of persons in the know, Stetson represented all parties in the deal: the New Haven, Thorne and Perry, and J. P. Morgan. Thorne and Perry had by then incorporated themselves, at Stetson's suggestion, and named their venture the Millbrook Company. Stetson's views on the wisdom of the arrangement are unrecorded, although he did caution Mellen that if Thorne and Perry were unable to clear the franchises, any amounts spent by them in the interim might be money lost.

Between October 1906 and October 1907, drawing on Special Account No. 2, Thorne and Perry spent $11 million buying up shares of the Westchester and Port Chester for the New Haven. Then suddenly, on October 31, 1907, Mellen received a call from Stetson to meet him at Thorne's Trust Company of America office in downtown Manhattan. That night the New Haven exercised its right to rescind the agreement with Thorne and Perry and took over the Millbrook Company from the two men.

Why the abrupt action? As it turned out, the fortunes of the various parties had intersected with the Panic of 1907, which took place that same October. Thorne's Trust Company of America had narrowly averted bankruptcy, saved only by an emergency loan that Morgan put together. But given the TCA's weak financial condition, Thorne was in no position to carry out his contract with the New Haven. The New Haven terminated its agreement with the Millbrook Company, Thorne and Perry resigned, and Special Account No. 2 was closed out.

The New Haven now owned a bushel of stock in the Westchester and Port Chester companies that Mellen thought was worth about "10 cents a pound." All the New Haven had to show for the money it had advanced was an unbuilt railroad, a couple of franchises of doubtful validity running parallel to each other and only a few hundred yards from the New Haven, plus some real estate and minor construction.

At a meeting on November 9, the rest of the New Haven board for the first time learned of the contract with the Millbrook Company, the creation of Special Account No. 2, and the payment of $11 million to Thorne and Perry over the previous year. They approved a brief report and resolution, drafted by Stetson, to ratify what had taken place. Surprisingly, the report contained no itemization of where or how the money was spent. Nonetheless, per their usual practice, the directors rubber-stamped the recommended action without discussion.

But they had severe misgivings. Mellen and the other directors were astonished by the lack of detail in the report, and it was only what Mellen called "cowardice" that prevented them from saying anything during the meeting. Mellen acquiesced in Morgan's judgment because "he was a man of such tremendous force and success... I felt that I was in the wrong in nine cases out of ten when he disagreed with me." Besides, Morgan was in the midst of an emergency—trying to save not only Thorne's trust company but the entire US financial system. It was no time to question the great man's judgment.

After the meeting, though, Mellen met privately with Morgan and told him he thought the report should have provided more information. A visibly agitated Morgan said, "Did not Mr. Stetson draw that vote?" Mellen said yes, he supposed so. "Do you think you know more how it ought to be done than he does?" Morgan asked. Mellen allowed as how he did not, and left feeling humiliated.

A group of the directors who had silently voted their approval gathered in Mellen's office after the meeting to protest. They said they were incredulous that the New Haven had spent so much money on an unbuilt railroad. ("Holy Caesarea Philippi, what in the world have you been doing with $11,000,000 of money?" one director exclaimed to Mellen.) But when Mellen offered to appoint any of them a committee of one to go to Morgan and find out, they said, "Not on your life."

A few weeks after the meeting, Mellen received a letter from Stetson's newly elected law partner and nephew, Allen Wardwell, concerning the Westchester. Mellen wrote a note to himself at the bottom of the letter saying, "I am sick and disgusted with this whole matter. I see nothing but trouble and loss to come from it, and I much fear many reputations will be damaged, and I shall probably in the end be the goat." He was right: The Westchester became a cause célèbre, and with Morgan dead the burden of explaining it fell to Mellen.

By the time of the ICC hearings in 1914, the New Haven had spent $36 million to make the Westchester railroad operational (it had opened in 1912). This was far in excess of the $5 million the directors had originally anticipated it would cost. The railroad was also losing $1.25 million a year, with estimates it would need to earn four and a half times what it was making in order to pay for itself. Mellen told the ICC that the New Haven's going into the Westchester was "an awful blunder, and it seemed to me almost a crime at times."

The ICC inquiry exposed numerous irregularities surrounding the Westchester transaction, including payments of bribes by Mellen to politicians on "Fourteenth Street" (Tammany Hall), to finally clear up the franchise issues. The legal impediments magically disappeared and the two franchises were combined into one by the end of 1909, allowing construction to proceed.

In addition, Thorne and Perry received unusually favorable treatment: They were overpaid on their contract, as alleged by the ICC, by more than $1 million. Yet Stetson, who drafted the contract, advised that the New Haven had no claim it could enforce against the Millbrook Company. "Mr. Stetson said there could not be anything done about it; there was no use pursuing it," Mellen testified.

Thorne and Perry also claimed $500,000 in damages for New Haven's termination of its contract with the Millbrook Company. The two promoters contended they were deprived of the opportunity to finish their work and earn additional commissions. Upon Stetson's recommendation the New Haven paid the pair $275,000 to settle the claim, which Mellen felt they did not deserve.

Folk, the ICC counsel, pressed Mellen on whether he should have accepted Stetson's advice on these matters, seeing as how Stetson had represented both Thorne and Perry and the New Haven. It led to the following colloquy:

MELLEN: Mr. Stetson was a very high-class man.

FOLK: Is he high enough class to represent both sides at the same time?

MELLEN: I would trust him with anything. . . . I do not care who else he represented or looked out for; my interest, in my judgment, would be fully protected by Mr. Stetson. . . . I have unlimited confidence that he would never do or advise a thing that he did not conscientiously believe was right.

· · ·

FOLK: Did you think at that time that his connection to Mr. Thorne as attorney might affect his judgment in any way?

MELLEN: Mr. Stetson has told me many times, and it is a matter of record, that his first duty was to the New Haven Railroad, and Mr. Thorne and Mr. Perry accepted him with the understanding that he was first to look after the New Haven Railroad. . . . When he told me he would stand first for the New Haven Railroad I did not care who he stood second for.

Stetson submitted a statement to the newspapers clarifying that he had only represented Thorne and Perry when they were acting as agents for the New Haven, and that whenever their interests conflicted he acted exclusively for the New Haven or J. P. Morgan & Co. He said he recalled only two transactions in which Thorne and Perry had separate and individual interests and that in those cases they had their own lawyer advising them.

Still, Folk had a point. Stetson had represented all parties in drafting the original documents governing the deal, as to which some ambiguity developed. When disputes arose under the contract, it was legitimate to question whether Stetson's advice to the New Haven as to its rights (or lack thereof) against Thorne and Perry could be completely dispassionate.

No one was ever able to ascertain what happened to the $11 million paid to Thorne and Perry because the Millbrook Company had not supplied vouchers or any other documentation detailing its expenses. And Thorne had burned all his books and records when he retired in 1912—personally tossing them into his furnace—making it impossible to reconstruct what had happened.

Exactly why Morgan seemed so intent on pushing the Westchester project, especially in such secrecy, remains something of a mystery. A related question is why the normally meticulous Stetson crafted a legal setup that was uncharacteristically untidy.

As New Haven chronicler John Weller has pointed out, the Panic of 1907 provides only a partial explanation for what he calls "the most conspicuously wasteful of all the Morgan-Mellen regime's improvident adventures." Although cancellation of the Thorne and Perry contract in 1907 undoubtedly was related to Morgan's efforts to bail out Thorne's trust company, the contract Stetson drafted predated the panic by a year. Thorne and Perry had already spent the $11 million by the time the bank runs started.

The true reasons behind the Westchester initiative must lie in the graves of those most directly involved: Morgan, Stetson, Thorne, and Perry. Most likely, Morgan had a bold vision of the Westchester as a high-speed, state-of-the-art, luxury railroad (which it did become) connecting New York City with one of its most rapidly growing suburban areas. He was willing to spend whatever it took to preempt any future competition in the area. With no imminent competitive threat, though, selling the idea to even as supine a board as the New Haven's might have been difficult. So the project was stealthily pushed through until it became a fait accompli.

Morgan had always looked to Stetson, not to tell him what he could *not* do but to advise him how he *could* do legally what he wanted. Whether Stetson shared any of Mellen's discomfort with the transaction is not known, but he did what was necessary to move the deal forward as Morgan commanded. Highly publicized megadeals such as US Steel needed to be structured tight as a drum; the Westchester was a good bit looser.

When it came time for the New Haven directors to testify about the Westchester deal in 1914, though, they could hardly justify it as being designed to eliminate all conceivable competition. By that time the government was planning an antitrust suit against the New Haven and criminal indictments against its directors, and it would have been a virtual admission of liability to so testify. They needed a better answer. And there was one well-known lawyer who came out of nowhere to offer them one.

—————◦《◎》◦—————

The front-page *New York Times* story on June 4, 1914, reported that the day's ICC hearings on the New Haven "were enlivened by the appearance of William Nelson Cromwell as attorney for the witnesses." When the ICC's Folk finished examining seventy-six-year-old director James Elton from Connecticut, Cromwell simply jumped in and started asking him questions. Although Cromwell was not representing Elton, he said he wanted to help elucidate "one or two items" Elton had not fully recalled.

It quickly became apparent that Cromwell, who represented a few other New Haven directors, was trying to establish a defense for them based on a principle later known as the "business judgment rule." The rule would not become firmly established until a few years later, in a Michigan court case involving Henry Ford. But the idea was, and remains, that absent bad faith or self-dealing, directors of a corporation are not liable for mere errors of judgment in managing the business as long as they exercise their duties honestly and with due care.

Even though the rule did not yet have a name, Cromwell intuitively grasped its significance and took the opportunity to invoke it through Elton's testimony. In his direct testimony to ICC counsel Folk, Elton admitted that he never understood what was going on in the board meetings and that he never asked any questions, instead relying on Mellen and Morgan. He thought the Westchester had been a "really extravagant" undertaking and that when its problems came to light, he realized he "had lived to be almost 76 years old [only] to find out that I belonged to the damn fool family."

But under Cromwell's friendly questioning, Elton suddenly became a font of wisdom. He explained that the Westchester deal had a legitimate rationale behind it—the relief of "congestion" at Grand Central Terminal. The New Haven had to pay Grand Central a service charge for every passenger it delivered into the station and the cost, then up to $3 million, was escalating. The Westchester could help reduce this charge by bringing passengers from as far away as White Plains (on one branch) and New Rochelle and Port Chester (on the other) to the Bronx, where, by walking a couple of blocks or taking a shuttle, they could transfer to the downtown elevated train. Later, following completion of a planned subway extension to East 180th Street, passengers could transfer directly across the platform to the downtown subway.

Because commuters arriving at Grand Central on the New Haven usually had to take a subway downtown anyway to their places of work, it was thought that they would trade a direct ride to Grand Central Terminal for a lower fare and faster, more comfortable ride into the Bronx on the Westchester. From the Bronx, for another nickel, they could take public transportation to a station close to their office. And the New Haven would avoid paying the Grand Central service charge.

Cromwell asked Elton a series of leading questions to develop this argument. "At that time the terminal charges of the Grand Central had grown to be very onerous, and the object was to relieve that, not only to diminish the cost of it, but to facilitate the service?" he asked. "Yes," Elton replied. "So that the acquisition of what we call here the Westchester properties was one of policy then?" Cromwell inquired. "It certainly was. It was not any crazy scheme," Elton testified.

CROMWELL: You were buying for the future, for the development you felt was bound to come?

ELTON: Yes.

CROMWELL: And which you still believe is going to come?

ELTON: Yes, it has got to come.

CROMWELL: It is a part of the great terminal situation in New York?

ELTON: Yes.

CROMWELL: The foothold in the city?

ELTON: Yes.

At that point a recess was called, and when Elton retook the stand, the puzzled ICC chairman said, "Mr. Cromwell, I am not quite clear as to whom you represent in this matter." Cromwell responded that he represented the next witness, director William Skinner, and some other unnamed directors as well, whereupon, before anyone could stop him, he went on questioning Elton. In typical Cromwellian fashion he concluded his examination with a long-winded, almost shamelessly leading question (really a speech) directly tracking the business judgment rule:

CROMWELL: I want to enlighten the record upon some points, and a few only, which I feel the evidence is somewhat lacking on—but I understand from what you have said that you, in passing upon the purchase and all of the purchases which Gov. Folk has brought to your attention, you have been guided, first, by the information brought before the board by President Mellen, with so much care and detail, as I have no doubt he did, as is his well-known characteristic, but you were also governed by your confidence in his judgment, and finally, you were governed by your belief in the prospective value of the properties which you purchased . . . and their increased value as they would come into the New Haven system?

ELTON: Yes.

When Cromwell's client Skinner took the stand, Cromwell brought out additional facts designed to absolve the directors of responsibility for the New Haven fiasco. Skinner testified, for example, that constant agitation and investigations by the states of Massachusetts and Connecticut had hampered the railroad's ability to obtain long-term financing. Cromwell also had Skinner confirm he never personally engaged in any transaction with the New Haven or any of its subsidiaries, had never made a dollar of profit on the New Haven, and as a stockholder had lost money along with everyone else. "In all these years you have been a stockholder [were you] doing what your judgment suggested was the best thing to do at the time?" Cromwell asked in conclusion. "Absolutely," Skinner said.

It was a foregone conclusion the ICC would skewer the New Haven directors in its final report, but Cromwell was locking in testimony and creating a record for inevitable future litigation. And if anything, the ICC report was even more scathing than anticipated. It called the New Haven "one of the most glaring instances of maladministration revealed in all the history of American railroading."

The ICC singled out the Westchester as "a story of the profligate waste of corporate funds." Brushing aside the congestion rationale, the ICC asserted that if the New Haven wanted an entrance into Manhattan via the subway, it could have built a transfer station somewhere in the Bronx connecting commuters to the New Haven's existing lines. Furthermore, the congestion rationale was offered only after the fact, as there was no evidence it was discussed by the New Haven directors at the time of the Westchester purchase. The ICC concluded the Westchester deal was just another Morgan effort to destroy competition.

The ICC reserved its severest criticism for the directors themselves. "The man who holds directors' positions in a dozen corporations may be thoroughly honest in his relations with each, but it is not practicable for him to give the stockholders of each corporation the full benefit of his ability and energy," the ICC stated. "There are too many ornamental directors and too many who have such childlike faith in the man at the head that they are ready to endorse or approve anything he may do." The report called the directors criminally negligent and recommended that the government bring civil and criminal antitrust charges against them, and that they be required to reimburse stockholder losses through civil suits.

Subsequently, the Justice Department sued the New Haven for antitrust violations and indicted twenty-one individuals, all of them present or former directors, including outside lawyer Lewis Cass Ledyard and in-house counsel Edward Robbins (but not Charles Mellen, who had been given immunity for his testimony). Directors Elton and Skinner, because they testified under oath before the ICC, were found entitled to the same immunity as Mellen. Perhaps that had been Cromwell's plan for them all along.

Frank Stetson, who was never a director of the New Haven, and whose only involvement with the railroad had been as counsel to the Westchester special committee, was not sued. Nor was he among the fifty persons named as unindicted coconspirators to violate the antitrust laws—a list that included Mellen, J. P. Morgan, and Thorne and Perry.

The criminal trials ended in acquittals for some directors and hung juries for five others, including Ledyard and Robbins, who had assured the directors they were not violating the antitrust laws. The government said it would retry the five but never did. A $150 million stockholder suit against the directors was eventually settled for $2.5 million.

After President Wilson instructed the filing of an antitrust suit against the New Haven itself, the railroad entered into a consent decree in October 1914 to dispose of various properties. Cravath partner Hines negotiated it with the government. Under the consent decree the Boston & Maine was to have been sold, but it never was.

The Westchester did become the gold-plated railroad its promoters had envisioned, but it never made money and went into bankruptcy in 1937. The popularity of the automobile with suburbanites, which J. P. Morgan had not foreseen, contributed to the Westchester's downfall. The Bronx never became the commercial center some had anticipated based on the continual northward movement of Manhattan business. And Westchester commuters did not like ending their train ride in the middle of the Bronx, only to have to take a long subway ride into Manhattan. They preferred emerging in the majestic new Grand Central that opened in 1913, replacing the outmoded terminal.

Despite the mixed results of later prosecutions and lawsuits, the New Haven scandal was a seminal event in the history of the Progressive Era. The ICC report vindicated Louis Brandeis in his warnings against interlocking corporate directorates, banker control of industrial corporations, financial recklessness, and corporate bigness itself. The New Haven provided the final impetus for passage of the last reform legislation of the era—the Clayton Antitrust Act of 1914 and the Federal Trade Commission Act of that same year. Both acts, supported by President Wilson as part of his New Freedom program, were designed to add teeth and greater specificity to the Sherman Act and to give the government greater power to stop monopolies before they formed.

The Clayton Act, in addition to outlawing interlocking directorates among competing companies, declared three specific practices illegal: (1) price discrimination; (2) corporate mergers with competing companies; and (3) exclusive dealing (tying) contracts, in which a seller conditions the sale of one of its products on the buyer also buying a different (tied) product. However, these three prohibitions had caveats: They applied only when a court determined that the challenged practice might tend to substantially lessen competition or create a monopoly in any line of business.

The FTC Act created the Federal Trade Commission, a five-member body appointed by the president with Senate approval. A sort of detective agency, the FTC was given subpoena power to investigate alleged "unfair methods of competition" (an undefined term), and to issue cease and desist orders, subject to court review. The commissioners were to be experts who could gather information and assist the attorney general in crafting antitrust consent decrees and shaping policy.

The Clayton and FTC Acts were the products of political compromise and, as such, did not go as far as some corporate critics such as Louis Brandeis would have liked. After being watered down, neither statute contained criminal penalties, which remained available only under the Sherman Act. Shareholders and other private parties could sue under the Clayton Act but not under the FTC Act. And the key language of the statutes—"unfair" methods of competition, and practices with a "tendency" to "substantially lessen" competition—were not much more specific than the rule of reason standard under the Sherman Act.

But when the FTC and Clayton Acts became law in September and October 1914, respectively, the twenty-five-year raging national debate over federal antitrust policy came to an end. The new laws contained something for everyone. They were consistent with Brandeis's refusal to accept monopolies as inevitable and gave the government new powers to proactively prevent them. Frank Stetson, Victor Morawetz, and other corporate lawyers had wanted more concrete guidance for their clients under the antitrust laws, and the supplemental legislation provided a measure of additional clarity.

Roosevelt adherents got their federal commission and greater publicity for corporate practices, but not federal licensing of corporations, preclearance of their contracts, or price controls. The courts remained the ultimate arbiters of what was fair and reasonable under the antitrust laws, the position most vigorously pushed by Taft and Wickersham in years past.[*]

By the end of 1914 the Progressive Era, in terms of big business reform, had come to a close. President Wilson declared, "The antagonism between business and government is over. The Government and businessmen are ready to meet each other half way in a common effort to square business methods with both public opinion and the law." After passage of the FTC and Clayton Acts, Frank Stetson, once a foe of federal antitrust legislation, publicly stated that the Wilson administration "deserves unmistakable approval."

Thereafter, the Trust Question receded from the center of national politics, although it remained an issue for lawyers to litigate, case by case, in the years to come. In no presidential election since 1912 has federal antitrust policy been the dominant, or even a major, issue. The Clayton and FTC Acts have been amended from time to time, either to close loopholes or to add new protections or exemptions. The enthusiasm for antitrust enforcement has waxed and waned over many presidential administrations. And the names of the players have changed: Google and Amazon have replaced US Steel and Standard Oil as the largest corporate behemoths. But the fundamental legal regime established in 1914—over which lawyers like Stetson, Cravath, Wickersham, and Untermyer had fought for so many years—remains in place today.

———— ◦(◉)◦ ————

For the white shoe corporate lawyers who came to prominence during the Progressive Era, the year 1914 saw several other milestones. William Hornblower became the first of that group to die, at age sixty-three, just a few weeks after being appointed to the New York Court of Appeals. The highest court in New York, it was then second in influence only to the US Supreme Court, to which Hornblower had been nominated but denied confirmation. That was not his only disappointment in life: His first wife died young, he

[*]The group that came up short was organized labor. The original Clayton Act, despite some vague assurances, did not give labor unions the clear, unqualified exemption from the antitrust laws they had sought. Later Supreme Court decisions did create an exemption for most union activities.

lost a teenage daughter, and his son, a published poet, committed suicide a year before Hornblower's own death. Yet Hornblower was happily remarried to his late wife's sister, enjoyed a stellar career, and left a million-dollar estate to his wife and surviving son, who was also a lawyer and poet. The honorary pallbearers at Hornblower's funeral included Frank Stetson and George Wickersham. Paul Cravath, who had begun his career working under Hornblower at the Carter firm, was present as well.*

Cravath suffered another setback in 1914 when, for the second time on the same site, his Long Island home was destroyed by fire. The sixty-room structure burned, at a loss of $250,000, while Cravath was in Europe. Afterward he sold the land and rebuilt a third Veraton, again named for his daughter, on another nearby property in Locust Valley. He threw himself into the project with his customary energy and with the same fierce passion for detail and perfection he brought to his legal work. He feuded with architects and landscapers and repeatedly fired workmen who did not satisfy him. But he ended up with the house he wanted: a beautifully crafted, neo-Georgian, redbrick mansion, with lavish gardens to satisfy his growing hobby of horticulture, a stable for his show horses, and a large, terraced music room to reflect his interest in opera.

On August 15, 1914, the Panama Canal opened for traffic, almost twenty years after William Nelson Cromwell had begun his instrumental work on the project. Cromwell did not make the opening ceremony, but his old nemesis, Philippe Bunau-Varilla, went to the isthmus to cross the canal on a steamer a fortnight before the official inauguration, to which he had not been invited.

And on August 3, 1914, the same day that Bunau-Varilla crossed the canal, Germany and France declared war on each other.

---

*Hornblower's law firm, which he formed after leaving Carter's, evolved into Willkie Farr & Gallagher, named for Wendell Willkie, who joined the old Hornblower firm after losing the 1940 presidential election to Franklin Roosevelt. It carries the same name today.

Chapter 18

Preparedness

After Great Britain entered the war against Germany on August 4, President Wilson formally proclaimed the United States neutral and said Americans "must be impartial in thought as well as in action." That was something Paul Cravath and his white shoe brethren would never be able to abide.

By ancestry, friendships, travel experience, and worldview, the leading Anglo-Saxon lawyers of Wall Street unreservedly favored the Allied cause from the beginning of the war. They perceived the war as a struggle between good and evil—between the liberal Western democracies, represented by England and France, and the despotic, militaristic German and Austro-Hungarian Empires. To men such as Cravath, Elihu Root, George Wickersham, and William Nelson Cromwell, one side was right, the other wrong, and there was no room for neutrality.

After the German army overran neutral Belgium and invaded France, the top Wall Street lawyers gave early and often to various charitable causes: Belgian relief, French war orphans, blinded soldiers, and displaced Poles, among others. Cromwell, semiretired by this time, spent most of the World War I years in France, a country he loved and admired since his Panama Canal days. He gave money to build homes for the wounded and a school for four hundred war-orphaned children. To make books available for those blinded in the war, he had a braille press installed in the old mansion of the Clermont-Tonnerre noble family, near the Arc de Triomphe in Paris.

William Guthrie, a fellow Francophile and fluent in the language from his early education in France, organized the American Society for the Relief of French War Orphans. It sent more than $400,000 to France before American entry in the war. Guthrie was appointed a Grand Officer of the

French Legion of Honor, as was Cromwell, who eventually received the Grand Cross, the Legion's supreme award.

The culturally connected Cravaths raised money in the United States by bringing in international stars. In November 1914, to aid destitute women and children of the world, Paul Cravath helped arrange a benefit theater performance starring British actress Stella (Mrs. Patrick) Campbell, who originated the role of Eliza Doolittle in George Bernard Shaw's *Pygmalion*. The following April, Cravath's wife, Agnes, sponsored a benefit concert for the impoverished families of Parisian musicians, with Pablo Casals as the guest cellist. Cravath later raised money to aid the families of British lawyers who were fighting and dying in Europe for what he called "the principles of liberty for which it has long been the glory of our profession to sustain."

But money and charity were not enough. Hopes that the war would be short were quickly dashed, and the staunchest Allied partisans argued that the United States needed to immediately build up its naval and land forces in preparation for America's likely entry into the contest. The Preparedness Movement, as it was called, came into flower in early 1915. It was led almost entirely by prominent Republicans, including ex-president Theodore Roosevelt, Elihu Root, General Leonard Wood, Massachusetts senator Henry Cabot Lodge, and Henry L. Stimson, secretary of war under Taft and a law partner and protégé of Root's.

Among the other leading Wall Street lawyers advocating preparedness were Cravath, Wickersham (by then back in private practice), and eighty-three-year-old Joseph Choate, the former US ambassador to the United Kingdom. Jack Morgan, head of his father's old firm, was unabashedly pro-Allied and interventionist, as were the other Morgan partners.

These and like-minded men came to form the "Atlanticist" foreign policy establishment of the United States—primarily upper-class lawyers, bankers, academics, and East Coast politicians committed to what has been called "Anglophile internationalism." They were a small but influential group of Anglo-Saxon Protestants who believed the United States had inherited England's role as the conciliator, and if necessary, enforcer, of international disputes. Although some of them, such as Roosevelt, Root, and Lodge, had long been nationalist-interventionists in foreign policy, for others, such as Cravath, World War I served as what one study has called "an epiphany, triggering previously dormant Anglophile and internationalist leanings."

As a group they favored universal conscripted military service for every eighteen-year-old male, a buildup of the woefully small United States army, and an officer corps drawn from the "best" professional men. Almost spontaneously, the preparedness advocates organized a privately funded summer military camp at Plattsburgh, in upstate New York, to train potential officers.

When the first camp opened there in August 1915, eleven hundred bankers, lawyers, doctors, and businessmen—a number of them former Ivy League college football stars—showed up for training. They spent ten-hour days on the shores of Lake Champlain, drilling with Springfield rifles and bayonets, digging trenches with picks and shovels, and performing KP duty. They hiked the Adirondacks and learned cavalry, field artillery, and military engineering.

The preparedness campaign, along with the highly publicized "Plattsburg Movement," as it was then known, were annoyances to President Wilson during the early stages of the European War. They violated the spirit, if not the letter, of his neutrality policy.

As a US senator, in an era when bipartisanship was still the norm in foreign policy, Elihu Root had to be careful not to be seen as flouting Wilson's policy. But he was not at all neutral, believing instead that Germany was "the great disturber of peace in the world." Friends pleaded with Root to make his feelings known, but Root was waiting for the right moment, which he was sure would come. Root laid blame for the war wholly on Germany and was convinced most Americans believed likewise.

Although Charles Evans Hughes's position on the Supreme Court prevented him from speaking out publicly, he, too, was deeply sympathetic to the Allied cause. Hughes privately criticized Wilson for not acting more vigorously against Germany and for not adequately readying the United States for war. Hughes's son would later become an enthusiastic recruit at the Plattsburgh training camp.

Henry Stimson, as a former (and future) war secretary and secretary of state, supported Wilson on neutrality early in the war but still advocated preparedness. And his loyalties were clear. The Allies were fighting for

Western civilization, he wrote, while Germany was trying to destroy that very civilization.

Although almost all the luminaries among Wall Street's lawyers favored military preparedness, if not immediate American intervention, there were exceptions. In March 1915, Frank Stetson was one of thirty signers of a letter from Andrew Carnegie's Church Peace Union, appealing to the churches and clergy of America not to be partisan and to avoid pressing for increased armaments. "I am a pacifist," Stetson wrote to a debate organizer who wanted Stetson to speak in favor of the United States doubling its standing army. Stetson responded that he was opposed to the increase, although to the extent the country maintained an army he thought it should be efficient. Stetson also was a vice president of Carnegie's New York Peace Society, which advocated a postwar body to enforce the peace.

Like millions of German Americans, Samuel Untermyer sympathized with his ancestral homeland. In 1903 he had praised German industrial progress and called Kaiser Wilhelm "the most remarkable of all captains of industry of modern times." German protectionism, Untermyer said, had shielded its young industries while they grew strong, placing the country in close competition with the United States for future world economic leadership. By contrast, Untermyer claimed, Britain's free trade policy had ruined its domestic industries.

When war broke out in August 1914, Untermyer and his family were vacationing in the spa town of Carlsbad in Austria-Hungary. After arriving safely in London, he spent two weeks helping thousands of stranded Americans obtain safe passage home. On his arrival in New York on the White Star liner *Baltic*, Untermyer gave an interview to the *New York Times* in which he blamed Russian mobilization for provoking the war and asserted "there was no more ardent champion of peace than Germany." More pro-German than anti-English, Untermyer trained his fire on Russia, Britain's ally, because of the Russian czar's anti-Jewish pogroms.

Before America's entry into the war, Untermyer strongly supported American neutrality and opposed the Preparedness Movement. He also lent his considerable lawyering and marketing skills to the German cause. Untermyer became an unpaid counselor to the German embassy in Washington and secretly assisted its propaganda campaign, once arranging for the German ambassador to state in an interview that a break in diplomatic relations between the United States and Germany would mean war, which helped extend relations for several months.

Untermyer also represented the German government in investing in American newspapers to influence public opinion and in trying to buy others, including the *New York Sun*, which ended up going to another purchaser. Untermyer was identified as one of the German government's most important American friends in papers found inside a briefcase stolen from a German agent while he was riding an elevated train in New York. The German ambassador and his staff were also frequent and honored guests at Greystone, Untermyer's Hudson River estate.

Although most Americans came to view Germany as the aggressor in World War I, they remained firmly in the neutrality camp for more than two years. German Americans, Irish Americans (who detested the British), and Scandinavian American farmers, particularly in the upper Midwest, opposed United States involvement in the European war. So did most rural citizens, women, and church leaders. Anglophile interventionists such as Cravath were still just a vocal minority.

The sinking of the passenger liner *Lusitania* in May 1915 by a German U-boat, with the loss of 1,198 lives, 128 of them American, turned public opinion further against Germany, but not to the point that Americans desired to join the war. Root, who had retired from the Senate in March, believed the United States should have entered the war on the Allied side after the *Lusitania* outrage, although he continued to keep his views private. But Wilson, despite issuing stern warnings to Germany, declared the United States "too proud to fight," and for the time being that view prevailed.

To many Americans, the elite Anglophile internationalists and their Preparedness Movement were synonymous with warmongering. And with something else: war profiteering. Antiwar critics pointed out that companies such as US Steel, Bethlehem Steel, and Westinghouse, controlled by bankers such as J. P. Morgan & Co. and represented by lawyers such as Cravath, were profiting enormously from munitions contracts with the Allies and would make even more money if the United States were to join the conflict. The lucrative contracts also sent these companies' stock prices soaring. No embargo prevented American manufacturers from selling munitions to warring countries, but war contracts did raise issues under Wilson's neutrality policy. Cravath's inclination was to advise his clients to go ahead with the deals without examining the question too closely.

But Cravath's client connections drew public scorn, particularly in the isolationist Midwest. In June 1915, as a member of the Navy League, Cravath was pushing the government to raise $500 million to build a greater army and navy. Noting Cravath's presence at a Navy League luncheon, a Minnesota newspaper observed that Westinghouse, which made shrapnel and shells, and on whose board Cravath sat, was "one of the deadliest of the 'war stocks'" on the stock exchange.

The former governor of South Dakota also attacked Cravath for his Westinghouse connection, as did Wisconsin senator Robert La Follette, who sarcastically referred to the Navy League as a group of "dollar-scarred heroes." A labor union newspaper in Duluth, Minnesota, said that "'Preparedness' fairly reeks with the smell of private profits." The money trust had become the "war trust," the paper wrote, and Cravath and the manufacturers he represented were seeking a government market for their "engines of death."

Frank Stetson's pacifism did not insulate him from similar criticism. An Illinois editorial writer called out Stetson as one of the Wall Street men profiting directly or indirectly from munitions sales. This was a reference to Stetson's help in arranging J. P. Morgan & Co.'s $500 million loan to the British and French governments, the biggest foreign loan in history and the largest securities issue ever floated in the United States. England and France used the money raised from US investors to buy war supplies from US manufacturers. The Morgan firm also served as sole fiscal agent for the British and French governments in purchasing the US-made materials on their behalf. Perhaps because he was too busy, or his firm lacked expertise in the area, Stetson turned down the chance to represent the House of Morgan in its purchasing role. The legal work went instead to the Wall Street firm of White & Case, whose cofounder had close ties to a Morgan partner.

Stetson did not decline the work out of any philosophical objection to munitions sales. As a member of New York's Peace Society, he publicly opposed pro-German proposals for an embargo of armament shipments from the United States to the Allied nations. Stetson argued, curiously, that an embargo would actually increase the world arms race because if foreign countries were prevented from buying war supplies from overseas, they would have to invest enormous sums to create their own. Whether Stetson's position was influenced by his admitted fondness for England or, as one critic alleged, his close relations with the Morgan firm can only be pondered.

On the pro-German side of the issue, Samuel Untermyer argued, although unsuccessfully, that if munitions sales to the Allies could not be banned, they should be heavily taxed. Untermyer's wife, Minnie, who was active in the peace movement, also thought it unfair that England, while blockading humanitarian aid to Germany, was free to buy war supplies from overseas. She urged, also without success, that the US government obtain Great Britain's consent to lift the British blockade to permit dried milk to be sent to starving German babies.

As expected, virtually all the Morgan-arranged $500 million Anglo-French loan was plowed back into American steel mills, gunpowder plants, tool works, and other plants whose smokestacks belched "as they fed the slaughter in Europe," wrote Frederick Lewis Allen. The transaction helped stimulate the American economy and began to turn the United States from a debtor to a creditor nation. But because it tied American money so closely to Allied war fortunes, it spurred feelings by some that the Morgan bank and its representatives had blood on their hands.

Some even charged that the entire war was undertaken so J. P. Morgan & Co. could make money off it. Allen Wardwell, who worked on the Anglo-French loan as a partner in Stetson's firm, thought the claim ridiculous. "There isn't much doubt where the sympathy of the Morgan firm was, or for that matter of most American bankers and businessmen," he later said, "but the war wasn't created for their own interest." Still, the charges stung, and when the Morgan firm began receiving a flood of hate mail, Jack Morgan vetoed a proposal by Paul Cravath to form a political action committee to propagandize for the Allied cause.

Wilson's secretary of state, the pacifist William Jennings Bryan, told the president that the Morgan loan was inconsistent with the spirit of neutrality, and Wilson initially agreed. But after the *Lusitania* sinking, Bryan resigned in protest over what he considered the overly belligerent tone of Wilson's protest notes to Germany. Bryan also objected that Wilson's messages were unaccompanied by requests for mediation or simultaneous warnings against England's use of passenger ships to carry explosives, as the *Lusitania* had done.

Bryan's replacement was the hawkish State Department legal advisor Robert Lansing, an authority on international law and an Anglophile. Lansing convinced Wilson to view the Anglo-French loan as providing "credits" for American goods. At least as a semantic matter, that placed the aid outside the neutrality policy's prohibition on loans to foreign governments.

Lansing, whose father-in-law, John W. Foster, was a former US secretary of state, was also the uncle of a future secretary of state. And Lansing's nephew, John Foster Dulles, was destined to become the most important successor to William Nelson Cromwell as leader of the influential Sullivan & Cromwell law firm.

It would have been difficult to find a more logical man than John Foster Dulles to spearhead the high-powered corporate and international law practice William Nelson Cromwell had built. Dulles's background was similar to that of many top white shoe lawyers of Wall Street of the previous generation, but more cosmopolitan. Like Stetson, Root, and Charles Evans Hughes, Dulles hailed from upstate New York, having been born in Watertown in 1888. Like Hughes's and Cravath's, his father was a Protestant minister.

But Dulles entered a world of international adventure at an earlier age than any of them. His father invited many missionary guests to their home, where Dulles heard tales of faraway, exotic lands. His grandfather, John W. Foster, was minister to Mexico, then Russia, then Spain, before he was appointed secretary of state under Benjamin Harrison. In that position, Foster helped bring about the overthrow of the Hawaiian monarchy under Queen Liliuokalani.

After leaving office, John W. Foster began a private international law practice in Washington, DC, lobbying for large corporations that sought global trade favors, representing foreign legations, and serving presidents on diplomatic missions. It was the same kind of work Sullivan & Cromwell performed with regard to the Panama Canal.

Young Foster (the name Dulles went by) grew up spending many hours at the feet, and later the dinner table, of his grandfather at the Foster mansion near Dupont Circle in Washington. He met presidents, Supreme Court justices, foreign ambassadors, and State Department officials and became schooled in high-level politics and diplomacy. At age nineteen, he attended the Second Hague Peace Conference in the Netherlands, serving as a secretary-clerk for the Chinese delegation, which his grandfather represented.

The following year Foster graduated valedictorian from Princeton, where he took a constitutional government class from Professor Woodrow Wilson, then president of the university. After a year of graduate study at the Sorbonne, Foster disappointed his parents by not entering the Presbyterian ministry, but the solemn and pious young man resolved to become a "Christian lawyer." Eschewing the typical Ivy League route, he chose to attend George Washington University Law School so he could live with his grandfather and take advantage of his Washington connections.

The decision almost derailed Foster's career. After law school, Foster wanted to work in New York for a prestigious Wall Street firm, preferably one with an international practice. But when he went to apply for a job, no white shoe firm would hire him. The elite firms considered only law school graduates from Harvard, Yale, or Columbia. But John W. Foster, who had clerked for Sullivan & Cromwell's senior cofounder, Algernon Sydney Sullivan, in Ohio in the 1850s, appealed to Cromwell on his grandson's behalf. "Isn't the memory of an old association enough to give this young man a chance?" the former secretary of state asked. Cromwell overruled his partners, who had rejected Foster's application, and hired him as clerk in 1911 at $12.50 a week.

Dulles found the everyday work of a young office lawyer boring, and he did not much enjoy spending late nights dissecting esoteric points of mortgage law and similar subjects. But he loved traveling to places like the British West Indies (where, however, he contracted malaria) and representing US clients with interests in foreign ventures such as tropical fruit companies,

Cuban banks, and Peruvian mines. He gained an understanding of the global economy and the benefits of free international trade.

When World War I broke out, Foster went to Europe to arrange war-risk insurance for Sullivan & Cromwell clients such as the American Cotton Oil Company and the Holland America Line. He represented the American subsidiary of German drug manufacturer Merck & Co., and also looked after the interests of G. H. Mumm & Co., a German-owned producer of French champagne. He counseled French banks conducting war finance operations in the United States. John Foster Dulles was becoming his law firm's next William Nelson Cromwell, and he would spend most of the next forty years developing a Cromwellian practice.

While staying in London, Dulles concluded Germany was guilty of "ruthless murdering and torturing [of] noncombatants—women, children and neutrals." He was enraged by the *Lusitania* sinking, which took the life of a Sullivan & Cromwell client, a millionaire hotelier whose widow made it back to America with Dulles's help. Dulles was thus entirely in sympathy with the pro-Allied leanings of his "Uncle Bert" Lansing, the secretary of state. In time, Lansing would select his nephew for some important secret US war missions, providing early training for Dulles's future career as a foreign intriguer. The State Department intelligence operation Lansing developed would also employ Dulles's younger brother, Allen, himself a future Sullivan & Cromwell lawyer and, eventually, America's head spy.

⸻

"It is hard just now to keep interested in anything except the war in Europe," Elihu Root wrote to Henry Stimson after the outbreak of hostilities. Indeed, the war consumed Americans' attention and dwarfed almost all other issues. Still, Root, Stimson, and other Wall Street lawyers found time for other matters of importance. One was the question of women's suffrage.

In 1915, Root presided over a New York State constitutional convention to consider a series of amendments, mostly designed to improve state government through modest reforms. George Wickersham was the majority floor leader for the amendments, which Root described as a "conservative constructive program." One of the proposed amendments was to give New York women the right to vote. Root was personally opposed to the amendment but agreed to have it submitted separately to the state's voters in a November referendum.

As early as 1894, Root was on record as opposing women's suffrage. He contended that politics involved contention and agitation, which were "adverse to the true character of woman. . . . Woman in strife becomes hard, harsh, unlovable, repulsive; as far removed from that gentle creature to whom we all owe allegiance and to whom we confess submission."

Although such words today sound at best antiquated, the sentiment behind them was not uncommon even among the highly educated, generally broad-minded members of the New York bar. When the question was placed on the state ballot in 1915, Henry Stimson wrote that suffrage was "not a natural right" akin to life, liberty, or the pursuit of happiness. He argued that giving women the vote would make government less efficient and competent because women totally lacked political and business experience. " 'To be the man of the family' means learning the hard lessons of self-support and protection of others which are the foundation of government," Stimson wrote. Even without the vote, he maintained, "the peculiar capacities of woman—her keener sympathy and special knowledge of various matters—can be brought to the assistance of government with sufficient influence to produce the needed reforms."

George Wickersham, Frank Stetson, and William Guthrie also opposed the suffrage amendment in a letter they signed, along with Stimson, three days before the November referendum. Only a small minority of women wanted the vote, they further asserted. Although accurate polling did not exist then, it was certainly the case that many women were anti-suffrage. Stetson's wife, Elizabeth, was a longtime member of the New York State Association Opposed to Woman Suffrage, an influential women's group on whose all-male advisory board Stetson served.

The Stetsons supported many worthy causes, such as the State Charities Aid Association, the Prison Association, the Women's Hospital, the Lincoln Hospital and Home (for poor people of color), the New York Babies Hospital, and the Legal Aid Society, which made legal representation available to indigents. Stetson favored giving Episcopal women the vote in parish elections, and he supported allowing women into Columbia Law School. But when it came to women's suffrage he was decidedly retrogressive.

Paul Cravath's views on women's suffrage are unrecorded, as are William Nelson Cromwell's. But Cromwell did contribute materially, if indirectly, to the pro-suffrage cause through his successful defense of the will of Mrs. Frank Leslie—the surviving wife of a well-known illustrated magazine publisher—who died in 1914. Her will, drafted by Cromwell, left $1.7 million to her friend, the suffragist leader Carrie Chapman Catt, to further the cause. Relatives challenged the will, alleging among things that Mrs. Leslie, who claimed to be a baroness, was in fact the illegitimate daughter of slaves. But the bulk of the estate ended up going to the suffrage movement.

New York State voters rejected the suffrage amendment in November 1915 by 57 to 43 percent, and the other proposed constitutional changes, which attracted a variety of opposition, were defeated as well. But the suffrage amendment would pass in 1917 with 54 percent of the vote. It obtained a boost from the money the suffragists eventually received from Mrs. Leslie's estate.

<hr>

Two months after the 1915 referendum, Woodrow Wilson, fresh off his honeymoon with the second Mrs. Wilson, nominated Louis Brandeis to fill a vacancy on the United States Supreme Court. The news came as a thunderbolt. Virulent opposition formed immediately from Wall Street and conservative Republicans, who accused Wilson of choosing a radical to curry favor with progressives for his upcoming reelection campaign. Six former presidents of the American Bar Association, including Root and William Howard Taft, signed a letter stating that taking into consideration Brandeis's "reputation, character and professional career," he was unfit to serve on the Supreme Court. Root had drafted the protest at the behest of George Wickersham, who, like Taft, had never forgiven Brandeis for publicly embarrassing them by exposing their backdating of a report during the 1911 Ballinger-Pinchot affair.

Taft, who had hoped to receive the nomination himself, called Brandeis "a muckraker, an emotionalist for his own purposes, a socialist . . . a hypocrite . . . who is utterly unscrupulous." Personal animus, as opposed to Brandeis's religion, seems to have motivated Taft, who, as president, had appointed the first Jewish judge to a federal judgeship. Later, as chief justice,

Taft would develop a warm personal relationship with Brandeis, although they would clash over their political and judicial philosophies.

Root's reasons for opposing Brandeis are more difficult to discern. He, too, had sparred with Brandeis during the Ballinger controversy and resented what he perceived as Brandeis's attacks on Taft's integrity. Root claimed Brandeis lacked the moral standards a Supreme Court justice should possess. That reasoning sounds suspiciously like a cover for anti-Semitism. Brandeis certainly could be ruthless and antagonistic, but so were many of the white shoe lawyers in defense of their clients' interests. Of course, Republican conservatives such as Root likely would have objected to any nominee who held Brandeis's liberal, antibusiness views. The *Wall Street Journal* predictably was against confirmation, but so was Adolph Ochs's *New York Times*, which had endorsed Wilson for president in 1912 and would do so again in 1916. The *Times* deplored the Brandeis nomination because of what it termed his "preconceived and known opinions" advocating social justice.

Wilson had wanted to appoint Brandeis as his attorney general in 1913 but decided not to in the face of Wall Street opposition, giving the post to James C. McReynolds instead. This time Wilson did not back down. After a contentious nomination fight that lasted several months, Brandeis was finally confirmed on June 1, 1916, by a Senate vote of 47–22. He took the bench as the nation's first Jewish Supreme Court justice, serving alongside his old nemesis McReynolds. A true anti-Semite, McReynolds did not speak to Brandeis for three years after the latter's appointment, and once refused to be photographed next to him when a group photograph of the court was taken.

The same week Brandeis took his seat on the bench, Charles Evans Hughes stepped down from his. Reluctantly, as he would always insist, and only out of a sense of duty, Hughes accepted the Republican nomination for president to run against Wilson. He was concerned about the precedent it would set for a sitting Supreme Court justice to run for president, but unlike in 1912, when his name was mentioned as a compromise candidate, he did not say he would decline the 1916 nomination if it were tendered.

The Hughes forces beat back all challengers at the convention, including Elihu Root, who finally, also against his inclination, had allowed friends to put his name forward as the "ablest living American." Hughes received important support from George Wickersham, who conceded Root's superior qualifications but doubted he could win in November. Theodore Roosevelt, who secured the Bull Moose Party nomination again, had hoped to be nominated by the Republicans as well. But Roosevelt's brand of progressivism had run out of steam, and he opted not to make another third-party bid. Instead he endorsed Hughes, although without great enthusiasm, and the Progressive Party disintegrated.

Hughes was widely regarded as the best candidate to unite the more conservative wing of the Republican Party, represented by Root, and the progressives who had bolted the party for Roosevelt in 1912. In his six years on the Supreme Court, Hughes had compiled a moderately progressive record and authored several landmark decisions that strengthened federal regulatory power and weakened the underpinnings of laissez-faire capitalism.

His most influential opinions were in a pair of railroad rate cases—the *Minnesota Rate* cases and the *Shreveport* case—which expanded the reach of the Constitution's Commerce Clause and established the supremacy of federal jurisdiction over the states in matters of interstate transportation. Samuel Untermyer applauded Hughes's *Shreveport* decision as one of "far-reaching importance" and "a long step in the direction of effective Government control." As an advocate of states' rights, Frank Stetson said the decision, although logical, presaged a broadening of central power beyond what the writers of the Constitution had contemplated. Both men's views were prescient, as the railroad rate cases laid the groundwork for later Supreme Court rulings sustaining New Deal legislation under the Commerce Clause, such as the National Labor Relations Act.

Hughes also took a generally liberal attitude on social welfare legislation. He wrote majority opinions upholding a statute prohibiting the employment of children under sixteen years of age in certain hazardous occupations and a California law forbidding the employment of women in selected establishments for more than eight hours a day. He authored a case striking down an Alabama "peonage" statute that authorized jailing a person who failed to fulfill a contract for personal services after accepting advance payment; Hughes held that the law violated the involuntary servitude clause of the

Thirteenth Amendment. Hughes also wrote the famous *Dr. Miles* antitrust case that forbade manufacturers from requiring their wholesale dealers or retailers to sell their products above a specified minimum price—known as vertical resale price maintenance. The case stood for nearly a century before being overruled in 2007.

Supreme Court historian Alexander Bickel has called Hughes "a leader, a fresh and in some ways a liberated intellect" during his tenure as an associate justice. But it would not be the relative liberalism or progressivism of Hughes and Wilson, or their views on antitrust, that dominated the 1916 election. The overriding issue was the World War and whether the United States should enter it. Wilson's supporters campaigned on the slogan "He kept us out of war." They asserted that Hughes, if elected, would embroil the country in the bloody European conflict, or maybe in Mexico, where Wilson had sent General John Pershing to capture Pancho Villa.

A popular American song of the day was "I Didn't Raise My Boy to Be a Soldier." Hughes tried to downplay the issue of war and focused on the more neutral issue of preparedness, which was gaining traction. Theodore Roosevelt was almost daily chiding Wilson for an inadequate national defense. Continued German provocations at sea prompted Secretary of State Lansing to call for a severance of diplomatic relations, which Wilson resisted. Lansing's twenty-eight-year-old nephew, Sullivan & Cromwell associate John Foster Dulles, wrote a stinging letter to the *New York Times* accusing Germany of repudiating its pledge not to sink merchant vessels.

Under pressure to act, Wilson gradually began such steps as expanding the National Guard and creating a Reserve Officers' Training Corps. He also called for a day of special patriotic exercises to take place on June 14, 1916—Flag Day. The message in celebration after celebration that month would be twofold: "Americanism" and preparedness.

Wilson was likely influenced to issue his proclamation by a huge Citizens' Preparedness Parade in New York City on May 13, 1916. In what was called the largest civilian parade ever held in the country, an estimated 145,000 people from all nationalities and walks of life—businessmen, factory workers, farmers—including many women, marched up Broadway and Fifth Avenue for twelve hours, sixteen abreast, led by an enormous, ninety-five-foot flag, to demand preparedness.

At 6:40 P.M. a lawyers' division passed the reviewing stand, where Mayor John Purroy Mitchel, General Leonard Wood, Elihu Root, and Joseph Choate watched. Among the frock-coated, silk-hatted attorneys parading before them was one whose attendance seemed curious: the self-described pacifist Francis Lynde Stetson. Recently turned seventy, Stetson was perhaps just showing solidarity with his longtime bar colleagues.

Paul Cravath was not listed among the many marchers, but if he was absent it was not for lack of interest in the Preparedness Movement. Indeed, he would soon make his commitment known in the most concrete manner. In July he went to London to study war conditions in England. The more he saw of the army that was training there, the more ambitious he became to see the fighting in France. On August 17 he boarded a military train at Charing Cross Station, then crossed the English Channel on a transport ship along with three thousand soldiers, officers, nurses, and surgeons. They were convoyed by two torpedo destroyers and landed in Boulogne, near Calais.

Ever since February, the largest and longest battle of the war had been taking place near a small town in northeastern France. With the battle still in progress, Cravath decided that however dangerous it might be, he needed to view the war up close and personally. He was taken by a gray army motorcar to British General Headquarters at an undisclosed location in northern France. He surveyed thirty square miles of deserted battlefield and surrounding farms and villages, where he saw the haunted looks on the faces of women and children in mourning. And then he moved closer to the fighting, eventually making his way to the western front and a place called Verdun.

Chapter 19

Over There

GERMANS FIRE AT PAUL CRAVATH blared the *New-York Tribune* head-line, and it was not an exaggeration. The *Tribune* story contained the report of an Associated Press correspondent who was allowed to tour the Allied trenches just west of Verdun on September 2, 1916, accompanied by Cravath and a Russian Assembly member. The French-dug tunnel in the Argonne Forest ran forty-five feet underground, to within yards of the German trenches, at one of the hardest-fought points near Verdun.

Cravath had to bend his six-foot-four frame in half to struggle through the tunnel and its ankle-deep water. When the visiting party emerged from the tunnel into the frontline French trenches, the German trenches were plainly visible on the crest, just three hundred yards away.

It had been a quiet day, the French commandant told his visitors—just two men injured in mine explosions, compared with forty to sixty men killed or injured on most days by the mines the enemy dug underneath the Allied trenches. Cravath spotted a line of French soldiers who had moved up to within ten yards of the Germans, crouching behind boulders with their ri-fles ready. When Cravath told the commandant that he could make out a German soldier by his uniform and round cap, the Frenchman replied, "And he sees you, too. You have been under fire."

The commandant then led the touring party to a more secure location, but they could still hear shells whizzing and bursting above them, one of which struck a few hundred feet away, throwing up trees, earth, and clouds of smoke. On the way back to the French headquarters in the bombarded town of Verdun, abandoned by all civilians, the group caught other sights of war: French soldiers digging graves, German prisoners being marched along two by two, airplane hangars covered with canvas, and the occasional large vehicle bearing the sign AMERICAN AMBULANCE CORPS.

Cravath was back in New York in mid-September after two months in France, where he also visited the front of the bloody battle of the Somme, in which more than one million men were killed or wounded. Interviewed by the *New York Times* upon his return, Cravath praised the accomplishments of the French and British armies, as well as their governments and people, but said it would be a year or more before the Allies could achieve their goal of crushing "Prussian militarism."

Cravath also harshly criticized Woodrow Wilson's policy of neutrality, for which he said the masses in Great Britain despised the United States. He said he had never realized, until then, how important an Allied victory was for America and how dangerous it was for the United States to remain aloof from the struggle and risk imperiling its friendship with England and France. He asserted that "the Allies *must* win because their cause is a righteous cause—because they are fighting for the salvation of Christendom."

Although Cravath had never been one to campaign publicly for his preferred political candidates, he turned out this time for his former law partner Charles Evans Hughes. On the night of November 4, five days before the presidential election, Cravath led a lawyers' group as part of a torchlight parade through the streets of New York by sixty-five thousand members of the Hughes Business Men's League. The Republican candidate himself rode at the head of the march, which ended at the reviewing stand at the Union League Club, a bastion of upper-crust Republicanism to which Cravath belonged, and which was just two blocks from Cravath's town house on East Thirty-Ninth Street.

The parade came two days after Wilson addressed a group of Wilson-friendly businessmen at a luncheon at the Waldorf-Astoria, where the president assailed certain reactionary elements on Wall Street for resisting necessary social and economic reforms. Singling out Wall Street lawyers, Wilson said, "Brains have been burned out acting as brakes." His remarks prompted Frank Stetson, who had been planning on publishing a letter in support of Wilson, to nix the idea. Stetson later explained to Wilson supporter Harry Garfield that after Wilson "specifically and severely criticized my Wall Street associates . . . I felt that I could not in loyalty publish this letter." But Stetson was also a loyal Democrat, and although he did not reward Wilson with a public endorsement, he almost certainly voted for him.

The day after Wilson attacked Wall Street men, Wall Street oddsmakers made Hughes a ten-to-seven favorite to win the election. The Republican Party still dominated national politics, having won four of the previous five presidential elections. Hughes led in the early returns and, with the *New York Times* flashing his election, he went to bed at midnight believing he had won. But Wilson eked out a 277-254 electoral college victory in the early-morning hours after California went to him by 3,800 votes, out of a million cast. Legend holds that when a reporter called on Hughes for his reaction, he was told by an aide that "the president is asleep and cannot be disturbed," to which the reporter replied, "Tell him when he wakes up he's no longer president."

Hughes had run a disorganized, inconsistent, and uninspiring campaign. His tone was negative, not constructive. He emphasized issues like business efficiency and the tariff (he favored a high, protective one) that had little resonance with voters. He opposed programs popular with organized labor, such as an eight-hour work law for railroad employees. His criticisms of Wilson's alleged weakness against German provocations and lack of military preparedness also played into the hands of those who saw Hughes as the candidate of war. It did not help that Theodore Roosevelt, his most visible supporter, seemed to advocate more for war than for Hughes.

The qualities that had served Hughes well as a corporate lawyer and Supreme Court justice—his coldly intellectual approach to problems, his thorough, methodical analysis of issues—hampered him as a presidential candidate. His speaking style was dry and legalistic. His nickname, the "human icicle," while unfairly ignoring his lighter private side, stuck to him in public. Wilson was an intellectual, too, but he was warm and witty on the campaign trail, capable of soaring, even fiery oratory, and he had a better instinct for the public mood.

Hughes might have fared better had he emulated his wife, Antoinette, the daughter of Walter Carter, the senior partner for whom Hughes had first worked as a young lawyer. Tall, slender Antoinette Carter (she exceeded her husband in height) had attended Wellesley, supported women's suffrage, and was described as the sort of woman who was always busy. It was she who had most encouraged Hughes to run for president when he was reluctant to do so. She became the first wife of a presidential candidate to accompany her husband on an extended campaign tour and did her best to enliven his campaign with her charm and sunny disposition. At times she donned a miner's hat or other outfits appropriate to the occasion. Hughes called her his greatest asset.

Social issues played little role in the outcome of the 1916 election. The segregationist Wilson was less sympathetic to the plight of African Americans than was Hughes, who was endorsed by black rights groups. But race relations were barely an issue in the campaign. Hughes also supported a federal women's suffrage amendment, while Wilson did not (he favored state-by-state amendments). A special campaign train carrying well-known progressive women labeled "Hughesettes" crossed the country in Hughes's support. But of the twelve states that allowed women to vote, ten ended up casting their ballots for Wilson, likely based on the peace issue.

Hughes himself attributed his defeat to Democratic fearmongering. He cited large, ubiquitous posters luridly displaying the carnage of war while a horrified mother and her children looked on from the sidelines. A last-minute paid advertisement in leading newspapers told Americans they were "alive and happy—not cannon fodder!" Would it be "Wilson and Peace with Honor?" the ad asked, or "Hughes with Roosevelt and War?" The voters chose peace.

Two months after his defeat, Hughes spoke at a dinner at the Waldorf-Astoria given by the New York State Bar Association to welcome him back as a fellow lawyer and private citizen. Hughes said he had no wounds to exhibit and wanted no sympathy. He had resigned from the Supreme Court out of a feeling of duty and had no regrets for having done so. Elihu Root said he was glad Hughes was there but wished "he were somewhere else," which drew loud applause from the others who had hoped for Hughes's election.

The one discordant note was struck by Frank Stetson, who welcomed Hughes cordially but expressed regret at the precedent Hughes had established in resigning from the Supreme Court to run for office. That action, Stetson said, entailed "embarrassment for future judges, and a great public loss." Stetson asserted that any future Supreme Court justices who declined to issue an irrevocable commitment not to enter any political contests would subject themselves to criticism that their judicial decisions were politically motivated. In fact, no sitting Supreme Court justice since Hughes has resigned to run for office.

———◆———

The great irony of the 1916 election is that one month after Wilson's inauguration, America was at war. The action was prompted by Germany's announced intention to resume unrestricted submarine warfare, and by the decoded Zimmermann telegram, in which Germany promised to help Mexico recover Texas, Arizona, and New Mexico if it entered a military alliance against the United States. On April 2, 1917, Wilson asked Congress for a declaration of war, which quickly passed both houses. Cravath thought the president's address to Congress showed an "unexpectedly firm and vigorous tone." Root later offered a reason for the president's resolve: "Wilson said to me just after we declared war, 'They bragged publicly in the Reichstag that they made a fool of me in the submarine affair, and I couldn't stand that.'"

Three weeks before the declaration, Hughes, as president of the Union League Club, appointed a committee on defense and national service, to which Root and Cravath were named. The club "virtually declared war a little ahead of the Government," Hughes wrote. After the general session, Hughes, Root, and Theodore Roosevelt sat down for a small group discussion. By this time Root and Roosevelt had reconciled their differences from 1912, at least on the surface, because of their mutual support of preparedness. But Roosevelt's bitterness still lingered, so the conversation was awkward. Roosevelt told the group he wanted Wilson to give him a military command to go to Europe, solemnly adding that if he went, he was sure he would not come back alive. There was silence for a moment, Hughes recalled, until "Root spoke up, with his unfailing humor, remarking, 'Theodore, if you can make Wilson believe that you will not come back, he will let you go.' And the tension was relieved."

In late March, a mass meeting of fifteen hundred New Yorkers at the Metropolitan Opera House celebrated the recent abdication of the Russian czar, Nicholas II, in favor of a provisional government that offered promise of a democratic republic. Those in attendance cheered the reading of a letter from Root predicting the German and Austro-Hungarian royal monarchies would meet the same fate as the Romanovs in Russia. The attendees adopted a resolution, drafted by Hughes and Joseph Choate, "rejoicing in the triumph of democracy in Russia" and congratulating the Wilson administration for having "officially welcomed New Russia to the sisterhood of free countries." The mass meeting's honorary vice presidents included Stimson, Cravath, and Cravath's former litigation adversary Thomas Alva Edison.

Three days after the United States formally entered the war, Root made an emotional speech to New York's Republican Club in which he called on his party to show complete loyalty to the Wilson administration. "We must have no criticism now," he declared. "The fate of our country is involved." Speaking extemporaneously, he admonished his fellow Republicans to banish from their heart "every feeling of partisanship, of party prejudice." They needed to put aside their loss in the recent election, he said, and accept that "for four years to come the Democrats will be in control in Washington, and as we love our country we must give to that party our whole-hearted, earnest, sincere support, just as if every man there was a Republican." For the longtime Republican partisan Root, it was among his finest hours.

Root rode home that night with his friend James R. Sheffield, the president of the Republican Club and a supporter of Root's failed bid for the 1916 nomination. After a few minutes of silence Root put his hand on Sheffield's knee and said, "We're in it, thank God, we're in it!" Paul Cravath wrote to a French friend of his great relief that America was finally in the war and that "we . . . can now stand up straight and look Frenchmen and Englishmen squarely in the face." Previously critical of Wilson for his "mental and moral isolation," Cravath now praised the president's "vigorous stand in favor of close and effective cooperation with France and England in achieving common victory by the complete defeat of Germany."

Wall Street's lawyers rapidly enrolled in the war effort. James Byrne, the former colleague of Cravath, Hughes, and Hornblower, and the legal star of the butler-did-it Rice murder case, went to Italy as a Red Cross major.

Henry Stimson, who had spent a month at the Plattsburgh training camp the previous summer, enlisted and was made a field artillery officer in France and eventually, at age fifty, a lieutenant colonel. As white shoe as

they came—Phillips Academy, Skull and Bones at Yale, Harvard Law—
Stimson spent a year in Europe thinking of "nothing but how to kill
Germans."

Wilson was eager for leading Wall Street Republican lawyers to have
visible roles in the war effort, both to emphasize nonpartisanship and to take
advantage of their competence in handling complicated and sensitive matters. Under Wilson's appointment, Elihu Root traveled to Russia in June
1917 on a goodwill and fact-finding mission to the new provisional government. The United States was hoping Russia would keep its army in the field
against Germany on the eastern front.

Root's wife saw to it that he was supplied with 250 cigars, two cases of
his favorite Haig & Haig scotch, and 200 gallons of Poland Spring water, so
that her seventy-two-year-old husband would drink what he was used to and
nothing else. Root recommended an extensive publicity campaign to
counter German propaganda, plus substantial supplies for the Russian government. The public relations effort, featuring Root's speeches, had no impact; he had little understanding of the revolutionary forces at play in Russia,
and he was too bourgeois for Russian tastes. (Root in revolutionary Russia
was "as welcome as the smallpox," said the head of the American Red Cross
group there.)

Root was also overly optimistic about the moderate Kerensky government, and he never met with the Bolsheviks or their leader, Lenin. Wilson
judged the mission a failure and blamed Root, creating lingering bitterness
between the two men. Russia did stay in the fight for the time being, but the
sacrifices of war led to growing unrest on the part of the peasants, workers,
and army. After the October Revolution, Lenin would conclude a separate
peace treaty with Germany and withdraw the Russian army from the field.

Not everyone in the United States was eager to serve, either. In the early
months of the war, after Congress passed the Selective Service Act, Charles
Evans Hughes headed New York City's draft appeals board, which was del-
uged with requests for exemptions and noncombatant status. Hughes often
worked past midnight for the appeals board, which received four thousand
pieces of mail a day and decided an average of a thousand cases daily.
Hughes was unwilling to keep a stamp with his signature on hand because
its use might mean the death of a man; instead, he personally signed the

papers for every man who went into the military service or was exempted. Later in the war, at President Wilson's request, Hughes headed an inquiry into delays in the production of aircraft, taking testimony from more than two hundred witnesses and producing suggestions for speeding up the process.

George Wickersham served under Hughes on the New York City draft appeals board. Although as hawkish as any of his legal brethren, Wickersham proposed federal legislation to prevent all the sons of one family from being drafted into the army. (This *Saving Private Ryan*-like rule was not adopted.) Wickersham was later appointed by Wilson to the War Trade Board, which controlled US exports and imports of war supplies. In that position he made a confidential investigation of alleged irregularities in the purchase of materials for use in Cuba.

Just after the United States declared war, Paul Cravath, as chairman of a Lawyers' Defense Committee, helped organize a citizens' group calling for ten thousand additional men to bring the state militia up to fighting strength. In October 1917, following the wedding of his daughter to an officer then in training at the Plattsburgh camp, Cravath headed back to Europe. He was named counsel to the Treasury Department on its mission to the Inter-Allied Council on War Purchases and Finance, which coordinated war purchases among the United States and the Allies. Wilson wanted a Wall Street Republican to serve on the mission, and the president personally telephoned Cravath to approve his appointment.

Cravath spent much of the next year shuttling between Britain and France to help coordinate Allied war purchases. He was often called upon to smooth ruffled feathers and mediate differences of opinion on war policy among various officials. He took the British side on issues such as the foreign exchange rate to be used in wartime advances made by the United States. As he explained, "Our fortunes in this war are so closely tied up with those of the allies that we are almost as deeply concerned in maintaining British credit as are the British themselves. Therefore, if at little, if any cost to ourselves we can very materially strengthen British credit it seems to me to be to our advantage to do so."

Cravath dealt regularly with famed British economist and treasury official John Maynard Keynes, who told a colleague, "Our great standby is Cravath, who is perfectly admirable in every way and the savior of all difficult situations. The cause of the allies owes a great deal to his wise, upright and straightforward character." On the other hand, a US treasury official complained that Cravath "was indiscreet, told almost everything, and disposed to be too pro-British."

Cravath met the king and queen of England at Buckingham Palace, and when the queen asked him to explain the work he was doing as lawyer to the mission, Cravath half-jokingly replied that it was to tell the Inter-Allied Council how to do what it wanted to do "with the least amount of illegality." Cravath recalled that when speaking with the queen he forgot to say "Your Majesty," instead calling her "you," and that he had kept both hands in his pockets, as was his habit. On a side trip to Italy, which had joined the Allied war effort, Cravath sat at dinner at the right of the Italian king and found him in surprisingly close touch with the military situation in his country.

During his official sojourn in Europe, Cravath made several more visits to the battlefront, again coming under bombardment, this time by German planes. He also did not hesitate to involve himself in political and military matters. When American soldiers began arriving at the front, Cravath urged the British prime minister, David Lloyd George, to downplay the announcement that Britain was ending military conscription in Ireland. Cravath was afraid Americans might think the war was to be won with American lives rather than Irish ones.

Cravath also thought General John Pershing was overburdened with responsibility for both the military and business sides of the army, and too ambitious in his bid to keep the American army independent of the British and French. Cravath consistently advocated a unified Allied military command and was happy to see French marshal Foch eventually designated as Allied commander in chief.

As soon as war was declared, one of Cravath's young partners, thirty-eight-year-old Russell C. Leffingwell, a graduate of the Yonkers Military Institute, entered the Plattsburgh officers' training camp and bought his uniform. Two years earlier, having grown disenchanted with large corporate law firm practice and its time demands, Leffingwell thought of leaving the Cravath firm to pursue a career in teaching or writing. Cravath managed to convince the former *Columbia Law Review* editor to stay after allowing him a six-month winter sabbatical at Lake George.

Now Cravath interceded again to steer him away from a military path and toward a government position Cravath thought would make better use of his partner's talents. Although Leffingwell was a solid Republican, Cravath helped find him a place in Wilson's Treasury Department as assistant secretary. Leffingwell was soon given charge of a program to float financial securities to the public to raise money for the war. They were christened Liberty Bonds.

The Liberty Loan program, promoted by such celebrities as Charlie Chaplin, Mary Pickford, and Douglas Fairbanks, proved to be an enormous success. The loan campaigns were "ingeniously contrived, intricately organized, and advertised with an altogether unprecedented patriotic ballyhoo," wrote Frederick Lewis Allen. After the war, when Leffingwell left the Cravath firm for good to become a partner in J. P. Morgan & Co., the *New York Times* wrote that Leffingwell deserved greater credit than any one man for the successful Liberty Loan program.

After the United States entered the war, William Nelson Cromwell became an even more fervent supporter of the Allied cause. He continued raising money for France's war victims while living out of an upstairs suite at the Ritz Hotel in Paris, designated the "Cromwell Bureau," where he had his meals delivered to him. Two secretaries and a bookkeeper worked out of a room below.

By this time, the sixty-three-year-old Cromwell's practice was mostly limited to trusteeships and executorships and large will contests. He came to feel that some of his partners back in New York, or else the firm's clients, wished he were devoting more time to home office matters. He was chagrined that they did not seem to share his conviction that the country's interests were paramount.

When Cromwell's partners reassured him that they in fact genuinely appreciated his overseas service, he wired back to say he was happy to be corrected. "If you lived in this atmosphere and daily witnessed the magnificent universal sacrifices, sufferings, sorrow, you feel as I do that mere personal gain is unworthy and that nothing now counts but humanity and the Allied cause," he wrote.

One Sullivan & Cromwell lawyer whose enthusiasm for the war effort Cromwell need not have worried about was John Foster Dulles. Officially, the twenty-nine-year-old Dulles was on leave to the State Department in Washington, working for Secretary of State Robert Lansing, his "Uncle Bert." Unofficially, Dulles continued to represent the interests of Sullivan & Cromwell clients.

In February 1917 a liberal revolution against the conservative government in Cuba endangered the property of thirteen Sullivan & Cromwell clients who owned $170 million worth of Cuban sugar plantations. Dulles and Lansing sided with the claims of the liberals, who accused the government of stealing the most recent election, and who controlled areas near the sugar fields. President Wilson maintained support for the pro-American existing Cuban government led by the Conservative Party. Nonetheless, Dulles persuaded his uncle to send two fast destroyers to Cuba to maintain order, and with Wilson's authorization 1,600 Marines landed on the island and quieted the uprising. It would not be the last time Dulles intervened in a foreign nation's affairs. The Marines would remain in Cuba until 1922; meanwhile, Cuba declared war on Germany the day after the United States did.

In late March 1917, Lansing sent his nephew Dulles on a confidential mission to Central America to urge the leaders of those countries to align themselves with the United States against Germany as soon as the American Congress acted. In Nicaragua, Dulles met with recently elected president Emiliano Chamorro, whom he had come to know while representing American and British bankers in that country. Chamorro's Conservative Party had received United States help in attaining power in 1916, partly influenced by good words Dulles had put in to Uncle Bert on Chamorro's behalf. Dulles worked hard to see Chamorro elected that fall, despite Lansing's warnings that it was "a delicate question to interfere in any way" in the Nicaraguan vote. Chamorro thanked Dulles profusely and was able to return the favor. Although Dulles found strong anti-American feelings in Nicaragua when he went there in the spring of 1917, Chamorro bucked public opinion to break relations with Germany on May 8, 1917. A year later Nicaragua declared war on the Central Powers.

In Costa Rica, a brutal dictator, General Federico Tinoco, had seized power in a coup supported by one of Sullivan & Cromwell's US clients, the United Fruit Company, which dominated the banana trade in Central America. Eager to obtain official United States recognition, Tinoco severed diplomatic and economic relations with Germany in February 1917 and declared war on April 7. Dulles urged his uncle to formally recognize Tinoco, arguing that he was friendlier to the United States than any other Central American leader. But Wilson declined because Tinoco had taken power by force from a democratic government.

Dulles's last stop was Panama, where wartime control of the canal was crucial. Dulles told the Panamanians that if they did not ally themselves with the United States, then under the new federal income tax law the Treasury Department might have to start taking taxes out of the $250,000 it was paying Panama annually under the canal treaty. The Panamanian government declared war on Germany and agreed to protect the canal for Allied shipping.

After returning to Washington in late May 1917, Dulles applied for admission to officers' training school but was turned down because of poor eyesight. He enlisted anyway in the US Army and was made a captain and eventually a major, working mostly in military intelligence. Later appointed to the War Trade Board, Dulles became enmeshed in the thorny issue of relations with Russia after the October 1917 Revolution, when the Bolsheviks toppled the provisional Kerensky government and afterward dropped out of the war against the Central Powers.

Dulles's brother, Allen (or Allie, as he was called), was still a few years away from joining Sullivan & Cromwell, which he would do after earning a law degree from George Washington University in 1926. But his wartime service would prepare him well for a future career in covert operations. More of a rakish bon vivant than his serious-minded brother, Allie, who, unlike Foster, was still single, was a notorious womanizer and risk-taker. He held a diplomatic post at Vienna during the war, and later in Bern, Switzerland, where he became a spymaster, gathering intelligence and writing reports for the State Department on German troop movements and zeppelin bomber factory locations. While in Bern, he was informed by British intelligence agents that a Czech woman he was dating—a co-employee with access to his code room—had been blackmailed by the Austrians into serving as a spy. The British agents decided she needed to be liquidated, so Allie dutifully delivered her to them after taking her to dinner one night. She was never heard from again, but Allie, a future head of the CIA, certainly would be.

------━◉━------

The Bolshevik takeover in October 1917 greatly complicated matters for Allen Wardwell, a corporate partner in Stetson's firm who had gone to Russia in July 1917 on a humanitarian Red Cross mission. Wardwell would later be nicknamed "the Bolshevik of Wall Street," and although the moniker was wildly overblown, Wardwell's amazing, yearlong Russian adventure did set him apart from Wilson, Root, and other establishment figures who remained unremittingly hostile to the new Soviet government.

Forty-four years old in 1917, Allen Wardwell was the youngest child of a Buffalo oil dealer who grew rich working for John D. Rockefeller in the petroleum business in New York City, where he became treasurer of Standard Oil in 1890. Raised Presbyterian, young Wardwell grew up in a comfortable environment on Manhattan's Upper East Side and in a town house on West Fifty-Eighth Street, traveled and lived abroad for a time as a child, and learned to play the piano. He graduated from Yale College and Harvard Law School, and in 1898 began a clerkship with his step-uncle Frank Stetson.

Allen inherited a streak of idealism from his father, a director of the National Temperance Society who ran for mayor of New York on the Prohibition ticket and helped organize the Red Cross. As a result, Allen Wardwell had a social conscience that was easily pricked. As a young lawyer he successfully defended the Erie Railroad against a negligence claim by an immigrant employee who spoke no English and who had lost both legs in an accident; the "no compensation" jury verdict always troubled Wardwell in later years.

Wardwell channeled his philanthropic impulses into the Legal Aid Society and became its treasurer in 1913. In December 1916, after the society's pro-German president was pressured into resigning, Wardwell convinced Charles Evans Hughes to take over as president, and the two of them revitalized an institution that had nearly collapsed because of adverse publicity. Wardwell, who had previously thought of Hughes as a cold fish, never had the same feeling again.

Like many Wall Street lawyers, even those whose interests lay more in the humanities, Wardwell found the law complicated and challenging but rarely dull. Even the most routine technical work often called for creativity. "There is hardly any case of any moment which isn't different from every other case," Wardwell said. "An opinion may be eighty percent right, but twenty percent is guesswork in a great many cases. The choice between a great many alternatives is left to the lawyer and that is where his wisdom really comes in. It's not a mechanical performance by any means."

By the time the United States declared war in 1917, Wardwell was the partner in charge of day-to-day management of the Stetson firm. Stetson's health had been declining for several years and he was now reserving most of his limited energy for Williams College matters. Stetson's wife, Lizzie, an invalid and nearly blind, died in April 1917, and in September the widower adopted their twenty-two-year-old secretary, Margery Lee, as his daughter. The news raised some eyebrows, and even Margery Lee's father expressed surprise when he learned of the adoption. Stetson explained to a reporter that his wife "had been very fond of Miss Lee" and that the young woman had become like a member of the family. Stetson wrote to a friend a few months later to say, "I now know how delightful a daughter can be."

During his year in Russia, Wardwell became manager of the mission to distribute food, clothing, and medical supplies to needy Russians. He made several harrowing train trips in which the cars were occasionally halted to be searched by the authorities, or by bandits who dragged people off to be shot. At one point the train had to stop because the body of a Russian man was lying on the track with his throat cut out.

Eventually, Wardwell traveled with a bodyguard and an interpreter, carrying letters from Trotsky and other Bolshevik officials to guarantee him and his party safe passage. Generally, though, trains bearing the Red Cross logo were waved through checkpoints, and the Russian people and soldiers warmly welcomed Wardwell and his colleagues with the kissing of cheeks.

At the Kremlin, Wardwell met Lenin, with whom he conversed in English, and found him to be the real brains behind the Bolshevik movement. Lenin broke off relations with the American ambassador but still treated the American Red Cross officials cordially. That was ironic given that the Red Cross mission was dominated by capitalists—Wall Street bankers and lawyers. Indeed, when a postwar Red Scare gripped the United States, the original director of the 1917 mission defended the patriotism of the Red Cross effort by pointing out that Wardwell and the mission's secretary, Thomas Thacher of the Simpson Thacher law firm, were "conservative lawyers of privilege and position in the City of New York."

While in Russia, Wardwell was escorted to the opera in the royal carriage and sat in the box of the deposed czar. A member of the imperial family gave him a guided tour of the czar's private home, where books, toys, and clothing were still in the same place as when the Romanovs were arrested. Yet danger was never far away. On Christmas Eve 1917, Wardwell witnessed shooting in the streets of Petrograd (St. Petersburg) and was forced to take cover in the Winter Palace.

The mission came to an end when, in the summer of 1918, Wilson quietly sent more than ten thousand American troops on expeditions to northern Russia and Siberia to fight alongside the French and British in support of anti-Bolshevik forces. Ostensibly the intervention was to protect Allied military stores, rescue a stranded Czech legion, and pressure the Germans with an eastern front. More generally, Wilson hoped to bolster anticommunist sentiment among the populace and facilitate the creation of a democratic Russia. The incursion, which lasted until 1920 and cost more than four hundred American lives, was ultimately unsuccessful and contributed to Soviet distrust of American intentions. Regardless, with Americans now fighting Bolsheviks, the Red Cross decided it needed to leave.

Wardwell stayed behind for weeks to interview inmates at Bolshevik prisons and hospitals and to protest brutalities and arbitrary arrests. Although the Bolsheviks allowed him to travel freely, they became increasingly testy, accusing him of ignoring Allied atrocities that, Russian officials claimed, were far worse and more frequent than those Wardwell was charging them with. Deciding it was time for him to leave, too, Wardwell traveled to the safety of Stockholm in October 1918 and returned to New

York after Armistice Day. His request to be allowed to return to Moscow to try to improve relations with the United States was denied. But he would go back to Russia on similar missions in future years.

———⊷⦿⊶———

Bolshevik control of Russia would soon lead to US government suppression of free speech and crackdowns on communists, socialists, and anarchists. Throughout the war, though, the Americans most singled out for censure were those of German ancestry. Even to have a German-sounding name exposed one to suspicion. Sauerkraut became "liberty cabbage," and hamburgers, "liberty steaks." Theaters refused to put on German operas, or had them performed in English.

Elihu Root supported a ban on teaching German in the public schools in New York. Although German was the second most commonly spoken language in the country, and "strong considerations from an educational point of view" favored teaching it, Root argued that "one does not intentionally introduce the young to bad company, or subject them to demoralizing influences that can be avoided." He asserted that "to be a strong and united nation we must be a one-language people" and that anything done to make it easier to read and speak German rather than English would retard "the process of Americanization which is so essential." He also supported banning German teachers or employees from the public schools because they were failing to teach "what the Country means, what our American institutions mean."

In August 1918, Cravath had to defend one of his longtime partners, Carl de Gersdorff, against suggestions made by some to President Wilson that because of the man's German ancestry he was pro-German. In a lengthy letter to Wilson's treasury secretary, Cravath stated that although de Gersdorff had been neutral early in the war, and perhaps even in sympathy with the country of his father's birth, he had never taken part in any pro-German activities, "if for no other reason than out of deference for the pronounced pro-ally sympathies of all of his partners."

As the war progressed, de Gersdorff told Cravath and others that he had reluctantly concluded that for the good of the world Germany had to be defeated. De Gersdorff's son-in-law entered the army early in the war, and his seventeen-year-old son, then taking military training, planned to enter as soon as he turned eighteen. The charges against de Gersdorff went nowhere.

Samuel Untermyer had a more difficult time of it. He was not only accused of disloyalty but also came under government investigation, as did his relatives, for their German leanings. Untermyer spoke out against government attempts to outlaw German-language newspapers in the United States and to seize property owned by German American businesses. On behalf of friends and clients, he protested often to A. Mitchell Palmer (the congressman David Lamar had impersonated in 1913), who now headed an office created by Wilson to expropriate enemy-owned property in the United States. One property custodian official called Untermyer the ablest pro-German propagandist in America during the war.

Untermyer actively sought to refute the insinuations that he was less than patriotic. He organized the Jewish League of American Patriots, which secured Jewish recruits for the army. He went on speaking tours for the Liberty Loan program and bought at least $3.5 million in Liberty Bonds, reportedly more than any single American citizen. He pointed out that since the outbreak of war he had been aggressively and consistently pro-American and a warm supporter of every Wilson administration policy. His oldest son and one of his nephews joined the army, though another nephew was rejected for service after volunteering.

Untermyer's youngest son, however, dodged the draft by buying a farm to obtain an exemption. And Untermyer's wife, Minnie, who was of German Protestant lineage, bitterly resented his spending so much money on Liberty Bonds. As Richard Hawkins, a frequent chronicler of Untermyer's career, has written, "Untermyer's patriotism was the result of necessity not conviction."

After the United States entered the war, Untermyer ceased his pro-German propagandizing and joined the chorus of Germany bashers. He called Germany "the enemy of freedom, the focus of anti-Semitism, the prompter of the Russian autocracy, the old persecutor and oppressor of the Jews." When Germany made peace proposals in September 1918,

Untermyer insisted the war be prosecuted to military victory to prevent future German efforts to dominate the world. "There is just one way to dislodge that obsession," he said, "and that is by smashing it to smithereens by the same weapons by which it is maintained."

Untermyer's enemies remained unconvinced of his sincerity, and in congressional hearings just after the war, Untermyer was evasive, and sometimes misleading, when questioned about his pro-German activities earlier in the war. But no acts of disloyalty to America were ever pinned upon him, and in later years, after the rise of Nazi Germany, he came to regret the German propagandizing he had done before America entered the Great War.

———◦◦◦———

Untermyer certainly did not regret the aggressively anti–Wall Street crusade he had conducted prior to the war, but the attitude of government toward big business, particularly in the area of antitrust, was considerably muted by war's end. Part of the reason was that antitrust furor had been quieted by enactment of Wilson's New Freedom program, including the Clayton and FTC Acts, in 1914. But in addition, the government was reluctant to interfere with businesses essential to wartime industrial production. A month after Congress declared war, the Supreme Court adjourned scheduled arguments in the International Harvester and US Steel antitrust cases, and the Wilson administration suspended active prosecution of both companies until later. Although International Harvester had been found guilty of antitrust violations by a lower federal court in 1914, a consent decree entered in 1918, negotiated by Cravath, was largely a slap on the wrist.

World War I solidified the notion that government and big business could coexist and even help each other. The war required an extraordinary level of collaboration between the two, including coordination of production, allocation of raw materials, and controls over prices. Wilson created the War Industrial Board to direct production of materials, centralize purchases, and restrict unnecessary competition. Indeed, the government went so far as to nationalize the railroads and the nation's communications systems: telegraph, telephone, cable, and wireless. By consolidating railroads, the government was able to eliminate many redundancies and save more than $100 million. The late J. P. Morgan and E. H. Harriman, both of whom preferred cooperation to competition, might have said, "I told you so."

The successful war effort changed American attitudes toward large-scale cooperative endeavors, bureaucratic management, and specialization, a development that corresponded with the societal search for order that had been taking place for some years. It was a goal Paul Cravath had pursued when he created a more structured and efficient law firm management system. It was the same impulse that had led to the building of a more economical interocean route through the Panama Canal.

But the Great War's impact went much further. The war also profoundly affected the people who survived it, especially those who, like Cravath, had witnessed its horrors directly. Cravath called his mission in Europe "the most interesting work of my life and, I trust, of some service to the government." But he was genuinely shocked by what he had seen in the trenches, writing in December 1917 that he had "never had any experience in my life which has left in my memory a more depressing impression than this visit to the battlefronts in winter."

Cravath was in London on Armistice Day, November 11, 1918, and heard the bells of Westminster and Saint Paul's ring that morning to signal the war's end. Back in New York in February 1919, Cravath wrote to the British ambassador to the United States to say, "Though I have been hard at work practicing law for six weeks, I still cannot shake off the feeling that by being away from London I am away from home." He had made many close friends there, including Herbert Asquith, the Liberal British prime minister for the first half of the war, and his wife, Margot, who recalled Cravath as her "tall and beloved American friend." For maintaining close American relations with the British authorities, Cravath was given the Distinguished Service Medal by General Pershing. The French government decorated Cravath with a special war cross and made him a Chevalier (Knight) of the Legion of Honor.

The Paul Cravath who returned from World War I was, in the words of his partner Robert Swaine, "a much more human person than the prewar Cravath."

He acquired tolerance. He learned that few men are unfailing in their judgments and he became less sure of his own and less insistent that everything be done his way. He mellowed and was less irascible; there were fewer outbursts of temper—though he had not lost his passion for perfection and could fly into quick anger at incompetent or slovenly work, or when he thought a flare-up good tactics.

His whole outlook on life broadened. His public contacts expanded. . . . He gave increasing attention to broad problems of Negro education and race relations, and particularly to his work as chairman of the board of trustees of Fisk University, the Negro school founded by his father.

There was one other cause to which Cravath turned his immediate attention upon his return. For more than four years he had been consumed by thoughts of war. Now he would enlist in the effort to secure international peace.

Chapter 20

To End All Wars

John Foster Dulles was still an associate with Sullivan & Cromwell when he joined Woodrow Wilson and the American delegation to the Paris Peace Conference to conclude a treaty to end the war. Just thirty years old, Dulles would be negotiating over the future of the world.

Feeding off his experience on the War Trade Board, Dulles attached himself as counsel to the American delegation to the Reparations Commission, the section of the conference dealing with payments by the defeated powers to the Allied nations. The American team he advised consisted of four eminent economic experts, all of them Dulles's elders: financier Bernard Baruch, Assistant Treasury Secretary Norman Davis, J. P. Morgan partner Thomas Lamont, and former Democratic national chairman Vance C. McCormick, who had also served as chairman of the War Trade Board. Among their British counterparts was John Maynard Keynes.

In January 1919, Dulles crossed the Atlantic, spending much of the voyage playing bridge with Assistant Navy Secretary Franklin D. Roosevelt, who was also en route to the conference. Dulles set himself up in the Hôtel de Crillon in Paris, where the American delegation was staying and where his wife, Janet, joined him in March. Dulles's younger brother, Allen, was there, too, as a technical advisor to the State Department on the redrawing of European territorial boundaries.

Although he worked extremely hard in Paris, Dulles enjoyed a busy social life there as well. He hosted lavish entertainments in his uncle's secretary of state suite at the Crillon, and lunches and dinners at the Ritz Hotel for his delegation colleagues and for William Nelson Cromwell. One of the dinners cost him $110 (almost $1,500 in 2019 money), but because his boss Cromwell and other luminaries attended, it was still "worth it, don't you think?" Dulles wrote to his wife.

Most of Dulles's time was spent in lengthy sessions at the French Ministry of Finance on the rue de Rivoli or at the foreign ministry on the Quai d'Orsay, where the leaders of the Big Four Allied powers met. As legal counsel, Dulles did most of the drafting and much of the oral presentation of the American position on reparations. For eight months he worked practically seven days a week, frequently into the morning hours and sometimes all night. He attended countless small group meetings and private working lunches in addition to the formal sessions. The rigorous regimen was necessary because the reparations issue, as American delegate Thomas Lamont put it, "caused more trouble, contention, hard feeling and delay at the Peace Conference than any other point of the Treaty of Versailles."

The United States and the European Allies approached the issue from starkly different viewpoints. The Allies wanted the maximum possible financial penalty imposed on Germany, both to punish it for past conduct and to cripple its ability ever to make war again. The American negotiators wanted the reparations to be moderate and realistic—not just an amount that Germany *should* pay but what it *could* pay.

To the American delegation the issue was more practical than moral. They recognized what Dulles called "the critical financial situation of Europe," and accordingly they sought to restore economic order to the postwar world. The Americans believed that if the reparations burden placed on Germany was too crushing it would threaten the financial and political stability of Allied Europe.

In addition, the Allies owed the United States about $13 billion, and their ability to repay that amount, and to buy additional goods from American companies, depended on the successful financial rehabilitation of Europe. As a matter of common sense, Dulles argued, any good businessman would want to help reorganize "a valued customer deeply indebted to him and temporarily embarrassed." Even Wilson the idealist spoke in pragmatic terms. As he told Congress, "Our industries, our credits, our productive capacity, our economic processes are inextricably interwoven with those of other nations and peoples."

Hovering above the reparations issue was America's ever-present dread of bolshevism. Wilson feared an economically prostrate Germany might embrace bolshevism, just as Russia had. Paul Cravath, who frequently weighed in with suggestions as an unofficial advisor, cautioned that the Allies should not so burden Germany "as to force her people into revolution." Cravath thought that in the long run it was better for the Allies to err on the side of leniency than to impose a paralyzing debt burden that would breed German resentment for a generation or more. At a minimum, he said, the Allies needed to leave Germany with sufficient working capital and assets to maintain its solvency.

The victorious European Allies, however, were in no mood to be lenient. The British came to the peace conference seeking about $90 billion in German reparations, while the French were demanding $200 billion. Both Britain and France were unwilling to set a time limit; in their view, Germany had to make good on its reparations obligation however long it took. After crunching the numbers, however, Dulles and his colleagues concluded Germany could pay at most $25 billion to $30 billion. To provide certainty, the United States wanted a fixed sum specified in the peace treaty. The Americans also pressed for a time limit, arguing it was unrealistic to expect the German people to shoulder such a large financial burden for more than twenty-five to thirty years.

The debate between the Americans and Allies centered on the question of what became known as "war costs." The French and British estimates included *all* costs arising from the war—not only loss or damage to private or public property but also everything the Allied governments spent on arms, ships, planes, and supplies in fighting the war. Consistent with international law, the Americans sought to limit compensation to damage caused by the German military to the Allied nations' civilians and their property. As examples, Dulles cited deportation of civilians, attacks on undefended towns, and the sinking of merchant vessels without warning.

Dulles also forcefully advanced an argument favored by Wilson—that in what became known as the Pre-Armistice Agreement of November 5, 1918, the Allies ceased hostilities on the condition Germany agree to pay for civilian damages only. Three months later, Wilson refused to agree to include all war costs in the reparations bill, not because he considered it unjust but because it was too late. Donning his lawyer's hat, Dulles likened the Pre-Armistice Agreement to a contract the Allies were not at liberty to break.

Along with his more senior colleagues, Dulles was at the very center of the discussions with the European Allies over war costs. The often-bitter debate landed Dulles in a "scrap" with David Lloyd George, the British prime minister, as Janet Dulles recorded in her diary. Her husband also found himself in a "row with the French" over war costs, she noted.

To deflect the Allies' fire, Dulles devised a way to drive a wedge between them. He pointed out that if all war costs were included, France and Belgium would receive a much lower percentage of the overall reparations than the British. That was because Britain had shouldered most of the military costs of war while the French and Belgians suffered greater damage to civilian population and property. The argument helped bring the intransigent French on board.

The Americans ultimately won the war costs argument, but at a price. Both France and Great Britain agreed to limit German reparations to civilian losses, provided Germany unequivocally accepted moral responsibility for the entire cost of the war. That is, Germany would recognize its theoretical liability to pay all war costs, limited only by its practical ability to pay. Dulles incorporated this concept in what came to be known as the "war guilt" clause. Germany objected to the clause but the Allies refused to remove it.

The now infamous war guilt clause led to great bitterness on the part of the German people, who never believed that Germany alone was responsible for World War I. Three decades later, as US secretary of state, Dulles himself expressed regret that the humiliation Germany felt over the war guilt clause was one of the conditions that led to World War II. But he also was proud that the exclusion of war costs "was both legally and morally right and practically indispensable to preventing the reparation charge from becoming a grotesque figure."

The war costs argument was the only major reparations point the American negotiators ended up winning. Dulles and his colleagues vigorously resisted a British proposal to include pensions for disabled veterans and war widows in the "civilian" damage category, but Wilson capitulated on the point. At a conference with Wilson at the president's hotel, the American delegates pointed out that as a legal matter war pensions could not be considered civilian damages. Dulles added that the British proposal was illogical, to which Wilson responded that the young lawyer was being overly legalistic. "I don't give a damn for logic," Wilson thundered. "I am going to include pensions."

Nor did the Americans prevail in their desire for a fixed reparations figure. The final price tag, set by an expert commission two years after the treaty was signed, was $33 billion, a figure closer to the American estimate than to the wildly inflated Allied demands. But Dulles and Cravath, among others, thought it was still far too high, particularly since it was to be paid in gold. The Americans had contemplated that half the German obligation would be payable in paper marks, and only half in hard money. And the obligation contained no time limit.

Cravath called it a "Carthaginian peace" (after the harsh peace imposed on Carthage by ancient Rome). He wrote to Judge Learned Hand to say, "There are limits beyond which a government cannot force its people to slave and sacrifice." In fact, a recalcitrant Germany ended up making good on only about 15 percent of the $33 billion obligation. The debt was later twice renegotiated, and further payments were ultimately suspended following the Great Depression and Hitler's rise to power.

Historians continue to debate whether the German reparations were unpayable in financial terms. But there is little doubt Germany lacked the political will to pay them. And although John Foster Dulles was disappointed with the resolution of the reparations issue, he emerged from the negotiations with invaluable foreign policy experience and as a full-fledged player on the international scene.

Five months into his mission in Paris, with the German treaty still under negotiation, Dulles wanted to return to New York to resume work at Sullivan & Cromwell, where he hoped to make partner. The American Commission to Negotiate Peace cabled the law firm to insist that Dulles "not go quite yet because . . . we consider his presence here of the utmost importance. . . . His work here has been of the highest order from the start." The American negotiators expressed hope that an extension of Dulles's stay in Paris would not harm his partnership chances back home, to which the law firm responded, "You can assure him his interest will not be prejudiced by doing so."

At this point in his life, Dulles was seen as an earnest, levelheaded young professional—far from his later Cold War image as a hawkish, inflexible anti-communist. The Dulles of 1919 embraced much of Woodrow Wilson's idealistic worldview. And despite their heated exchange over pensions, Dulles and Wilson developed a great fondness and respect for each other in Paris. Dulles idolized the president, a fellow Presbyterian whose moralistic streak and high-minded principles appealed to the pious young man. Wilson, in turn, was impressed with his secretary of state's precocious nephew.

After the final treaty with Germany was signed at Versailles in June 1919, Wilson wrote to Dulles to "beg very earnestly that you make arrangements to remain in Europe." Wilson asked Dulles to act as the principal American negotiator of the reparations and financial clauses of the treaties with the other Central Powers (Austria, Hungary, Bulgaria, and Turkey). "My request is justified by the confidence we have all learned to feel in your judgment and ability, and I am acting upon the opinion of the men with whom you have been collaborating, as well as upon my own," Wilson wrote. Again Dulles stayed, while the four US delegates to the Reparations Commission (Baruch, Davis, Lamont, and McCormick) returned home, satisfied to leave the unfinished business in Dulles's hands.

Dulles took the American lead on the remaining reparations negotiations with the smaller powers. Meanwhile, his portfolio expanded: He participated in discussions concerning the return of stolen works of art, the treatment of German prisoners of war held by the United States, commercial trade with Bolshevik Russia, and the occupation of the Rhineland. Dulles also conferred frequently with Herbert Hoover, who was in Europe advising on food relief issues. Near the end of his stay, Dulles managed to take an afternoon off to play golf at the exclusive Saint-Cloud course just outside Paris.

Dulles finally came home at the end of August 1919. To his great chagrin, the US Senate refused to appoint an American representative to the expert commission charged with determining the final amount and form of Germany's payment under the treaty. By that time, the Senate was caught up in a debate over whether to ratify the Versailles treaty, and the senators who opposed ratification did not want to approve any form of American participation. Dulles considered the Senate's refusal shortsighted because, whether the United States ratified the treaty or not, it had a strong self-interest in being part of the post-treaty reparations discussions.

Shortly after Dulles's return to New York, he was promoted to a full partner in Sullivan & Cromwell. There he resumed his career as an international lawyer and, within a few years, succeeded William Nelson Cromwell as operating head of the firm. Along with his friend John W. Davis, the US ambassador to Great Britain, who soon joined the Stetson firm, Dulles became a leader of the next generation of Wall Street's white shoe lawyers.

For Dulles personally, the future seemed bright indeed. The prospects for American participation in the postwar new world order, however, were considerably less rosy.

———◉———

Paul Cravath and his internationalist colleagues were almost unanimous in their support of a League of Nations. But Cravath, Root, Hughes, and other leading Wall Street lawyers expressed reservations about the particular League negotiated by President Wilson. And although they were only private citizens at this point, this small band of white shoe lawyers had an outsize impact on the debate over America's entry into the League.

The entire League process had started off on the wrong foot. Almost immediately after Armistice Day, Wilson announced he would personally go as head of the American delegation to the Paris Peace Conference. Cravath and others, including Wilson's own secretary of state, Robert Lansing, considered that a mistake. They thought Wilson would be more effective staying home and issuing lofty proclamations from the White House, going over the heads of the conference attendees with direct appeals to world opinion. By sitting down at the table with such leaders as Britain's Lloyd George and France's Georges Clemenceau, Wilson would be seen as just another negotiator.

George Wickersham even argued that if Wilson was out of the country for an extended time, it would trigger the disability clause of the Constitution, under which the duties of the presidency devolve to the vice president while the president is unable to serve. Frank Stetson publicly defended Wilson's decision, saying the president was in the best position to determine if he should go to Paris. A confirmed Wilsonian by this time, Stetson privately wrote to a friend, "I am in favor of establishment of a League of Nations and I am not an adverse critic of the President."

Wilson also incurred the opposition party's wrath by declining to include any prominent Republicans in the American delegation to the peace conference. The logical choice was Root, whom the president's closest advisors recommended. But Wilson thought him too conservative. Probably more important, the two men intensely disliked each other. While in the Senate, Root had implacably opposed Wilson's progressive New Freedom program, including the Federal Reserve Act, the Clayton Antitrust Act, and the Federal Trade Commission Act. Wilson held Root responsible for the failure of the 1917 Russian mission, even though Wilson had chosen him to head it, and Root resented Wilson for his thankless attitude. Root called the mission "a grandstand play" by the president, ruefully adding, "I was willing to be the instrument."

Charles Evans Hughes would have provided bipartisan credibility to the American peace delegation, but the possibility of a 1920 rematch with Wilson probably precluded his participation. Cravath would have made a good choice, but there is nothing to indicate Wilson ever considered him. Instead Wilson chose the nominally Republican Henry White, a career diplomat with no political base. Congressional Republicans dismissed White as completely inadequate. Their ire was compounded by Wilson's decision not to consult the Senate, and its Republican majority leaders, on the treaty negotiations.

Wilson further insisted the League of Nations Covenant be made part of the overall peace treaty that dealt with reparations, German disarmament, and the reassignment of German territorial boundaries. Henry Cabot Lodge, the Republican leader in the Senate, wanted the League Covenant delinked from the more general treaty; that way, if the United States declined to join the League, it could still sign a peace treaty with the Allied and Central Powers. But Root, who played a moderating role in the debates over the League, convinced Republican senators they could vote to ratify the peace treaty, including the League Covenant, while expressing whatever reservations they deemed appropriate. Root did not believe any such reservations would require the express consent of the other signing parties or renegotiation of the treaty itself.

Root had great influence with his fellow Republicans. He was the party's elder statesman and intellectual leader, he had been secretary of state and war, and he had served in the Senate with most of the Republicans who were still members of that body. Hughes, Wickersham, Cravath, and other pro-League Republicans agreed with Root's view that the Senate could ratify the peace treaty with reservations without affecting the treaty's validity, at least in the absence of specific objections from the Allies.

The Republican "reservationists" quickly became the key voting bloc in the Senate. They held a position in between the Democrats, who favored ratification without qualifications, and the "irreconcilables"—Republican isolationists, mostly from western states, who were opposed to a League of Nations in any form.

Cravath, Root, and other reservationists believed the United States should play an active role in preserving the postwar peace. Cravath envisioned the League of Nations as a vehicle for formal, ongoing economic cooperation between the United States and Great Britain—the two nations that, in his view, had the greatest power to enforce peace. Cravath also wanted a specific Anglo-American guarantee of France's security against future German aggression.

As befit their profession, the leading Wall Street lawyers favored arbitration of international disputes, development of a body of international law, and a world court. But they did not want to commit the United States to collective military action against any and all future aggressor nations. That placed them at odds with the version of the League advocated by Woodrow Wilson.

The crux of the dispute was over the famous Article X of the League Covenant. It required League members to protect the territorial integrity and political independence of any member attacked or threatened by military aggression. In case of such aggression or its threat, the League Council was to "advise upon the means by which this obligation shall be fulfilled."

A related article (XVI) provided that in the event of aggression, the Council, consisting of five permanent members (the United States, the United Kingdom, France, Italy, and Japan), plus four nonpermanent members periodically elected, would recommend the specific armed forces the various members would contribute to any collective security action. Whether the Council's recommendations required unanimity or merely a majority was left ambiguous, but certainly there would be moral pressure on any reluctant nation to go along with the advice of a clear majority.

The League Covenant did not automatically require full-scale war as the only possible response to aggression, nor did it preclude the peaceful resolution of territorial questions by negotiation or conciliation. But American opponents objected that the League would usurp the exclusive right of the US Congress to declare war. William Guthrie, for example, insisted it was "not our business or duty . . . to maintain peace in Europe, Africa, and Asia" or to "sacrifice American lives and American treasure in quarrels" that did not affect America's national interest. Although not opposed in principle to some form of world body, Guthrie cautioned that the advocates of internationalism should not be allowed to diminish American nationalism and independence.

More moderate reservationists made a subtler argument—that Article X was illusory. They pointed out that Congress would never declare war if American public opinion was opposed. Americans had no interest, for example, in going to war to defend Poland against a Russian invasion, or to intervene militarily on behalf of Serbia. By requiring member nations to assume sweeping, vague promises of future military action they were unlikely to keep when the time came, Article X would only lead to dashed expectations, and therefore was counterproductive. "Nothing can be worse in international affairs than to make agreements and break them," Root wrote.

As Hughes and Cravath argued, if the United States agreed to Article X, and later failed to join other member nations in a peacekeeping action, the US would be viewed as having reneged on its League obligations. On the other hand, if America decided it needed to go to war to aid a country under attack, as it did in World War I, it could do so in the absence of Article X.

The reservationists also objected that Article X would freeze the territorial status quo established by the victorious Allies. Any nation in possession of disputed territory could refuse to compromise, secure in the knowledge that the League would come to its defense in case its borders were threatened. That could entangle the United States in wars to defend claims of dubious validity or fairness; Cravath called them "arbitrary and irrational boundaries."

Addressing the Union League Club, Hughes said Article X unwisely attempted to make permanent the changes arranged at the peace conference in a dynamic world to which no one could set bounds. It therefore ascribed a prescience and wisdom to the League that no institution in the history of the world had ever possessed. "It is in the teeth of experience," he said. As Root similarly observed, "Change and growth are the law of life, and no generation can impose its will in regard to the growth of nations and the distribution of power upon succeeding generations."

Wilson, on the other hand, saw the guarantee of territorial integrity as a guard against British and French imperialism. Article X, in his view, provided protection for new, small states and colonial mandates, mostly controlled by Britain and France, that colonialists might be tempted to annex by force.

Wall Street internationalists such as Root and Cravath were highly interested in the question of whether and under what circumstances the United States might intervene in Europe to preserve order. By contrast, they gave little thought to the aspirations of colonial peoples in Asia, Africa, and Latin America. A few years later, after visiting India, the Anglophile Cravath would extol Britain's "benevolent, just and enlightened rule" of the Indian people, who were "hopelessly unfitted for self-government." Cravath recognized that the British attitude of "patronizing superiority and racial aloofness" made them little beloved in India. But he believed the strong nations of the world needed to rule the governments of "depressed races" and "the backward and undeveloped nations until they can be trusted to rule themselves."

Such prejudices were common among the American foreign policy elite. And lest Wilson be viewed as a wholly enlightened avatar of self-determination, he and his Paris delegation ignored the petition of a twenty-eight-year-old Vietnamese nationalist seeking independence for the people of French Indochina. The budding young communist, a later antagonist of the Dulles brothers, soon took the name Ho Chi Minh.

The League reservationists had other objections to the treaty Wilson brought back home. They said it gave insufficient sanctity to the Monroe Doctrine, which posited an American sphere of influence in the Western Hemisphere. Critics also charged that the Paris treaty failed to make clear that American domestic matters (code for immigration policy) were beyond the League's jurisdiction. They further insisted the treaty grant the United States the unqualified right to withdraw from the League after proper notice.

Wilson returned to Paris and negotiated treaty amendments to address these concerns. But he refused to compromise any further, particularly regarding Article X. To Wilson, the collective security guarantee was the heart of the League and without it the League would become merely a "debating society." To the reservationists, Article X was the main problem, and it needed to be excised or substantially modified.

At first glance, the respective positions seemed like a reversal of those held before America's entry into the European war. Wilson, the erstwhile proponent of neutrality, now favored a virtual commitment by the United States to fight in foreign wars to defend invaded nations. Meanwhile, prewar preparedness advocates, who sought earlier US intervention in World War I, now feared embroiling America in foreign entanglements.

Wilson resolved the apparent contradiction by saying he was trying to prevent wars of the type that broke out in 1914. His Republican critics argued that no one could foretell, if the United States was called upon to intervene in future disputes, that it would be aiding a just cause, as it did in siding with the Allies against Germany. Because Congress still had to declare war, it would either feel pressured by the League to do so, without exercising its independent judgment, or it would be charged with failing to support the League's collective security actions in places, like the Balkans, where the United States had little at stake.

The Wall Street lawyers expressing such concerns were sincere both in their desire for a League and in their objections to Article X. Hughes saw "a plain need for a League for Nations," but he considered Article X a grave mistake and a trouble breeder. There was a middle ground, he said, "between aloofness and injurious commitments." Root likewise called the League a great opportunity that should not be wasted, but Article X, in his view, was "mischievous." Cravath also strongly favored ratification provided the treaty confirmed America's right to refrain from sending an army or navy to settle European disputes against its will.

However sincere their concerns, the objections voiced by respected lawyers such as Root, Hughes, and Cravath were used as intellectual cover by partisan Republican politicians who opposed Wilson for personal or political reasons. Henry Cabot Lodge, in particular, had a visceral hatred of Wilson and contempt for his utopian approach to world affairs. Lodge was determined either to kill the League or to emasculate it with conditions that he was confident Wilson would never accept, or that would humiliate the president and his party if they did accept them. Although Lodge claimed to favor a league of some sort, he wanted to alter Wilson's treaty to the point it would be regarded as a Republican document. He could then claim the Republicans had rewritten the treaty to save the country from Wilson's folly.

Although in poor health, Wilson decided to take the issue to the people in a speaking tour through the Midwest and West, where isolationist sentiment was strongest. During the exhausting, eight-thousand-mile trip over twenty-two days, Wilson suffered two small strokes, then a major one in Washington in October 1919 that paralyzed the left side of his face and body. According to the popular if exaggerated story, Wilson's wife, Edith, became the de facto president for the five months he was incapacitated (he would never fully recover). Confined to his quarters and surrounded by only his wife, doctors, and closest friends, Wilson became moody, petulant, and at times delusional. His physical and mental state, as well as his pride of authorship, made him unwilling to accept a single wording change to Article X. He instructed Senate Democrats to vote against any treaty containing Republican-sponsored reservations or amendments.

On November 19, 1919, the Senate voted on the treaty, first on a version with fourteen reservations offered by Lodge. One of the reservations exempted the United States from Article X absent a specific congressional declaration of war. Lodge also specified that three of the four other Allied powers had to expressly consent to the reservations, a requirement that Root believed unwise, as he thought their affirmative consent unnecessary.

With Democrats and Republican irreconcilables voting against it, the treaty garnered only 39 yes votes against 55 nays, well short of the two-thirds majority needed for ratification. A clean treaty without reservations was then put to a vote and was defeated, 53–38, with the Cabot-led Republicans joining the irreconcilables in opposition.

Cravath was crestfallen. "I am so irritated over the tactics of the Republican Senators that I would be willing to give up being a Republican if that would not force me to join the party of Wilson," he wrote to Lord Buckmaster, his British friend and former colleague on the Inter-Allied Council. Cravath differed from Root and Hughes in that he favored ratification, with or without reservations. He preferred Wilson's treaty, with all its flaws, to no treaty at all. "I have never felt keener disappointment over any public event than over the failure of my country to become a party to the Treaty and a member of the League of Nations that it created," he later wrote.

Cravath chided Wilson for refusing to compromise. He said that power and adulation had gone to the president's head and that he had been determined for the treaty to go down in history as a Wilson peace. Cravath called it "a pathetic fate for the man who recently held the fate of the world in his hands" and who had shown "qualities approaching greatness" in leading the country during the war. Still, Cravath hoped that a treaty with reservations could be resubmitted and passed by the Senate and that the Allies would accept it. "The future of the world seems to me to be full of danger unless the League of Nations can be set up with American participation," he wrote.

Elihu Root, too, refused to give up on the League. Root detested Wilson almost as much as Lodge did, but, unlike Lodge, Root did not allow his personal feelings to blind him to the need to forge a compromise. Root spent several months formulating various face-saving modifications he thought Wilson and Senate Republicans might accept. But Wilson remained unwilling to budge on Article X, and Lodge responded by strengthening the earlier reservations. For example, Lodge made congressional authorization a requirement not only for military action but for any collective action, including an economic boycott. American public opinion, originally in favor of the League, had turned increasingly isolationist, and Lodge saw no reason to move in Wilson's direction.

On a renewed vote in March 1920, the League again went down to defeat. A group of Democrats who wanted some form of league, even with Lodge's reservations, defied Wilson and joined Republican reservationists to vote in favor. But the treaty fell seven votes short of ratification. The United States had refused to join the League of Nations.

Root, Cravath, Hughes, and their fellow Wall Street lawyers primarily blamed Wilson for the failure. They believed that if the president had been willing to accept modest compromises months earlier, the outcome would have been different. Great Britain had signaled it had no objection to Lodge's Article X reservation; in fact, Cravath claimed he was told by "the highest British authorities" that they did not like Article X because it made them guarantors of "every one of the ill-formed nations set up in the Treaty of Versailles." But, the British told Cravath, Wilson had forced Article X upon them.

Hughes maintained that if Wilson had accepted the Article X reservation and no others, the treaty would have overwhelmingly passed the Senate. But as time went on the debate became so bitter that, as Hughes put it, "the early opportunity to accomplish something worthwhile was lost."

Root cited Wilson's "willful self-sufficient pride" and stubbornness as the major stumbling blocks to ratification. But Lodge was also guilty of intransigence in the League debates, and he used Root and other moderates to camouflage his intentions. Root himself later expressed concern to Lodge that the Republicans might justly be accused of using subterfuge to achieve their real goal of killing the treaty altogether.

By failing to ratify the Treaty of Versailles, the United States technically remained at war with Germany, although the Treaty of Berlin formally established peace between the two countries a year later. Wilson also signed a separate treaty under which the United States and Great Britain agreed to come to the aid of France in the event of an unprovoked attack by Germany—an idea Cravath had strongly advocated. But, for whatever reason, Wilson never pushed for its ratification and it died a quiet death.

The League seemed a broken dream. The Wall Street lawyers who had crafted so many great American corporations over the years were unable to broker a deal to create the largest and arguably most important organization the world had ever known. They would try again, but not until after the 1920 presidential election. Cravath told Lord Buckmaster he thought a new Republican administration could bring America into active participation in world affairs, provided the Republicans did not "commit the folly of nominating some conspicuous reactionary like Senator Harding."

Chapter 21

Normalcy

A curious consequence of the Senate's failure to ratify the Treaty of Versailles was that Americans were not allowed to buy beer.

Earlier during the war, ostensibly to conserve food, Congress had passed an emergency measure forbidding the use of grain in producing distilled spirits, and President Wilson issued a series of proclamations extending the ban to the production of beer and malt liquor. Then, just days after the November 1918 Armistice that ended hostilities, in what sounded like a contradiction in terms, Congress passed the Wartime Prohibition Act. It forbade the manufacture and sale of "intoxicating liquors" until the president formally proclaimed the war at an end and demobilization complete.

To contest the law, in March 1919 an association of German brewers in the United States hired Elihu Root and William Guthrie to represent them. Newspapers quipped that "Hires Root Beer" had been changed to "Beer Hires Root." The most prominent of the brewers fighting the government was Colonel Jacob Ruppert, owner of the New York Yankees, who later that year would purchase Babe Ruth's contract from the Boston Red Sox.

Root and Guthrie faced two challenges: first, the temporary wartime measure, and second, the Eighteenth Amendment to the Constitution, ratified by the states in January 1919, which established Prohibition to permanently outlaw the manufacture and sale of alcohol. The two lawyers faced an uphill battle, as the temperance movement had swept the country, and anti-German sentiment was strong in the wake of World War I.

Although the Wartime Prohibition Act did not define "intoxicating," the Internal Revenue Service, which was charged with enforcement, ruled that any beverage with more than one half of 1 percent alcohol by volume fit the definition. Root and Guthrie advised the brewers to ignore the IRS and to go ahead and make beer limited to 2.75 percent alcohol by weight (3.3 percent by volume), which the lawyers said could not be considered intoxicating.

Root and Guthrie also argued the Wartime Prohibition Act was unconstitutional because the war was over and the statute could no longer be supported as an emergency measure. As Root told a New York federal court, President Wilson said demobilization had progressed so far that he considered it safe to resume the manufacture and sale of wine and beer. The IRS, Root asserted, threatened nothing less than the destruction of the entire brewery business.

Root and Guthrie had some initial success in obtaining injunctions to prevent the IRS from enforcing its interpretive ruling, but Congress acted to strengthen the wartime ban. In October 1919 it passed the Volstead Act over Wilson's veto. The act amended the Wartime Prohibition Act and provided guidelines for federal enforcement of the Prohibition amendment for when it would take effect in January 1920 (delayed until a year after ratification). The Volstead Act declared illegal the manufacture and sale of beverages with an alcohol content of 0.5 percent or higher, consistent with the IRS view. If the Volstead Act was valid, then it no longer mattered whether 2.75 percent beer could be considered intoxicating, because it would be banned regardless.

Ruppert and his fellow brewers took their case to the Supreme Court, again represented by Root and Guthrie. Both of these conservative lawyers had deep philosophical objections to Prohibition, which at heart was a progressive, reformist movement. They were offended by the notion that a matter traditionally handled through state and local legislation should be transferred to the federal government by way of a constitutional amendment.

Root, a scotch drinker, also was outraged that the government should attempt to regulate his personal habits. "Temperance," he would later write, "means moderation through self-control. When one is grown up compulsion creates revulsion. You cannot make man just through the law, you cannot make man merciful through the law, you cannot make man affectionate through the law." Responding to those who spoke constantly of the evils of the saloon, Root told a friend that Prohibition "takes away the chief pleasure in life for millions of men who have never been trained to get their pleasure from art, or literature, or sports, or reform movements." He observed that "millions of men who do the hard labor of the world have been in the habit of meeting their fellows over a glass of beer, and finding in that way the chief relaxation and comfort of very dull grey lives." These were well-intentioned if patrician sentiments, coming from a man far more comfortable with the educated and propertied classes than with the working man.

The Supreme Court considered both the Wartime Prohibition Act's ban on beer and the constitutionality of the Eighteenth Amendment itself. As to the former, the Root-Guthrie argument that the war was over was met with an inconvenient fact: The Senate had not ratified the peace treaty with Germany, so America was still technically at war. Not only that, but President Wilson still had American troops in Siberia, and he had not formally proclaimed demobilization to be complete. In an opinion by Louis Brandeis, the Supreme Court upheld the ban on beer as a valid exercise of the constitutional war power.

The more important case was the challenge to the Prohibition amendment. Root and Guthrie had two main arguments. The first, advanced by Root, was that the Constitution did not allow for "legislative" amendments, such as the Prohibition Act, which purported to regulate the life of the individual. The Constitution could no more be amended to make liquor illegal than it could to establish a state religion or to eliminate the right of due process, Root asserted. He was in the unenviable position of having to argue that a constitutional amendment passed by two-thirds of Congress and ratified by three-fourths of the states was somehow itself unconstitutional.

Guthrie thought little of Root's argument, so he pushed a different one. He contended that the peculiar wording of the Eighteenth Amendment, which gave Congress and the states "concurrent power" to enforce its provisions, meant each state had to approve the enforcement of Prohibition within its own borders.

Most lawyers considered these arguments to be long shots. Charles Evans Hughes thought them so weak that he turned down a retainer from the liquor interests and instead filed an amicus curiae ("friend of the court") brief, on behalf of twenty-one state attorneys general, supporting the amendment. "While I thought the amendment unwise as a matter of policy," Hughes later wrote, "I took not the slightest stock in the view advanced by Mr. Root that the people had no power to adopt such a constitutional amendment if they saw fit."

But Root believed passionately in his case. At the argument before the Supreme Court in March 1920, he was intent on filling up the last six minutes of the court's time before it adjourned at 4:30 P.M. He put his glasses in his pocket, drew himself up to his full height, and pointed his finger at Chief Justice White as all nine justices fixed their eyes upon Root. Rather histrionically, Root told the justices that if they upheld the Prohibition amendment, "the government of the United States, as we have known it, will have ceased to exist. . . . In that case, Your Honors, John Marshall need never have sat upon your bench." The clock read half past four.

The Supreme Court soundly rejected the alcohol manufacturers' challenge to the Prohibition amendment and the related Volstead Act. All nine justices dismissed Root's argument as without merit, and seven of the nine rejected Guthrie's "concurrent enforcement" argument. Prohibition, already in force in many dry states and localities, was now the law of the land.

Almost immediately, Americans looked for ways to continue their drinking. One of John Foster Dulles's early assignments as a Sullivan & Cromwell partner was to obtain the return of two cases of rare French champagne William Nelson Cromwell had bought in France before Prohibition took effect but which US customs officials confiscated in New York. "Above all, we must not do anything which would subject us to criticism or even to serious doubt as to the course of conduct," Cromwell warned Dulles. The crates sat in a New Jersey warehouse for more than a year before they were finally released to Cromwell.

As it turned out, Prohibition was a short-lived experiment, repealed in 1933 by the Twenty-First Amendment. Feeling vindicated, Root entered the bar at the Century Club, planted his foot on the rail, and declared, "This is a step in the right direction."

———◈———

Attorney General A. Mitchell Palmer, an enthusiastic supporter of Prohibition, had become a household name in the few years since he was so little recognized that David Lamar was able to impersonate him over the telephone. The "Palmer Raids" of November 1919 and January 1920, organized by Palmer's young assistant, J. Edgar Hoover, were well known for their arrests and deportations of hundreds of socialists, communists, and anarchists, almost all of them aliens. The radical activist Emma Goldman, previously stripped of her citizenship, was among 249 alleged subversives sent by ship to Russia. The government crackdowns were conducted under the authority of the immigration laws and the Sedition Act of 1918, which extended the reach of the Espionage Act of 1917 to cover disloyal speech.

The threat was not imaginary; the year 1919 had seen a series of anarchist mail bombings targeted at prominent Americans, including Palmer himself, who was nearly killed in an explosion at his home. But the government's response, including thousands of warrantless arrests and brutal treatment of suspects, was wildly indiscriminate and disproportionate.

Still, the Palmer Raids were popular with the press and the public, and the politically ambitious Palmer hoped they would catapult him to the 1920 Democratic presidential nomination. President Wilson did nothing to stop them, although some claim he was either unaware of the raids or too incapacitated by his stroke to deal with the situation. Apart from civil liberties groups, scattered churchmen, legal academicians, and some Justice Department officials, few Americans voiced serious objections to the raids at the time.

Although they were reluctant to say so publicly, some of Wall Street's leading lawyers expressed concern that the raids or deportations had gone too far. Privately, Cravath deplored the "ruthless and indiscriminate exercise of governmental power" and the danger of injustice to innocent persons. Undersecretary of State Frank Polk, a corporate lawyer who soon became the law partner of John W. Davis and Allen Wardwell, probably expressed the common view among his colleagues when he wrote to Davis, "I am a little afraid he [Palmer] is overdoing this deportation business."

Samuel Untermyer publicly criticized Palmer's mass deportations and assaults on personal liberty, but not until a year after the last raids, by which time the Red Scare had died down. Among prominent white shoe lawyers, Frank Stetson was probably the most philosophically opposed to government infringement of civil liberties, but Stetson, partially paralyzed by thrombosis (blood clotting), was an invalid and sliding into dementia. William Guthrie, a staunch opponent of federal interference in business, enthusiastically welcomed the Palmer Raids, citing the "poisonous propaganda" of bolshevism and the "highly contagious" disease of socialism. In a fiery speech to the Union League Club, he blamed seditious agitators for hundreds of recent strikes across the country by workers with "unreasonable demands."

The hysteria extended to the state level. In January 1920, the New York State Assembly took the unprecedented step of refusing to seat five socialist assemblymen elected the previous November. That was finally too much for Charles Evans Hughes, who led a plea by New York's city and state bar associations to reinstate the five suspended assemblymen. He was joined in protest by George Wickersham and Allen Wardwell, while William Guthrie led the bar association opposition to Hughes.

The resolution Hughes secured from the city bar, by a vote of 174-117, called the assembly's action un-American for excluding duly elected representatives merely because of their membership in the Socialist Party and not because of any personal unfitness. "The peaceful means of political expression through the ballot box . . . should not be denied or constituencies disenfranchised because of political opinion," the resolution stated.

To the state bar association, which voted for reinstatement by only 131-100, Hughes asserted the assembly's action in the name of hatred of bolshevism was "the most Bolshevist Act ever performed in this state." He recalled a time when church members were disqualified from holding office because of their religion, and thus he warned the tables might one day be turned on capitalists, who could be denied the right to sit in the legislature under a dictatorship of the proletariat.

Guthrie argued that it was both the right and the duty of the assembly to deny office to the socialists because they could not truthfully take the oath promising to support and defend the state and national constitutions. His view prevailed in the legislature, which expelled the socialists and passed a law outlawing the Socialist Party. Hughes's group was not even given a hearing in Albany, and Hughes—the former governor of the state, Supreme Court justice, and presidential nominee—was all but charged with disloyalty himself. Even the Union League Club, of which Hughes was president, overwhelmingly backed the assembly action. Hughes called the entire episode "nothing short of a calamity."

For Hughes, it was a period not only of soul searching but of tragedy. Just days after the assembly expelled the five socialists, Hughes's eldest daughter, suffering from advanced tuberculosis, died at age twenty-eight. Her death may have emboldened Hughes to speak out for the principles he cherished, as evidenced by his speech several weeks later at the one-hundredth anniversary of Harvard Law School. Appearing to take aim directly, if not by name, at the Palmer Raids and deportations, Hughes referred to recent "violations of personal rights which savor of the worst practices of tyranny." He lamented that:

> We went to war for liberty and democracy, with the result that we fed the autocratic appetite. We have seen the war powers, which are essential to the preservation of the nation in time of war, exercised broadly after the military exigency had passed and in conditions for which they were never intended, and we may well wonder, in view of the precedents now established, whether constitutional government as heretofore maintained in this Republic could survive another great war even victoriously waged.

At least one cause Hughes supported—women's suffrage—did achieve success at this time. Two months after Hughes's speech, Tennessee became the thirty-sixth and last of the requisite three-fourths of the states to ratify the Nineteenth Amendment to the Constitution, which Hughes had championed in the 1916 presidential campaign.

The 1920 presidential election was the first in which women were allowed to vote. Their choice was between two former Ohio newspaper publishers: Republican senator Warren Harding, running on a ticket with Calvin Coolidge; and Ohio governor James M. Cox for the Democrats, whose running mate was Franklin D. Roosevelt.

The campaign continued the debate over the League of Nations, but most voters were losing interest in the League amid Harding's call for a return to "normalcy." Harding was the overwhelming favorite because, after years of upheaval, tumultuous change, and war, the nation was ready for a rest. As Frank Polk wrote to John W. Davis, the American people "don't give a darn about peace treaties, or suffering Europe. They are interested in the high cost of living, the baseball season and the difficulty of getting something to drink."

Paul Cravath originally opposed Harding's nomination, as did Root, who thought the Ohio senator lacked the caliber for the presidency. But they campaigned hard for the Republican nominee as the best hope for bringing America into the League of Nations. Cox gave unqualified support to Wilson's League, but Republican supporters of the League foresaw only continued congressional gridlock on the League issue if a Democrat were elected. Cravath, Root, and other internationalists viewed their task as ensuring Harding committed to joining the League with the Senate reservations.

Harding did not make their job easy. He wobbled back and forth on the issue, at times endorsing a vague association of nations as an alternative to Wilson's League, and at other times, in a bow to the irreconcilables, seeming to declare the League dead. Cravath grew disillusioned with Harding's vacillation, and Root was frustrated by Lodge's refusal to press Harding to pledge support for a League with reservations—even the very reservations that bore Senator Lodge's name. Meanwhile, the irreconcilables feared Root might trick the malleable Harding into a strong endorsement of the League.

Sensing the political winds, Lodge was drifting increasingly from the reservationist into the irreconcilable camp. Root, trying to stem that tide, constantly stressed that the issue should not be league versus no league but the Wilson League, unchanged, against an Americanized league that did not obligate the nation to take collective military action. But at the Republican convention, Lodge prevailed upon his friend Root to draft a party platform containing only an ambiguous statement of support for an international association, and Root obliged him for the sake of party unity.

In a statement released to the press on October 15, 1920, shortly before the election, thirty-one prominent internationalists, most of them Republicans, urged the election of Harding as the best means of securing American entry into the League. It was drafted by Root and Cravath and signed by them, along with Hughes, Wickersham, Henry Stimson, and others who supported a league without Article X. Cravath worked behind the scenes to make the statement as internationalist in tone as possible.

The Statement of the 31, as it became known, had no impact on the outcome; Harding had the election well in hand and would win it in a landslide. But the statement did help solidify support among Republican members of the foreign policy elite who were uneasy with Harding's frequent nods to isolationism. Cravath feared that Harding's reluctance to endorse the League was "driving to the support of Cox thousands of the more intelligent voters, particularly women, who normally should support the Republican Party." Writing privately to Columbia University president Nicholas Murray Butler, a fellow signatory, Cravath said he was pleased that their group was able to make a much more definite declaration of Harding's position on the League than the candidate was able to make himself.

Wilsonians have long denounced the Statement of the 31 as a disingenuous effort to mislead voters into thinking Harding favored the League, and its signers as partisans who prostituted their principles to favor their party. Defenders of the statement maintained it was designed less for the voters than for Harding and his isolationist supporters—to remind them of the party's commitment to a league, if not *the* League, and to hold them to it.

If that was the goal it did not work. With Lodge's active concurrence, Harding abandoned the league concept after taking office. League supporters such as Root, Cravath, and Wickersham had been sandbagged, but they were naive to think that Harding, a man of little intellect or ideology, would feel bound by principle.

Hughes, whom Harding chose as his secretary of state (after rejecting Root as "an elder statesman of a different generation"), was also disappointed in the new administration's failure to push for either a league with reservations or even a nebulous world association such as Harding had previously endorsed. But Hughes reluctantly concluded that isolationist sentiment had grown so strong that it was politically futile to continue to make the case for American membership in an international body. With no prospect of Senate ratification of the Treaty of Versailles, Hughes negotiated a separate peace treaty with Germany to officially end the war.

Over the summer of 1920, Cravath visited Germany to assess the mood there, and he found the German people unrepentant. They did not consider themselves morally bound to the Treaty of Versailles, which they viewed as harsh and vindictive and as having been signed by their government only under duress.

Back in New York, Cravath reported on his trip in a speech to the League of Free Nations Association. His words were both ominous and prescient. Cravath warned that if the United States failed to engage with its western allies, a new alliance of Germany, Russia, and "another power, further to the east, and not lacking in military qualities," would form for the purpose of dominating the world.

Chapter 22

"The Last Great Epoch"

On December 5, 1920, Francis Lynde Stetson, the prototypical white shoe corporate lawyer of his era, died at age seventy-eight at his Manhattan residence. The honorary pallbearers at his funeral, held at the Episcopal Church of the Incarnation in New York, included Elihu Root, Victor Morawetz, and J. P. Morgan Jr. Of his estate, valued at roughly $3 million (almost $40 million in 2019 dollars), Stetson left a third to Williams College, where he was buried alongside his wife in the school cemetery. He also left a substantial trust fund to his adopted daughter, Margery, who tended to him in his final years.

Stetson did live long enough to see the legality of his biggest and most important corporate deal sustained. US Steel had won its antitrust case in the lower courts in 1915 on the grounds that under the "rule of reason" it had not acted with an illegal intent to monopolize. The government appealed but put the case on hold, with the Supreme Court's consent, pending the outcome of World War I. Finally, in March 1920, two decades after Stetson had organized the company for J. P. Morgan Sr., the Supreme Court affirmed the lower court decision and ruled in favor of US Steel. By that time, the company's share of the steel production market was below 50 percent, and the high court found that whatever intent it had at its formation, US Steel no longer had monopoly power.

In the White House meeting in 1902 in which J. P. Morgan offered to have his man Stetson fix up any legally problematic deals, Theodore Roosevelt said the government would not prosecute US Steel unless it had broken the law. Now the Supreme Court said that it had not. The US Steel decision vindicated the Roosevelt view that big was not necessarily bad if no unfair or improper conduct was found. Trust-busting for its own sake was officially over. The president for whom the term was coined had died in January 1919, but he would have approved of the result.

With the victory by US Steel, the last of the mega antitrust cases that began in 1902 with Roosevelt's suit against the Northern Securities Company had failed. The 1920s would see a renewed merger wave and, under Harding, Coolidge, and Hoover, a hands-off attitude toward big business, as compared with that in the Progressive Era. But there was no going back to the law of the jungle under which the robber barons had operated. Between 1890 and 1920 the rules had changed forever, and the foundations had been laid for an even greater expansion of federal regulation in later decades.

The postwar America that emerged in the 1920s was completely transformed from the one that existed when the white shoe law firms came into prominence in the late nineteenth century. Gone was the economy dominated by farmers and small, local proprietors; increasingly they had been superseded by large, bureaucratic industrial concerns, run by a new class of managerial professionals, just as the law firms that served those same businesses had grown in size, organization, and efficiency. The unbridled laissez-faire capitalism that reigned in the Gilded Age—marked by a "public be damned" attitude—had also melted away.

But neither had the country adopted the state-sponsored socialism, with public ownership of corporations, advocated by more radical leaders in the United States and Europe. Instead the American economic system remained essentially one of private enterprise and individual initiative, but subject to heightened government oversight and regulation by technical and legal experts. Even a young socialist lawyer working in Cravath's office in 1910 saw no contradiction between his utopian ideals and representing capitalists. "If there was going to be a socialist world, anyway," recalled Nicholas Kelley decades later, "those industries would have to be built up."

In the thirty years between 1890 and 1920, the steering of a middle course between unchecked capitalism and state socialism owed much to the elite Wall Street lawyers and their firms. As they were members of the establishment, their principal task was to maintain the status quo and to protect their large corporate clients. And in this they largely succeeded. But they also quietly influenced their clients to change with the times to prevent more radical changes from below. As Cravath had written to Theodore Roosevelt back in 1906, to gain protection from radicalism, the owners of great corporations had to agree to reforms and "accept justice uncomplainingly."

With the white shoe lawyers' help, the capitalist system at home had been considerably tamed. In the years to come, the search for international order would prove more elusive. Internationalists such as Cravath would spend the next two decades in the wilderness as America turned increasingly isolationist, even as the German military threat that Cravath warned against in 1920 grew. The internationalists would not become ascendant until December 7, 1941, a day that Cravath did not live to see. But the groundwork for the post–World War II international order was largely laid in World War I by the establishment figures, many of them Wall Street lawyers, who had urged America's participation in the war and the subsequent League of Nations.

In the decades following 1920, Wall Street's white shoe lawyers continued to serve as trusted counselors to government and business leaders. The growth of the regulatory state and the global economy made them indispensable to their private corporate clients. But the influence of Wall Street lawyers, as public men, began to recede in the 1960s. Their place as intimate presidential advisors was increasingly taken by academics, businessmen, and career diplomats. By the end of the sixties, the lawyers with the greatest sway over national policy were those practicing before the federal government in Washington, DC. The last prominent Wall Street lawyer to serve at the highest levels of the president's cabinet was Cyrus Vance in the 1970s.

The 1980s saw the collapse of the liberal Rockefeller wing of the Republican Party, previously led by Wall Street lawyers such as Wendell Willkie and Thomas Dewey, which had long been a recruiting ground for members of the Eastern foreign policy establishment. The loosening of the monopoly once held by WASPs in America's power centers, which had remained strong through the 1950s, and the waning of the WASP elite social culture by the end of the twentieth century further contributed to the decline of the white shoe brand.

As a group, Wall Street lawyers remain a powerful force within the corporate world they inhabit. They are just as bright, hardworking, and creative as their predecessors. And if they are not as wealthy as the richest of the early corporate lawyers, they are well paid indeed. Today's top corporate law firm leaders run very large enterprises—highly profitable, multinational concerns of thousands of attorneys and staff—rendering quaint the early-twentieth-century perception of a firm of two dozen lawyers as a law factory.

But just as the J. P. Morgans, E. H. Harrimans, and Thomas Fortune Ryans of the world are never to return, neither will America again witness a coterie of such lawyers as Paul Cravath, William Nelson Cromwell, Francis Lynde Stetson, Elihu Root, and their white shoe brethren. These figures pioneered a new legal world when the field of corporate law was virgin territory. Operating only as private citizens, at times almost singlehandedly, they could achieve the extraordinary: create a great interocean waterway or a massive city transportation system, or lead the debates on constitutional amendments and international treaties.

Their advice was eagerly sought by robber barons and presidents alike, and they were known to the public to a greater degree than any present-day corporate lawyer. Stetson was recognized as Morgan's lawyer, Cromwell as Harriman's, and Cravath as Westinghouse's. Few people in 2019 could name the most trusted attorney for Facebook's CEO Mark Zuckerberg or for Amazon's Jeff Bezos (and they wouldn't be Wall Street lawyers, anyway).

Paradoxically, time seems to move most slowly during eras of rapid change. The eventful years between 1890 and 1920, during which Wall Street's great lawyers played such a large role, were one of those eras. Writing to his partners around 1918, William Nelson Cromwell said, "We are living in a period when each day is as a year and each year has the significance of a hundred." It was, he ventured, "probably the last great epoch in which we of maturity will ever be participants." Indeed, it was the epoch of the white shoe lawyers, and in the hundred years since he wrote those words, we have never seen its like.

Epilogue

Paul Cravath, who turned sixty in 1921, had lost little of his legendary energy. He continued his iron rule of his law firm, which remained among the top echelon in New York and is known today as Cravath, Swaine & Moore, celebrating its two-hundredth anniversary in 2019.

Increasingly, Cravath devoted himself to world politics, long trips abroad, collecting foreign art, and gardening and horse shows at his country home. He publicly advocated reducing sanctions on Germany and canceling Allied war debts to the United States so Europe could remove the economic millstone around its neck. He supported arms control agreements, which, to his relief, the United States signed, as well as the World Court, which the United States did not join. In 1921, after the United States abandoned the League of Nations, Cravath cofounded the Council on Foreign Relations to promote cooperation between the United States and foreign countries.

Somewhat surprisingly, Cravath urged United States recognition of Soviet Russia. He reasoned that the communist government was there to stay and both nations could profit by resuming trade with each other. He even called the Soviet system a "fascinating experiment" on a trip to Moscow and Leningrad in 1928.

In 1929, a few months before the stock market crash, Cravath created a bit of a stir at a dinner of the New York Economic Club, where the subject was "Is Big Business a Menace?" His surprising response was, "Of course it is. It is perhaps the most serious menace of our age in its social consequences upon American life." He said big business was the product of fundamental forces that had been accumulating over many years, principally "the mania of our age for organization, efficiency and volume." It is not clear if Cravath appreciated the irony of his having done much to drive his own profession in that same direction.

In 1932 Cravath became chairman of the Metropolitan Opera. (His marriage to onetime opera singer Agnes Huntington had ended amicably in separation in 1926, though they never divorced.) Ever the corporate deal-maker, he helped merge the New York Symphony Society and Philharmonic Society to become the New York Philharmonic, of which he served as a director and vice president. He took music appreciation lessons to better understand the operas and symphonies he had long enjoyed.

During the 1930s Cravath adopted a moderate stance on domestic issues. Although he characterized Roosevelt's early New Deal measures as radical, Cravath refrained from the vitriolic criticism of the president that most of his conservative Wall Street colleagues regularly engaged in—the "New York standpatters" as Cravath called them. When Elihu Root and William Guthrie vigorously opposed a federal constitutional amendment to regulate child labor, Cravath joined President Roosevelt and others in supporting it. Cravath also spoke out in favor of government subsidies for low-rent housing to eliminate slums.

Cravath's main interest, however, was in international affairs. He again favored American military support of Britain and France to meet the threat of war from Germany, which was rearming after repudiating the reparations obligations Cravath had thought were too high in the first place. There were some things the modern world could not allow to happen, Cravath said, and one of them was the domination of the world by Nazi Germany. He predicted that sooner or later France and Britain would have to fight Germany, but he reluctantly concluded that the United States was unlikely to enter another European war barring some dramatic event, like the sinking of the battleship *Maine*, that would enrage the American people.

On July 1, 1940, two weeks shy of his seventy-ninth birthday, Cravath died of a heart attack at his Long Island home. More than a thousand people, including opera singers, bankers, and businessmen, attended the funeral in Locust Valley. A small group from the Fisk Jubilee Singers, which Cravath and his father had once toured Europe with, sang spirituals, and a string quartet from the Metropolitan Opera Orchestra played some of Cravath's favorite selections.

Cravath's *New York Times* obituary called him "one of the last representatives of the original industrial giants who forged the links of America's vast business corporations." The *New-York Tribune* described him as a relentless fighter on behalf of his clients and more of a leader than a follower. "In recent years he had become somewhat a figure of the past—his very appearance suggested an older New York," the *Tribune* added.

A *Times* editorial said, "Just when the efficient organization of great business enterprises began to be in most demand, Mr. Cravath had exactly the talent or genius required. He was one of the most accomplished and eminent of that school of lawyer who are as much business men and who blend with the legal mind a certain imagination, vision, foresight. . . . His was a fortunate as well as useful life."

Paul Cravath was an influential corporate lawyer and a significant if largely behind-the-scenes player on the international stage during his illustrious career. His greatest legacy, however, remains the law firm and innovative management system he began when paper clips were still new. Today, thousands of practicing and aspiring lawyers with no knowledge of the actual man nonetheless recognize the name Cravath as representing the very pinnacle of their profession.

If **Charles Evans Hughes** never became as renowned a corporate lawyer as his Wall Street colleagues, his career as a public servant and government official surpassed all of theirs, with the possible exception of Elihu Root's. As Harding's secretary of state, Hughes led the 1922 Washington Naval Conference, the first international disarmament conference in history. Overcoming strong opposition from admirals at home, Hughes engineered several treaties that ended the building of new battleship fleets and curbed Japanese naval expansion in the Pacific. Although the structure did not last (an increasingly militaristic Japan withdrew from participation in 1936), the treaties Hughes negotiated served to reduce armaments and maintain calm in the tension-filled atmosphere following World War I.

Hughes resigned as secretary of state after Calvin Coolidge, who succeeded to the presidency upon Harding's death in 1923, was elected to a full term in 1924. Hughes returned to private practice in New York City, earning as much as $400,000 a year, and was named president of the American Bar Association. From 1928 to 1930 he sat as a judge on the Permanent Court of International Justice, or World Court, established under the League of

Nations, although the United States did not accept the court's jurisdiction over it.

Hughes's high reputation today stems mainly from his service as chief justice of the United States Supreme Court from 1930 to 1941. Although President Hoover considered the sixty-eight-year-old Hughes the obvious choice, the appointment was bitterly opposed by those who viewed Hughes as a partisan Republican and defender of corporate interests.

During the initial stages of the New Deal, Hughes sided with the court's conservative justices in striking down such legislation as the National Industrial Recovery Act, which gave the president the authority to issue fair competition codes, including wage and price controls, for private industry, and protected collective bargaining rights for unions. But things changed after Roosevelt's landslide reelection in 1936, followed by his unsuccessful court-packing plan in 1937, which Hughes helped kill. The Supreme Court suddenly began upholding popular economic legislation such as the Social Security Act, the National Labor Relations (Wagner) Act, and state minimum-wage laws. In these cases, Hughes voted with Louis Brandeis and the other liberal justices to sustain Roosevelt's programs, leading many to assume the court was bowing to public opinion. Hughes always denied this and maintained that the justices decided every case on its merits.

Hughes was a consistent enforcer of the Bill of Rights. In keeping with his defense of free speech for socialists, he wrote the majority opinion in *Near v. Minnesota*, decided in 1931, which held that prior restraint against the press is unconstitutional. The case established a precedent followed forty years later when the Supreme Court refused to enjoin publication of the Pentagon Papers by the *New York Times* and *Washington Post*. In the cases involving the Scottsboro Boys, a group of black youths accused of raping two white women, Hughes held that the defendants had been denied due process because of the exclusion of African Americans from the Alabama jury.

Most scholars rank Hughes among the top two or three most influential chief justices in US history, just behind John Marshall. Under Hughes's leadership, the Supreme Court effected a constitutional revolution that laid to rest the economic philosophy of laissez-faire as a legal principle, clearing the way for most of the progressive economic legislation passed by Congress in subsequent years.

Hughes ran a tight ship in the judicial conferences, during which, according to Brandeis, the chief justice "did virtually all the speaking." Hughes used his prestige, moral authority, and political skills to bring other justices around to his thinking. When Justice Owen Roberts agreed, after Hughes's lobbying, to provide the deciding vote to uphold the minimum-wage law, Hughes almost hugged him. It was a rare display of emotion by the man once called the "human icicle."

Hughes maintained cordial relations with Roosevelt, notwithstanding their opposing party affiliations. When Hughes was unable to attend a state dinner for the visiting King George and Queen Elizabeth in 1939, Roosevelt personally called Mrs. Hughes to invite her and seated her next to the king. In 1941, after Hughes administered the oath of office to Roosevelt for the third time, he told the president he had a mischievous desire to break the solemnity of the occasion by remarking, "Franklin, don't you think this is getting to be a little monotonous!"

Later that same year, Hughes retired from the court, at age seventy-nine, because of declining health. He died in 1948 at a Cape Cod resort where he had gone to convalesce. He had been deeply affected by the death three years earlier of his wife, Antoinette, whose father, Walter Carter, had given Hughes his start as a Wall Street lawyer. The last original member of Carter, Hughes & Cravath was now gone, too. But the firm, which evolved into Hughes Hubbard & Reed, one of the leading law firms on Wall Street, still bears the name of its most famous member.*

In 1920, **Elihu Root** drafted the blueprint for the World Court in The Hague, long a project close to his heart, then spent fifteen years trying to persuade the United States to join it. But, as with the League of Nations, Root found that isolationist sentiment and fears of the loss of American sov-

---

*By the time of Hughes's death in 1948, a number of other currently prominent Wall Street law firms were operating in New York under the names of their founding or most influential partners. A partial list, by the shortened forms of names by which they became better known, includes (from oldest to youngest) Curtis-Mallet; Milbank Tweed; Paul Weiss; Proskauer Rose; Stroock & Stroock; Fried Frank; Chadbourne & Parke; Cahill Gordon; Patterson Belknap; Debevoise & Plimpton; Weil Gotshal; Cleary Gottlieb; and Skadden Arps.

ereignty were too strong to overcome. The refusal by the United States to join the World Court was probably the greatest disappointment of Root's long career.

Root was scornful of Roosevelt's New Deal; he considered its initiatives too fast, anti-business, and an infringement of property and individual rights. But because he held no official position, and was nearing ninety, Root's views on domestic issues no longer had much influence.

Having outlived most of his contemporaries, Root spent his last years quietly, among family and a few remaining friends, at his home in Clinton, New York, at the foot of the Adirondacks. The Federal-style house sat on the campus of Hamilton College, his alma mater, where his father had taught mathematics and where Root had grown up.

For many years Root served as "of counsel," a mostly honorary position, to a law firm founded by his son, Elihu Root Jr. The Root Clark firm, as it was known, later recruited twice-defeated Republican presidential candidate Thomas E. Dewey as a partner, and the firm, in shortened form, was renamed Dewey Ballantine. It operated as one of the top white shoe law firms in New York for fifty years.*

Elihu Root Sr. died in Manhattan in 1937 at the age of ninety-one. He was buried at Hamilton College on a hill overlooking the Mohawk Valley. He had lived through the Civil War, the Spanish-American War, the Progressive Era, World War I, and the Great Depression. He started out representing robber barons and streetcar owners and ended up as the most respected elder statesman in America.

Root maintained his characteristic wit to the end, saying he had endured the infirmities of age with cheerfulness "based upon a clear understanding that the only way to avoid them is by dying young, which I have neglected to do." He said that as a lawyer he could not prove a case for the existence of God, but as an individual he believed there was a God and he had no fear of death.

A towering figure in American life in the early twentieth century, Root

---

*A disastrous merger in 2007 between Dewey Ballantine and another large Wall Street firm, LeBoeuf, Lamb, landed the new firm in bankruptcy and led to criminal indictments of a number of former law firm executives, followed by split jury verdicts.

is little remembered by most Americans today. Nor has he maintained the status among historians enjoyed by his more junior and liberal-minded contemporary, Charles Evans Hughes, the other intellectual leader of the Republican Party in those years.

As a conservative in an age of progressivism, Root was out of step with his times. Although not a reactionary, Root was more intent on preserving the existing order than in enacting reforms pushed by those he regarded as do-gooders. Both in his private legal practice and as a public servant, he approached problems from a logical and technical standpoint, rather than from a moral one. A superb conciliator of opposing views, Root was less successful in articulating a vision of his own. While praising Root's integrity and fair-mindedness, his most recent biographer, writing in 1954, thought Root's conservative cause could have benefited from "a little more daring, imagination, and faith in the people than Root was able to contribute."

If Root had a fondest dream as a lawyer, it was to see breaches of international law treated the same as violations of domestic criminal law—as offenses against the entire community, punishable by a body with authority over the lawbreaker. Ironically, for the cautiously conservative Root, it was a lofty, almost utopian aspiration, and one that remains unfulfilled today.

William D. Guthrie, one of the few white shoe lawyers who could almost make Elihu Root seem progressive, never changed his reactionary stripes. As late as 1934, a year before his death, Guthrie gave a radio address opposing the New York State Legislature's ratification of a federal child labor constitutional amendment granting Congress the power to regulate the working conditions of persons under age eighteen. Guthrie thought the amendment even more pernicious than Prohibition; he predicted hordes of government agents would invade private homes and farms to dictate the terms of unpaid physical labor. The amendment was never ratified but was largely rendered moot by the Fair Labor Standards Act of 1938, upheld by the Supreme Court in 1941. Guthrie would not have approved.

Until 1922, Guthrie taught constitutional law at Columbia University, prompting an attack a year later from writer Upton Sinclair in a study on higher education. "William D. Guthrie . . . a corporation lawyer, rich, smooth, hard, and ignorant, was selected to come once a week during half a semester, and give a lecture interpreting the constitution as . . . a permanent bulwark against any kind of change in property relations," wrote the author of *The Jungle*.

For someone who, by consensus, had a thoroughly disagreeable personality, Guthrie managed to be chosen by his peers for important positions within the profession. (He did write warm, personal notes to colleagues on their landmark birthdays, which probably helped.) He was elected president of the New York State Bar Association in 1921 and became president of the city bar association in 1926. In those capacities he successfully fought against proposals for a mandatory self-governing bar in which all the state's lawyers, as opposed to the courts or an elite group of lawyers, would set standards of admission and control discipline of their members. Guthrie objected that it would give too much democratic power to undesirable elements, meaning foreign immigrant lawyers, most of whom were Jewish.

In 1924, President Coolidge considered appointing Guthrie to the Supreme Court but was dissuaded by Columbia University president Nicholas Murray Butler. Guthrie had an "ultra-legalistic mind," Butler told Coolidge, "which made him approach new and strange problems with stiff inflexibility." A historian of the New York City Bar Association sums up Guthrie as a "man driven and crippled by his ambitions which, for all his brilliance, he could never achieve because his temper, his selfishness and his snobbery always tripped him up."

Guthrie had one major legal triumph in his later years, and it came in a landmark Supreme Court case protecting individual freedoms. Retained by Catholic groups, Guthrie challenged an Oregon law that required all school-age children to attend public schools.

In *Pierce v. Society of Sisters*, a 1925 decision hailed as the Magna Carta of parochial-school cases, the Supreme Court unanimously declared the Oregon law unconstitutional. It was held to be a violation of individual liberty under the due process clause of the Fourteenth Amendment to the Constitution. Guthrie, a devout Catholic, centered his winning argument on the fundamental right of parents to control the education of their children. (The freedom of religion clause of the First Amendment did not apply at that time to the states, only to federal government action.)

Adopting Guthrie's reasoning, the court stated, "The child is not the mere creature of the state; those who nurture him and direct his destiny have the right, coupled with the high duty, to recognize and prepare him for additional obligations." The opinion was written by Justice James McReynolds, the conservative jurist who had been brought into the Cravath firm in 1906 to replace the departing Guthrie.

Pierce has been recognized as an early decision establishing a right of privacy under the Constitution. Guthrie probably would have objected, though, to the subsequent extension of the principle. Decades later, citing *Pierce* as precedent, the Supreme Court invalidated state laws against contraception, abortion, sodomy, and same-sex marriage as infringements of fundamental individual rights of privacy.

Guthrie remained active as a lawyer his entire life, although his final years were spent as a solo practitioner, as no one wanted to partner with him. He died of a heart attack in December 1935, at age seventy-six, at his Long Island estate, Meudon. The funeral was held at St. Patrick's Cathedral; the honorary pallbearers included several giants of the bar: William Nelson Cromwell, Elihu Root, George Wickersham, and John W. Davis.

One prominent lawyer, however, was conspicuous by his absence. Paul Cravath, Guthrie's former partner, had never forgiven him for writing letters to the grievance committee and bar association in support of the ethics complaint against Cravath in the Metropolitan transit matter a quarter century earlier. But Cravath could not escape his old colleague and neighbor entirely: Guthrie and his wife were buried together in Locust Valley Cemetery, where Cravath was interred five years later in a solo plot less than two hundred yards away.

In the years following World War I, **Samuel Untermyer** continued his role as a legal gadfly. He represented the people's interest in a variety of highly publicized matters, often without pay. He conducted a state legislative investigation into corruption in the building trades industry in New York and uncovered union extortion of construction firms; numerous union officials and employers were indicted and went to jail. Representing the city transit system, Untermyer secured continuation of the five-cent subway fare in a fight with private subway operators. He also fought for greater transparency by the New York Stock Exchange and eventually helped achieve federal regulation of the stock exchange.

After Henry Ford published a widely distributed article blaming most of the world's problems on Jews, Untermyer brought a libel suit on behalf of a Jewish newspaper editor aggrieved by Ford's claims. Untermyer obtained for his client a formal retraction and apology from Ford, as well as a $75,000 payment. The auto magnate agreed to settle when he could no longer avoid having to testify and face Untermyer's cross-examination.

A founder of the reorganized American Jewish Congress in 1922, Untermyer's concern for Jewish causes made him an outspoken early critic of Hitler's Nazi regime. Untermyer had propagandized for Germany before American entry into World War I but he would not make the same mistake again. In 1933, after Hitler's appointment as German chancellor, Untermyer led a movement to boycott German goods. He persuaded New York mayor Fiorello La Guardia not to use German steel in building the Triborough Bridge, and on a passenger voyage to Bermuda, Untermyer staged a one-man protest over the German-made table decorations he found at the captain's table. Untermyer's anti-Nazi boycott was largely unsuccessful, partly because American Jewry was divided over it, but it did expose Hitler's treatment of the Jews to the American public. As early as 1934, Untermyer predicted that Hitler could eventually move from persecution to mass extermination of the Jews.

Never much one for sleep, Untermyer continued working fourteen- to sixteen-hour days into his seventies. A *New Yorker* profile explained that "big enemies keep him young." But he also had many notable friends, including Albert Einstein and New York mayor Jimmy Walker. After he began representing Hollywood movie producers, Untermyer bought a winter home in Palm Springs to entertain his clients nearer to Los Angeles. He had four other residences: his garden estate in Yonkers, a hotel suite in Manhattan, a bungalow in Atlantic City, and a houseboat in Florida.

Untermyer's work as a Wall Street lawyer had made him fabulously wealthy, and he had no use for the philosophies of bolshevism or socialism. He remained a progressive Democrat and declared in 1935 that the age of exploitation of labor was over. Henceforth, he maintained, labor would receive its just share of the wealth it created. He added, however, that "capitalism will survive."

After an extended illness, Untermyer died in Palm Springs in 1940 at the age of eighty-one. He had been a Wall Street pioneer. At the outset of his career, and for decades after, Jewish lawyers were excluded from the white shoe firms, forcing even the most talented of them to form their own all-Jewish law firms, as Untermyer did, if they wanted to practice high-level corporate law. But by the time Untermyer's own firm dissolved in the mid-1980s, the phenomenon of the "Jewish law firm" had largely disappeared from Wall Street. Jewish lawyers were now routinely practicing in the old white shoe firms (which were no longer really white shoe) or in mixed firms that were never white shoe to begin with.

Untermyer bequeathed his Yonkers estate, now known as Untermyer Park, to the people of New York. He was buried in Woodlawn Cemetery in the Bronx, next to his wife, Minnie, who preceded him in death by sixteen years. It is perhaps a blessing that Untermyer did not live to see the genocide in Europe he had feared might come.

The most erudite of the prominent white shoe lawyers, and the best liked among his peers, **George Wickersham** was constantly in demand as an after-dinner speaker and toastmaster. His competence and leadership skills also landed him a steady stream of positions as the head of many significant organizations and causes. As his law partner Henry W. Taft said, Wickersham "was never content to be a passenger in the boat, but was always willing either to row or to steer."

In 1922 Wickersham organized and then served as longtime president of the American Law Institute, created to introduce greater certainty into the law; its many treatises on the common law, known as Restatements, are familiar to every law student, lawyer, and judge. Wickersham later served as president of both the Council on Foreign Relations, which he helped found, and the Japan Society, which promoted conciliation between the United States and the Far East power. He was a president of the Hungarian-American Society and the American Society of the French Legion of Honor. He headed an international arbitration panel to resolve disputes arising under negotiated plans to reduce German reparations in the 1920s. A senior warden and vestryman in the Episcopal Church, Wickersham led the fundraising effort to build the Cathedral of Saint John the Divine in New York City, the fifth largest Christian church in the world.

When Reginald Vanderbilt, great-grandson of the commodore, died in

1925, he left behind a $7 million estate, a twenty-year-old wife, and an eighteen-month-old daughter, Gloria. Wickersham was named the child's guardian and oversaw her $4,000-per-month allowance for the next decade. His service ended after a guardianship fight ensued between Gloria's neglectful mother and the girl's aunt, Gertrude Vanderbilt Whitney, who prevailed in a celebrated court case.

The crowning point of Wickersham's career came in 1929 when President Herbert Hoover appointed him to chair the National Commission on Law Observance and Enforcement, popularly known as the Wickersham Commission. The expert panel, the first presidential commission of its kind, was formed to investigate the rise of organized crime during the Roaring Twenties (the Saint Valentine's Day Massacre in Chicago had taken place earlier that year). Among its charges was to determine whether Prohibition, which had spawned bootleggers, speakeasies, and violent gangsters, should be repealed.

After two years of study, the Wickersham Commission released a multivolume report that, at more than a million words, was so voluminous that Will Rogers joked that people were using it to feed goats in Texas. The report recommended numerous improvements in law enforcement, including ending the practice of "third degree" interrogations, better professional training for police forces, and greater use of probation and parole over incarceration. But the report's conclusions in those areas were dwarfed, in the public mind, by the harsh comments directed at Prohibition.

Although the commission did not advocate immediate repeal, it found that the Prohibition Act was widely disregarded, had been inadequately enforced, and possibly was unenforceable. It castigated the police for failing to detect and arrest criminals guilty of murders and sensational bank robberies. For the time being, the commission recommended more aggressive enforcement of the anti-alcohol laws. But the report provided ammunition to the many critics of Prohibition, and two years later the "noble experiment" came to an end.

George W. Wickersham died in January 1936, at age seventy-seven, little more than two years after the repeal of Prohibition. He was riding in a taxicab in midtown Manhattan when he collapsed of a fatal heart attack. He was on his way to lunch at the Century Club, whose members would greatly miss their convivial and learned friend. Today his name remains part of Cadwalader, Wickersham & Taft, the oldest law firm in New York City.

William Nelson Cromwell spent the last decades of his life trying his best to give his money away. By the mid-1920s, he was living in Paris on a semipermanent basis, taking an apartment next to the Bois de Boulogne and employing a staff of six. He made large donations to revive the renowned lace industry of the Valenciennes region, an area in northern France near Belgium that had been destroyed in World War I. Cromwell funded a French scientific research group and spread gifts to farmers and villages throughout the country. Another contribution—totaling a million dollars— went to build a memorial to the American volunteer aviators of the Lafayette Escadrille killed in the war.

Cromwell also financed a Museum of the Legion of Honor along the banks of the Seine in Paris, although he objected violently to the portrait painted of him for the opening ceremony. Complaining that any amateur could have done a better job, he had the painting removed and shipped back to New York. More to his liking was a marble bust that the city of Bailleul, France, in the lacemaking region, placed in his honor in 1925.

Back in New York, Cromwell's major project was construction of a new home for the New York County Lawyers' Association, of which he served as president from 1927 to 1930. Although Cromwell had joined William Guthrie in opposing a mandatory, inclusive bar association to govern itself, he wanted bigger quarters for the group. Cromwell furnished the land and half a million dollars to build the county bar home on Vesey Street in lower Manhattan. Designed by famed architect Cass Gilbert, the sturdy structure remains the bar association's home to this day, having survived the September 11, 2001, attacks on the World Trade Center just two blocks away.

In 1930, the same year the county bar building was dedicated, Cromwell established the William Nelson Cromwell Foundation for research in American legal history, with an emphasis on the colonial period. The foundation continues to award yearly prizes and research fellowships to early-career scholars.

In 1931, Cromwell's wife, the former Jennie Osgood, died in New York at age eighty. She maintained a lower public profile than perhaps any of the top white shoe lawyers' spouses, and the marriage produced no children. According to one source, Cromwell's partners suspected he kept a much younger mistress—a longtime secretary of his in Paris and later New York—but what little evidence exists on the subject is equivocal at best.

Cromwell died in New York on July 19, 1948, at the age of ninety-four, the oldest of the original group of corporation lawyers to have come to prominence at the end of the nineteenth century and the early part of the twentieth. "He was a bright star in a brilliant constellation of lawyers of that era," said one eulogist. A crowd of more than five hundred attended his funeral at St. Bartholomew's Church in New York, at which both John Foster and Allen Dulles served as pallbearers. The French ambassador to the United States sent the consul general to represent Cromwell's beloved France. Cromwell was buried in Woodlawn Cemetery next to his wife.

For all his efforts to reduce his fortune during his lifetime, Cromwell still had an estate valued at $19 million at his death (equivalent to nearly $200 million in today's dollars). Almost all the money went to roughly fifty different charities: legal groups, colleges and universities, churches, hospitals, art and cultural institutions, and war relief and welfare organizations. The largest single beneficiary, at more than $1 million, was Cromwell's law school alma mater, Columbia University.

Under the will, which Cromwell drafted himself, less than $300,000 went to individuals: $85,000 each to two first cousins, his only surviving relatives; $35,000 to each of two former secretaries (one of them his reputed mistress); and smaller amounts to various former law firm staff employees and home servants. Helen Keller received a small bequest as a token of Cromwell's admiration for the woman he had worked with on so many causes for the blind.

Cromwell's law partner Arthur Dean wrote that "in an age of individualists he was a personality of exceptional color and vigor." In a foreword to the same work, Cromwell's protégé John Foster Dulles described him as a trailblazer: "He saw the need of a breakthrough from practices which were parochial and routine and unnecessarily restrictive of the creative impulses of his time." Indeed, there had been no more creative white shoe lawyer in his time than William Nelson Cromwell.

John Foster Dulles was anointed as sole managing partner of Sullivan

& Cromwell in 1927, chosen by William Nelson Cromwell to run what had become the largest and most influential law firm on Wall Street. Not yet forty years old, Dulles was the world's leading international business lawyer and one of its highest paid, earning around $300,000 a year, or more than $4 million in 2019 dollars. He could have made even more money, but he repeatedly turned down raises, preferring to spread the wealth to his junior partners.

Dulles was a less autocratic manager than Cromwell, delegated more, and was more popular with the associates. He considerably expanded Sullivan & Cromwell's hiring and opened offices in Berlin and Buenos Aires. An incessant doodler and pipe smoker, Dulles continued drinking gin throughout Prohibition, stirring it with his index finger, as was his habit.

For Dulles, private enterprise and multinationalism went hand in hand. During the 1920s and early 1930s, Dulles arranged billions of dollars in loans from his banking clients to governments and corporations in Latin America, the Middle East, China, and Europe. By far the majority of these loans were placed in Germany, which Dulles continued to believe needed help rebuilding, and which provided a fertile source of business for Sullivan & Cromwell's lender and investor clients.

Many of the international loans went sour during the Great Depression, but Dulles and his firm continued to earn large fees restructuring and refinancing the debt for their clients. Dulles personally attended debt conferences in Berlin in 1933 and 1934 in an effort to salvage the wreckage for his clients who held German bonds and securities, but the German government effectively repudiated its obligations to American investors.

Because Dulles's financial dealings with Germany continued after Hitler seized power, he has been accused of colluding to prop up the Nazi regime. Among other things, critics pointed to the fact that Sullivan & Cromwell's cablegrams from its Berlin office bore the salutation "Heil Hitler!" as required by German government regulations. The partners back in New York, three of whom were Jewish (unusual for white shoe firms at the time), became uneasy with the firm's German connections, and in 1935 they voted, over Dulles's objection, to close the Berlin office. Dulles's brother, Allen, by then also a Sullivan & Cromwell partner, prevailed upon Foster that it was no longer possible to honorably practice law in Germany.

Dulles always denied the charges of Nazi collaboration, and there is no evidence that he willingly or directly represented German businesses or nationals who provided support to Hitler's government. But throughout the 1930s Dulles was instrumental in creating and strengthening major international cartels to allow certain of his clients to control the production of nickel and chemicals in conjunction with the German conglomerate IG Farben. As a cartel member, Farben benefited from access to the group's resources and the agreements to divide territories.

Farben was never a Sullivan & Cromwell client, and before 1933 it was attacked by the Nazis as a tool of international capitalist Jews. But its wartime contracting work for the German government, including licensing the pesticides used in the Holocaust gas chambers, was another embarrassing fact for Dulles. And in the period leading up to World War II, Dulles successfully blocked the Canadian government's effort to restrict his client International Nickel's export of nickel to Farben, which enabled Germany to stockpile a material critical in the manufacture of stainless steel and armor plate.

Because Dulles's legal work only indirectly aided the Nazi military buildup, he was able to disclaim any intention to do so. It was harder for him to disavow his own words and actions. He continued to visit Berlin and meet with high-ranking businessmen for several years after the closing of the firm's office there. He also made various public statements rationalizing the Third Reich. In 1935, for example, as Germany was rearming, Dulles praised it for having, by unilateral action, "taken back her freedom of action." He expressed admiration for Hitler's rise from humble beginnings to the leadership of a great nation, and he attacked Churchill and Roosevelt as warmongers. In a speech in March 1939, a week after Hitler seized Czechoslovakia, Dulles said "only hysteria" accounted for the notion that Germany, Italy, or Japan was contemplating war against the United States.

Dulles also had his firm draw up the papers incorporating the New York chapter of the infamous America First Committee, the noninterventionist group led by Charles Lindbergh that was prone to anti-Semitic, pro-Nazi rhetoric. As late as February 1941, Dulles was providing the committee with free legal advice. He later explained that he did so only as a courtesy to a banking client, but both Dulles and his wife were still donating money to America First a month before Pearl Harbor.

Prior to America's entry into the war, Dulles took pains to insist he was not an isolationist, and he condemned as repugnant the violence, cruelty, and intolerance of the leaders of Germany, Italy, and Japan. But in blaming the existing system of international relations, rather than the Axis powers themselves, for the breakdown of the world order, Dulles implied a moral equivalence even those close to him, including his brother and law partners, found disturbing.

One of Dulles's Jewish partners wrote him a long memorandum admonishing him for publicly advocating the view that Germany's position was morally equal or even superior to that of the Allies. The firm's lawyers, by contrast, were entirely patriotic: More than half of them, including four partners, enlisted after Pearl Harbor. One forty-year-old partner, Rogers Lamont, even resigned in 1939 to volunteer to fight in Europe; he was killed at Dunkirk, becoming the first American officer in the British army to die in the war.

Dulles's blind spot when it came to Nazi Germany was largely traceable to his faith that it stood as a bulwark against communism, which Dulles considered the greatest evil in the world. He was almost as vehement a critic of Roosevelt's New Deal, which Dulles viewed as a threat to free enterprise. He opposed the 1933 Securities Act, the first major federal legislation to regulate the offer and sale of securities. But at Roosevelt's request, and with William Nelson Cromwell's blessing, Dulles's more conciliatory partner Arthur Dean drafted amendments and negotiated changes to the original bill that made it more palatable to Wall Street, if not to Dulles. Dean also served on the committee that recommended the creation of the SEC and the Securities Exchange Act of 1934, which made it possible for investors to sue for fraudulent stock sales. Dulles did not like that law any better.

Dulles could never reconcile himself to America's growing administrative and welfare state. After Congress passed a 1935 law to break up public utility holding companies, he advised his clients to resist "with all your might" and to refuse compliance pending a ruling by the Supreme Court, which he said would surely strike the law down as unconstitutional. It did not, but the new law, like the Securities Act and other federal regulations, created more business for Sullivan & Cromwell and its fellow white shoe firms.

During World War II and in the immediate postwar years, Dulles turned his attention back to international affairs. Having previously supported the failed League of Nations, he assisted in drafting the preamble to the new United Nations Charter and served as a delegate to the early UN General Assemblies. He expressed grave misgivings about the United States' atomic bomb attacks on Japan, saying that if the United States, as a Christian nation, felt morally free to use such weapons, other nations would, too. (After the Soviet Union acquired the bomb, however, he supported a policy of deterrence and massive retaliation.) Dulles also played an integral role in negotiating the treaty with Japan to end American occupation and restore Japanese sovereignty.

Dulles served as the chief foreign policy advisor to Thomas E. Dewey in Dewey's unsuccessful 1944 and 1948 campaigns for president, and when Dewey, as New York's governor, appointed Dulles to a US Senate vacancy in 1949, Dulles resigned from Sullivan & Cromwell to take the seat. He lost a special election later that year to the Democratic former governor of New York, Herbert Lehman, following a campaign in which Dulles and his supporters colored the opposition as Reds; his opponents responded by raising his prewar Nazi connections.

Dulles's hard-line views toward the Soviet Union were inspired by his deep religious convictions. As a member of the Federal Council of Churches, Dulles spoke out frequently against godless communism. He assailed the Truman administration's policy of containment as inadequate and urged a more aggressive policy of rollback and liberation of people under communist rule.

After Eisenhower's election in 1952, the new president chose Dulles as his secretary of state. Dulles served in that position from 1953 until shortly before his death, in 1959, at age seventy-one, from colon cancer. After an official funeral at Washington's National Cathedral attended by world leaders, his coffin was taken in a horse-drawn caisson to Arlington National Cemetery, where he was buried on a hilltop looking down at the Lincoln Memorial and Washington Monument.

Dulles is of course most remembered for his controversial tenure as secretary of state. Volumes have been written about his actions as a Cold Warrior, including his instigation, along with his brother, Allen, the CIA director during the same period, of various covert operations to topple or undermine communist or left-leaning foreign governments. US-sponsored coups deposed nationalist leaders in Iran (in favor of the shah) and in Guatemala (to the benefit of Sullivan & Cromwell client United Fruit Company). Similar interventions in Vietnam and Indonesia proved unsuccessful. Dulles strengthened the NATO alliance and formed a similar one in Southeast Asia, both of which provided for collective action against aggressors reminiscent of the League of Nations.

It is debatable whether Dulles or Eisenhower was the true architect of American foreign policy in the 1950s. Likewise, opinions differ on whether Dulles was primarily a pragmatic realist, an inspirational free-world leader, or a stern ideologue whose closed-mindedness perpetuated an era of unnecessary confrontation with the Soviet Union and China.

It cannot be disputed, though, that the worldview Dulles brought to the secretary of state position was deeply influenced by the nearly forty years he had spent as a white shoe corporate lawyer. As both the leading international business lawyer and foreign diplomat of his day, Dulles equated American international business interests with the American national interest. Dulles's career saw the marriage of liberal internationalism and corporate globalism. The resulting philosophy, promoted by Dulles, became commonplace on Wall Street and in Washington and remains prevalent to this day. For that reason alone, and for better or worse, John Foster Dulles had a large hand in shaping the American twentieth century.

ACKNOWLEDGMENTS

In many ways credit for the idea for this book belongs to my former partner at Willkie Farr & Gallagher, the late Rick Posen, who in early 2004 asked me to write a history of our law firm. The result, *"One Firm": A Short History of Willkie Farr & Gallagher LLP, 1888-* was a mostly reverent, occasionally irreverent, chronology of a Wall Street law firm that traced its origins to 1888.

Thirteen years later it occurred to me to expand the concept into a book about other New York City white shoe law firms that attained prominence in the late nineteenth century. It fell to my longtime agent, Jim Donovan, to give shape to the idea and to encourage me to focus on the handful of powerful and colorful personalities profiled in these pages and the formative period of 1890 to 1920, during which their influence as builders of American big business was greatest. Thanks to Jim for his typically savvy guidance and to his able colleague Melissa Shultz.

Several former Willkie Farr colleagues provided helpful suggestions and commented on large portions of the manuscript. As usual, Larry Kamin read the book from cover to cover and helped me with the big picture as well as with editorial advice. Bill Rooney, one of the top antitrust lawyers in New York, gave me useful direction in that area. Gary Malone, another Willkie Farr alumnus and antitrust specialist, took his excellent eye and pen to many chapters. John Dutt did likewise. And Hal Kennedy, Willkie's veteran managing attorney, with whom I collaborated on our firm's history, provided much encouragement and support.

Special thanks go to Susan Freyberg Wolfert, a freelance writer friend who edited the book with consistently professional care and attention and offered helpful overall advice. Dave Larkin also earned my high commendation for his proficient work on the book.

I wish to thank Debbie Glessner and the library staff at Willkie Farr for their help and hospitality.

Richard Hawkins generously shared his extensive writings on Samuel Untermyer with me. Lelia Mander gave me valuable information about her great-grandfather Allen Wardwell. Writer-historian John Rousmaniere offered insights on how to think and write about the great early Wall Street lawyers.

I am grateful to the following libraries and archives for their resources and assistance:

New York: New York Public Library; Columbia University Rare Book and Manuscript Library; New-York Historical Society; the Morgan Library and Museum.

Washington, DC: Library of Congress, Manuscript Division; Smithsonian National Museum of American History; National Archives and Records Administration.

Massachusetts: Baker Library Historical Collections, Harvard Business School; Houghton Library, Harvard University; Williams College Archives and Special Collections; Amherst College Archives and Special Collections.

New Jersey: Princeton University Library, Department of Rare Books and Special Collections.

Maryland: National Archives II, College Park.

Connecticut: Yale University Library, Manuscripts and Archives.

Ohio: Jacob Rader Marcus Center of the American Jewish Archives, Cincinnati.

Finally, I wish to thank my editor at Dutton, Brent Howard, for his judicious editing of the manuscript and his enthusiasm for the book. It was a pleasure working with him and with the Dutton/Penguin Random House team, including his assistant, Cassidy Sachs; designer Francesca Belanger; copy editor Maureen Klier; and editorial assistant Maddy Newquist.

ABBREVIATIONS

MANUSCRIPT COLLECTIONS

Butler Papers, Columbia University: Nicholas Murray Butler Papers, Columbia University Rare Book and Manuscript Library

B-V Papers, LOC: Philippe Bunau-Varilla Papers, Library of Congress, Manuscript Division

Davis Papers, Yale: John William Davis Papers, Yale University Library, Manuscripts and Archives

JFD Papers, Princeton: John Foster Dulles Papers, Public Policy Papers, Department of Rare Books and Special Collections, Princeton University Library

Morrow Papers, Amherst College: Dwight W. Morrow Papers, Amherst College Archives and Special Collections

Perkins Papers, Columbia University: George W. Perkins Sr. Papers, Columbia University Rare Book and Manuscript Library

Root Papers, LOC: Elihu Root Papers, Library of Congress, Manuscript Division

Stetson Papers, Williams College: Francis Lynde Stetson Papers, Williams College Archives and Special Collections

Stewart Collection, LOC: Emily A. Stewart Collection of Elihu Root Material, Library of Congress, Manuscript Division

Taft Papers, LOC: William Howard Taft Papers, Library of Congress, Manuscript Division

TR Papers, LOC: Theodore Roosevelt Papers, Library of Congress, Manuscript Division

Villard Collection, Harvard Business School: Henry Villard Collection, Baker Library Historical Collections, Harvard Business School

Wilson Papers, LOC: Woodrow Wilson Papers, Library of Congress, Manuscript Division

BOOKS AND OTHER PUBLICATIONS

Dean: Arthur H. Dean, *William Nelson Cromwell, 1854-1948: An American Pioneer in Corporation, Comparative and International Law* (New York: Ad Press, 1957)

Hughes Notes: *The Autobiographical Notes of Charles Evans Hughes,* ed. David J. Danelski and Joseph S. Tulchin (Cambridge, MA: Harvard University Press, 1973)

Jessup, 1: Philip C. Jessup, *Elihu Root,* vol. 1, *1845-1909* (New York: Dodd, Mead, 1938)

Jessup, 2: Philip C. Jessup, *Elihu Root,* vol. 2, *1905-1937* (New York: Dodd, Mead, 1938)

Lisagor & Lipsius: Nancy Lisagor and Frank Lipsius, *A Law unto Itself: The Untold Story of the Law Firm of Sullivan & Cromwell* (1988; repr., New York: Paragon House, 1989)

Rousmaniere: John Rousmaniere, *Called in to Consultation: The History of an American Law Firm; Davis Polk & Wardwell, 1849-1993* (Stamford, CT: privately printed, 1999)

Swaine, 1: Robert T. Swaine, *The Cravath Firm and Its Predecessors, 1819-1947,* vol. 1, *The Predecessor Firms, 1819-1906* (1946; repr., Clark, NJ: Lawbook Exchange, 2012)

Swaine, 2: Robert T. Swaine, *The Cravath Firm and Its Predecessors, 1819-1947,* vol. 2, *The Cravath Firm Since 1906* (1948; repr., Clark, NJ: Lawbook Exchange, 2012)

NOTES

Prologue: New High Priests for a New Century

1 **In 1899 . . . cofounded by William H. Seward:** Swaine, 1:ii, ix, 1-3, 573. The original predecessor firm, founded in 1819 by Richard M. Blatchford in New York City, merged in 1854 with a firm in Auburn, New York, cofounded by Seward.

1 **The standard paper clip:** Sara Goldsmith, "The Perfection of the Paper Clip," *Slate*, May 22, 2012, http://www.slate.com/articles/life/design/2012/05/the _history_of_the_paper_clip_it_was_invented_in_1899_it_hasn_t_been _improved_upon_since_.html.

1 **rubber bands:** Rousmaniere, 81; Dean, 28.

1 **no filing system . . . office boy's head:** Swaine, 1:364-365, 658.

1 **After the first elevator . . . just stayed home:** Swaine, 1:448.

1 **When the first telephones . . . in the boroughs:** Dean, 27-28, 117-118; Rousmaniere, 84; Swaine, 1:448-449; *Davis Polk Wardwell Sunderland & Kiendl: A Background with Figures* (New York: privately printed, 1965), 22, 34 (available at Williams College Archives and Special Collections).

1 **"some of the older partners . . . by hand":** J. F. Dulles, foreword to Dean, iii.

1-2 **Lawyers were also slow . . . to replace male copyists:** Richard Polt, *The Typewriter Revolution: A Typist's Companion for the 21st Century* (New York: Countryman Press, 2015), 67-69; J. F. Dulles, foreword to Dean, iii; Dean, 29; Rousmaniere, 80; William John Curtis, *Memoirs of William John Curtis* (Portland, ME: Mosher Press, 1928), 55; Swaine, 1:364-365, 449-451; *Davis Polk: Background with Figures*, 22; Lawrence M. Friedman, *A History of American Law*, 3rd ed. (New York: Simon & Schuster, 2005), 273, 464.

2 **The first thing he did . . . to run it:** Swaine, 1:658.

2 **the typical law office . . . legal work of the firm:** Swaine, 2:6; Rousmaniere, 4; James Willard Hurst, *The Growth of American Law: The Law Makers* (1950; repr., Clark, NJ: Lawbook Exchange, 2004), 256-257, 280-283, 306; Friedman, *History of American Law*, 237-238; Wayne K. Hobson, *The American Legal Profession and the Organizational Society, 1890-1930* (New York: Garland Publishing, 1986), 105, 249.

Until the twentieth century, bar examinations often were perfunctory and oral. New York State held its first written bar examination in 1895 and made passage a condition to admission, but graduation from a law school was not a prerequisite to taking the exam. Time spent clerking in a law office counted toward the required three years of legal study (two years for college graduates) needed before one could take the exam. Friedman, *History of American Law*, 236-237, 498-499; Hurst, *Growth of American Law*, 281-284; Hobson, *American Legal Profession*, 251-252; Austen G. Fox, "Two Years' Experience of the New York State Board of Law Examiners," in *Report of the Nineteenth Annual Meeting of the American Bar Association* (Philadelphia: Dando Printing, 1896), 545-561.

3 **"white shoe" firms:** William Safire, "Gimme the Ol' White Shoe," *New York Times Magazine*, Nov. 9, 1997; Paul Hoffman, *Lions in the Street: The Inside Story of the Great Wall Street Law Firms* (New York: Saturday Review Press/E. P. Dutton, 1973), 20.

3 **From the early nineteenth century . . . chief domain the conference room:** Marc Galanter and Thomas Palay, "The Transformation of the Big Law Firm," in *Lawyers' Ideals/Lawyers' Practices: Transformations in the American Legal Profession*, ed. Robert L. Nelson, David M. Trubek, and Rayman L. Solomon (Ithaca, NY: Cornell University Press, 1992), 34-35; Hurst, *Growth of American Law*, 298, 302-305; Beryl Harold Levy, *Corporation Lawyer . . . Saint or Sinner?: The New Role of the Lawyer in Modern Society* (Philadelphia: Chilton Company, 1961), 17-26; Wayne K. Hobson, "Symbol of the New Profession: Emergence of the Large Law Firm, 1870-1915," in *The New High Priests: Lawyers in Post-Civil War America*, ed. Gerard W. Gawalt (Westport, CT: Greenwood Press, 1984), 3-9, 16, 21; George Whitney Martin, *Causes and Conflicts: The Centennial History of the Association of the Bar of the City of New York, 1870-1970* (New York: Fordham University Press, 1997), 191; Dean, 52-53, 165-166; Swaine, 1:369-371; *Davis Polk: Background with Figures*, 42-43; Frederick T. Birchall, "William Nelson Cromwell: The Man Who Made the Panama Canal Possible," *Leslie's Monthly Magazine*, May 1904, 173; Nathan L. Miller, in *Addresses on the Occasion of a Meeting in Memory of William Nelson Cromwell* (New York: Association of the Bar of the City of New York and New York County Lawyers' Association, Jan. 16, 1949), 11-12.

4 **Francis Lynde Stetson . . . the "attorney general":** Rousmaniere, viii; Jean Strouse, *Morgan: American Financier* (1999; repr., New York: Random House, 2014), 430.

4 **classic small-town boy . . . love of books and music:** Swaine, 1:579-583; *Erie County (OH) Reporter*, Nov. 24, 1892; Milton Mackaye, "Public Man," *New Yorker*, Jan. 2, 1932, 22.

5 **"brilliant" . . . "mischief-maker":** Swaine, 1:585-586.

5 **ambition . . . took an apprentice clerkship:** Swaine, 1:586-587.

5 **"a collector . . . progenitor of many law firms":** Otto E. Koegel, *Walter S.*

Carter: Collector of Young Masters, or the Progenitor of Many Law Firms (New York: Round Table Press, 1953).

5 Carter developed a reputation . . . illustrious careers: Ibid., 1–12, 102–111; Hobson, "Symbol of the New Profession," 17, 19.

5 "a veritable nursery . . . kids": Koegel, *Walter S. Carter*, 362 (first quotation), 3, 102 (second quotation).

6 William Hornblower: Harold Gallagher, "Books for Lawyers," *American Bar Association Journal* 40, no. 9 (September 1954): 777–778; *Richmond (VA) Times-Dispatch*, June 17, 1906; *New York Times*, Sept. 5, 20, 1893, June 17, 1914; John Oller, *"One Firm": A Short History of Willkie Farr & Gallagher LLP, 1888–* (New York: Willkie Farr & Gallagher LLP, 2004), 3–4, 7; "William Butler Hornblower," in *Prominent and Progressive Americans: An Encyclopedia of Contemporaneous Biography*, comp. Mitchell C. Harrison (New York: New-York Tribune, 1902), 1:170–171.

6 "seven thousand dollars . . . in COAL": Hughes Notes, 59.

6 he came to believe . . . Cravath chose to stay: Hughes Notes, 72–75; Swaine, 1:588; Oller, "One Firm," 1, 7.

6 To cement the deal . . . "and I'll join": Hughes Notes, 73.

6 extroverted personality . . . "glittering presence": Swaine, 1:573–574 (quotations), 2:479; *New York Times*, July 2, 1940.

7 his first major client . . . George Westinghouse's companies: Swaine, 1:588–589; Hughes Notes, 84.

7 1890 to 1916 . . . internationalist foreign policy: Martin J. Sklar, *The Corporate Reconstruction of American Capitalism, 1890–1916: The Market, the Law, and Politics* (1988; repr., Cambridge: Cambridge University Press, 1993), 1.

7 "prayerfully within the law": Samuel Untermyer, "What Every Present-Day Lawyer Should Know," *Annals of the American Political and Social Science* 167 (May 1933): 173.

7 Finley Peter Dunne . . . triumphal arch: Henry Steele Commager, *The American Mind: An Interpretation of American Thought and Character Since the 1880's* (New Haven, CT: Yale University Press, 1950), 53.

8 "In a . . . familiar to all of us": Levy, *Corporation Lawyer*, 45.

8 harness the growth of corporate capitalism: Jason Weixelbaum, "Harnessing the Growth of Corporate Capitalism: Sullivan & Cromwell and Its Influence on Late Nineteenth-Century American Business," Jason Weixelbaum Publications and Research, Dec. 25, 2010, https://jasonweixelbaum.wordpress.com/2010/12/25/harnessing-the-growth-of-corporate-capitalism-sullivan-cromwell-and-its-influence-on-late-nineteenth-century-american-business/#_ftn7.

9 "search for order" . . . organizational society: Robert W. Wiebe, *The Search for Order, 1877–1920* (New York: Macmillan, 1967); Hobson, *American Legal*

Profession, 2-3; Louis Galambos, "The Emerging Organizational Synthesis in Modern American History," *Business History Review* 44, no. 3 (Autumn 1970): 279-290. See also William J. Novak, "The Legal Origins of the Modern American State," in *Looking Back at Law's Century*, ed. Austin Sarat, Bryant Garth, and Robert A. Kagan (Ithaca, NY: Cornell University Press, 2002), 249-283.

Chapter 1: Boy Wonder

11 Pittsburgh-based Westinghouse . . . light bulb war: Jill Jonnes, *Empires of Light: Edison, Tesla, Westinghouse, and the Race to Electrify the World* (2003; repr., New York: Random House, 2004), 117-124, 150-151, 179, 237-240, 243, 259; Maury Klein, *The Power Makers: Steam, Electricity, and the Men Who Invented Modern America* (New York: Bloomsbury, 2008), 326.

12 War of (Electric) Currents . . . dense population centers: Jonnes, *Empires of Light*, 139, 147-148, 150; Mark Essig, *Edison & the Electric Chair: A Story of Life and Death* (New York: Walker Books, 2004), 113.

12 safety . . . danger of electrocution: Essig, *Edison & the Electric Chair*, 64, 69, 105; *New York Times*, Jan. 26, 1891; Vincze Miklós, "Photos from the Days When Thousands of Cables Crowded the Skies," Gizmodo.com, Sept. 3, 2014, http://io9.gizmodo.com/photos-from-the-days-when-thousands-of -cables-crowded-t-1629961917; Edwin G. Burrows and Mike Wallace, *Gotham: A History of New York to 1898* (Oxford: Oxford University Press, 1999), 1065-1067.

12 dozens of people were killed . . . unsuspecting children: *New York Herald*, Dec. 11, 1889; *New York Times*, Oct. 9, 1889, May 19, 1890; Jonnes, *Empires of Light*, 142-143.

13 Electric Wire Panic . . . axes and clippers to the lines: *New York Times*, May 31, June 27, Oct. 15, 17, 18, 25, Dec. 17, 1889, Feb. 18, Mar. 15, 21, 23, 27, 29, May 19, Oct. 17, 1890, Feb. 28, May 16, 1891; *New-York Tribune*, Oct. 15, 29, Dec. 14, 1889; *New York Herald*, Oct. 16, Dec. 11, 20, 1889, Feb. 27, Mar. 6, 21, 29, May 22, 1890, Apr. 1, May 29, June 30, 1891; *New York World*, Oct. 29, 1889. See also Klein, *Power Makers*, 325; Burrows and Wallace, *Gotham*, 1068; Hughes Notes, 84-85; United States Illuminating Co. v. Grant, 7 N.Y.S. 788 (App. Div. 1st Dep't 1889); Armstrong v. Grant, 9 N.Y.S. 388 (App. Div. 1st Dep't 1890); Manhattan Electric Light Co. v. Grant, 9 N.Y.S. 942 (App. Div. 1st Dep't 1890).

13 ROASTED IN A NETWORK OF WIRES . . . charred body: *New York Times*, Oct. 12, 1889; Jonnes, *Empires of Light*, 198-199.

13 Cravath immediately agreed . . . own set of problems: *New-York Tribune*, Oct. 15, 1889; *New York Times*, Oct. 15, 1889.

13 Westinghouse came at once from Pittsburgh . . . and all day on Sundays: Swaine, 1:589.

14 Edison had lobbied . . . burned him to death: Jonnes, *Empires of Light*, 171–178, 188, 197, 211–213; Essig, *Edison & the Electric Chair*, 152–156, 167–169; Quentin R. Skrabec Jr., *George Westinghouse: Gentle Genius* (New York: Algora, 2007), 120; *New-York Tribune*, Apr. 30, 1890; Swaine, 1:589; *New York Times*, Aug. 7, 1890; *New York World*, Aug. 9, 1890.

14 "the mysterious character . . . expense of human life": *New York Herald*, Aug. 7, 1890.

14 "they would have done better using an axe": Skrabec, *George Westinghouse: Gentle Genius*, 120.

14 Cravath, who was assisted . . . transferred to the Thomson-Houston group: Swaine, 1:589; Koegel, *Walter S. Carter*, 66; Hughes Notes, 84–87; Randall E. Stross, *The Wizard of Menlo Park: How Thomas Alva Edison Invented the Modern World* (New York: Crown, 2007), 183–188; Jonnes, *Empires of Light*, 233–243; Klein, *Power Makers*, 325; Strouse, *Morgan*, 231n, 312–314; Rousmaniere, 36, 49–50 (as to Stetson); Robert L. Bradley Jr., *Edison to Enron: Energy Markets and Political Strategies* (New York: Scrivener/John Wiley, 2011), 56–59.

15 After Cravath helped . . . stave off a bankruptcy proceeding: *New York Times*, Jan. 16, 1891; *Chicago Tribune*, Jan. 17, 1891; Henry G. Prout, *A Life of George Westinghouse* (New York: Charles Scribner's, 1922), 280; Jonnes, *Empires of Light*, 219–224, 235–239.

15 Westinghouse went on . . . by Stetson: Klein, *Power Makers*, chaps. 15, 16; Jonnes, *Empires of Light*, 280; Rousmaniere, 34–37.

15 agreed to cross-license patents . . . Westinghouse nominees: Skrabec, *George Westinghouse: Gentle Genius*, 190–191; Swaine, 1:650, 769–770.

15 "not so much a great lawyer . . . legal mind": *New York Times*, July 2, 1940. See also Koegel, *Walter S. Carter*, 67.

15 Cravath had left Walter Carter . . . Piping Rock Club: Swaine, 1:589, 591, 677; *New York Times*, Oct. 29, 30, Nov. 16, 1892, May 5, Oct. 9, 1911, July 2, 1940, Mar. 5, 1989; *Washington Daily Republican* (Wilmington, DE), Nov. 16, 1892; Graham Moore, *The Last Days of Night* (New York: Random House, 2016), 361; "Agnes B. Huntington Cravath," Find a Grave, July 8, 2012, https://www.findagrave.com/memorial/93305271/agnes-b.-cravath; Robert B. MacKay, Anthony Baker, and Carol A. Traynor, eds., *Long Island Country Houses and Their Architects, 1860–1940* (New York: Society for the Preservation of Long Island Antiquities/W. W. Norton, 1997), 59.

15 In 1899 Cravath moved . . . William Dameron Guthrie: Swaine, 1:359–361, 384, 386, 459, 490, 518–536, 539, 552, 572–573, 590, 669, 709; *Richmond* (VA) *Times-Dispatch*, June 17, 1906; *New York Times*, Dec. 9, 1935; Hurst, *Growth of American Law*, 350–351.

16 Guthrie was a brilliant . . . Guthrie, Cravath & Henderson: Swaine, 1:459 (first quotation), 659, 665, 675–676, 775–779; *Reminiscences of Allen Ward-*

well, 1952, Columbia Center for Oral History Archives, Columbia University Rare Book and Manuscript Library, 79; Robert W. Gordon, "'The Ideal and the Actual in the Law': Fantasies and Practices of New York City Lawyers, 1870-1910," in Gawalt, *New High Priests*, 65; *Harper's Weekly*, Aug. 29, 1891, 662 (second quotation); Paul J. Mateyunas, *Long Island's Gold Coast* (Charleston, SC: Arcadia, 2012), 16, 77.

Chapter 2: "Send Your Man to My Man"

17   **As J. P. Morgan . . . invulnerable to legal attack:** Ron Chernow, *The House of Morgan: An American Banking Dynasty and the Rise of Modern Finance* (New York: Grove Press, 1990), 106; Strouse, *Morgan*, 440-441; Edmund Morris, *Theodore Rex* (New York: Random House, 2001), 91; Doris Kearns Goodwin, *The Bully Pulpit: Theodore Roosevelt, William Howard Taft, and the Golden Age of Journalism* (New York: Simon & Schuster, 2013), 297-299; *New York Times*, Feb. 20, 21, 1902; *Omaha* (NE) *Daily Bee*, Aug. 13, 1911.

17   **friend of the president's father . . . influential classes:** David McCullough, *Mornings on Horseback: The Story of an Extraordinary Family, a Vanished Way of Life, and the Unique Child Who Became Theodore Roosevelt* (1981; repr., New York: Simon & Schuster, 1982), 252, 363-364; Chernow, *House of Morgan*, 82; Morris, *Theodore Rex*, 29.

17   **The financial markets were equally stunned:** Goodwin, *Bully Pulpit*, 297; *New York Times*, Feb. 21, 23, 1902; Richard B. Baker, Carola Frydman, and Eric Hilt, "From Plutocracy to Progressivism?: The Assassination of President McKinley as a Turning Point in American History" (Boston University Working Paper, September 2014), 21-24.

17   **During the presidency . . . 98 percent:** Baker, Frydman, and Hilt, "From Plutocracy to Progressivism?," 4-9, 22; Goodwin, *Bully Pulpit*, 218; Strouse, *Morgan*, 395-396; United States v. E. C. Knight Co., 156 U.S. 1 (1895). The technical ruling in the *Knight* case was that the manufacture of sugar was not part of interstate commerce. The sugar "trust" was actually a New Jersey holding company, a form of corporate consolidation discussed later in the text. César J. Ayala, *American Sugar Kingdom: The Plantation Economy of the Spanish Caribbean, 1898-1934* (Chapel Hill: University of North Carolina Press, 1999), 38-39.

18   **Hanna called him a "damned cowboy":** Goodwin, *Bully Pulpit*, 292.

18   **What especially galled Morgan . . . "fix it up":** Strouse, *Morgan*, 440-441; Chernow, *House of Morgan*, 106; Swaine, 1:710-711; Baker, Frydman, and Hilt, "From Plutocracy to Progressivism?," 9, 21-24. See also Maury Klein, *The Life and Legend of E. H. Harriman* (Chapel Hill: University of North Carolina Press, 2000), 308-310.

18 Stetson was born . . . horse-drawn tram system: Rousmaniere, 18-23; *Davis Polk: Background with Figures*, 11-12; Stetson to Samuel J. Tilden, Nov. 22, 1870, Stetson Papers, Williams College, box 1, folder 8; *New York Times*, Dec. 20, 1920.

19 Bangs . . . older theatrical school: Rousmaniere, 1, 9-15, 23.

19 "I don't think . . . a word": *Davis Polk: Background with Figures*, 12.

19 One of Stetson's earliest cases . . . launched Roosevelt's career: *Davis Polk: Background with Figures*, 14-15; Rousmaniere, 23; Goodwin, *Bully Pulpit*, 71-75.

19 After Bangs's death . . . second term in 1892: Rousmaniere, 24-26; *Davis Polk: Background with Figures*, 23-24, 28.

20 Five feet seven . . . warm and congenial: Rousmaniere, 41, 67-68; *Richmond* (VA) *Times-Dispatch*, June 17, 1906; Stetson to Cottrell & Leonard, May 22, 1901, Stetson Papers, Williams College, box 1, folder 18 (physical measurements).

20 knew exactly what he wanted done . . . "didn't let things go by": Wardwell, *Reminiscences*, 80, 82.

20 In college . . . owed letters: Spreadsheet, c. July 1867, Stetson Papers, Williams College, box 1, folder 5a.

20 "I've always said . . . incomparably logical": Wardwell, *Reminiscences*, 41, 80.

20 Stetson first came . . . using Stetson exclusively: Rousmaniere, 39-40; *Davis Polk: Background with Figures*, 17, 27; Strouse, *Morgan*, 249-250.

21 "our regular attorney in everything": Rousmaniere, 40 (quotation). See also Strouse, *Morgan*, 4, 430.

21 "Good morning . . . Mr. Stetson!": Levy, *Corporation Lawyer*, 79.

21 Translating Morgan's . . . AT&T: Rousmaniere, 36, 49-51, 104; Vincent P. Carosso and Rose C. Carosso, *The Morgans: Private International Bankers, 1854-1913* (Cambridge, MA: Harvard University Press, 1987), 366-367, 422, 483.

21 "all the usual protections and loopholes": J. P. Morgan to George W. Perkins, July 26, 1902, Perkins Papers, Columbia University, box 5.

21 In 1895 . . . replenish its reserves: Strouse, *Morgan*, 343-344; Jonnes, *Empires of Light*, 322; *Davis Polk Wardwell Gardiner & Reed: Some of the Antecedents* (New York: privately printed, 1935), 21, available at HeinOnline; *New York Evening World*, Feb. 13, 1895. Traditional accounts hold that Morgan was the one who recalled the old Civil War enabling statute, but Strouse persuasively argues it was almost certainly Stetson or one of his partners who found the old law on the books.

21 $50,000-a-year retainer . . . earned $301,997: *Astorian* (Astoria, OR), Oct. 27, 1904; Jonnes, *Empires of Light*, 323; Rousmaniere, 106-108.

21 "the greatest of the new school . . . merely a lawyer": *Omaha* (NE) *Daily Bee*, Aug. 13, 1911.

21 Stetson and his wife . . . 4 East Seventy-Fourth Street: George W. Stetson

and Nelson M. Stetson, compilers, *Stetson Kindred of America, Inc.: Account of Second Reunion and Other Data* (Medford, MA: J. C. Miller Jr., 1907), 86, 94, 99; Tom Miller, "The 1899 Francis Stetson House—No. 4 E. 74th Street," Daytonian in Manhattan: The Stories Behind the Buildings, Statues and Other Points of Interest That Make Manhattan Fascinating, Feb. 28, 2013, http://daytoninmanhattan.blogspot.com/2013/02/the-1899-francis-stetson-house-no-4-e.html.

22 thousand-acre country home: *New York Times*, Jan. 30, 1907, Nov. 30, 1921; Rousmaniere, 127.

22 attended the wedding: Strouse, *Morgan*, 388–389.

22 good friends with . . . Andrew Carnegie: Carnegie to Stetson, Feb. 12, Nov. 14, 1895, June 20, 1900, Stetson Papers, Williams College, box 1, folders 14, 16; Rousmaniere, 37, 45.

22 "perhaps the most . . . in American history": Chernow, *House of Morgan*, 88.

22 most dominant railroad moguls . . . outbid Harriman: James Wilford Garner, "The Northern Securities Case," *Annals of the American Academy of Political and Social Science* 24 (July 1904): 125–127; Chernow, *House of Morgan*, 91; Strouse, *Morgan*, 418–421; Rousmaniere, 114–115; Cyrus Adler, *Jacob H. Schiff: His Life and Letters* (New York: Doubleday, 1928), 1:102–106.

22 "buy the mare . . . filly": Matthew Josephson, *The Robber Barons: The Classic Account of the Influential Capitalists Who Transformed America's Future* (1934; repr., San Diego: Harcourt Brace, 2008), 436.

22 Harriman began secretly . . . causing the market: Chernow, *House of Morgan*, 91–92; Josephson, *Robber Barons*, 438–441; Strouse, *Morgan*, 419–421; *New York Times*, May 9, 10, 1901; Adler, *Schiff*, 1:106.

22 "the greatest general panic . . . has ever known": *New York Times*, May 10, 1901.

23 Unable to tolerate . . . proposed a truce: Garner, "The Northern Securities Case," 128; Josephson, *Robber Barons*, 442–444; Lloyd J. Mercer, *E. H. Harriman: Master Railroader* (1985; repr., Washington, DC: BeardBooks, 2003), 95; Adler, *Schiff*, 1:110.

23 Stetson's legerdemain . . . unwanted suitors: Rousmaniere, 112; Josephson, *Robber Barons*, 442.

23 a minnow . . . "spew him out": Balthasar Henry Meyer, "A History of the Northern Securities Case," *Bulletin of the University of Wisconsin* 142 (July 1906): 232.

23 Harriman agreed . . . $400 million: Rousmaniere, 113–115; Strouse, *Morgan*, 426–427, 431–432; Meyer, "History of the Northern Securities Case," 232–241; Alfred D. Chandler Jr., *The Visible Hand: The Managerial Revolution in American Business* (1977; repr., Cambridge, MA: Belknap Press of Harvard University Press, 2002), 173–174; Garner, "The Northern Securities Case," 129.

23 **$1.4 billion ... Stetson was appointed:** Swaine, 1:688-689; Strouse, *Morgan*, 404; Rousmaniere, 106-108; *Davis Polk: Background with Figures*, 31-32.

24 **"the people must act ... commercial slavery":** *Minneapolis Journal*, Nov. 20, 1901. See also Goodwin, *Bully Pulpit*, 295-298.

24 **Roosevelt was ... instructed Knox:** Goodwin, *Bully Pulpit*, 298-299; Strouse, *Morgan*, 440.

24 **Morgan's most beloved corporate child:** Chernow, *House of Morgan*, 106.

24 **"unless we find out ... we regard as wrong":** Joseph Bucklin Bishop, *Theodore Roosevelt and His Time, Shown in His Own Letters* (New York: Charles Scribner's, 1920), 1:184.

24 **created as holding companies ... legal loophole:** Baker, Frydman, and Hilt, "From Plutocracy to Progressivism?," 5n4, 22n32; Tony Freyer, *Regulating Big Business: Antitrust in Great Britain and America, 1880-1990* (1992; repr., Cambridge: Cambridge University Press, 2008), 25, 36-37, 41, 135, 137, 154-155; Meyer, "History of the Northern Securities Case," 264-265; Weixelbaum, "Harnessing the Growth," text at nn38-41; Barak Orbach and Grace Campbell Rebling, "The Antitrust Curse of Bigness," *Southern California Law Review* 85, no. 3 (March 2012): 605-624; Lawrence E. Mitchell, *The Speculation Economy: How Finance Triumphed over Industry* (San Francisco: Berrett-Koehler, 2008), 42-45; Ayala, *American Sugar Kingdom*, 38-39.

Chapter 3: "The Physician of Wall Street"

25 **"who taught the robber barons how to rob":** Lisagor & Lipsius, 31.

25 **flashing blue eyes ... "a rather theatrical look":** *New York World*, Oct. 4, 1908 (quotation); *Richmond* (VA) *Times-Dispatch*, June 17, 1906; Stephen Kinzer, *Overthrow: America's Century of Regime Change from Hawaii to Iraq* (2006; repr., New York: Times Books, 2007), 57-58; Dean, 47; Cromwell to Henry Villard, Mar. 10, 1891, Henry Villard Papers, 1604-1948 (MS Am 1322), Houghton Library, Harvard University.

25 **"no life insurance agent could beat him":** *New York World*, Oct. 4, 1908.

25 **more a doer ... a dissector of the law:** Miller, in *Addresses, Memory of William Nelson Cromwell*, 11.

25 **never saw a business problem ... creative lawyering:** Dean, 96-97.

25 **Born in Brooklyn ... bears that name today:** Dean, 4-7, 24, 42; William Piel Jr. and Martha Moore, compilers, *Lamplighters: The Sullivan & Cromwell Lawyers, April 2, 1879, to April 2, 1979* (New York: Sullivan & Cromwell, 1981), 36-39; Lisagor & Lipsius, 16, 19-21; *Chicago Tribune*, Mar. 4, 1906.

26 **Sullivan ... was apprehensive:** Lisagor & Lipsius, 16-17; Weixelbaum, "Harnessing the Growth," n27.

26 **Cromwell ... no such qualms:** Lisagor & Lipsius, 16-17, 23.

26 **"the physician of Wall Street":** *Omaha* (NE) *Daily Bee*, Aug. 13, 1911. See

also *New York Times*, Jan. 19, 1908; Dean, 113; Birchall, "William Nelson Cromwell," 172-173 ("great negotiator" of Wall Street).

26 **Henry Villard . . . Ulysses S. Grant:** Henry Villard, *Memoirs of Henry Villard: Journalist and Financier, 1835-1900* (Boston: Houghton, Mifflin, 1904), 2:297-300, 309-311; Alexandra Villard de Borchgrave and John Cullen, *Villard: The Life and Times of an American Titan* (New York: Nan A. Talese, 2001), 329-334.

26 **Northern Pacific collapsed . . . denied was "tricky":** Lisagor & Lipsius, 30; *New York Times*, Nov. 13, 1900; Josephson, *Robber Barons*, 247; Cromwell to C. A. Spofford, July 14, 1885, Villard Collection, Harvard Business School, box 23, folder 199 (quotation); Cromwell to Spofford, Sept. 25, 1885, ibid., folder 200; assignment dated October 15, 1885, ibid., folder 202.

26 **"What we needed . . . working it out":** Cromwell to Villard, Dec. 15, 1885, ibid., folder 198.

26 **"advice and guidance permanently":** Cromwell to Villard, Feb. 28, 1886, ibid., folder 202.

26 **"I was imbued . . . so interested in them":** Ibid.

27 **"in a very bitter . . . without severe mutilation":** Cromwell to Villard, Dec. 29, 1885, ibid., folder 198.

27 **"I boldly assented . . . That killed it":** Ibid.

27 **"the only one thing . . . inclined to dodge":** Ibid.

27 **Villard returned . . . world cartel:** Lisagor & Lipsius, 59; Skrabec, *George Westinghouse: Gentle Genius*, 121-124; Jonnes, *Empires of Light*, 166, 225; Villard, *Memoirs*, 2:325-326; Strouse, *Morgan*, 254-255, 312-313.

27 **J. P. Morgan . . . counseled by Frank Stetson:** Jonnes, *Empires of Light*, 5, 225; Bradley, *Edison to Enron*, 40-41, 54; Rousmaniere, 36, 49-50.

27 **Cromwell and Stetson joined forces . . . Morgan interests:** Swaine, 1:496-497; Rousmaniere, 88-92; *Davis Polk: Background with Figures*, 28-30, 33; David A. Skeel Jr., *Debt's Dominion: A History of Bankruptcy Law in America* (Princeton, NJ: Princeton University Press, 2001), 63-69, 102; Swaine, 2:168; Francis Lynde Stetson et al., *Some Legal Phases of Corporate Financing, Reorganization, and Regulation* (New York: Macmillan, 1917), viii (quotation).

28 **Two years earlier . . . fee of $260,000:** *New York Times*, Nov. 12, 1890, Jan. 6, May 9, 16, 1891, Nov. 13, 1900; Lisagor & Lipsius, 29; Villard, *Memoirs*, 2:343, 357.

28 **"Cromwell Plan" . . . when the crisis passed:** Dean, 88-92; Lisagor & Lipsius, 31; Weixelbaum, "Harnessing the Growth," text at n73.

28 **knack for numbers . . . different rooms:** Dean, 52; Josephson, *Robber Barons*, 382.

28 **"the severest task . . . in [Northern Pacific] matters":** Rousmaniere, 93.

28 **Shrewdly, he . . . "File":** Swaine, 1:496-498; Dean, 93 (quotation).

28 holders were made whole: Villard, *Memoirs*, 2:367–369.

29 "the pirates . . . vessel's wall": Cromwell to George Siemens, Aug. 31, 1894, Villard Collection, Harvard Business School, box 43, folder 323.

29 he emerged . . . "hocus-pocus legal tactics": Rousmaniere, 94 (quotation); Strouse, *Morgan*, 418–419; Weixelbaum, "Harnessing the Growth," text at n75.

29 "**Morganized**": Stephen J. Lubben, "Railroad Receiverships and Modern Bankruptcy Theory," *Cornell Law Review* 89, no. 6 (September 2004): 1430–1431 and n57. At the turn of the century, railroad receiverships tended to allow large existing securities holders, such as mortgage bondholders and shareholders, to maintain their position in the reorganized railroad at the expense of unsecured general creditors. Ibid., 1445; Skeel, *Debt's Dominion*, 67. However, in 1913, in a case in which Stetson was on the losing side, the Supreme Court held that a general unsecured creditor left out of the original Northern Pacific reorganization for the benefit of shareholders could recover his debt from the new, reorganized company. Northern Pacific Ry. v. Boyd, 228 U.S. 482 (1913). The *Boyd* doctrine was a precursor to the absolute priority rule, which prohibits a bankrupt entity from paying shareholders or a lower-priority class of creditors before a higher-priority class is paid in full.

The *Boyd* case greatly complicated the reorganization process and was attacked by Paul Cravath as "a veritable demon incarnate standing across the path" of reorganizers. But leading bankruptcy lawyers such as Cravath and Stetson quickly adapted to the new regime and maintained their dominance in receivership practice. Skeel, *Debt's Dominion*, 67 (quotation), 68; Rousmaniere, 93–94; Swaine, 2:167–184; Dean, 95–97. See also Alexander M. Bickel and Benno C. Schmidt Jr., *History of the Supreme Court of the United States*, vol. 9, *The Judiciary and Responsible Government, 1910–21* (New York: Macmillan, 1984), 340, 364, 716; Paul D. Cravath, "The Reorganization of Corporations; Bondholders' and Stockholders' Protective Committees; Reorganization Committees; and the Voluntary Recapitalization of Corporations," in Stetson et al., *Some Legal Phases*, 191–198.

29 **Morgan turned to Cromwell . . . $2 million worth of stock**: Dean, 105–106; Lisagor & Lipsius, 34–35; *New York Times*, Feb. 21, 1902; *St. Paul* (MN) *Globe*, Mar. 12, 1902.

29 **Cromwell would later claim . . . given Morgan the idea**: Curtis, *Memoirs*, 83–84.

29 **Cromwell had seen . . . was becoming vulnerable**: Dean, 98–99; Orbach and Rebling, "Antitrust Curse," 609–614.

29 **In one celebrated case . . . "sharp practice"**: Dean, 99; Lisagor & Lipsius, 28; *New York Times*, Feb. 10, 1889 (quotation).

29 **His tactic ended up . . . new stratagem**: William G. Roy, *Socializing Capital: The Rise of the Large Industrial Corporation in America* (Princeton, NJ:

Princeton University Press, 1997), 201; *New York Times*, June 22, 23, Oct. 19, Nov. 2, 5, 1889. Dean, Lisagor, and Lipsius appear to have conflated the Rhode Island and New Jersey maneuvers, apparently on the basis of Curtis's memoirs, which were written almost thirty years after the fact. See Curtis, *Memoirs*, 80–82.

29 Until 1888 . . . skirt the antitrust laws: Dean, 98–101; Roy, *Socializing Capital*, 201–203; Lisagor & Lipsius, 27; Chandler, *Visible Hand*, 319–320; Weixelbaum, "Harnessing the Growth," text at nn38–41, 45; Freyer, *Regulating Big Business*, 25, 36–37, 41, 133, 135–137, 154–155; Mitchell, *Speculation Economy*, 42–45; Ayala, *American Sugar Kingdom*, 38–39.

30 Cromwell locked . . . $50,000 for a single night's work: Clarence W. Barron, *More They Told Barron: Conversations and Revelations of an American Pepys in Wall Street*, ed. Arthur Pound and Samuel Taylor Moore (New York: Harper, 1931), 4.

30 seven hundred corporations . . . money in circulation: Lisagor & Lipsius, 27; Dean, 101.

30 burdened with excessive debt . . . much of it watered stock: Swaine, 1:667, 688; *New York Times*, Apr. 24, 1908; Strouse, *Morgan*, 405–407; Gabriel Kolko, *The Triumph of Conservatism: A Reinterpretation of American History, 1900–1916* (New York: Free Press, 1963), 22–24; Freyer, *Regulating Big Business*, 39; Mitchell, *Speculation Economy*, 58–78. Mitchell argues the real problem with stock watering was it concealed monopoly profits promoters received by suppressing competition.

31 Both Cromwell and Stetson were retained: *St. Paul* (MN) *Globe*, Mar. 12, 1902.

Chapter 4: "Beware of Mr. Cromwell"

32 "villainous": *The Story of Panama: Hearings on the Rainey Resolution Before the Committee on Foreign Affairs of the House of Representatives* (Washington, DC: Government Printing Office, 1913), 654. The "story" recounted in these hearings is largely told by two correspondents for the *New York World* who were enemies of Cromwell: Earl Harding, who put together a "Compilation of Facts" for the defense of a 1908 criminal libel suit filed by the Roosevelt administration against the *World*—a suit Cromwell supported—and Henry Hall, who testified during the 1912 hearings and made liberal use of Harding's compilation. Ibid., 73, 103ff, 630ff. Philippe Bunau-Varilla, another harsh Cromwell critic, also made a submission to the committee, titled "Statement on Behalf of Historical Truth," written in 1912. Ibid., 10–43.

32 "corrupt": Charles D. Ameringer, "The Panama Canal Lobby of Philippe Bunau-Varilla and William Nelson Cromwell," *American Historical Review* 68, no. 2 (January 1963): 359.

32 "the rape of the Isthmus": *Story of Panama*, 140.

32 "the most dangerous man . . . since the days of Aaron Burr": Ibid., 61-62.

32 "remarkably cheap at the price": Ibid., 507.

33 Cromwell's clients . . . New Panama Canal Company: Ibid., 140; Dean, 129.

33 Ferdinand de Lesseps . . . proud French people: Dean, 127-129; *Report of the Isthmian Canal Commission, 1899-1901*, S. Doc. No. 54, 57th Cong., 1st Sess. (Washington, DC: Government Printing Office, 1901), 196–197; Ralph Emmet Avery, *America's Triumph at Panama: Panorama and Story of the Construction and Operation of the World's Giant Waterway from Ocean to Ocean* (Chicago: L. W. Walter Co., 1913), 45-68. Citations to *Isthmian Canal Commission* are to the original report in 1901; a later version, including maps and charts, was published in 1904.

33 Cromwell had no association . . . hired as US counsel: Dean, 129-130; *Story of Panama*, 4-5, 140-141; David McCullough, *The Path Between the Seas: The Creation of the Panama Canal, 1870-1914* (New York: Simon & Schuster, 1977), 273; Curtis, *Memoirs*, 86.

33 penalty shareholders: Ameringer, "Panama Canal Lobby," 348; McCullough, *Path Between*, 288-289.

33 Wyse Concession . . . to 1904: *Isthmian Canal Commission*, 56, 78, 81, 83; *Story of Panama*, 52, 79, 139.

34 some additional digging . . . find a buyer: *Isthmian Canal Commission*, 84-85; Ameringer, "Panama Canal Lobby," 348.

34 "almost unanimous opinion . . . American canal": *Story of Panama*, 210.

34 Congress overwhelmingly supported . . . political unrest: Ibid., 210; Dean, 131; Curtis, *Memoirs*, 88; Lisagor & Lipsius, 40; Morris, *Theodore Rex*, 67.

34 "a scandalous affair . . . evil was spoken": *Story of Panama*, 210.

34 "Public opinion demanded . . . vanished dream": Ibid., 209. See also Curtis, *Memoirs*, 87-88.

34 Cromwell stayed in the shadows . . . public case for Panama: *Story of Panama*, 143-149, 214-218; Dwight Carroll Miner, *The Fight for the Panama Route: The Story of the Spooner Act and the Hay-Herrán Treaty* (1940; repr., New York: Octagon, 1966), 80-82, 85.

35 Panama did hold . . . advantages: *Isthmian Canal Commission*, 81-82, 99-101, 165-166, 258-261; John Taliaferro, *All the Great Prizes: The Life of John Hay, from Lincoln to Roosevelt* (New York: Simon & Schuster, 2013), 425; *New York Times*, Jan. 21, 1902; McCullough, *Path Between*, 283, 322; Morris, *Theodore Rex*, 84.

35 "different, open, audacious, aggressive": *Story of Panama*, 214 (quotation), 219-220.

35 "Napoleonic strategy": Ibid., 217.

35 organized a press bureau . . . "political department": Ibid., 148, 220; Lisagor & Lipsius, 42 (quotation); McCullough, *Path Between*, 273; *Los Angeles Times*, Aug. 16, 1904.

35 "one of . . . confidential agent": *Story of Panama*, 336.

35 Farnham . . . "accomplished her ruin": Peter James Hudson, *Bankers and Empire: How Wall Street Colonized the Caribbean* (Chicago: University of Chicago Press, 2017), 87.

35 Farnham sent a corps . . . pro-Panama material: *Los Angeles Times*, Aug. 16, 1904; Hudson, *Bankers and Empire*, 87; *Story of Panama*, 223-224.

36 "thousand and one efforts . . . Panama route": *Story of Panama*, 221.

36 John Tyler Morgan . . . "the veneer of its crafty diplomacy": Ibid., 222, 631.

36 "he would have believed . . . any crime or offense": Curtis, *Memoirs*, 98.

36 "took charge . . . Panama Canal Co.": *Story of Panama*, 632.

36 48-6 . . . "fate of Panama was sealed": Ibid., 224.

36 hit upon a plan . . . Reed convinced the House: Ibid., 224-225; Curtis, *Memoirs*, 91-92; Miner, *Fight*, 88.

36 But wily Senator Morgan . . . appropriated $10 million: *Story of Panama*, 225, 632; Miner, *Fight*, 89.

37 There was no question . . . was going to pass: *Story of Panama*, 225; Curtis, *Memoirs*, 91, 93.

37 "The supporters of Nicaragua . . . by the conferees": *Story of Panama*, 226.

37 At the last minute . . . million-dollar appropriation: Ibid., 153-154, 225-227, 229-230, 632; Curtis, *Memoirs*, 92; Dean, 132-134; Miner, *Fight*, 89-90, 92-93; *Hearings Before the Committee on Interoceanic Canals of the United States Senate* (Washington, DC: Government Printing Office, 1906), 2:1146-1154; McCullough, *Path Between*, 273-274; Cromwell to T. Roosevelt, Dec. 9, 1908, TR Papers, LOC, reel 86.

37 composition of the commission . . . George S. Morison: *Story of Panama*, 152, 227, 632-633; Curtis, *Memoirs*, 93; McCullough, *Path Between*, 274.

38 had intended to begin . . . a final breakfast: George S. Morison, diary for 1899, George Morison Papers, Smithsonian National Museum of American History, Series 1.2, box 6, folder 4 (quotations); *Story of Panama*, 152-153, 227-228; *Isthmian Canal Commission*, 15; McCullough, *Path Between*, 274-276; Curtis, *Memoirs*, 93-94; Lisagor & Lipsius, 40, 42.

39 Back in Washington . . . their hesitations: *Story of Panama*, 231.

39 ubiquitous . . . driven by his desire: Ibid., 633, 651.

39 unwilling to name a price . . . unqualified American control: Ibid., 162, 229, 231, 240, 636; Curtis, *Memoirs*, 93-94; Dean, 136; *Isthmian Canal Commission*, 198-199, 205-208; Lisagor & Lipsius, 43; Philippe Bunau-Varilla, *Panama: The Creation, Destruction, and Resurrection* (1913; repr., New York: McBride, Nast, 1914), 205-206.

39 Mark Hanna . . . became a dedicated supporter: Curtis, *Memoirs*, 96; Miner, *Fight*, 103; Birchall, "William Nelson Cromwell," 174-175.

39 he obtained a change . . . donated $60,000: Curtis, *Memoirs*, 96-97; *Story of Panama*, 157-158; Miner, *Fight*, 102-103; Taliaferro, *All the Great Prizes*,

428. Bunau-Varilla, the source for the alleged $60,000 payment, later denied it. *Story of Panama*, 42.

40 **They argued . . . no need to wait:** *Story of Panama*, 231-235, 241; Miner, *Fight*, 94-95; Curtis, *Memoirs*, 94.

40 **Admiral Walker also made clear . . . vicinity of $60 million:** Curtis, *Memoirs*, 94-95; Bunau-Varilla, *Panama*, 206; *Story of Panama*, 241-242.

40 **Hutin fired him . . . spending too much:** *Story of Panama*, 164, 241-242; Miner, *Fight*, 112; McCullough, *Path Between*, 292.

40 **From July 1901 . . . Roosevelt confirmed:** *Story of Panama*, 164, 243; Curtis, *Memoirs*, 94; McCullough, *Path Between*, 292; Henry F. Pringle, *Theodore Roosevelt: A Biography* (New York: Harcourt, Brace, 1931), 302, 306.

40 **worth $109 million . . . $40 million:** *Isthmian Canal Commission*, 101-103, 209, 261-263.

40 **$144 million . . . $253 million:** Ibid., 99, 261, 263.

40 **Walker broke off . . . Nicaragua plan:** Ibid., 13, 241, 263; *Story of Panama*, 164; Miner, *Fight*, 104, 115-116.

41 **Committees in both . . . Clayton-Bulwer Treaty:** *Story of Panama*, 164-165, 243-244; Lisagor & Lipsius, 44; McCullough, *Path Between*, 265.

41 **Hutin resigned . . . sentiment of the 250 shareholders:** *Story of Panama*, 14, 243; Curtis, *Memoirs*, 95; *New York Times*, Dec. 22, 1901.

41 **Bô cabled Washington . . . $40 million:** Ameringer, "Panama Canal Lobby," 349; McCullough, *Path Between*, 266, 294; Lisagor & Lipsius, 44; Gabriel J. Loizillon, *The Bunau-Varilla Brothers and the Panama Canal* (2008; repr., Panama: Lulu.com, 2016), 211.

41 **voted 309-2:** *Story of Panama*, 244.

41 **deserved another look . . . Morgan was stunned:** Ibid., 166-167, 244, 637; Taliaferro, *All the Great Prizes*, 425; McCullough, *Path Between*, 266-267; *New York Times*, Jan. 17, 19, 20, 21, 1902; Morris, *Theodore Rex*, 84.

42 **Hanna . . . sought to bring Cromwell back:** Ameringer, "Panama Canal Lobby," 350.

42 **Bunau-Varilla . . . forced to subscribe:** *Story of Panama*, 6; Ameringer, "Panama Canal Lobby," 347-348; McCullough, *Path Between*, 288-289, 401. Bunau-Varilla's personal share was about $110,000, his brother's about $300,000. *Story of Panama*, 35; Loizillon, *Bunau-Varilla Brothers*, 138-148, 335.

42 **"Great Adventure":** Taliaferro, *All the Great Prizes*, 426.

42 **"the work of the French genius":** Bunau-Varilla, *Panama*, 429.

42 **cultivated manner . . . effective propagandist:** McCullough, *Path Between*, 162.

42 **did not meet until January 1902 . . . working independently:** *Story of Panama*, 22; Ameringer, "Panama Canal Lobby," 348-350; Loizillon, *Bunau-Varilla Brothers*, 159-164, 180-183, 189. Bunau-Varilla claimed to have had

long and frequent conferences with some of the Walker Commission members, separate from Cromwell, while the commission was in Paris in 1899. But the Bunau-Varilla Papers in the Library of Congress, as well as George Morison's meticulous diary, indicate Bunau-Varilla had little or no substantive discussions with them at that time.

42 came to tour . . . Tiffany clock: Bunau-Varilla, *Panama*, 173–178; McCullough, *Path Between*, 281–288; Loizillon, *Bunau-Varilla Brothers*, 6, 31, 89, 125–127, 147–149, 198, 335.

43 "never let go of . . . had converted him": *Story of Panama*, 5.

43 claimed converts was Mark Hanna . . . "convinced me": Bunau-Varilla, *Panama*, 184–186. Hanna's biographer lends some credence to the claim, although the source of his information was probably Bunau-Varilla himself. Herbert Croly, *Marcus Alonzo Hanna: His Life and Work* (New York: Macmillan, 1912), 381.

43 audience with Senator Morgan . . . to his face: Bunau-Varilla, *Panama*, 187–188.

43 "the lawyer Cromwell" . . . messenger: Bunau-Varilla, *Panama*, 221, 402, 428.

43 Cromwell's enemies . . . Cromwell's pawn: *Story of Panama*, 3–4; Ameringer, "Panama Canal Lobby," 346.

43 "had no use for Bunau-Varilla . . . meddlesome intruder": Dean, 140, 147; Curtis, *Memoirs*, 102.

43 two men worked together . . . mentioned his name: Ameringer, "Panama Canal Lobby," 347, 351–360; *Story of Panama*, 10–43, 507; Loizillon, *Bunau-Varilla Brothers*, 182. The exact amount of Cromwell's fee for his representation of the New Canal Company has never been ascertained. It appears he made about $225,000 in total, consisting of about $100,000 in fees earned on retainer from 1896 to 1906, plus $125,000 awarded in the 1907 arbitration. *New York World*, Oct. 4, 1908; *New York Times*, Dec. 15, 1908; Loizillon, *Bunau-Varilla Brothers*, 235, 317. Press reports of a $1 million to $2 million fee were common but wildly inaccurate.

44 They were first introduced . . . January 22, 1902: Ameringer, "Panama Canal Lobby," 350; *Story of Panama*, 22.

44 urgent cable . . . to his wife: Bunau-Varilla to [Ida] Bunovarilla, Paris [cable address], Jan. 23, 1902, B-V Papers, LOC, box 4; *Story of Panama*, 22; Ameringer, "Panama Canal Lobby," 350.

44 "alienate sympathies . . . the situation": Bunau-Varilla to [Maurice] Bunovarilla, Paris [cable address], Jan. 26, 1902, B-V Papers, LOC, box 4 (quotation); Ameringer, "Panama Canal Lobby," 350–351; *Story of Panama*, 22.

44 "Your affair was settled . . . Felicitations": Bunau-Varilla to Cromwell, Jan. 27, 1902, B-V Papers, LOC, box 4.

44 placed on a short leash: *Story of Panama*, 23, 244–245; Loizillon, *Bunau-Varilla Brothers*, 214.

44 "Not an hour . . . will give you details": Cromwell to Bunau-Varilla, Jan. 27, 1902, B-V Papers, LOC, box 4.

44 Senator Spooner introduced . . . Cromwell claimed he inspired: *Story of Panama*, 169–170. Miner concludes that the Spooner bill was instigated by Roosevelt. Miner, *Fight*, 123–124.

44 "He is wonderful . . . I have seen him when he wanted to": Spooner to William J. Curtis, Dec. 5, 1894, Villard Collection, Harvard Business School, box 58, folder 395.

45 final floor debate . . . "Hannama Canal": McCullough, *Path Between*, 318–323 (quotation); Miner, *Fight*, 147; Cromwell to Bunau-Varilla, June 6, 1902, B-V Papers, LOC, box 5.

45 Cromwell and Bunau-Varilla supplied Hanna . . . every member of Congress: *Story of Panama*, 71, 180–181, 261, 646, 652; Ameringer, "Panama Canal Lobby," 355–358; Taliaferro, *All the Great Prizes*, 433; Bunau-Varilla to Elmer Dover, Apr. 6, 14, May 13, 1902; Dover to Bunau-Varilla, Apr. 7, 1902; Bunau-Varilla to Cromwell, May 31, 1902; Cromwell to Bunau-Varilla, May 31, June 3, 6, 1902; Bunau-Varilla to Hanna, May 10, 12, 1902, B-V Papers, LOC, boxes 4, 5.

45 one intriguing argument . . . continued smoking and rumbling: *Story of Panama*, 181, 642–643; McCullough, *Path Between*, 283, 285, 315–318; Ameringer, "Panama Canal Lobby," 357–359; Loizillon, *Bunau-Varilla Brothers*, 229; *New York Times*, June 7, 1902.

45 Cromwell's press bureau planted . . . "the earth's surface": *New York Sun*, May 14, 15, 1902; Kinzer, *Overthrow*, 59.

45 Mount Pelée . . . A simultaneous eruption: Kinzer, *Overthrow*, 58–59; McCullough, *Path Between*, 316–318.

45 With Cromwell and Bunau-Varilla watching . . . "corrupt Panama scheme": Ameringer, "Panama Canal Lobby," 358–359, quoting *New York Journal*, June 7, 1902; *New York Times*, June 6, 7, 1902; McCullough, *Path Between*, 319–323; Cromwell to Bunau-Varilla, June 3, 1902, B-V Papers, LOC, box 5; Miner, *Fight*, 151–154; Croly, *Marcus Alonzo Hanna*, 382–384, 449. The *Journal* reporter was James Creelman, who had famously attributed to Hearst the statement to artist Frederic Remington in Cuba, shortly before the sinking of the battleship *Maine* in Havana harbor, "You furnish the pictures, and I'll furnish the war." James Creelman, *On the Great Highway: The Wanderings and Adventures of a Special Correspondent* (Boston: Lothrop, 1901), 178.

46 managed to blunt the volcano scare . . . since 1835: Bunau-Varilla, *Panama*, 245–246; McCullough, *Path Between*, 318, 323.

46 Bunau-Varilla had an inspiration . . . sent them to every senator: Bunau-Varilla, *Panama*, 246–247.

46 On June 19, 1902 . . . "Our bill passed": Cromwell to Bunau-Varilla, June

26, 1902, B-V Papers, LOC, box 5 (quotation); Ameringer, "Panama Canal Lobby," 362; *Story of Panama*, 180-181; Miner, *Fight*, 154-156.

46 largest real estate deal in history: McCullough, *Path Between*, 337, 400.

47 "I trace this man . . . Beware of Mr. Cromwell": *Story of Panama*, 652.

Chapter 5: The Cravath System

48 request for an extra window . . . architects refused: Swaine, 1:557.

48 nitric acid fumes . . . unobstructed views: Swaine, 1:557, 773; Tom Miller, "The Lost Assay Office—No. 30 Wall Street," Daytonian in Manhattan: The Stories Behind the Buildings, Statues and Other Points of Interest That Make Manhattan Fascinating, May 23, 2016, http://daytoninmanhattan.blogspot .com/2016/05/the-lost-assay-office-no-30-wall-street.html.

48 Guthrie had no problem . . . not going to interfere: Swaine, 1:773, 777.

48 mentor Walter Carter: Ibid., 3.

49 would remain in favor for the rest of the century: Galanter and Palay, "Transformation of the Big Law Firm," 33-37; Erwin O. Smigel, *The Wall Street Lawyer: Professional Organization Man?* (New York: Free Press of Glencoe, 1964), 114-116; Hoffman, *Lions in the Street*, 5-7; Paul Hoffman, *Lions of the Eighties: The Inside Story of the Powerhouse Law Firms* (Garden City, NY: Doubleday, 1982), 9-12; James B. Stewart, *The Partners: Inside America's Most Powerful Law Firms* (1983; repr., New York: Warner Books, 1984), 55.

49 Cravath's first principle . . . law review: Swaine, 2:2-3. As late as 1960 more than 70 percent of lawyers at large Wall Street firms graduated from Harvard, Yale, or Columbia Law Schools. Smigel, *Wall Street Lawyer*, 39.

49 "somewhat eccentric—not to say stuffy": Swaine, 2:3.

49 Cravath did not want bland eggheads . . . "sweatshops": Ibid., 3; *Reminiscences of Nicholas Kelley*, 1953, Columbia Center for Oral History Archives, Columbia University Rare Book and Manuscript Library, 55-56, 59-60; Smigel, *Wall Street Lawyer*, 102-104; Eli Wald, "The Rise and Fall of the WASP and Jewish Law Firms," *Stanford Law Review* 60, no. 6 (April 2008): 1831 (quotation).

50 highest going rate . . . $2,000 after five years: Swaine, 2:6 and n1.

50 In return, associates . . . Charitable, educational: Ibid., 9.

50 As to the training . . . different lawyering styles: Ibid., 4. Under the rotation system as it developed at Cravath and other firms, beginning lawyers choose one of a number of specialized departments such as corporate, litigation, tax, or trusts and estates and rotate within their department of choice. Cravath, Swaine & Moore LLP, "The Rotation System," 2017, https://www.cravath.com/rota tionsystem; Smigel, *Wall Street Lawyer*, 239, 242.

50 "not thrown into deep water . . . taught strokes": Swaine, 2:4.

50 watched a more senior . . . in detail: Ibid., 4-5.

50 "geniuses selected" . . . independent responsibility: Dean, 33 (quotation);
Lisagor & Lipsius, 32.

50 tenure policy . . . a drag on the system: Swaine, 2:7; Galanter and Palay,
"Transformation of the Big Law Firm," 40-41; Hoffman, Lions in the Street, 7;
Hoffman, Lions of the Eighties, 10-11; Smigel, Wall Street Lawyer, 64, 77, 85.
As these authors point out, the "up or out" system was not enforced at all firms
as strictly as the phrase would imply. Firms occasionally allowed passed-over
associates to extend their tenures or even become permanent associates.

51 Cravath firm took care of its own . . . profession altogether: Swaine, 2:7-8;
Smigel, Wall Street Lawyer, 64-65, 74-75, 86-90, 130-136; Galanter and
Palay, "Transformation of the Big Law Firm," 40-41.

51 almost always homegrown . . . rest of the century: Swaine, 2:8; Wald,
"WASP and Jewish Law Firms," 1821; Galanter and Palay, "Transformation of
the Big Law Firm," 38, 50-52; Hoffman, Lions in the Street, 60-61; Hoffman,
Lions of the Eighties, 10-11, 32; Smigel, Wall Street Lawyer, 42, 90-91.

51 If an associate did make partner . . . considered bad form: Galanter and
Palay, "Transformation of the Big Law Firm," 39, 41-43; Wald, "WASP and
Jewish Law Firms," 1821; Hoffman, Lions in the Street, 72, 84-85. The ten-
dency of large corporate clients not to switch law firms had eroded by the 1980s.
Hoffman, Lions of the Eighties, 28-29.

51 Under the old nineteenth-century model . . . make less: Galanter and
Palay, "Transformation of the Big Law Firm," 33-34, 42 and n21; Hoffman,
Lions in the Street, 58-59; Smigel, Wall Street Lawyer, 228-230.

52 even at Cravath . . . and worth: Swaine, 2:9-10; Hoffman, Lions in the
Street, 59.

52 "as long as I get my half": Bill Henderson, "How Most Law Firms Misapply
the 'Cravath System,'" Legal Profession Blog, July 28, 2008, http://lawprofessors
.typepad.com/legal_profession/2008/07/part-ii-how-mos.html#.

52 client of one partner . . . shared profits, shared work: Swaine, 2:10;
Galanter and Palay, "Transformation of the Big Law Firm," 33-34.

52 created a meritocracy . . . from the bottom: Swaine, 2:265; Wald, "WASP
and Jewish Law Firms," 1807-1809.

52 religious and cultural identity . . . directly into their ranks: Wald, "WASP
and Jewish Law Firms," 1804-1805 and nn3-4; ibid., 1811, 1824-1832,
1836-1839, 1853-1858; Robert W. Gordon, "Legal Thought and Legal Practice in the Age of American Enterprise, 1870-1920," in Professions and Professional Ideologies in America, ed. Gerald L. Geison (Chapel Hill: University of
North Carolina Press, 1983), 77; Smigel, Wall Street Lawyer, 37-40, 44-47,
65-67, 350; Hoffman, Lions in the Street, 134-137; Hoffman, Lions of the
Eighties, 202-204; Galanter and Palay, "Transformation of the Big Law Firm,"
39. Sullivan & Cromwell was somewhat unusual in that it had a Jewish partner

in 1894 and three in the 1920s. Lisagor & Lipsius, 58–59; Dean, 42. The Seward firm had one Jewish partner in the 1890s, Victor Morawetz, who left before Cravath's arrival. Swaine, 1:381–384, 562–564.

53 **Women did not enter . . . remains tiny:** Hoffman, *Lions in the Street*, 137–140; Stephanie Francis Ward, "Women Lawyers at Wall Street Firms Are Rarely Partners, Study Finds," *ABA Journal*, Apr. 21, 2016, http://www .abajournal.com/news/article/women_lawyers_at_wall_street_firms_rarely _promoted_to_partner_study_finds; Elizabeth Olson, "Women and Blacks Make Little Progress at Big Law Firms," *New York Times*, Nov. 19, 2015; Smigel, *Wall Street Lawyer*, 45–47. Different claims are advanced for the first woman partner in a Wall Street law firm. The New York Women's Bar Association credits Soia Mentschikoff, who became a partner in Spence, Windels, Walser, Hotchkiss & Angell in 1944. Catherine Noyes Lee, named a partner by Cadwalader, Wickersham & Taft in 1942, after eighteen years of practice there, is claimed by that firm as the first woman partner in a major Wall Street firm. The Cravath firm, which hired its first female attorney in 1943, elected its first female partner, Christine Beshar, in 1971. *New York Times*, Jan. 19, 2018. The 1970s saw a number of other Wall Street law firms name their first woman partner.

In 2017, a woman of Pakistani descent, Faiza Saeed, took over as the Cravath firm's first female presiding partner, making her one of only three women at the head of a top US law firm. Seth Stern, "The Dealmaker: Top M&A Attorney Faiza Saeed Is Cravath's Presiding Partner," May 18, 2017, *Harvard Law Bulletin* (Spring 2017), https://today.law.harvard.edu/the -dealmaker.

54 **when Cravath took over . . . more than a thousand attorneys:** Swaine, 2:122 and n2, 2:313; "America's Largest 350 Law Firms," Internet Legal Research Group, 2016, https://www.ilrg.com/nlj250.

54 **"You have a client . . . they go elsewhere":** *Reminiscences of John William Davis, 1954*, Columbia Center for Oral History Archives, Columbia University Rare Book and Manuscript Library, 157, 159–160. See also Wald, "WASP and Jewish Law Firms," 1825–1826; Wardwell, *Reminiscences*, 54–59.

54 **strong executive direction . . . autocratic leaders:** Swaine, 2:12; Hoffman, *Lions in the Street*, 52.

55 **Cravath was legendary . . . seldom got another:** Swaine, 2:124.

55 **"In those years . . . to suit him":** Ibid., 125.

55 **Overconfident . . . was expected:** Swaine, 1:574, 2:127.

55 **Swaine tells a story . . . never mentioned again:** Swaine, 2:125–126.

56 **"Many young men . . . ones he advanced":** Ibid., 127.

56 **"disliked him heartily . . . done his way":** Mackaye, "Public Man," 23.

56 **"I always had the feeling . . . go up and see him":** Wardwell, *Reminiscences*, 86.

56 **"Seldom was he a party . . . those he could not convince":** Swaine, 1:573.

57 "with as much courtesy . . . verdict for defendants": *Davis Polk: Background with Figures*, 43.

57 perpetual calm and smiling countenance: Ibid., 43.

57 One of his colleagues . . . in name only: Ibid., 44; William Henry Harbaugh, *Lawyer's Lawyer: The Life of John W. Davis* (New York: Oxford University Press, 1973), 187.

57 resisted the teamwork . . . death of the three name partners: Rousmaniere, 41, 75-77; *Davis Polk: Background with Figures*, 44; Hobson, "Symbol of the New Profession," 8; Wardwell, *Reminiscences*, 39-41.

57 after Stetson's death . . . more Cravath-like system: Rousmaniere, 77.

57 He went around his office . . . for reuse: Dean, 116.

58 He distrusted the mails . . . "no thought of misadventure": Ibid., 117.

58 Once he was taking a French visitor . . . "they all rose and bowed": Ibid., 33. See also J. F. Dulles, foreword to Dean, iii (Bullpen).

58 Cromwell kept an impressive suite . . . extra one hanging behind: Hoffman, *Lions in the Street*, 23; Lisagor & Lipsius, 29-30, 32; *Richmond (VA) Times-Dispatch*, June 17, 1906, Dec. 31, 1911; Dean, 47.

58 "conceited, arrogant, dictatorial . . . so much time talking": *Reminiscences of Eustace Seligman, 1975*, Columbia Center for Oral History Archives, Columbia University Rare Book and Manuscript Library, 229-231. The page references are to those written in pencil on the transcript of the April 8, 1975, taped interview.

Chapter 6: "The Respectable Person"

60 "professional revolutionist": *Story of Panama*, 62.

60 Philippe Bunau-Varilla . . . would declare Cromwell innocent: Ibid., 40.

60 William Curtis . . . nervous breakdown: Curtis, *Memoirs*, 101-102, 128-129; Piel and Moore, *Lamplighters*, 42.

60 "revealed nothing . . . the revolution": Dean, 149; see ibid., 147.

60 What Dean failed to mention . . . huge gap: McCullough, *Path Between*, 339, 637n339.

60 Spooner Act . . . "reasonable time": Miner, *Fight*, 156, 408-409.

61 The official negotiator . . . Unofficially, Cromwell: Taliaferro, *All the Great Prizes*, 429-432; McCullough, *Path Between*, 329-330, 337; Miner, *Fight*, 109, 126-130, 159, 193; *Story of Panama*, 178-179, 272; Curtis, *Memoirs*, 101.

61 That draft . . . for all practical purposes: Miner, *Fight*, 141-142, 397-407; *Story of Panama*, 141-142, 175-178, 256-257.

61 Concha was a proud . . . pressed for various changes: McCullough, *Path Between*, 330-331; Taliaferro, *All the Great Prizes*, 430-432, 441; Miner, *Fight*, 138-142, 182-186, 211-215.

61 Cromwell was able to convince Hay: *Story of Panama*, 190, 268-269; Miner, *Fight*, 214-216.

61 In November 1902 . . . sailed back to Colombia: McCullough, *Path Between*, 331; Miner, *Fight*, 184-188; Taliaferro, *All the Great Prizes*, 441; *Story of Panama*, 315-316.

62 Tomás Herrán . . . deadline of January 5, 1903: Taliaferro, *All the Great Prizes*, 442-443; Miner, *Fight*, 188-191; *Story of Panama*, 270, 316-318.

62 Cromwell was in despair . . . round the clock: *Story of Panama*, 270-271.

62 Cromwell brokered . . . presented him with the pen: Ibid., 272; Bunau-Varilla, *Panama*, 256-257; Miner, *Fight*, 195, 411-426.

63 "You want to be . . . stick close to Cromwell": Mark Sullivan, *Our Times, 1900-1925: America Finding Herself* (New York: Charles Scribner's, 1928), 2:319.

63 US Senate ratified . . . worked successfully to defeat: *Story of Panama*, 273-275, 328-329; Miner, *Fight*, 198-199.

63 To convince senators . . . a little secret: *Story of Panama*, 273-274.

63 "Do not sign canal treaty . . . letter of today": Ibid., 322 (quotation); Miner, *Fight*, 196.

63 strenuous opposition . . . Yankee imperialism: Miner, *Fight*, 256-258, 264-266, 314-317, 411-426; Taliaferro, *All the Great Prizes*, 470; Pringle, *Theodore Roosevelt*, 310-311; Beaupré to Hay, May 4, 1903, in *Diplomatic History of the Panama Canal*, S. Doc. No. 474, 63rd Cong., 2nd Sess. (Washington, DC: Government Printing Office, 1914), 388-389.

63 they wanted more money . . . quarter to a half: Miner, *Fight*, 261-264, 281-282, 296, 327-328; Taliaferro, *All the Great Prizes*, 471; *Story of Panama*, 52, 277-278, 283, 635; Loizillon, *Bunau-Varilla Brothers*, 216; Beaupré to Hay, May 4, 1903, in *Diplomatic History*, 389.

63 Cromwell knew which buttons . . . ratify the treaty as signed: *Story of Panama*, 279, 336-339.

64 "contemptible little creatures": T. Roosevelt to Hay, July 14, 1903, quoted in Pringle, *Theodore Roosevelt*, 311.

64 "bandits": Pringle, *Theodore Roosevelt*, 313.

64 "We may have to give . . . those jack rabbits": T. Roosevelt to Hay, Aug. 17, 1903, quoted in Pringle, *Theodore Roosevelt*, 311.

64 "greedy little anthropoids": Hay to T. Roosevelt, Aug. 22, 1903, quoted in Taliaferro, *All the Great Prizes*, 473.

64 On June 13, 1903 . . . about their plans: Morris, *Theodore Rex*, 241-242; *Story of Panama*, 344-346; Miner, *Fight*, 293.

64 *World* ran an article . . . fueling suspicions: *New York World*, June 14, 1903, quoted in *Story of Panama*, 345.

64 By mid-June 1903 . . . to which he was privy: *Story of Panama*, 281, 347, 676; Miner, *Fight*, 287; McCullough, *Path Between*, 337.

65 The ringleader . . . became titular heads: McCullough, *Path Between,* 342–343; Miner, *Fight,* 337–338; *Story of Panama,* 349–350; *New-York Tribune,* Nov. 18, Dec. 21, 1903.

65 Beers . . . "persons of high position and influence": Miner, *Fight,* 337; *Story of Panama,* 28, 349, 677–678 (quotation); Bunau-Varilla, *Panama,* 290.

65 "promised everything to him": *Story of Panama,* 28; see Bunau-Varilla, *Panama,* 290.

65 "go the limit" . . . cable code: *Story of Panama,* 349 (quotation), 357–359, 678; Miner, *Fight,* 339, 347; McCullough, *Path Between,* 343–344.

66 Amador took an inexpensive room: *Story of Panama,* 359; McCullough, *Path Between,* 345.

66 José Gabriel Duque . . . import-export business: *Story of Panama,* 385, 690; Miner, *Fight,* 291–292; Loizillon, *Bunau-Varilla Brothers,* 247.

66 Duque's motives . . . "fire brigade": *Story of Panama,* 382, 392, 678; Miner, *Fight,* 354, 360.

66 Duque maintained . . . went with Farnham: *Story of Panama,* 359–360, 690–692; *Trow's General Directory of the Boroughs of Manhattan and the Bronx, City of New York, for the Year Ending July 1, 1904* (New York: Trow Directory, 1903), 43 (Andreas & Company).

67 Cromwell supposedly offered . . . agreed to take a night train: *Story of Panama,* 359–361, 372, 385, 690–691; Miner, *Fight,* 348; Dean, 27–28, 117–118 (Cromwell's dislike of the telephone).

67 Duque proceeded to disclose: *Story of Panama,* 360, 691.

67 He also informed Herrán . . . Amador was in New York: Loizillon, *Bunau-Varilla Brothers,* 248, citing Olmedo Beluche, *La verdadera historia de la separación de 1903: Reflexiones en torno al centenario* (Panamá: Imprenta Articsa), 44, http://bdigital.binal.ac.pa/bdp/laverdaderahistoriadelaseparacion.pdf; *Story of Panama,* 692.

67 strong supporter . . . spur to ratification: Miner, *Fight,* 291; McCullough, *Path Between,* 346; Taliaferro, *All the Great Prizes,* 477.

67 Herrán cabled Bogotá . . . French concession rights: *Story of Panama,* 283, 361–363, 692, 694.

68 "a thousand offers . . . assisting": Ibid., 362, 693.

68 But in their second meeting . . . shooed out of the office: Ibid., 362, 692–694; Bunau-Varilla, *Panama,* 291.

68 "Disappointed; await letters" . . . "Hope": *Story of Panama,* 364–365.

68 Bunau-Varilla would always insist . . . friend's estate near West Point: *Story of Panama,* 27–28; Bunau-Varilla, *Panama,* 288–289; Loizillon, *Bunau-Varilla Brothers,* 250–251.

68 Others have suspected . . . replace him in America: McCullough, *Path Between,* 349; *Story of Panama,* 696; Miner, *Fight,* 356; Loizillon, *Bunau-Varilla Brothers,* 249. Loizillon discounts the possibility that Cromwell

summoned Bunau-Varilla and speculates that Hay's assistant secretary of state, Francis Loomis, supposedly a good friend of Bunau-Varilla's, cabled him in France. Roosevelt biographer Edmund Morris, however, writes that Loomis and Bunau-Varilla did not become close friends until after 1904. Morris, *Theodore Rex*, 665n274.

69 basket of fruit . . . "French and American genius": Bunau-Varilla to Cromwell, July 3, 1902, B-V Papers, LOC, box 5.

69 meet for a dinner: Cromwell to Bunau-Varilla, Aug. 14, 1902, ibid.

69 On September 24 . . . wife had designed: *Story of Panama*, 28–29; Bunau-Varilla, *Panama*, 289–291; Miner, *Fight*, 357; Taliaferro, *All the Great Prizes*, 478, 481; Loizillon, *Bunau-Varilla Brothers*, 254–256, 265.

69 "never saw the shadow": *Story of Panama*, 30.

69 "cold-bloodedly to their fate": Ibid., 29.

69 Cromwell stopped answering . . . until November 17: Ibid., 29, 282, 475, 694, 723.

69 *Nashville* . . . had sent all the rolling stock: Taliaferro, *All the Great Prizes*, 487; Bunau-Varilla, *Panama*, 335; McCullough, *Path Between*, 363; *Story of Panama*, 385; Loizillon, *Bunau-Varilla Brothers*, 258; *New York Times*, Nov. 5, 1903.

70 Shaler . . . force and effect of law: *New-York Tribune*, Jan. 2, 1904.

70 when he insisted . . . They were arrested: Miner, *Fight*, 360–362; McCullough, *Path Between*, 366, 368–371; *Story of Panama*, 385–394.

70 At dusk . . . without a shot: *Story of Panama*, 394–397; *New-York Tribune*, Nov. 18, 1903; *New York Times*, Nov. 6, 18, 1903; Loizillon, *Bunau-Varilla Brothers*, 258. There was one casualty: Mr. Wong Kong Yee, a native of China, who, while eating dinner, was killed by one of the half-dozen shells lobbed into Panama City by a Colombian gunboat, mostly for show. *Story of Panama*, 396–397; Taliaferro, *All the Great Prizes*, 489; William D. McCain, *The United States and the Republic of Panama* (Durham, NC: Duke University Press, 1937), 16.

71 "to the entire exclusion . . . sovereign rights": Taliaferro, *All the Great Prizes*, 494–496; Miner, *Fight*, 377 (quotation); Loizillon, *Bunau-Varilla Brothers*, 262–265.

71 he had pressed Hay . . . Amador's "childish" desire: Bunau-Varilla, *Panama*, 357–360, 372, 374 (quotation at 358); *Story of Panama*, 475; Loizillon, *Bunau-Varilla Brothers*, 261; *New York Times*, Nov. 18, 1903.

71 by lingering with Cromwell . . . died at age sixty-six: Bunau-Varilla, *Panama*, 371, 378–379; McCullough, *Path Between*, 394–398; *Story of Panama*, 475, 722–723; Loizillon, *Bunau-Varilla Brothers*, 264–267; *New York Times*, Nov. 18, 1903.

72 offered Bunau-Varilla . . . express his congratulations: Bunau-Varilla, *Panama*, 402, 428; *Story of Panama*, 30.

72 private memoirs . . . perhaps not at all: Curtis, *Memoirs*, 103–104; see *New York Times*, Nov. 10, 11, 1903.

72 "I wish you would tell him . . . 'skin our own skunk' ": Curtis, *Memoirs*, 104–105.

72 confidential message: Curtis, *Memoirs*, 105; Ameringer, "Panama Canal Lobby," 363.

73 "We are advised that they have *full powers* . . . *I hope it is*": Curtis to Bunau-Varilla, [Nov. 10], 1903, B-V Papers, LOC, box 6; Ameringer, "Panama Canal Lobby," 363 (latter emphasis added).

73 Bunau-Varilla would be excoriated . . . enemy of the people: *New York Times*, Jan. 18, 1904; *New York Sun*, Jan. 20, 1904; Loizillon, *Bunau-Varilla Brothers*, 6.

73 first flag . . . designed a new one: *Story of Panama*, 377, 384, 725.

73 gave a luncheon . . . names appeared on the menu card: Ibid., 731.

74 invest the $10 million . . . official diplomats: Dean, 151; Lisagor & Lipsius, 50; McCullough, *Path Between*, 399–400; *Hearings Before the Committee on Interoceanic Canals of the United States Senate* (Washington, DC: Government Printing Office, 1906), 1:578.

74 managed to have another client . . . shareholders received nothing: McCullough, *Path Between*, 400–401; Lisagor & Lipsius, 50; Loizillon, *Bunau-Varilla Brothers*, 271–272, 335; Cromwell to T. Roosevelt, Dec. 9, 1908, TR Papers, LOC, reel 86.

74 "perfectly willing . . . have the revolution occur": Curtis, *Memoirs*, 103. See also Dean, 147.

74 But they also knew . . . their railroad property: *Story of Panama*, 283; Curtis, *Memoirs*, 101–102; Dean, 147.

74 "a typical revolutionist . . . the fun of the game": Morris, *Theodore Rex*, 274.

75 La Persona Respectable ("the respectable person"): *Story of Panama*, 29.

75 "the responsible person": Ibid., 348, 677, 694.

75 "my canal": Carol W. Gelderman, *Louis Auchincloss: A Writer's Life*, rev. ed. (Columbia: University of South Carolina Press, 2007), 77.

75 was brusque with researchers . . . "man of mystery": Dean, 120.

75 may even have relished the "most dangerous man" moniker: Ibid., 148.

75 "walk around New York . . . 'Panama Infamy' ": T. Roosevelt to William Roscoe Thayer, July 2, 1905, in *The Letters of Theodore Roosevelt: The Days of Armageddon, 1900–1914*, ed. Elting E. Morison (Cambridge, MA: Harvard University Press, 1954), 8:944.

Chapter 7: A Gordian Knot

76 Supreme Court issued: Northern Securities Company v. United States, 193 U.S. 197 (1904). The prevailing "plurality" opinion of four justices adhered to

earlier rulings, in United States v. Trans-Missouri Freight Association, 166 U.S. 290 (1897), and United States v. Joint Traffic Association, 171 U.S. 505 (1898), which held that all restraints of trade, not just unreasonable ones, violated the Sherman Act. In his separate concurring opinion in *Northern Securities*, Justice David Brewer agreed with the plurality that the Northern Securities Company needed to be broken up, but only because its contracts were unreasonable restraints of trade.

76   Although Frank Stetson . . . he was pessimistic: Rousmaniere, 115, 119.

76   huge victory . . . since the Civil War: Goodwin, *Bully Pulpit*, 398–400.

76   "the most powerful men . . . before the law": Quoted in Freyer, *Regulating Big Business*, 113–114.

77   lynch mob mentality . . . Constitution Club: Francis Lynde Stetson, "The Government and the Corporations," *Atlantic Monthly*, July 1912, 35; Rousmaniere, 122–124; *Control of Corporations, Persons, and Firms Engaged in Interstate Commerce: Hearings Before the Committee on Interstate Commerce, United States Senate, 62nd Cong., pursuant to S. Res. 98, November 29, 1911* (Washington, DC: Government Printing Office, 1911), 957 (quotation), 964–968 (hereafter, *1911 Senate Hearings, Control of Corporations*); *The Commoner* (Lincoln, NE), Mar. 25, 1904; *Guthrie Daily Leader* (Guthrie, OK), Aug. 23, 1904.

77   Roosevelt knew and respected . . . private correspondence: See, for example, T. Roosevelt to Stetson, Feb. 9, 1900, Mar. 8, 1901, Dec. 29, 1904, June 12, 1905, Dec. 19, 1906, TR Papers, LOC, reels 323, 325, 336, 338, 344; T. Roosevelt to Hornblower, Aug. 27, 1900, July 6, 1906, TR Papers, LOC, reels 324, 342.

77   "There are many reasons . . . anything you ask": T. Roosevelt to Stetson, Mar. 8, 1901, TR Papers, LOC, reel 325.

77   "the big corporation people . . . corporation attitude": *The Letters of Theodore Roosevelt: The Square Deal, 1901–1905*, ed. Elting E. Morison (Cambridge, MA: Harvard University Press, 1951), 3:648.

77   Stetson was a realist . . . began cautioning: Rousmaniere, 119, 122; *1911 Senate Hearings, Control of Corporations*, 959–961, 965–967.

77   "You can't fight a community": Rousmaniere, 123.

77   "My client . . . never will do anything wrong": *1911 Senate Hearings, Control of Corporations*, 967.

77   he devised a plan . . . stick it to E. H. Harriman: Rousmaniere, 119–120.

78   Harriman favored . . . filed suit: Ibid.; Meyer, "History of the Northern Securities Case," 290–292; Mercer, *Master Railroader*, 96; Klein, *E. H. Harriman*, 313–314; *Minneapolis Journal*, Apr. 13, 1904; Wardwell, *Reminiscences*, 90.

78   Harriman's first choice . . . was Elihu Root: Rousmaniere, 119.

78   lion of the New York City bar . . . defended the infamous Boss Tweed: *Washington* (DC) *Herald*, Jan. 11, 1914; *New York Times Magazine*, July 30,

1899; Morris, *Theodore Rex*, 13, 127; Hurst, *Growth of American Law*, 368-369; Richard W. Leopold, *Elihu Root and the Conservative Tradition*, ed. Oscar Handlin (Boston: Little, Brown, 1954), 10-12, 15-17; Jessup, 1:184-185; Jessup conversation with Root, July 26, 1934, Stewart Collection, LOC, box 2, folder "New York Prominence" (Sugar Trust); Jessup conversations with Root, May 4, 1930, July 26, 1934, ibid., box 1, folder "Early Years in New York 1866-1880" (Tweed).

79 "that wicked man . . . heart is against him": Jessup, 1:87.

79 Root's answer . . . "no matter how vile the criminal": Ibid., 93.

79 Root preferred to think . . . clients out of litigation: Jessup conversation with Root, May 4, 1930, Stewart Collection, LOC, folder "Early Years in New York 1866-1880"; Hurst, *Growth of American Law*, 368-369; Hobson, *American Legal Profession*, 91; Jessup, 1:123, 2:304; Jessup conversation with Root, Nov. 10, 1930, Stewart Collection, LOC, box 1, folder "Law Practice." See also Leopold, *Root*, 13-19, 179.

79 "about half . . . should stop": Jessup, 1:133.

79 client-friendly version . . . wanted to do: Hurst, *Growth of American Law*, 345; Jessup, 1:185.

79 his only weakness was for cigars: James Brown Scott, "Elihu Root: An Appreciation," *Proceedings of the American Society of International Law at Its Annual Meeting (1921-1969)* 31 (April 29-May 1, 1937): 8; Jessup, 2:360.

79 "You have shown . . . guilty of rape": Jessup, 1:404-405.

80 as early as 1894 . . . campaign contributions: Melvin I. Urofsky, "Campaign Finance Reform Before 1971," *Albany Government Law Review* 1 (2008): 13-14.

80 "In view of . . . further acquaintance": Jessup, 1:202.

80 "The office of being . . . only one I ever cared about": Jessup conversation with Root, Sept. 20, 1930, Stewart Collection, LOC, box 1, folder "Law Practice."

80 "a thousand new interests": Jessup, 1:218. See also Leopold, *Root*, 23-24.

80 "became a happier woman . . . new contacts": Jessup conversation with Root, Sept. 20, 1930, Stewart Collection, LOC, box 1, folder "Law Practice."

80 had played a pivotal role . . . neutral arbitration: Jessup, 1:272-277; Strouse, *Morgan*, 448-451.

81 "there is no such thing as a lawful strike": Cromwell to George Siemens, July 7, 1894, Villard Collection, Harvard Business School, box 43, folder 323.

81 Root tried hard to convince . . . best interests in mind: Kolko, *Triumph of Conservatism*, 73, 76.

81 Just two hours before . . . $75,000 retainer: Jessup, 1:434.

81 Harriman then tapped William Guthrie . . . defeated a private shareholder suit: Rousmaniere, 119; Swaine, 1:709; *Richmond* (VA) *Times-Dispatch*, June 17, 1906.

81 Root had turned down . . . would rather make less money: Root to Guthrie, May 22, 1900, in Hobson, "Symbol of the New Profession," 9, 24n20.

81 about a dozen lawyers: Swaine, 1:657.

81 Guthrie . . . on behalf of Harriman: Rousmaniere, 119; Swaine, 1:713; *Minneapolis Journal*, Apr. 13, 1904.

81 Johnson . . . "the greatest lawyer in the English-speaking world": *New York Times*, Apr. 15, 1917. See also *New York Times*, Jan. 19, 1908; Hobson, "Symbol of the New Profession," 15; Wardwell, *Reminiscences*, 92.

81 The venerable . . . value of his services: *Richmond* (VA) *Times-Dispatch*, June 17, 1906; Sklar, *Corporate Reconstruction*, 124n86; *New York Times*, Apr. 15, 1917; Hurst, *Growth of American Law*, 349, 368; Curtis, *Memoirs*, 197.

82 "small of stature . . . masterful": *Minneapolis Journal*, Apr. 13, 1904.

82 But the argument . . . relief from the courts: Rousmaniere, 120; Swaine, 1:713-715; Meyer, "History of the Northern Securities Case," 292-304.

82 "co-sinners": *Minneapolis Journal*, Apr. 13, 1904.

82 Supreme Court . . . in favor of Hill and Morgan: Harriman v. Northern Securities Co., 197 U.S. 244 (1905); *New York Times*, Mar. 7, 1905.

82 Harriman's loss . . . $50 million: Klein, *E. H. Harriman*, 388; Josephson, *Robber Barons*, 450. See also Mercer, *Master Railroader*, 97-99.

82 unsympathetic a figure . . . quest for power: Klein, *E. H. Harriman*, xv, 13, 44; Patricia Beard, *After the Ball: Gilded Age Secrets, Boardroom Betrayals, and the Party That Ignited the Great Wall Street Scandal of 1905* (New York: HarperCollins, 2003), 100-101; Strouse, *Morgan*, 420; Chernow, *House of Morgan*, 89; *The Nation*, Mar. 21, 1907, 255.

83 He once boasted . . . heartily reciprocated: Klein, *E. H. Harriman*, 369-370; Beard, *After the Ball*, 147.

83 cold Tuesday night . . . Sherry's: *New-York Tribune*, Feb. 1, 1905.

83 took in more money . . . "sacred trust": Robert E. Mutch, *Buying the Vote: A History of Campaign Finance Reform* (Oxford: Oxford University Press, 2014), 33; John Rousmaniere, *The Life and Times of the Equitable* (New York: Equitable Companies, 1995), 75; Beard, *After the Ball*, 4 (quotation).

83 James Hazen Hyde . . . all things France: Beard, *After the Ball*, 3, 6, 44-45, 68-69, 107, 124-125, 133-136; Swaine, 1:750, 754-755nn1, 2; Rousmaniere, *Equitable*, 83, 91.

84 costume party . . . seven the next morning: *New-York Tribune*, Feb. 1, 1905 (quotation); Beard, *After the Ball*, 4, 171-178.

84 Soon rumors started . . . could have gone to the Equitable: Beard, *After the Ball*, 4, 178; Mutch, *Buying the Vote*, 34-41; Rousmaniere, *Equitable*, 79, 85, 92-93; *Staunton* (VA) *Spectator and Vindicator*, Jan. 1, 1906.

85 James W. Alexander . . . alienating his mentor: Mutch, *Buying the Vote*, 35-36; Swaine, 1:750-751; Beard, *After the Ball*, 184-186, 190 (quotation); Rousmaniere, *Equitable*, 91-100.

85 The Equitable board . . . Root and John G. Johnson: Swaine, 1:751; Beard, *After the Ball*, 191-193; *New York Times*, Feb. 17, 1905; Hughes Notes, 108-109.

86 The newspapers . . . merge the two insurers: *New York World*, Feb. 16, Apr. 3, 1905; Ric Burns and James Sanders, with Lisa Ades, *New York: An Illustrated History* (New York: Knopf, 1999), 231 (Equitable Building); Beard, *After the Ball*, 190-196, 284; Rousmaniere, *Equitable*, 50, 96; Strouse, *Morgan*, 545.

86 appointed a committee . . . Guthrie resigned: Swaine, 1:751-752; *New York Times*, Feb. 16, 1905; Strouse, *Morgan*, 544; Rousmaniere, *Equitable*, 97-98.

86 "such a damnable scandal . . . the Equitable": Swaine, 1:753.

86 Root was so consumed . . . agreed: Jessup, 1:438. In the Supreme Court case, Root, representing Thomas Fortune Ryan's Metropolitan Street Railway Company, unsuccessfully challenged the constitutionality of New York's franchise tax law. Ibid., 434-435. Some sources mistakenly state that the postponed argument was the one in the Northern Securities dissolution proceeding, which had already been argued and decided when Root requested the postponement.

86 An internal investigation . . . Harriman denied it: Beard, *After the Ball*, 238-252; *New York Times*, June 14, 1905; Rousmaniere, *Equitable*, 100-101; *Testimony Taken Before the Joint Committee of the Senate and Assembly of the State of New York to Investigate and Examine into the Business of Life Insurance Companies Doing Business in the State of New York* (Albany, NY: Brandon Printing, 1905), 4:3012-3016, 3021-3023, 3098-3100 (hereafter, *Armstrong Hearings*).

86 now rudderless company . . . verge of collapse: *New-York Tribune*, June 10, 1905.

87 Thomas Fortune Ryan . . . mild-mannered Southerner: Swaine, 1:721-723, 753; Klein, *E. H. Harriman*, 338; Strouse, *Morgan*, 544-545; *New York Times*, June 18, 1905, May 19, 1907; *New York Sun*, July 2, 1905; Edwin Slipek Jr., "The Tycoon: The Story of Thomas Fortune Ryan, and His Legacy in Richmond," *Style Weekly*, Jan. 19, 2005, http://www.styleweekly.com/rich mond/the-tycoon/Content?oid=1378337twp; James Blaine Walker, *Fifty Years of Rapid Transit, 1864-1917* (New York: Law Printing, 1918), 192.

87 "the sphinx of Wall Street . . . Who is Thomas F. Ryan?": *New York Times*, June 18, 1905.

87 "the most adroit . . . ever known": *New York Times*, May 19, 1907. See also Mutch, *Buying the Vote*, 30-31.

87 Root had been instrumental . . . watered stock: Burrows and Wallace, *Gotham*, 1057; Walker, *Fifty Years of Rapid Transit*, 193; Josephson, *Robber Barons*, 385-386; Leopold, *Root*, 17.

87 Ryan later opined . . . not a dollar: *New York Times*, Apr. 24, 1908.

87 Ryan was looking to expand . . . and vice versa: Swaine, 1:729-730; Walker, *Fifty Years of Rapid Transit*, 192-198.

88 "rapid transit . . . every citizen": Walker, *Fifty Years of Rapid Transit*, 196.

88 Cravath appeared regularly . . . Brooklyn transportation system: Swaine, 1:730; *New York Times*, Mar. 31, Apr. 21, May 27, 28, 30, 1905; Walker, *Fifty Years of Rapid Transit*, 186, 197.

88 After the death . . . three Rodin busts: Beard, *After the Ball*, 260; John H. Davis, *The Guggenheims: An American Epic* (New York: William Morrow, 1978), 112.

88 "the frightful losses . . . had ever seen": *Armstrong Hearings*, 5:4554, 4562.

88 After conferring with Root and Cravath . . . an idea: Ibid., 4556–4557.

88 June 8, 1905 . . . "baronial stronghold": *Armstrong Hearings*, 6:4801; Swaine, 1:753; Beard, *After the Ball*, 261 (but misdating meeting as June 9); *New York Times*, June 18, 1905 (quotation).

89 502 shares . . . dividends on his stock: Swaine, 1:750, 753–754; *New York World*, June 10, 1905; *New York Times*, June 10, 16, 1905; *Armstrong Hearings*, 5:4553–4559, 4563; Rousmaniere, *Equitable*, 102–104; *Daily Morning Journal and Courier* (New Haven, CT), June 16, 1905; Francis Ellington Leupp, *George Westinghouse: His Life and Achievements* (Boston: Little, Brown, 1919), 200–201.

89 He agreed to Ryan's terms, and Cravath was tasked: *Armstrong Hearings*, 6:4801; Beard, *After the Ball*, 263.

89 "a fostering eye . . . exigency may require": *New York World*, Mar. 22, 1906. See also Cravath to Root, Sept. 13, 1905 ("Mr. Ryan is anxious that I should talk with you regarding one or two matters involving him and the Equitable"), Root Papers, LOC, box 40.

89 Equitable board approved . . . officers resigned: *New-York Tribune*, June 10, 1905; *New York World*, June 10, 1905.

89 "wolf and lamb" situation: *New York World*, June 11, 1905.

89 Others, though, applauded: *New York Times*, June 10, 18, July 20, 1905; *New-York Tribune*, June 10, 1905.

89 "the man who cut . . . Equitable tangle": *New York Times*, June 18, 1905.

Chapter 8: "I Turned My Back on Cravath"

90 June 9, 1905 . . . "rather staggering": *Armstrong Hearings*, 6:5135–5136.

90 had plenty of money . . . told him so: Ibid., 5137–5138.

90 Ryan promised . . . wait to hear from Ryan: Ibid., 5140–5141.

90 "I went there . . . and walked away": Ibid., 5141.

91 "Mr. Root had insisted . . . announcement to me": Ibid., 5141. See also Klein, *E. H. Harriman*, 44 (Harriman's height).

91 Cravath was retained . . . not be scapegoated: Swaine, 1:755–757.

91 Charles Evans Hughes . . . complex matters: Ibid., 587–588, 756–757; *New*

York Times, Aug. 28, 1948; Hughes Notes, xiii, 16, 24–26, 49–53, 56–67, 80–81, 88–97.

92 **speed reader with a photographic memory:** Dexter Perkins, *Charles Evans Hughes and American Democratic Statesmanship*, ed. Oscar Handlin (Boston: Little, Brown, 1956), xvi–xvii.

92 **"Many nights Hughes and I . . . still reading":** Merlo J. Pusey, *Charles Evans Hughes* (New York: Macmillan, 1951), 1:81.

92 **"His was an intellectual moralism . . . the facts":** Mark Sullivan, *Our Times, 1900-1925: Pre-War America* (New York: Charles Scribner's, 1930), 3:54.

92 **"he cut me off . . . the word 'if' ":** Davis, *Reminiscences*, 100.

92 **Hughes was more engaging . . . witty conversationalist:** Pusey, *Hughes*, 1:174–175, 221, 339; *New York Times*, Aug. 28, 1948.

92 **tense and high-strung . . . to improve his efficiency:** Hughes Notes, 176–177.

92 **Hughes frequently worked himself . . . European vacations:** Hughes Notes, 114–115; Perkins, *Charles Evans Hughes*, xvii; Bickel and Schmidt, *Supreme Court*, 399.

92 **He was reluctant . . . hurried home:** Hughes Notes, 121–122 and n7.

93 **"the scandal . . . one sustained event":** Mark J. Roe, "Foundations of Corporate Finance: The 1906 Pacification of the Insurance Industry," *Columbia Law Review* 93, no. 3 (April 1993): 657.

93 **Hughes soberly and methodically . . . newspaper reader:** Ibid., 657; Swaine, 1:758; Mutch, *Buying the Vote*, 39–40; Rousmaniere, *Equitable*, 109–111; Martin, *Causes and Conflicts*, 197–199; *Staunton* (VA) *Spectator and Vindicator*, Jan. 1, 1906.

93 **He was so effective . . . Hughes declined:** Beard, *After the Ball*, 286–287; Hughes Notes, 128–131; Perkins, *Charles Evans Hughes*, 5.

93 **George W. Perkins . . . a bogus sale:** John A. Garraty, *Right-Hand Man: The Life of George W. Perkins* (New York: Harper, 1957), 171–172; Chernow, *House of Morgan*, 108–110.

94 **"Now . . . what the actual case is":** *Armstrong Hearings*, 1:771–772.

94 **"When you bargained . . . myself, probably":** *Armstrong Hearings*, 2:1219.

94 **got Perkins to admit . . . his own pocket:** *Armstrong Hearings*, 1:751–752, 759–760; Garraty, *Right-Hand Man*, 183, 190–193; Chernow, *House of Morgan*, 110; Perkins to Alexander Orr, Mar. 6, 1907, Perkins Papers, Columbia University, box 9. Perkins, who made the campaign contribution at the request of New York Life's chairman, asserted he was acting in what he considered the best interests of the company. Perkins to William Travers Jerome, Mar. 27, 1906, Perkins Papers, Columbia University, box 7. A second indictment of Perkins for falsifying company records to conceal New York Life's sale of railroad stocks was also later dismissed. Garraty, *Right-Hand Man*, 193–194.

94　Thomas Ryan was called . . . motives could not be questioned: *Armstrong Hearings*, 5:4555; Swaine, 1:753.

94　great public service . . . his own financial interests: *Armstrong Hearings*, 5:4562.

95　"Mr. E. H. Harriman desired . . . I refused": Ibid., 5:4566.

95　Ryan had made up his mind . . . quite strained: Ibid., 4566, 4573-4574.

95　"unofficial" and "private" conversation . . . not required to disclose: Ibid., 4567, 4569.

95　"My advice . . . I do under advice of counsel": Ibid., 4571-4572.

95　declined more than a dozen times: Ibid., 4566-4575.

95　RYAN WON'T TELL: *New York Times*, Dec. 9, 1905.

95　asked the county district attorney . . . $500 fine: *Armstrong Hearings*, 5:4792-4793; *New-York Tribune*, Dec. 9, 1905.

95　"of having shielded . . . supposed to wield": Cravath to Root, Dec. 12, 1905, Root Papers, LOC, box 40.

95　"There is nothing confidential . . . now": *New York Times*, Oct. 1, 1905.

96　Jerome concluded . . . Ryan would answer their questions: *Armstrong Hearings*, 5:4794. See also Cravath to Root, Dec. 12, 1905, Root Papers, LOC, box 40.

96　Ryan took the stand . . . now prepared to do: *Armstrong Hearings*, 6:4799.

96　about a meeting . . . on Monday, June 12: Ibid., 4801-4802, 5143.

96　As Ryan recounted . . . "would be against me": Ibid., 4800-4809 (quotation at 4806).

96　HARRIMAN WANTED HALF: *New-York Tribune*, Dec. 13, 1905.

96　HARRIMAN HOLD-UP . . . THREATENED TO RUIN ME—RYAN: Swaine, 1:759-760.

96　Cravath privately told Root . . . erred on the side of mildness: Cravath to Root, Dec. 12, 1905, Root Papers, LOC, box 40.

97　"I want you and this committee . . . 'absolutely independent'": *Armstrong Hearings*, 6:5142-5144.

97　"I may have said . . . may have done so": Ibid., 5144.

97　"Not yet": Ibid., 5153. See *New York Times*, Dec. 16, 1905.

97　issued a report . . . "rather drastic": Swaine, 1:760-761 (quotation).

97　legislature passed . . . going to jail: Beard, *After the Ball*, 10-11, 341, 348-349; Martin, *Causes and Conflicts*, 199; Swaine, 1:763-764; Roe, "Foundations of Corporate Finance," 639, 651; Mutch, *Buying the Vote*, 40, 45-47; Rousmaniere, *Equitable*, 111-112; *New York Times*, Feb. 1, 1906, Feb. 14, 1934 (fifty-six indictments). Some of the new legislative restrictions were loosened in the 1980s. Roe, "Foundations of Corporate Finance," 651, 667-682.

98　"to meet the suggestions . . . life insurance companies": Swaine, 1:763.

98　Cravath convinced the Equitable . . . another forty years: Ibid., 764-765; Roe, "Foundations of Corporate Finance," 663-664; Kolko, *Triumph of Conservatism*, 95-97.

98 "the first pervasive . . . in American finance": Rousmaniere, *Equitable*, 69.

98 industry's working bible . . . he kept it handy: Roe, "Foundations of Corporate Finance," 678.

98 Ryan thunderbolt . . . merging with rival: *New York Times*, Dec. 23, 24, 27, 1905.

98 "The community gasped . . . combined with them": Walker, *Fifty Years of Rapid Transit*, 198.

99 plan all along . . . force him to merge: Ibid., 193.

99 merger was bitterly attacked: Swaine, 1:731, 733; *New-York Tribune*, Feb. 21, 1906.

99 "corporation attorneys . . . financial freebooter": *New York Sun*, Oct. 2, 1906.

99 "I wish publicly to thank . . . for his opposition to me": Ibid.

99 "It has been disheartening . . . as it is foolish": T. Roosevelt to Cravath, Oct. 31, 1906, TR Papers, LOC, reel 343.

100 Roosevelt named Cravath . . . housing reform movement: *New York Times*, Apr. 17, 1900; Swaine, 1:576; Burns and Sanders, *New York*, 300; *Muskogee Cimeter* (Muskogee, Indiana Territory, OK), Nov. 16, 1906; *Housing Reform in New York City: A Report of the Tenement House Committee of the Charity Organization Society of the City of New York, 1911, 1912, 1913* (New York: M. B. Brown, 1914), 47.

100 "The adjustment of . . . Wall Street lawyer is surrounded": Cravath to T. Roosevelt, Nov. 7, 1906, TR Papers, LOC, reel 70.

101 "I wonder if you realize . . . Would you mind doing this?": T. Roosevelt to Cravath, Nov. 27, 1906, TR Papers, LOC, reel 343.

101 Hughes ended up . . . Moreland Act: Perkins, *Charles Evans Hughes*, 8–28.

101 SOME MODERN MILLIONAIRE . . . "dresses impressively": *Richmond* (VA) *Times-Dispatch*, June 17, 1906.

101 Guthrie had withdrawn . . . "made everyone about him jumpy": Swaine, 1:775 (quotation), 778.

102 becoming increasingly inconsiderate . . . perform the honors: Ibid., 776.

102 "was that of unbounded physical strength . . . his pace": Ibid., 777.

102 Guthrie came to resent . . . had never much cared for: Ibid., 777.

Chapter 9: "Nothing but a Paid Attorney"

103 digging had become stalled . . . versus lock system: McCullough, *Path Between*, 438–458, 485–489.

103 Morgan, a Southern Democrat . . . left him bitter: Thomas Adams Upchurch, "John Tyler Morgan," Encyclopedia of Alabama, last updated May 28, 2014, http://www.encyclopediaofalabama.org/article/h-1508.

104　The previous June . . . in the lurch: *New York Times*, June 30, 1905; *Hearings Before the Committee on Interoceanic Canals of the United States Senate* (Washington, DC: Government Printing Office, 1906), 1:550-555, 568-576, 2:1072, 1075 (hereafter, *1906 Canal Hearings*).

104　major reason . . . Cromwell's interference: *1906 Canal Hearings*, 1:551, 577-578; *New York Times*, Feb. 6, 1906.

104　"dangerous man . . . might not be willing to carry out": *1906 Canal Hearings*, 1:578-579.

104　radically different explanation . . . " 'my hat to you' ": *1906 Canal Hearings*, 2:1047, 1050.

104　"recording phonographically . . . every conversation": *1906 Canal Hearings*, 2:1070.

105　"In other words . . . the essence": Ibid., 1063.

105　"There are some subjects . . . worth treating lightly": Ibid., 1065.

105　he and Wallace grasped . . . sermonizing and sentimentality: Ibid., 1068, 1077; *New York Sun*, Feb. 27, 1906.

105　John F. Stevens . . . talked him into accepting: *1906 Canal Hearings*, 2:1074; McCullough, *Path Between*, 459-460.

105　"probably the most valuable . . . 'silver-tongued' attorney": McCullough, *Path Between*, 460.

106　"an honor": *1906 Canal Hearings*, 2:1103.

106　"Because of the broad instinct . . . unfortunately": Ibid., 1177-1178.

106　net worth . . . hundred million dollars: Ibid., 1103.

106　dodging . . . Morgan threatened: Ibid., 1130 (quotations), 1143-1145, 1187-1188, 1360-1362, 4:3059-3061, 3193-3195, 3207; *New York Times*, Feb. 28, Mar. 1, 3, 4, 1906; *New York Sun*, June 20, 1906.

106　Privately, Cromwell . . . his brother lawyers: Curtis, *Memoirs*, 197-198.

106　"How will the torturing . . . before them?": *New York Times*, Mar. 22, 1906. See *New York Times*, June 21, 1906.

106　"Let the dead past bury its dead": *New-York Tribune*, June 28, 1906.

107　"lower bar . . . and cultivation": Elihu Root, *Addresses on Government and Citizenship*, ed. Robert Bacon and James Brown Scott (Cambridge, MA: Harvard University Press, 1916), 497. See also Hobson, *American Legal Profession*, 283-284, 299.

107　Samuel Untermyer . . . many business introductions: *New York Times*, Mar. 17, 1940; Alva Johnston, "Little Giant 1," *New Yorker*, May 17, 1930; Mitchell, *Speculation Economy*, 220 (quotation); Richard A. Hawkins, "Samuel Untermyer (1858-1940)," in Immigrant Entrepreneurship: German-American Business Biographies, 1720 to the Present, vol. 2, ed. William J. Hausman (German Historical Institute, last modified Nov. 12, 2013), https://www .immigrantentrepreneurship.org/entry.php?rec=181#_edn20; Richard A. Hawkins, "The Marketing of Legal Services in the United States, 1855-1912:

A Case Study of Guggenheimer, Untermyer & Marshall of New York City and the Predecessor Partnerships," *American Journal of Legal History* 53 (April 2013): 247-255.

107 **"Between the Irish . . . men of our race":** Richard A. Hawkins, "The 'Jewish Threat' and the Origins of the American Surveillance State: A Case Study of the Untermyer Family," *Australian Journal of Jewish Studies* 24 (2010): 77.

107 **$100,000 a year . . . conceded a draw:** Johnston, "Little Giant 1," 30-32; *New York Times*, Mar. 17, 1940; Hawkins, "Immigrant Entrepreneurship."

108 **organize industrial trusts . . . close friends of the Untermyers':** Hawkins, "Samuel Untermyer."

108 **"Mr. Untermyer's firm . . . strong and influential":** Martin L. Friedland, *The Death of Old Man Rice: A True Story of Criminal Justice in America* (New York: New York University Press, 1996), 90.

108 **The firm's clients . . . disdained by elite lawyers:** Hawkins, "Marketing of Legal Services," 239-240, 249-252, 255-257.

108 **he was paid $775,000 . . . "Whew":** *New York Times*, Jan. 27, 1910.

108 **Nor was he welcome . . . hotels:** Hawkins, "The 'Jewish Threat,'" 77.

108 **113-acre estate . . . opened them to the public:** Geoffrey T. Hellman, "The Boutonnières of Mr. Untermyer," *New Yorker*, May 18, 1940, 54-64; Strouse, *Morgan*, 660.

108 **"managing genius":** Mitchell, *Speculation Economy*, 52. See also Hawkins, "The 'Jewish Threat,'" 104n19.

109 **young attorney . . . $5 million:** Strouse, *Morgan*, 660.

109 **US Shipbuilding . . . fairer deal could be worked out:** Swaine, 1:693-696; Robert Hessen, "Charles M. Schwab, President of United States Steel, 1901-1904," *Pennsylvania Magazine of History and Biography* 96 (April 1972): 208-212, 220-221, 224-227; Chernow, *House of Morgan*, 82-84; *New York Sun*, Jan. 11, 13, 1902 (Monte Carlo); Robert Hessen, *Steel Titan: The Life of Charles M. Schwab* (Pittsburgh: University of Pittsburgh Press, 1975), 148-162; *New York Times*, June 8, 1901, June 24, July 1, Aug. 18, 1903, Feb. 6, 1904; Curtis, *Memoirs*, 83-84 (as to Cromwell claiming credit for the US Steel idea). Schwab insisted the reports of his winnings at Monte Carlo were absurdly exaggerated. Schwab to George Perkins, Jan. 26, 30, 1902, Perkins Papers, Columbia University, box 6; Hessen, "Charles M. Schwab," 222.

110 **"It is almost ludicrous . . . in the press":** Swaine, 1:702 (quotation); *New York Times*, June 24, 1903.

110 **"Unfortunately, men who have none . . . men of honor":** Swaine, 1:698.

110 **blistering, four-hour . . . "Please, Mr. Schwab":** Ibid., 701 (quotation); *New York Times*, Jan. 8, 1904; Hessen, *Steel Titan*, 159-161.

110 **Schwab had looked foolish . . . sought to portray him:** *New York Times*, Jan. 8, 1904; Hessen, *Steel Titan*, 159-161; Swaine, 1:701.

110 **negotiated settlement . . . newly organized company:** Hessen, *Steel Titan*, 161;

Hessen, "Charles M. Schwab," 228; Swaine, 1:703; Arundel Cotter, *The Story of Bethlehem Steel* (New York: Moody Magazine and Book Company, 1916), 10-14.

110 Untermyer himself bought . . . and promoter: *Oregonian* (Portland, OR), Jan. 30, 1916; *New York Times*, Mar. 17, 1940.

111 he tapped . . . years to come: Swaine, 1:703-704, 2:197-200; *Washington* (DC) *Herald*, Oct. 6, 1915.

111 The Wells Fargo controversy . . . no jurisdiction to grant access: Klein, *E. H. Harriman*, 357-358; Lisagor & Lipsius, 37-38; *New York Times*, July 17, 19, 21, 27, 28, 31, 1906.

112 The battle then shifted . . . $175 when the fight began: *New York Times*, July 17, 28, 1906; Lisagor & Lipsius, 37-38. One of the soliciting agents who went door-to-door was twenty-seven-year-old Sullivan & Cromwell associate Hjalmar H. Boyesen II, the son of a famous Norwegian American author. Boyesen joined the law firm in 1904 out of Columbia Law School after working for several years as an editor for *Cosmopolitan* and other women's magazines. Piel and Moore, *Lamplighters*, 59-60; Lisagor & Lipsius, 37; *New York Times*, Oct. 5, 1895, July 17, 1906, Aug. 30, 1929; Herman W. Knox, ed., *Who's Who in New York, 1917-1918* (New York: Who's Who Publications, 1918), 113.

112 annual Wells Fargo meeting . . . discretion of the board: *New York Times*, Aug. 10, 1906; *New-York Tribune*, Aug. 10, 1906.

112 "a rapid-fire contest . . . Harriman champion": *New York Times*, Aug. 10, 1906.

113 "executive genius . . . we may not enter": Ibid.

113 comment would be derisively thrown back: *New York Times*, Nov. 5, 1906; Klein, *E. H. Harriman*, 358.

113 Cromwell proceeded cautiously . . . make a favorable impression: Morton Keller, *The Life Insurance Enterprise, 1855-1910: A Study in the Limits of Corporate Power* (1963; repr., Lincoln, NE: toExcel Press, 1999), 270.

113 hurled allegations . . . A LIVELY COURT DAY IN THE INSURANCE FIGHT: *New York Times*, Nov. 9, 10 (quotation), 1906; see Farrelly v. New York Life Ins. Co., 102 N.Y.S. 726 (Sup. Ct. N.Y. Co. 1906).

114 "My learned friend . . . with this suit": *New York Times*, Nov. 10, 1906 (quotations); *Farrelly*, 102 N.Y.S. 726.

114 "anybody who attempts . . . some good fish, too": *New York Times*, Nov. 10, 1906.

114 The court ruled . . . insufficient evidence: *Farrelly*, 102 N.Y.S. 726.

114 ANOTHER CHARGE DISPROVED—UNTERMYER LOSES OUT AGAIN: *The Insurance Field* 14, no. 23 (Dec. 6, 1906): 14.

114 election went forward . . . administration victory: *New York Times*, Dec. 19, 1906, Feb. 5, Apr. 29, 30, May 1, Sept. 30, Oct. 1, 1907; Keller, *Life Insurance Enterprise*, 271.

115 Untermyer received . . . support the company ticket: *New York Times*, Apr. 18, 1910.

115 "farce": *New York Times*, Apr. 19, 1910.

115 E. H. Harriman owed . . . harmonious railroad system: Klein, *E. H. Harriman*, 49–50, 62–67, 92–93, 211, 253, 255, 273, 348; *New York Times*, Sept. 10, 1909; Mercer, *Master Railroader*, 12–18.

116 prided himself . . . at the annual meeting: Klein, *E. H. Harriman*, 345, 349; *New York Times*, Feb. 22, Mar. 11, Apr. 3, July 7, 1906.

116 "Abe Lincoln type": *New York Times*, Mar. 11, 1906.

116 Although Fish himself . . . white tie and tails: Klein, *E. H. Harriman*, 346–347; *New York Times*, Apr. 22, 1906; Elizabeth Wharton Drexel Beresford Decies, *"King Lehr" and the Gilded Age* (Philadelphia: J. B. Lippincott, 1935), 150–151; Marissa Doyle, "Not the Nineteenth Century: Meet Mrs. Fish," NineteenTeen: Being a Teen in the Nineteenth Century, Jan. 31, 2012, http://nineteenteen.blogspot.com/2012/01/not-nineteenth-century-meet-mrs-fish.html.

116 Along with his bankers . . . mentor from office: Klein, *E. H. Harriman*, 346, 349; *New York Times*, Feb. 6, 22, 24, May 29, July 7, 8, 1906; Adler, *Schiff*, 1:122–123.

116 The commonly accepted story . . . plan to expel Fish: *New York Times*, Feb. 22, 24, 25, July 8, 1906; *New-York Tribune*, Feb. 24, Mar. 3, 1906; *Literary Digest*, Mar. 10, 1906, 353–354; Klein, *E. H. Harriman*, 345–346.

117 Others suggest . . . had to go: Klein, *E. H. Harriman*, 346–349; George Kennan, *E. H. Harriman: A Biography* (Boston: Houghton, Mifflin, 1922), 2:42–49.

117 Still another theory . . . too dull: Terrence Gavan, *The Barons of Newport: A Guide to the Gilded Age* (Newport, RI: Pineapple Publications, 1988), 42.

117 "I must be the judge . . . in these things": Frank A. Vanderlip, in collaboration with Boyden Sparkes, *From Farm Boy to Financier* (New York: D. Appleton-Century, 1935), 203–204.

117 Harriman could force . . . Fish proclaimed: Klein, *E. H. Harriman*, 349–351; *New York Times*, Oct. 18, 1906; Kennan, *Harriman: A Biography*, 2:53–55.

118 "I request that you fulfill" . . . courtesy was wasted on him: *New York Times*, Oct. 18, 1906.

118 On November 7 . . . replace Fish as president: *New York Times*, Nov. 8, 1906.

118 "Mr. E. H. Harriman . . . piratical high finance": Quoted in *New York Times*, Nov. 10, 1906.

118 "one of those ruthless . . . voting power": *New York Times*, Nov. 10, 1906. Fish would mount another proxy fight the following year in an effort to wrest

back control, but he lost his bid for reelection as a director and sold off all his stock. Dean, 103–105; *New York Times*, July 14, Sept. 24, 1907, Feb. 21, Mar. 4, June 25, 1908; Klein, *E. H. Harriman*, 353–354.

118 "The Colossus of Roads . . . excessive financial concentration": Quoted in *New York Times*, Nov. 9, 1906.

Chapter 10: "High Finance"

120 cofounder of the New Theatre: Swaine, 2:77–78; *New York Times*, Feb. 5, 1906.

120 He and his wife . . . steeplechase: *New York Times*, Nov. 15, 1906 (steeplechase), Feb. 3, 1907 (wedding).

120 Long Island neighbors . . . they bought: *New York Times*, Jan. 16, 1907.

120 Cravath became a major booster . . . zoning powers: MacKay, Baker, and Traynor, *Long Island Country Houses*, 26.

120 As part of their white shoe ethos . . . (Helen Keller was a personal friend): *New York Herald*, Dec. 6, 1920, *New York Times*, Dec. 6, 1920, July 20, 1948; Dean, 157–158.

121 real estate owners attacked . . . when he lived comfortably: *New York Times*, Sept. 13, 1901.

121 357,000 New York rooms . . . no windows: *Muskogee Cimeter* (Muskogee, Indiana Territory, OK), Nov. 16, 1906.

121 "three generations . . . unventilated boxes": Louis Heaton Pink, *Old Tenements and the New Law* (1907; repr., New York: Fred F. French, 1932), 3.

121 "unspeakably bad conditions": *New York Times*, Oct. 28, 1906.

121 Cravath would remain active . . . housing reform movement: Swaine, 2:264; *New York Times*, Sept. 17, 1911, Aug. 2, 1936.

121 $50 million French bank loan . . . Paris lending banks: *New York Times*, June 19, 1906; *New-York Tribune*, June 19, 1906; Swaine, 1:715–716; Dean, 111–112.

122 "malefactors of great wealth . . . their evil-doing": *New York Times*, Aug. 21, 1907.

122 In November 1906 . . . launching an investigation: *New York Times*, Nov. 10, 1906; Swaine, 2:21; *New-York Tribune*, Jan. 4, 1907.

122 But early court decisions . . . all but toothless: Friedman, *History of American Law*, 338–339; Marc Allen Eisner, *Regulatory Politics in Transition* (1993; repr., Baltimore: Johns Hopkins University Press, 2000), 50–55.

122 Elkins Act . . . Hepburn Act: Chandler, *Visible Hand*, 174–175; Eisner, *Regulatory Politics*, 55–56; Morris, *Theodore Rex*, 423, 433–435, 446–448; Goodwin, *Bully Pulpit*, 455–458.

122 one-man hunt . . . against E. H. Harriman: Kennan, *Harriman: A Biography*, 2:219, 228–229; Mercer, *Master Railroader*, 144–145.

122 major falling-out . . . main subjects of the ICC inquiry: Kennan, *Harriman: A Biography*, 2:203-227; Mutch, *Buying the Vote*, 29, 225n6; Klein, *E. H. Harriman*, 360-370; Mercer, *Master Railroader*, 146-148; Chandler, *Visible Hand*, 174-175; Swaine, 1:620, 2:21; *New York Times*, Nov. 10, 1906, Oct. 4, 1912.

123 Harriman was represented . . . John G. Milburn: Swaine, 2:21; *New York Times*, Aug. 12, 1930; Frank Friedel, *Franklin D. Roosevelt: The Apprenticeship* (Boston: Little, Brown, 1952), 82.

123 Cravath appeared . . . Harriman's attorney: Swaine, 2:21; *New York Times*, Apr. 5, 1907; Klein, *E. H. Harriman*, 13.

123 When Harriman bought the Alton . . . steep decline: Kennan, *Harriman: A Biography*, 2:230-240, 261-262; Swaine, 1:616-620; Mercer, *Master Railroader*, 105-116, 120-125; *New York Times*, May 3, 1909; Adler, *Schiff*, 1:131-136.

124 By rejiggering . . . cushion against future downturns: Klein, *E. H. Harriman*, 174-180; Mercer, *Master Railroader*, 17-18, 109-110, 125; *New York Times*, Feb. 26, 1907.

124 acquisition in 1899 . . . little if any criticism: Klein, *E. H. Harriman*, 174-175; Kennan, *Harriman: A Biography*, 2:229, 241.

124 "indefensible" . . . "scuttling": Kennan, *Harriman: A Biography*, 2:229 (quotations); Swaine, 1:620.

124 Although Cravath . . . Guthrie had done the legal work: Swaine, 1:617, 621, 2:21, 54; *New York Times*, Apr. 5, 1907.

125 Harriman responded . . . some sort of mistake: *New York Times*, Feb. 26, 1907. See also Klein, *E. H. Harriman*, 17, 179-180.

125 Cravath, better than anyone . . . perspective: *New York Times*, Apr. 5, 1907.

125 It was true . . . no relation to the actual market value: Ibid.; Friedman, *History of American Law*, 391-392; *Cambridge* (MA) *Tribune*, Sept. 16, 1922.

125 But as Cravath pointed out . . . "to make more valuable": *New York Times*, Apr. 5, 1907; Swaine, 2:23 (quotation). See also Mitchell, *Speculation Economy*, 69-70, 73-74.

125 Untermyer . . . "you never would have had a railroad built": Mitchell, *Speculation Economy*, 50-52, 70 (quotation).

125 Alton financing was no different . . . heightened scrutiny: Swaine, 2:23; *New York Times*, Apr. 5, 1907.

126 "my own individual judgment . . . when these securities were issued": Swaine, 2:24. See also *New York Times*, Apr. 5, 1907.

126 Cravath provided his analysis . . . to President Roosevelt: Adler, *Schiff*, 1:134.

126 the ICC in its final report . . . no violation of law: Kennan, *Harriman: A Biography*, 2:305-306; *New York Times*, May 3, 1909; Mercer, *Master Railroader*, 149-154; Klein, *E. H. Harriman*, 404.

126 "corporations were too free" . . . publicity would cure much: Swaine, 2:95-96.

126 Cromwell, too, urged . . . fuller disclosure: Dean, 113-115.

127 It would not be until 1920 . . . securities by railroads: Swaine, 2:25n1.

127 "no-par" stock . . . followed suit: Wardwell, *Reminiscences*, 52-53; James. A. Austin, "Stock Without Par Value," in *Utility Corporations: Summary Report of the Federal Trade Commission to the United States . . . On Holding and Operating Companies of Electric and Gas Utilities*, S. Doc. No. 92, 70th Cong., 1st Sess. (Washington, DC: Government Printing Office, 1935), 83-87; John J. Roche, "No Par Value Stock," *Marquette Law Review* 7, no. 2 (1923): 76; *New York Times*, Dec. 17, 1910; Rousmaniere, 55; *Davis Polk: Background with Figures*, 32, 35.

127 Roosevelt directed . . . Union Pacific and Southern Pacific: Swaine, 2:26; *New York Times*, Jan. 2, 26, 1908.

127 move driven more . . . did not serve the same territory: Maury Klein, *Union Pacific*, vol. 2, *1894-1969* (1989; repr., Minneapolis: University of Minnesota Press, 2006), 175-176, 193-196. See also Klein, *E. H. Harriman*, 404.

128 "If you would let me": Klein, *E. H. Harriman*, 401-402.

128 The Supreme Court . . . was then retained by the Union Pacific: United States v. Union Pacific R. Co., 226 U.S. 61 (1912); Swaine, 2:26; *New York Times*, Dec. 3, 1912, Apr. 24, June 26, 1913.

128 By the time . . . stomach cancer: *New York Times*, Sept. 10, 1909; Klein, *E. H. Harriman*, 434-441.

128 "When we laid . . . to replace": Adler, *Schiff*, 1:117.

128 ironic postscript . . . Morgan thus gained control: *New York Times*, Dec. 20, 1912, Mar. 18, 1913; Klein, *E. H. Harriman*, 341, 493n48; Rousmaniere, *Equitable*, 115-116. After Morgan's death in 1913, control of the Equitable passed to Coleman du Pont, who sold out for a profit when the Equitable was finally mutualized in 1914. Beard, *After the Ball*, 349-350; Rousmaniere, *Equitable*, 121.

129 "a symbol of rapacious capital": Mackaye, "Public Man," 21.

129 Despite the initial uproar . . . able to stand on its own: Swaine, 1:724-728, 2:45-47; *New York Times*, July 30, Sept. 22, 1907; Adler, *Schiff*, 1:165-167.

129 With the collapse of the Metropolitan . . . Cravath had overseen as counsel: Swaine, 1:722-723, 728, 2:46, 52-53, 64, 67n3; Adler, *Schiff*, 1:165-166.

129 William M. Ivins . . . second only to Charles Evans Hughes: *New York Times*, July 24, 1915.

130 First came the revelation . . . had been destroyed: *New York Times*, Aug. 23, Sept. 5, 1907.

130 sold . . . to a junkman: *New York Times*, Sept. 5, 1907.

130 "these gentlemen deliberately destroyed their own books": *New York Times*, Oct. 18, 1907.

130 "You say 'these gentlemen'" . . . "Well, I do": Ibid.

130 more serious charge . . . a plain mulcting: Swaine, 2:50–51; *New York Times*, Oct. 9, 19, 1907, Apr. 22, 1908, July 19, 1910.

131 nothing to indicate Cravath . . . important client Ryan: Swaine, 2:50 51; *New York Times*, Oct. 19, 1907.

131 suit was eventually settled: Swaine, 2:51; *New York Times*, Apr. 8, 1909.

131 Ryan denied knowing . . . heavily rebuked Jerome: Swaine, 2:51; *New York Times*, Dec. 12, 19, 1907, Jan. 28, Apr. 21, 1908, Dec. 12, 1914, Feb. 14, 1934.

132 Undaunted, Jerome continued . . . not provable crimes: Swaine, 2:51–52; *New York Times*, Feb. 28, Apr. 21, 25, June 17, Aug. 25, 1908, May 31, 1909.

132 HERE THEY ARE . . . king of the swindlers: *Daily People* (New York), Oct. 17, 1907.

132 That very day . . . retiring from all interest: *New York Times*, Oct. 17, 1907. See also *New York Times*, May 19, 1907.

133 *Lusitania* . . . breaking all speed records: *New York Times*, Oct. 11, 1907.

133 first wireless press message: *New York Times*, Oct. 17, 18, 1907.

133 on October 22 . . . bank crisis passed: *New York Times*, Oct. 22–26, Nov. 5, 1907, June 14, 1912; Chernow, *House of Morgan*, 122–128; Strouse, *Morgan*, 575–590 (quotation at 578); Goodwin, *Bully Pulpit*, 529–530; Swaine, 2:29–30; Mitchell, *Speculation Economy*, 168–169; Kolko, *Triumph of Conservatism*, 114–117, 155–156; Jessup, 2:184.

134 With Stetson's legal advice . . . prevent New York City: Garraty, *Right-Hand Man*, 206–209; Strouse, *Morgan*, 582.

134 Morgan drove himself . . . twenty cigars a day: Chernow, *House of Morgan*, 126.

134 Metropolitan surface transportation . . . whose owners blamed: Swaine, 2:29; Klein, *E. H. Harriman*, 406; Adolph Edwards, *The Roosevelt Panic of 1907* (New York: Anitrock, 1907), 66–68; Kennan, *E. H. Harriman: A Biography*, 2:311.

134 Pittsburgh-based Westinghouse companies . . . unwilling to bail out: *New York Times*, Oct. 24 (quotation), 26, 27, 1907; Swaine, 2:32–34; Prout, *Life of George Westinghouse*, 19; Skrabec, *George Westinghouse: Gentle Genius*, 8–11, 14–22.

135 Cravath raced to Pittsburgh . . . patient and showed forbearance: Swaine, 2:33; *New York Times*, Oct. 24, 1907.

135 Working with banks . . . "crossed it off wherever possible": Swaine, 2:33–38 (quotation).

135 It would take roughly a year . . . normal state of mind: *New York Times*, Nov. 21, 1908; Swaine, 2:40.

135 "the most remarkable . . . with which I am familiar": Swaine, 2:41. See also Koegel, *Walter S. Carter*, 383.

135 costing Westinghouse control . . . ended in failure: Swaine, 2:39, 41–42; Prout, *Life of George Westinghouse*, 19.

135 "My obligation . . . instrumental in carrying through": Swaine, 2:42.

135 Westinghouse continued . . . died in 1914: Swaine, 2:42; Skrabec, *George Westinghouse: Gentle Genius*, 234–236.

135 "No man I have known . . . foundations that he laid": Swaine, 2:43–44.

Chapter 11: "I Hope I Am a Wiser Man"

137 In January 1908 Cravath was sued . . . a very short-term loan: *New York Times*, Jan. 28, 1908, Jan. 25, 26, 1910; Swaine, 1:724, 2:57–58; Adler, *Schiff*, 1:167. See also *New York Times*, Mar. 22, 1906.

137 As Cravath testified . . . that could be the case even if: *New York Times*, Jan. 26, 1910; Swaine, 1:724, 2:46, 57–62; Adler, *Schiff*, 167–168. See also *New York World*, Mar. 2, 1908 (Cravath statement).

138 "looted" . . . conspiracy: Swaine, 2:58–59 (quotation).

138 Joseph Hodges Choate . . . hands in his pockets: *New-York Tribune*, May 14, 1893; *New York Times*, May 15, 1917.

138 He was sly . . . "skin merchant": Hughes Notes, 86.

138 Choate once upbraided him . . . time he could get: *Davis Polk: Background with Figures*, 20–21.

138 A past president . . . held until 1905: *New York Times*, May 15, 1917.

138 "There are people who think . . . you couldn't know": Wardwell, *Reminiscences*, 78.

139 In a related $5 million lawsuit . . . amply justified by the facts: *New York Times*, June 10, 1908 (quotations); Swaine, 2:53–56. The verbatim accounts by the *Times* and Swaine contain minor wording differences.

139 "Mr. Cravath, can you . . . Nothing else?": Swaine, 2:59.

140 "I think it was Mme. Roland . . . paved with good intentions": Swaine, 2:60–62. A nearly identical account appears in the *New York Times*, Jan. 26, 1910.

140 "with the force of a man" . . . first to shake his hand: *New York Times*, Jan. 26, 1910.

140 The $3 million suit was eventually settled . . . Cravath reportedly paid $100,000: *New York Times*, July 8, 9, 19, 1910; *New-York Tribune*, July 20, 24, 1910; Swaine, 2:63–64; Adler, *Schiff*, 1:163–169. Four of the individual defendants, including Ryan but not Cravath, also financed the $4 million paid by Interborough-Metropolitan by taking notes of that company.

140 Guthrie sided with . . . "not informed of the transactions": Swaine, 1:778,

2:52-53, 64-65 (quotation). See also *New York Times*, June 5, 1908 (Schiff testimony).

141 ethics complaint . . . Guthrie continued to attack: *New-York Tribune*, Jan. 12, 1912; *New York Sun*, Jan. 12, 1912; *New York Times*, Jan. 24, 1912; Swaine, 2:66-67, 67n3.

141 The grievance committee determined . . . "'beyond forgiveness'": Swaine, 2:67-68.

141 Swaine speculates . . . Cravath chose: Ibid., 52.

142 "to the public" . . . not only reasonable but moderate: Ibid.,52-53.

142 Guthrie maintained . . . had always been jealous: Swaine, 1:777-779.

142 Veraton . . . Meudon: Ibid., 675-676; Joan Harrison and Amy Dzija Driscoll, *Locust Valley* (Charleston, SC: Arcadia, 2012), 35, 42, 46-48; MacKay, Baker, and Traynor, *Long Island Country Houses*, 61, 188-189; Mateyunas, *Long Island's Gold Coast*, 77; "'Meudon,' the William Dameron Guthrie Estate, Lattingtown, N.Y.," The Country House, Feb. 20, 2015, http://halfpuddinghalfsauce.blogspot.com/2015/02/meudon-william-dameron-guthrie-estate.html.

142 Guthrie detested . . . "the best of the Bar": Paula Abrams, *Cross Purposes: Pierce v. Society of Sisters and the Struggle over Compulsory Public Education* (Ann Arbor: University of Michigan Press, 2009), 113-117.

142 devout Catholic . . . almost as much a rarity: Abrams, *Cross Purposes*, 117; *New York Times*, Dec. 9, 1935; Swaine, 1:361; Wald, "WASP and Jewish Law Firms," 1804n3; Hoffman, *Lions in the Street*, 137.

142 "which differ . . . from ourselves": Root, *Addresses on Government and Citizenship*, 516.

142 Wickersham warned . . . hordes: Jerold S. Auerbach, *Unequal Justice: Lawyers and Social Change in Modern America* (London: Oxford University Press, 1976), 121.

142 the term "immigrant" . . . Eastern European Jews: Edwin David Robertson, *Brethren and Sisters of the Bar: A Centennial History of the New York County Lawyers' Association* (Bronx, NY: Fordham University Press, 2008), 100n16. See also Auerbach, *Unequal Justice*, 50-51.

143 He did not hesitate . . . went too far: Gordon, "The Ideal and the Actual in the Law," 65; Robertson, *Brethren and Sisters*, 33-34, 45nn39, 41.

143 The Metropolitan experience . . . personal loyalties: Swaine, 2:125.

143 "When I came in there" . . . "a useful thing": Kelley, *Reminiscences*, 109. See Swaine, 2:xii.

143 Kelley, who had joined . . . Kelley Drye & Warren: Kelley, *Reminiscences*, 55, 57-58, 96, 114.

143 One lesson Cravath drew . . . acting as counsel: Swaine, 2:9-10, 68.

144 "Your criticism . . . ten years ago": Ibid., 67.

144 rule would routinely be subject . . . 1929: Ibid., 10, 264, 397, 417–418; Hoffman, *Lions in the Street*, 7, 84; Galanter and Palay, "Transformation of the Big Law Firm," 43.

Chapter 12: Conscience of a Conservative Lawyer

145 He went back . . . Japanese valet: Stetson to Harry A. Garfield, June 18, 1913, Stetson Papers, Williams College, box 9, folder 18; Stetson to H. N. Teague, June 16, 1913, June 18, 1914, Sept. 27, 1915, ibid., box 9, folder 18; box 11, folder 24; box 12, folder 4.

145 desired frequency of chimes . . . new dining table: Stetson to Henry Hopkins, June 17, 1907, Stetson Papers, Williams College, box 5, folder 9; Jerome Allen to Stetson, Nov. 5, 1906, ibid., box 4, folder 21; Stetson to Jerome Allen, Nov. 7, 1906, ibid.

145 dead elms on campus . . . where to plant: Stetson to Perry Smedley, Oct. 21, 1907, ibid., box 5, folder 15.

145 "I am more and more . . . with fellow students": Stetson to Willard E. Hoyt, July 2, 1909, ibid., box 6, folder 17.

146 Stetson's proposal . . . was unanimously adopted: Stetson to Harry A. Garfield, Jan. 17, 1908, and attachments, ibid., box 5, folder 18; *Report of Henry Hopkins, President of Williams College, for the Academic Year 1908, Presented at Commencement 1908*, 10 (available at Williams College Archives and Special Collections).

146 "good-humored persistence . . . riotous exuberance": Stetson to Harry A. Garfield, Jan. 17, 1908, and attachments, Stetson Papers, Williams College, box 5, folder 18. Stetson considered, but rejected, permitting additional games in case of a tie.

146 helping the American Bar Association . . . nearly every state bar association: Rousmaniere, 99–100; Hobson, *American Legal Profession*, 298; *New York Sun*, Apr. 2, 1908; James M. Altman, "Considering the A.B.A.'s 1908 Canons of Ethics," *Fordham Law Review* 71, no. 6 (2003): 2395–2508.

146 "shysters" . . . "into its ranks": *New York Times*, May 29, 1908. See also Auerbach, *Unequal Justice*, 41, 50.

146 One of the canons prohibited . . . lifeblood: Hawkins, "Marketing of Legal Services," 260.

146 "a mere commercial agent" . . . "insidious and secret": John R. Dos Passos, *The American Lawyer: As He Was, As He Is, As He Can Be* (New York: Banks Law, 1907), 33, 80.

147 "the protection of the people" . . . "'people's lawyer'": Louis D. Brandeis, "The Opportunity in the Law," address delivered May 4, 1905, to the Harvard Ethical Society, reprinted in Louis D. Brandeis, *Business: A Profession* (Boston: Small, Maynard, 1914), 321–325 (quotations at 321).

147 **Roscoe Pound . . . Woodrow Wilson:** Roscoe Pound, "The Causes of Popular Dissatisfaction with the Administration of Justice," *Reports of the American Bar Association* 29 (1906): 395–417; Woodrow Wilson, "The Lawyer and the Community," *North American Review*, November 1910, 604–622. See also Auerbach, *Unequal Justice*, 35.

147 **"The way Mr. Harriman . . . price of admission is too high":** Quoted in Levy, *Corporation Lawyer*, 12.

148 **In Stetson's view . . . "public or the press":** Francis Lynde Stetson, "The Lawyer's Livelihood," *Green Bag* 21, no. 2 (February 1909): 49–53, 56 (quotation).

148 **"I never conceived . . . well and good":** Davis, *Reminiscences*, 46–47.

148 **Stetson pushed for adoption . . . newer sets of rules:** Altman, "Considering the A.B.A.'s 1908 Canons of Ethics," 235–236n10, 297–300n373; Hurst, *Growth of American Law*, 329–330.

148 **to this day . . . bounds of the law:** See, for example, ABA Model Rules of Professional Conduct, Preamble 9 and Comment on Rule 1.3. The substance of the 1908 Code's Canon 32 is captured in current Model Rule 3.1. It permits a lawyer to make any nonfrivolous argument having a basis in law and fact, including "a good faith argument for an extension, modification or reversal of existing law."

148 **Cravath spoke . . . moral responsibility:** Swaine, 2:95.

149 **"I am conscious . . . condemn":** Jessup, 1:208.

149 **"the judicious and helpful advice . . . souls and consciences":** Stetson, "The Lawyer's Livelihood," 55.

149 **nobody was particularly happy . . . many blamed the Sherman Act:** Sklar, *Corporate Reconstruction*, 203–204; Mitchell, *Speculation Economy*, 169–172; Burton J. Hendrick, "The Battle Against the Sherman Law: How Capital and Labor Combine to Safeguard the Trust and Legalize the Boycott," *McClure's Magazine*, October 1908, 665, 679; Goodwin, *Bully Pulpit*, 530–531.

149 **"So long as the baiting . . . industrial affairs":** Adler, *Schiff*, 1:39.

150 **Among the biggest critics . . . an unheard-of sum:** Sklar, *Corporate Reconstruction*, 223–227; Hendrick, "Battle Against the Sherman Law," 673–676; Loewe v. Lawlor, 208 U.S. 274 (1908); Lawlor v. Loewe, 235 U.S. 523 (1915).

150 **even Theodore Roosevelt . . . or prosecute them if they were not:** Sklar, *Corporate Reconstruction*, 187–188, 193, 196–203, 249–250, 334–343; Kolko, *Triumph of Conservatism*, 127–129; Morris, *Theodore Rex*, 427; Morton Keller, *Regulating a New Economy: Public Policy and Economic Change in America, 1900–1933* (Cambridge, MA: Harvard University Press, 1990), 27–28; Oswald W. Knauth, "The Policy of the United States Towards Industrial Monopoly," in *Studies in History, Economics and Public Law* 56, no. 2, ed. faculty of political science of Columbia University (New York: Columbia University, 1914), 76–86.

151 National Civic Federation . . . looked to two eminent corporation lawyers: Sklar, *Corporate Reconstruction*, 204-205; Mitchell, *Speculation Economy*, 118, 173; Hendrick, "Battle Against the Sherman Law," 676-677.

152 Victor Morawetz . . . form US Steel: Swaine, 1:381-384, 460-461, 502-510, 562-564; *New York Times*, Apr. 21, 1911, May 19, 1938; *New-York Tribune*, Dec. 16, 1918; Eugene Fauntleroy Cordell, *Medical Annals of Maryland, 1799-1899* (Baltimore: Medical and Chirurgical Faculty of Maryland, 1903), 510-511; Marc McClure, "Victor Morawetz, Draftsman of Political-Economy: A Study in Constitutional Constraints and Solutions in the Era of Reform," Business and Economic History On-Line, vol. 13, 2015, 2-11, http://www.thebhc.org/sites/default/files/McClure_BEHO_Final%20Draft_0.pdf; "Violet Westcott Morawetz," Find a Grave, Jan. 20, 2012, https://www.findagrave.com/cgi-bin/fg.cgi?page=gr&GRid=83734776&ref=acom.

152 "perhaps the most accurate . . . come into contact": Stetson to John Haskell Hewitt, June 8, 1914, Stetson Papers, Williams College, box 10, folder 22.

152 In early 1908 . . . seeking a middle way: *New York Times*, Mar. 18, 1908; Swaine, 1:384, 563-564; McClure, "Victor Morawetz," 11-12.

153 Stetson and Morawetz produced a draft bill: McClure, "Victor Morawetz," 13-14; Sklar, *Corporate Reconstruction*, 229-233; Hendrick, "Battle Against the Sherman Law," 677.

153 But Roosevelt was not satisfied . . . political advantage to the Republican Party: Sklar, *Corporate Reconstruction*, 185-186, 219, 229-236; Stetson to George W. Perkins, Mar. 10, 13, 1908, Perkins Papers, Columbia University, box 9; Perkins to J. P. Morgan, Mar. 16, 1908, ibid.; *New York Sun*, Mar. 13, 1908; *New York Times*, Mar. 24, 1908.

154 Stetson and Morawetz continually attempted . . . said he would veto: Sklar, *Corporate Reconstruction*, 233-249; McClure, "Victor Morawetz," 14; Hendrick, "Battle Against the Sherman Law," 680.

154 "The more I think . . . worse than passing nothing": T. Roosevelt to Seth Low, Apr. 9, 1908, in *The Letters of Theodore Roosevelt: The Big Stick, 1905-1909*, ed. Elting E. Morison (Cambridge, MA: Harvard University Press, 1952), 6:997.

154 The public would view it . . . cave-in: Roosevelt to Low, Apr. 9, 1908, in Morison, *Roosevelt Letters*, 6:997; Hendrick, "Battle Against the Sherman Law," 680.

154 Roosevelt's view prevailed . . . subject to his approval: Sklar, *Corporate Reconstruction*, 238-249; Mitchell, *Speculation Economy*, 173-174; Hendrick, "Battle Against the Sherman Law," 678-680. The final bill as introduced in the House on March 23, 1908, appears in the James R. Garfield Papers, Library of Congress, Manuscript Division, box 128, folder 45. The same folder contains various prior drafts of the bill and related memoranda.

155 "statist" solution . . . public servants: Sklar, *Corporate Reconstruction*, 35-36, 173, 252-253.

155 Stetson and Morawetz distanced themselves . . . not be helpful: Sklar, *Corporate Reconstruction*, 233, 275n133; Rousmaniere, 123; Hendrick, "Battle Against the Sherman Law," 677; *Davis Polk: Background with Figures*, 21 (Garfield); Stetson to James R. Garfield, Feb. 15, 1908, James R. Garfield Papers, Library of Congress, Manuscript Division, box 128, folder 45.

155 "lukewarm": T. Roosevelt to Low, Apr. 9, 1908, in Morison, *Roosevelt Letters*, 6:997.

155 congressional opponents used . . . writing the final bill: Sklar, *Corporate Reconstruction*, 239 and n83, 245n91, 248-249, 283-284n154; Hendrick, "Battle Against the Sherman Law," 677, 680.

155 Hepburn amendments died . . . would take their chances: Sklar, *Corporate Reconstruction*, 249-285; Mitchell, *Speculation Economy*, 172; Freyer, *Regulating Big Business*, 114; Hendrick, "Battle Against the Sherman Law," 677-680; *New York Times*, Dec. 12, 1907, Mar. 24, 1908. Kolko argues that despite Roosevelt's public sympathy with labor, he abandoned support for the Hepburn amendments because he thought they might be interpreted to legalize the union boycott. The letter Kolko cites, though, indicates that Roosevelt's concerns about the labor aspects of the bill were secondary, and that he was equally afraid the bill might legalize the blacklist, an anti-union tactic used by employers. Kolko, *Triumph of Conservatism*, 134-138; see Sklar, *Corporate Reconstruction*, 275n134.

156 "Trust Question" . . . dominant issue: George W. Wickersham, *The Changing Order: Essays on Government, Monopoly, and Education, Written During a Period of Readjustment* (New York: G. P. Putnam's, 1914), 162 (quotation); Sklar, *Corporate Reconstruction*, 2-3, 5, 33, 179; Freyer, *Regulating Big Business*, 111.

Chapter 13: "The Scourge of Wall Street"

157 refused to take William Nelson Cromwell's money . . . any official capacity: Taft to Cromwell, Aug. 6, 1908, TR Papers, LOC, reel 84; Taft to T. Roosevelt, Aug. 5, 1908, ibid.; Cromwell to George R. Sheldon, July 29, 1908, ibid.; Cromwell to Taft, July 17, 1908, Taft Papers, LOC, reel 88 ("vacation" quotation); Taft to Cromwell, July 11, 20, 29, 1908, ibid., reels 473, 474, 475; *New York Times*, July 9, 10, 11, 19, Aug. 23, Nov. 12, 24, 1908, Oct. 3, 4, 15, 1912; Mutch, *Buying the Vote*, 29, 69, 225n6; Goodwin, *Bully Pulpit*, 552; Lisagor & Lipsius, 55. After Cromwell, without clearing it with Taft, arranged to become chairman of Taft's public advisory committee, Taft objected but allowed him to remain on the committee as its counsel. Taft to Cromwell, Aug. 6, 1908, TR Papers, LOC, reel 84; *New York Times*, Aug. 23, 1908.

157 Taft consulted . . . reviewed it with Cromwell: *New York Sun*, July 24, 1908; Jessup, 2:185. See also Cromwell to Taft, July 17, 1908, Taft Papers, LOC, reel 88; Taft to Cromwell, July 20, 1908, ibid., reel 474.

158 "breaches of trust" . . . if the courts were not inclined to do so: *New York Times*, July 29, 1908 (quotations). See also Knauth, "Policy of the United States," 86-88.

158 "The lawyers in New York . . . clients as a rule": Wardwell, *Reminiscences*, 123.

158 Taft's biggest contributors . . . Kuhn, Loeb gave: *New York Times*, Nov. 24, 1908; *New-York Tribune*, Nov. 24, 1908; Curtis, *Memoirs*, 148-159; Piel and Moore, *Lamplighters*, 42.

159 "gratifying": Stetson to Lewis Perry, Nov. 6, 1908, Stetson Papers, Williams College, box 6, folder 8.

159 "conservative progressivism": David Henry Burton, *Taft, Holmes, and the 1920s Court: An Appraisal* (Madison, NJ: Fairleigh Dickinson University Press, 1998), 80-82 (quotation).

159 he hosted a dinner . . . Sullivan & Cromwell Society: Lisagor & Lipsius, 57.

160 "the scourge of Wall Street": David H. Burton, introduction to William Howard Taft, *Essential Writings and Addresses*, ed. David H. Burton (Madison, NJ: Fairleigh Dickinson University Press, 1998), 23; David H. Burton, *Taft, Roosevelt, and the Limits of Friendship* (Madison, NJ: Fairleigh Dickinson University Press, 2005), 92.

160 George Woodward Wickersham . . . "pure materialism": Koegel, *Walter S. Carter*, 10, 326; Wickersham, *Changing Order*, 71-76 (quotation).

160 "give up the study . . . Blackstone": Wickersham, *Changing Order*, 71.

160 He obtained his law degree . . . Wickersham's practice: *New York Times*, Jan. 26, 1936, Aug. 12, 1945 (Henry W. Taft); *The Appeal* (St. Paul, MN), May 22, 1909; Henry W. Taft, *A Century and a Half at the New York Bar* (New York: privately printed, 1938), 284-286; Deborah S. Gardner, *Cadwalader, Wickersham & Taft: A Bicentennial History, 1792-1992* (New York: Cadwalader, Wickersham & Taft, 1994), 1, 6-8, 11-12.

160 "He is a corporation lawyer . . . I don't know": Taft to E. F. Baldwin, Dec. 24, 1908, quoted in Hobson, *American Legal Profession*, 92. See also *Topeka* (KS) *State Journal*, Dec. 18, 1908.

161 Wickersham was widely considered . . . on domestic affairs: Burton, *Taft, Holmes*, 81; Burton, *Taft, Roosevelt*, 92.

161 "expression of the will . . . his people": Wickersham, *Changing Order*, 82. See also Henry W. Taft, *Century and a Half*, 294, 296.

161 he was a student . . . as early as 1436: Wickersham, *Changing Order*, 1-16, 55-57, 64-65, 104-105; Henry W. Taft, *Century and a Half*, 283-284, 295.

161 met the needs . . . "who had but a humble share": Wickersham, *Changing Order*, 32.

161 Corporations had been given . . . curb their abuses: Ibid., 94–96.

161 "redeem the profession . . . selfish forces": Ibid., 98–99.

161 Wickersham instituted twice the number . . . a court trial: *The Federal Antitrust Law with Amendments: List of Cases Instituted by the United States and Citations of Cases Decided Thereunder or Relating Thereto, Jan. 1, 1914* (Washington, DC: Government Printing Office, 1914), 25–55; Wickersham, *Changing Order*, 162–167; Henry W. Taft, *Century and a Half*, 286–288; Sklar, *Corporate Reconstruction*, 151–152, 375–376.

162 Although Westinghouse and General Electric . . . end their arrangement: Swaine, 1:650, 769–770, 2:30–31, 44; Skrabec, *George Westinghouse: Gentle Genius*, 191.

162 Wickersham faced accusations . . . thirty-nine associated individuals: *New York Times*, Nov. 27, 1909, Mar. 29, Apr. 15, May 22, June 5, Sept. 18, 1910; *Chicago Tribune*, Dec. 25, 1909; *American Sugar Industry and Beet Sugar Gazette* 12, no. 1 (January 1910): 11; *Bills and Debates in Congress Relating to Trusts, 1902-1913*, 57th Cong., 2nd Sess. to 63rd Cong., 1st Sess., Inclusive, Dec. 1, 1902-Dec. 1, 1913 (Washington, DC: Government Printing Office, 1914), 2:2316, 2325–2328, 2346–2347, 2352–2353.

162 "Wickersham has out-radicaled . . . most feared member of the Administration": Frank Vanderlip to James Stillman, Feb. 3, June 3, 1910, quoted in Sklar, *Corporate Reconstruction*, 371.

163 "A man who owns . . . that can be devised": Wickersham to George W. Perkins, Feb. 19, 1910, Perkins Papers, Columbia University, box 10.

163 "the willful misrepresentation . . . to answer the call": Wickersham to Stetson, Sept. 5, 1910, Stetson Papers, Williams College, box 6, folder 11.

163 popular magazine: *Puck*, Oct. 18, 1911.

163 Publicly, Taft supported . . . his new cabinet: Hudson, *Bankers and Empire*, 127–128.

163 two most important antitrust cases . . . what kind of economic system: Standard Oil Company of New Jersey v. United States, 221 U.S. 1 (1911); United States v. American Tobacco Co., 221 U.S. 106 (1911); Kolko, *Triumph of Conservatism*, 125–127 (as to Root); Swaine, 1:436–437 (as to Morawetz), 640–641, 776 (as to Guthrie), 2:13 (as to McReynolds); *New York Times*, Jan. 8, 1911; Wickersham, *Changing Order*, 116–134; Adler, *Schiff*, 1:290; Bickel and Schmidt, *Supreme Court*, 87–98.

165 John Marshall Harlan . . . truly good society: Lisa Paddock, "John Marshall Harlan," American National Biography Online, February 2000, http://www.anb.org/articles/11/11-00385.html; Sklar, *Corporate Reconstruction*, 134, 139–140; *Standard Oil*, 221 U.S. at 83–84; *Northern Securities*, 193 U.S. at 331.

166 "It is rotten . . . chewing tobacco anymore": *New York Sun*, Jan. 11, 1911.

166 Edward Douglass White: *New York Times*, Dec. 12, 1910, May 19, 1921; Sklar, *Corporate Reconstruction*, 106, 140, 372.

166 "jovial monk": Isaac F. Marcosson, "The New Supreme Court," *Munsey's Magazine*, March 1911, 747.

166 The press had widely expected . . . Stetson vouched for him: Bickel and Schmidt, *Supreme Court*, 32–33; *New York Times*, Nov. 29, 1910; Rousmaniere, 100.

166 "who personally opposes vice . . . legalized robbery": *Green Bag* 22, no. 6 (June 1910): 326.

166 Taft did appoint Hughes . . . hoped to succeed White someday: *New-York Tribune*, Apr. 26, 1910; *New York Times*, Dec. 12, 1910; Bickel and Schmidt, *Supreme Court*, 26–30; Burton, *Taft, Holmes*, 80; Goodwin, *Bully Pulpit*, 748.

167 At the oral argument: *New York Sun*, Jan. 11, 12, 1911; *New York Times*, Jan. 12, 1911.

167 "safely substitute . . . left in trade?": Bickel and Schmidt, *Supreme Court*, 99n34.

167 Wickersham conceded . . . "sugar the devil himself": *New York Sun*, Jan. 11, 12, 1911; *New York Times*, Jan. 12, 1911 (quotation).

167 tension mounted . . . speculation as to the outcome: Bickel and Schmidt, *Supreme Court*, 97–98; *New York World*, Mar. 20, 1911; *New-York Tribune*, Apr. 25, 1911. See also *New York Sun*, Jan. 6, 1910.

167 "the business . . . at a standstill": *New York Times*, May 13, 1911.

167 "Nobody seemed to care . . . business in the Street": *New-York Tribune*, May 16, 1911.

167 May 15, 1911 . . . "rule of reason": *New York Times*, May 16, 1911; *New York Sun*, May 16, 1911; Sklar, *Corporate Reconstruction*, 373; Wickersham, *Changing Order*, 116–134; "Standard Ogre," *Economist*, Dec. 23, 1999; Freyer, *Regulating Big Business*, 138–141; Bickel and Schmidt, *Supreme Court*, 103–110; Chandler, *Visible Hand*, 350–351.

168 Wickersham called . . . heartily endorsed: *New York Times*, May 16, 30, 1911; *New York Sun*, May 16, 1911; Sklar, *Corporate Reconstruction*, 304, 380–381; Burton, *Taft, Holmes*, 82; Taft, *Essential Writings*, 428–432; Wickersham, *Changing Order*, 116–117, 121, 133–134, 141, 154; Bickel and Schmidt, *Supreme Court*, 111, 115–116, 127–128.

168 Taft had adopted . . . should be allowed: United States v. Addyston Pipe & Steel Co., 85 F. 271 (6th Cir. 1898), *aff'd*, 175 U.S. 211 (1899); Sklar, *Corporate Reconstruction*, 130–132, 367–368; William Howard Taft, *Third Annual Message to Congress*, Dec. 5, 1911, http://www.presidency.ucsb.edu/ws/index.php?pid=29552.

169 "had led clean lives . . . nothing to fear from the Sherman law": *New York Sun*, May 16, 1911.

169 Others reacted . . . a different angle: Bickel and Schmidt, *Supreme Court*, 112; *New York Sun*, May 16, 1911; *New York Times*, May 19, 1911.

169 "As an important business man . . . 'will conform to it'": *1911 Senate Hearings, Control of Corporations*, 958. See also ibid., 965-966.

169 Stetson resurrected . . . advance clearance: Ibid., 958-964.

169 "The law never . . . except a punishment": Ibid., 965-966.

169 "stopping . . . to go on": Ibid., 960.

170 "Will Samuel Untermyer . . . rebates and otherwise?": *Graham Guardian* (Safford, AZ), Jan. 19, 1912, quoting *New York World*.

170 Wickersham won another big victory . . . had to be broken up: Bickel and Schmidt, *Supreme Court*, 183-188; United States v. Union Pacific R.R., 226 U.S. 61 (1912); Klein, *Union Pacific*, 2:194-196; Swaine, 2:26.

170 certain amount of good . . . but only a federal corporation agency: *New York Times*, June 5, 1911.

170 Roosevelt added . . . might need to set prices: Ibid., Kolko, *Triumph of Conservatism*, 175-176.

170 a bridge too far . . . and for Taft: *1911 Senate Hearings, Control of Corporations*, 958, 963-964; Sklar, *Corporate Reconstruction*, 378.

170 Although Wickersham thought . . . bad business behavior: Wickersham, *Changing Order*, 66, 133-134, 153-161; Knauth, "Policy of the United States," 91-92; Sklar, *Corporate Reconstruction*, 376-377.

171 "complete and perfect the machinery": *New York Times*, July 29, 1908.

171 new railroad law . . . had not gone far or fast enough: Goodwin, *Bully Pulpit*, 632-633, 638; Burton, introduction to Taft, *Essential Writings*, 23-24; Burton, *Taft, Holmes*, 81-82.

171 "financial Armageddon": *Hawaiian Star* (Honolulu [Oahu]), Dec. 2, 1911.

171 In part, what incensed . . . lack of political tact: Bickel and Schmidt, *Supreme Court*, 144-146; Goodwin, *Bully Pulpit*, 667-669; Burton, *Taft, Roosevelt*, 91-92; George E. Mowry, *The Era of Theodore Roosevelt: 1900-1912* (New York: Harper, 1958), 288-290; Jessup, 2:184-185.

172 evidence that Wickersham . . . knew exactly what he was doing: Kolko, *Triumph of Conservatism*, 170-171.

172 "minor source of annoyance": Jessup, 2:184.

172 Wickersham played a key role . . . Taft admitted to Congress: Goodwin, *Bully Pulpit*, 605-627; Mowry, *Era of Theodore Roosevelt*, 250-259; Burton, introduction to Taft, *Essential Writings*, 23; Burton, *Taft, Holmes*, 25-26; Lewis J. Paper, *Brandeis: An Intimate Biography of Supreme Court Justice Louis D. Brandeis* (Englewood Cliffs, NJ: Prentice-Hall, 1983), 124-131; *New York Times*, May 13, 16, 22, 1910.

173 "My hat is in the ring": Goodwin, *Bully Pulpit*, 681.

173 had Wickersham launch . . . serious adverse consequences: Chernow, *House of Morgan*, 109, 148; Swaine, 1:705-706; Garraty, *Right-Hand Man*, 126-142, 246-247 (Cromwell quotation at 136); Bickel and Schmidt, *Supreme*

Court, 156–157; Cravath to Charles J. Bonaparte, Mar. 30, 1907 (National Archives and Records Administration, Record Group 122.2). George W. Perkins, J. P. Morgan's lieutenant and the chairman of Harvester's Finance Committee, is also credited with having persuaded Roosevelt not to prosecute. Kolko, *Triumph of Conservatism*, 119–122; Garraty, *Right-Hand Man*, 246–247.

173 **When Wickersham finally ... political advantage**: *New York Times*, Apr. 25, 26, 1912; Garraty, *Right-Hand Man*, 257–258; Perkins to William B. McKinley, Apr. 29, 1912, Perkins Papers, Columbia University, box 12.

Chapter 14: "A Civilization Which Is Called Christian"

175 **"the butler did it"**: Matt Soniak, "Why Do We Say, 'The Butler Did It'?," *Mental Floss*, May 22, 2013, http://mentalfloss.com/article/50679/why-do -we-say-butler-did-it. The phrase does not actually appear in *The Door* or in any of Rinehart's other books.

175 **James Byrne ... kill Rice with chloroform**: Oller, *One Firm*, 6; Friedland, *Death of Old Man Rice*, 39–41, 44–46, 68, 87–90; *San Francisco Call*, Nov. 2, 1900.

175 **The case began ... a lying criminal**: *New York Times*, Mar. 12, 13, 1907, Jan. 30, Feb. 5, 8, 11, 21, 27, Mar. 20, 26, 27, 28, 29, 1912; *New-York Tribune*, Apr. 5, 1907, Feb. 3, 21, Apr. 4, 1912, Jan. 8, 1913; *New York Sun*, Feb. 20, 21, Mar. 19, 20, Apr. 1, 1912; *New York World*, May 10, 1912; *Sacramento Union*, Feb. 14, 1912; *Chicago Day Book*, Feb. 15, 1912; *Daily People* (New York), Feb. 17, 1912; *Kingston* (NY) *Daily Freeman*, Feb. 20, 1912; John A. Dix, *Public Papers of the Governor, 1912* (Albany: J. B. Lyon, 1913), 363–381; Thomas Carmody, *Annual Report of the Attorney General of the State of New York, for the Year Ending Dec. 31, 1912* (Albany: J. B. Lyon, 1913), 1:322–329.

177 **Schiffs to board ... Olympic**: *New York Times*, Apr. 14, 1912.

177 **As for Brandt ... his native Sweden**: *New York Times*, Jan. 18, 22, 1913; *New-York Tribune*, Jan. 18, 1913; *San Francisco Call*, Jan. 18, 1913; *Bemidji* (MN) *Daily Journal*, Feb. 25, 1914; *New York Sun*, Feb. 22, 1914.

177 **Theodore Roosevelt believed ... only Elihu Root had the qualities**: Morris, *Theodore Rex*, 127; Jessup, 2:125.

177 **The two men's friendship ... implicit trust**: *New York Times*, Sept. 27, 28, Oct. 7, 1898, July 30, 1899; Morris, *Theodore Rex*, 13; Jessup, 1:197–200; Jessup conversations with Root, Jan. 23, July 26, 1934, Stewart Collection, LOC, box 2, folder "New York Prominence" (quotations).

178 **"he was often so with me" ... "just what he was going to say"**: Jessup conversation with Root, Nov. 9, 1935, Stewart Collection, LOC, box 2, folder "Theodore Roosevelt."

178 **Roosevelt thought him unelectable**: Jessup, 2:125.

178 **"a New York lawyer ... would not make an effective candidate"**: Jessup

conversation with Root, Sept. 2, 1935, Stewart Collection, LOC, box 2, folder "War Department."

178 "never thinks . . . as well as he did": Jessup, 2:185.

178 "so darn mad": Ibid., 184.

178 "make-believe strangle": *New York Times*, Aug. 20, 1912. See also Bickel and Schmidt, *Supreme Court*, 116-123; Kolko, *Triumph of Conservatism*, 169.

179 "Buy Standard Oil" . . . skyrocketed: Ron Chernow, *Titan: The Life of John D. Rockefeller, Sr.* (New York: Random House, 1998), 554 (quotation), 556.

179 New Nationalism: Sidney M. Milkis, "Why the Election of 1912 Changed America," *Claremont Review of Books* 3, no. 1 (Winter 2002-2003).

179 one particular issue . . . nor did he propose: *Chicago Tribune*, Apr. 7, 1912; Ives v. South Buffalo Railway Co., 201 N.Y. 271 (1911); Goodwin, *Bully Pulpit*, 679-680.

179 "a perfectly wild program": Jessup, 2:180.

179 "I could not have been for Roosevelt . . . rules of law": Ibid., 191.

180 "he wanted to hear . . . and then jump": Jessup conversation with Root, Nov. 15, 1933, Stewart Collection, LOC, box 2, folder "Theodore Roosevelt." See also Jessup, 2:185.

180 Root found that Taft . . . influenced to change it: Jessup conversation with Root, Nov. 15, 1933, Stewart Collection, LOC, box 2, folder "Theodore Roosevelt."

180 At the opening . . . had been stolen: *New York Times*, June 19, 20, 1912; Jessup, 2:188-189; Goodwin, *Bully Pulpit*, 704-706.

180 He labeled his old friend . . . reactionary policies: Jessup, 2:188.

180 Aided by Root's rulings . . . form a third party: *New York Times*, June 20, 22, 23, 1912; Goodwin, *Bully Pulpit*, 710-715.

181 "took part in . . . ballot box stuffer": Jessup, 2:203-204.

181 claim to the nomination was entirely valid: Ibid., 201. See also Root to William R. Thayer, May 21, 1919, Root Papers, LOC, box 137.

181 "triangulating" . . . not merely regulated: Jean M. Yarbrough, "The New Freedom," *Claremont Review of Books* 6, no. 1 (Winter 2005-2006) (quotation); Sklar, *Corporate Reconstruction*, 334-335, 359, 377, 381, 401, 420-421; Freyer, *Regulating Big Business*, 65-66, 117-118; Woodrow Wilson, *The New Freedom: A Call for the Emancipation of the Generous Energies of a People* (New York: Doubleday, 1913), 180 (Wilson quotation); Bickel and Schmidt, *Supreme Court*, 141-144; Frederick Lewis Allen, *The Lords of Creation* (New York: Harper, 1935), 164-167; Jeffrey Rosen, *Louis D. Brandeis: American Prophet* (New Haven, CT: Yale University Press, 2016), 62-65; Arthur S. Link, *Woodrow Wilson and the Progressive Era: 1910-1917* (New York: Harper, 1954), 16-22; Paul F. Boller Jr., *Presidential Campaigns* (New York: Oxford University Press, 1984), 191-196.

181 "Ours is . . . theirs a program of regulation": Bickel and Schmidt, *Supreme Court*, 142.

181 suggested the states themselves . . . holding companies: Allen, *Lords of Creation*, 166; Joseph F. Mahoney, "Backsliding Convert: Woodrow Wilson and the 'Seven Sisters,'" *American Quarterly* 18, no. 1 (Spring 1966): 71-80.

181 Frank Stetson would have preferred: Stetson initially favored Ohio governor Judson Harmon, Grover Cleveland's attorney general, who was viewed as Wall Street's candidate despite some more recent progressive leanings. *Caucasian* (Clinton, NC), Feb. 29, 1912; *The Commoner* (Lincoln, NE), Apr. 26, 1912; Burton J. Hendrick, "Judson Harmon: Progressive Candidate," *McClure's Magazine*, April 1912, 619-624.

182 "sucked into the maelstrom . . . system of the country": Wilson, "The Lawyer and the Community," 609.

182 Wilson urged lawyers . . . private corporate clients: Ibid., 606, 608-610, 614, 618, 622.

182 white shoe Democratic lawyers . . . gave money to Wilson: *New York Times*, Oct. 26, Nov. 26, 1912; Arthur S. Link, *Wilson*, vol. 1, *The Road to the White House* (1947; repr., Princeton University Press, 2015), 187n37.

182 "radical free trader": *1911 Senate Hearings, Control of Corporations*, 964.

182 Wall Street's Republican lawyers . . . biggest money contributors: *New York Times*, Oct. 27, 1912; *Washington* (DC) *Times*, July 17, 1912.

182 "a socialist at heart": *Las Vegas* (East Las Vegas, NM) *Optic*, Sept. 25, 1912; *Ogden* (UT) *Evening Standard*, Sept. 25, 1912.

182 "corporation lawyers . . . against the people": *New York Times*, Nov. 5, 1912.

182 Two decisions: In re Jacobs, 98 N.Y. 98 (1885); Knisley v. Pratt, 148 N.Y. 372 (N.Y. 1896); *New York Times*, Nov. 5, 1912 (Roosevelt quotation).

183 A conservative libertarian . . . senator Elihu Root: Rousmaniere, 122-123; *New York Times*, June 22, Aug. 15, 1909, Jan. 6, Feb. 11, Mar. 2, Apr. 14, Apr. 28, 1910, July 13, 1911; Stetson to Garrett Droppers, Aug. 16, 1910, Stetson Papers, Williams College, box 6, folder 10; Jessup, 2:226-231; Perkins, *Charles Evans Hughes*, 26.

183 supported prison reform . . . Williams College: Rousmaniere, 122-123; *New York Times*, Nov. 11, 1915, Jan. 9, 18, 1916.

183 "a statistician, a demagogue . . . Political Economy": Stetson to Hamilton W. Mabie, Sept. 30, 1907, Stetson Papers, Williams College, box 5, folder 14.

183 "the shocks between . . . or critical public": Kolko, *Triumph of Conservatism*, 178, 322n30, quoting Francis Lynde Stetson, "Address Before Williams College Good Government Club, May 8, 1912."

184 "clear, frank . . . political cant": George F. Parker to Stetson, July 15, 1912, Stetson Papers, Williams College, box 8, folder 19. See also Theodore H. Price to Stetson, July 23, 1912, ibid.; Junius Parker to Stetson, July 3, 1912, ibid., box

8, folder 18; Frank J. Mather Jr. to Stetson, July 5, 1912, ibid.; James E. Freeman to Stetson, July 8, 1912, ibid.

184 "would have been abhorrent": Stetson, "Government and the Corporations," 40.

184 "I owe the public nothing": *New York World*, May 11, 1901. Morgan biographer Jean Strouse asserts the quote was taken out of context. Strouse, *Morgan*, xi–xii.

184 "a civilization . . . a soul": Stetson, "Government and the Corporations," 41.

184 "Although we did not . . . his best lights": *Washington* (DC) *Times*, Aug. 9, 1912.

184 In his private legal practice . . . "ability to produce a magic result": Swaine, 2:11–12.

185 Schiff, supported Wilson: Link, *Wilson: Road to the White House*, 338, 479, 485; *New York Times*, Oct. 26, 1912.

185 attended the opening night . . . J. P. Morgan was in attendance: *New York Sun*, Nov. 12, 1912.

Chapter 15: "Money Cannot Buy It"

186 "I congratulate our country . . . unreservedly enlisted": Untermyer to Wilson, July 3, 1912, Wilson Papers, LOC, reel 28 (quotations); *New York Times*, Aug. 25, 1912.

186 check for $10,000: Link, *Wilson: Road to the White House*, 485; *New York Times*, Oct. 26, 1912.

186 "money oligarchy" . . . dangerous and vicious system: "Rising Against the 'Money Oligarchy,'" *Literary Digest*, Feb. 17, 1912, 315.

186 collies had bested Morgan's: *New York Times*, Nov. 30, 1906. See also "J. P. Morgan and Collies," Collies of the Meadow, Nov. 3, 2011, https://collies ofthemeadow.wordpress.com/2011/11/03/jp-morgan-and-collies.

187 anti-Semitism was well established: Strouse, *Morgan*, 218, 537–538; Chernow, *House of Morgan*, 74, 89–90.

187 likely to be most unpleasant: J. P. Morgan Jr. to Morgan Sr., Apr. 25, 1912, quoted in Strouse, *Morgan*, 9.

187 "underbred, disgusting . . . mountain lion": Bella de Costa Greene to Bernard Berenson, Oct. 30, 1912, quoted in Strouse, *Morgan*, 666.

187 Taft expressed his disgust . . . "the so-called 'Money Trust' Investigation": Hudson, *Bankers and Empire*, 127.

187 "ungentlemanly": Swaine, 1:698.

187 "diabolical" plot . . . unprofessional conduct: *New York Sun*, Apr. 26, 1910.

187 Cravath criticized Untermyer . . . too radical: Robertson, *Brethren and Sisters*, 33–34, 45nn39, 41.

187 Untermyer accepted . . . a dangerous concentration: Mitchell, *Speculation Economy*, 219, 222-223; Untermyer to Wilson, July 31, 1912, Wilson Papers, LOC, reel 29; *New York Times*, Apr. 23, May 7, June 11, 1912.

188 the "Trio" . . . Panic of 1907: Strouse, *Morgan*, 595, 597.

188 badly wanted an ambassador post . . . "get a whitewash for his character": Strouse, *Morgan*, 666 (quotation); Mitchell, *Speculation Economy*, 221; Hawkins, "Samuel Untermyer."

188 Wilson declined . . . any official post: Mitchell, *Speculation Economy*, 221, 332n24; Hawkins, "The 'Jewish Threat,'" 80, 104n19.

189 A significant obstacle . . . died in the Senate: Mitchell, *Speculation Economy*, 224.

189 Untermyer appealed . . . Wickersham advised: Mitchell, *Speculation Economy*, 224; *New York Times*, Sept. 24, Nov. 22, Dec. 30, 1912.

189 Taft eventually . . . the least important: Mitchell, *Speculation Economy*, 224; *New York Times*, Dec. 30, 1912.

189 Stetson advised Morgan he could refuse to cooperate: Chernow, *House of Morgan*, 150.

189 Morgan voluntarily accepted . . . go abroad: Strouse, *Morgan*, 667; Stetson to Untermyer, Oct. 28, 1912; Untermyer to Stetson, Nov. 4, 16, 1912, all in the Samuel Untermyer Papers, Jacob Rader Marcus Center of the American Jewish Archives, box 3, folder 2.

189 "there are many abuses . . . by legislation": Stetson to Untermyer, Oct. 28, 1912, Samuel Untermyer Papers, Jacob Rader Marcus Center of the American Jewish Archives, box 3, folder 2.

190 Untermyer did not accede . . . assured Stetson: Untermyer to Stetson, Oct. 29, Nov. 2, 4, 16, 19, 1912; Stetson to Untermyer, Oct. 28, Nov. 2, 4, 1912 (quotation), all in the Samuel Untermyer Papers, Jacob Rader Marcus Center of the American Jewish Archives, box 3, folder 2.

190 "It was as if . . . 'controlled American business?'": Frederick Lewis Allen, *The Great Pierpont Morgan: A Biography* (New York: Harper, 1949), 4.

190 Untermyer was caught off guard . . . some open seats: *New York Times*, Dec. 18, 19, 1912; Strouse, *Morgan*, 3-4.

191 Untermyer hurried . . . Trio now held sway: *New York Times*, Dec. 19, 1912; Strouse, *Morgan*, 9-10, 625-626, 667-668, 680; Rousmaniere, *Equitable*, 115-116; *Money Trust Investigation: Investigation of Financial and Monetary Conditions in the United States Under House Resolutions nos. 429 and 504 Before a Subcommittee of the Committee on Banking and Currency: Interlocking Directorates* (Washington, DC: Government Printing Office, 1913), 27; Rosen, *Louis Brandeis*, 67-70.

192 Baker and Stillman further agreed . . . off his hands: *Money Trust Investigation: Investigation of Financial and Monetary Conditions in the United*

States Under House Resolutions nos. 429 and 504 Before a Subcommittee of the Committee on Banking and Currency (Washington, DC: Government Printing Office, 1913), Part 15:1067–1068 (hereafter, *Pujo Hearings*); Rousmaniere, *Equitable*, 116.

192 Morgan seemed weary . . . until the next morning: *New York Times*, Dec. 19, 1912; Strouse, *Morgan*, 4–5, 9.

192 When the hearing resumed . . . riveted the attention: *New York Times*, Dec. 20, 1912; Hellman, "The Boutonnières of Mr. Untermyer," 57–58; *Boston Journal*, Dec. 20, 1912 (Cravath's presence).

192 "When a man has got a vast power" . . . "I do not feel it at all": *Pujo Hearings*, 15:1052.

193 "Your firm is run by you" . . . "Never have": Ibid., 1053–1054.

193 "You do not think you have any power" . . . "Not the slightest": Ibid., 1061.

194 "a little competition": Ibid., 1050.

194 "You can get a combination . . . but you cannot control money": Ibid., 1083.

194 "I should doubt it . . . They come": Ibid., 1056.

194 Morgan was warming . . . gauge their approval: *New York Times*, Dec. 20, 1912; Allen, *Lords of Creation*, 181; Strouse, *Morgan*, 9–10; *Richmond* (VA) *Times-Dispatch*, Apr. 1, 1913.

194 only about a million dollars' worth: *Pujo Hearings*, 15:1036; Strouse, *Morgan*, 10.

194 "No, sir . . . any danger in it at all": *Pujo Hearings*, 15:1047.

194 "Because I thought . . . all I have to say about it": Ibid., 1068–1069.

195 "If it is good business . . . I do it": Ibid., 1062.

195 asked Morgan whether it was possible . . . Morgan said he doubted: Ibid., 1062.

195 "Is not commercial credit" . . . "all the bonds in Christendom": Ibid., 1084.

196 At the end of his five hours . . . their courtesy: *Richmond* (VA) *Times-Dispatch*, Apr. 1, 1913; Strouse, *Morgan*, 671.

196 "Mr. Morgan was animated . . . incredible power": *New York Times*, Apr. 1, 1913.

196 congratulatory telegrams . . . "insolent persistence": Pierpont Morgan Papers, Pierpont Morgan Library Archives, box 7, folders 41–46 (quotation in Dec. 20, 1912, letter).

197 "When all is said and done . . . finances of the world?": *The Bellman*, Mar. 8, 1913.

197 "lost no prestige through . . . favorable impression": *New York Times*, Dec. 21, 1912.

197 "I give . . . up. I don't know": *Pujo Hearings*, 21:1566.

197 "You think everything is all right . . . Pretty nearly": Ibid., 1518.

197 "good hands" . . . "I think that is all": Ibid., 1567-1568; *New-York Tribune*, Jan. 11, 1913.

198 "a complete fiasco . . . may be so considered": *The Bellman*, Mar. 8, 1913.

198 "an established and well defined . . . these few men": *Report of the Committee Appointed Pursuant to House Resolutions 429 and 504 to Investigate the Concentration of Control of Money and Credit*, H. R. Rep. No. 1593, 62nd Cong., 3rd Sess. (Washington, DC: Government Printing Office, 1913), 129.

198 "What may be virtually . . . private hands": *Report of the Committee*, H. R. Rep. No. 1593, 26.

198 "he was being 'put upon' . . . 'crowding' him": Mark Sullivan, *Our Times, 1900-1925: The Turn of the Century* (New York: Charles Scribner's, 1926), 1:137.

198 Although the Pujo Committee . . . sluggish economy: Mitchell, *Speculation Economy*, 209-210, 219, 227-238, 262.

198 But the money trust investigation . . . Clayton Antitrust Act: Allen, *Lords of Creation*, 190-192; Chernow, *House of Morgan*, 156; A. Scott Berg, *Wilson* (New York: Simon & Schuster, 2013), 298-301, 315-316; Swaine, 1:563 (Morawetz), 2:103 and n1; *New York Times*, Mar. 17, 1940; McClure, "Victor Morawetz," 15-21.

199 Morgan sailed for Egypt . . . half-mast: Strouse, *Morgan*, 674-681; Chernow, *House of Morgan*, 157-158.

199 "And to think . . . rich man": Strouse, *Morgan*, 14-15.

199 Morgan's partners . . . blame squarely on Untermyer: Chernow, *House of Morgan*, 158; Edward M. Lamont, *The Ambassador from Wall Street: The Story of Thomas W. Lamont, J. P. Morgan's Chief Executive* (Lanham, MD: Madison Books, 1994), 56.

199 "the Pujo Committee Investigation killed . . . protecting coating": Barron, *More They Told Barron*, 157.

199 "miserable little things like that" . . . "the beast": Strouse, *Morgan*, 678-679.

Chapter 16: "The Wolf of Wall Street"

200 "the man with the mellifluous voice" . . . took the train to Washington: *Maintenance of a Lobby to Influence Legislation: Hearings Before a Subcommittee of the Committee on the Judiciary, United States Senate, June 13 to July 10, 1913*, 63rd Cong., 1st Sess. (Washington, DC: Government Printing Office, 1913), 2:1785-1787 (hereafter, *Lobby Hearings*); *New York Times*, Apr. 17, 1913 (Lauterbach); Edmund Morris, *The Rise of Theodore Roosevelt* (New York: Random House, 1979), 529, 537 ("Smooth Ed").

201 "I said to him . . . if I apply to you?": *Lobby Hearings*, 2:1786.

201 Lauterbach would say only . . . no good would come: Ibid., 1787.

201 At the same time . . . none of the men: *New York Times*, June 27, 28, July 3, 4, 8, 1913; *San Francisco Call*, July 3, 1913.

201 David Lamar . . . "nest of rascals": *New York Times*, Aug. 24, 1902, May 5, 1909, July 3, 1913, Oct. 28, 1923, Jan. 14, 16, 1934; *New York World*, May 1, 1916; *Lobby Hearings*, 2:1696-1697, 1713-1714, 1785-1787; George W. Perkins to J. P. Morgan, July 11, 1902 (quotation), Perkins Papers, Columbia University, box 5.

202 bond deal lawsuits . . . eventually defeated or settled: Swaine, 1:691-692; *Davis Polk: Background with Figures*, 32.

202 "extremely disagreeable . . . from the other side": Swaine, 1:692.

202 Lamar had better success . . . liberal allowance: Chernow, *Titan*, 356.

203 "Put up a bluff . . . The rest will be easy": *New York Times*, Oct. 28, 1923.

203 "He can just make a stock . . . He is wonderful": *New York Times*, May 5, 1909.

203 "more of an eagle . . . and was gone": *New York Times*, Oct. 28, 1923.

203 hired the gangster Monk Eastman . . . was hooted: *New York Times*, Jan. 14, 1934; Neil Hanson, *The Heroic Gangster: The Story of Monk Eastman, from the Streets of New York to the Battlefields of Europe and Back* (New York: Skyhorse, 2013), chapter 7.

203 convicted for impeding arms shipments . . . jumped bail: *New York Times*, May 21, 1917, Oct. 28, 1923; Barbara W. Tuchman, *The Zimmermann Telegram* (New York: Viking, 1958), 76.

203 insidious efforts . . . tariff reduction bill: *New York Times*, May 27, 1913.

204 "It was a pure fabrication . . . a perfect farce": *Lobby Hearings*, 2:1782.

204 "nothing but malicious mischief": Ibid., 1774.

204 Lamar testified that his main object . . . might rehabilitate himself: Ibid., 1706-1707, 1717-1718, 1721-1722, 1795, 2047-2050, 2057, 2066-2068; *New York Times*, June 27, 28, July 3, 4, 8, 9, 1913, Mar. 5, 1923; *San Francisco Call*, July 3, 1913.

204 Ledyard, a corporate lawyer . . . could "kiss six hands at one time": *New York Times*, Jan. 28, 1932; Barron, *More They Told Barron*, 170 (quotation); Wardwell, *Reminiscences*, 91.

204 "Palmer" . . . told Ledyard: *Lobby Hearings*, 2:1712, 1715-1716, 1737-1739; *New York Times*, June 27, July 3, 1913; *San Francisco Call*, July 3, 1913.

204 Lamar told Frank Stetson . . . he refused to bite: *Lobby Hearings*, 2:1734, 1782-1783; Bickel and Schmidt, *Supreme Court*, 154-155, 165-166.

204 "Mr. Stetson began to talk . . . not human": *Lobby Hearings*, 2:1783; see ibid., 2:1769.

205 Otto Kahn . . . Lauterbach said he was confident: Ibid., 1650-1651, 1655-1656, 1786.

205 Lauterbach was unaware . . . Ledyard had entrapped him: Ibid., 1903-1905, 1908-1909, 1941-1942, 1979, 2002-2003, 2036; *New York Times*, June 27, July 8, 1913.

205 They said they genuinely opposed . . . hoped to create congressional hostility: *Lobby Hearings*, 2:1647-1649, 1652-1654, 1658-1659, 1693, 1723-1724, 1731-1732, 1787, 1977-1978, 2098-2100. The plan, ultimately approved by McReynolds and Wilson, called for the Union Pacific to exchange its Southern Pacific stock for shares of the Baltimore & Ohio Railroad held by the Pennsylvania Railroad. Lauterbach and Lamar gave the newspapers a false story claiming the plan was part of an effort by Kuhn, Loeb to obtain control of multiple railroads. See also Bickel and Schmidt, *Supreme Court*, 187-188; Klein, *Union Pacific*, 2:196-200.

205 Lamar also fed the papers . . . "liar": *Lobby Hearings*, 2:1708-1709, 1732-1733; *San Francisco Call*, July 3, 1913 (quotation).

205 accountant . . . no improper accounting: *New York Times*, July 19, 1913.

206 "would own them . . . to any extent": *Lobby Hearings*, 2:1769; ibid., 1761-1762.

206 Lamar was indicted . . . had been unclear: *New York Times*, Nov. 8, Dec. 3, 4, 1914, May 2, 1916.

206 charges against Lauterbach . . . Hebrew Orphan Asylum: *New York Times*, Nov. 6, 1915, Mar. 5, 1923; Robertson, *Brethren and Sisters*, 69n11.

206 "I had had domestic difficulties . . . would have done me great good": *Lobby Hearings*, 2:1687.

206 He had a law office . . . "nothing else left for me": Ibid., 1979-1980.

206 he had inspired . . . try to blackmail: Ibid., 1712, 1714-1715, 1742, 1765, 1795-1800; *New York Times*, July 13, 1913.

207 using its own methods: *Lobby Hearings*, 2:2074-2075, 2082-2083, 2085; *New York Times*, July 9, 1913.

207 "I was sick of the persecution . . . set me in motion": *Lobby Hearings*, 2:1798.

207 "If these gentlemen . . . inclined to forgive them": Ibid., 1794.

207 One US congressman . . . Lamar's frauds paled: *New York Times*, Feb. 1, 1914.

207 "Who are the lawyers . . . money today?": *Springfield* (MA) *Republican*, July 15, 1914.

207 passage of a federal statute: *New York Times*, Feb. 11, 1914; Robertson, *Brethren and Sisters*, 69n11.

Chapter 17: "The Curse of Bigness"

208 It was the lifeblood . . . readily accepted Morgan's offer: John L. Weller, *The New Haven Railroad: Its Rise and Fall* (New York: Hastings House, 1969),

6, 45–49; Herbert H. Harwood Jr., *The New York, Westchester & Boston Railway: J. P. Morgan's Magnificent Mistake* (Bloomington: Indiana University Press, 2008), 14; Barron, *More They Told Barron*, 121.

209 "last of the railway czars": Chernow, *House of Morgan*, 174.

209 whip-smart . . . sarcasm: Weller, *New Haven Railroad*, 49.

209 "first class fellow" . . . contribution of $50,000: Carosso and Carosso, *The Morgans*, 858n1 (quotation); Weller, *New Haven Railroad*, 50.

209 "I took orders . . . don't you think he didn't!": Barron, *More They Told Barron*, 168.

209 "Call a vote. . . . We stood in awe of him": Garet Garrett, "Things That Were Mellen's and Things That Were Caesar's," *Everybody's Magazine*, July 1914, 98.

209 Morgan and Mellen both dominated . . . interlocking directorates: Strouse, *Morgan*, 615–616, 663n; Weller, *New Haven Railroad*, 50–51.

210 New Haven gained a virtual monopoly . . . disinclined to bring a prosecution: Chernow, *House of Morgan*, 174–175; Harwood, *New York, Westchester*, 14, 17; Weller, *New Haven Railroad*, 51, 64–66, 138; *Evidence Taken Before the Interstate Commerce Commission, Relative to the Financial Transactions of the New York, New Haven & Hartford Railroad Company, Together with the Report of the Commission Thereon*, S. Doc. No. 543, 63rd Cong., 2nd Sess. (Washington, DC: Government Printing Office, 1914), 1:765–767, 982, 1026, 1035–1036, 1100 (hereafter, *ICC Investigation*); Gabriel Kolko, *Railroads and Regulation, 1877–1916* (Princeton, NJ: Princeton University Press, 1965), 158–159.

210 Mellen had the New Haven "sell" . . . Billard as a stalking horse: Weller, *New Haven Railroad*, 138–142, 178–181; *ICC Investigation*, 1:16–24.

210 Louis Brandeis . . . accounting trickery: Rosen, *Louis Brandeis*, 50–53, 68–73 (quotation); Weller, *New Haven Railroad*, 7, 128–142; Chernow, *House of Morgan*, 176.

211 New Haven's capitalization . . . to $242 million: Weller, *New Haven Railroad*, 6–7; Strouse, *Morgan*, 616.

211 Morgan's custom . . . if he could eliminate competition: Weller, *New Haven Railroad*, 21; Allen, *Lords of Creation*, 172.

211 "had an instinct . . . only a banker": Garraty, *Right-Hand Man*, 136.

211 millstone . . . skipped its dividend payment: *ICC Investigation*, 1:921; Weller, *New Haven Railroad*, 149–159, 165; Chernow, *House of Morgan*, 178; *New York Times*, July 8, 9, Sept. 5, 6, 1913.

211 His son, Jack Jr. . . . Walker D. Hines: Chernow, *House of Morgan*, 177, 180–181; Weller, *New Haven Railroad*, 159, 162–169; Swaine, 2:13, 18–21, 157–158.

212 Brandeis pushed . . . "the Curse of Bigness": Weller, *New Haven Railroad*, 163, 166; Louis D. Brandeis, *Other People's Money, and How the Bankers Use It* (New York: Frederick A. Stokes, 1914), 189 (quotation); see ibid., 162.

212 Brandeis had played a part . . . two-faced: Weller, *New Haven Railroad*, 42-43, 132; Alpheus Thomas Mason, *Brandeis: A Free Man's Life* (New York: Viking, 1956), 221-226, 230-232; Freyer, *Regulating Big Business*, 157-158, 160-161, 164-165, 175, 191-193.

213 "age-long struggle between Jew and Gentile": Weller, *New Haven Railroad*, 149.

213 "The man with the hatchet . . . winning in the end": Mason, *Brandeis: A Free Man's Life*, 472.

213 Brandeis also earned the enmity . . . more important: Weller, *New Haven Railroad*, 168-170.

213 The Senate directed . . . Hines of the Cravath firm: Ibid., 167; Swaine, 2:158; *New York Times*, May 15, 1914; *ICC Investigation*, 1:107.

213 Stetson . . . made the banking firm's documents: *New York Times*, May 27, 29, 1914; *Springfield* (MA) *Republican*, May 28, 1914.

213 David Lamar . . . from the Senate gallery: Weller, *New Haven Railroad*, 170-172; *New York Times*, Feb. 26, 27, 1914. See also *New York Times*, Feb. 21, 1914.

213 subsidiaries . . . dummy directors: Chernow, *House of Morgan*, 175; Weller, *New Haven Railroad*, 65, 90, 180.

214 "Diamond Jim" Brady . . . "I wear a few jewels": Weller, *New Haven Railroad*, 2, 45, 50, 55, 66-67, 138, 151-153; *ICC Investigation*, 1:352-362 (quotation); *New York Times*, May 2, 1914.

214 Mellen took the stand . . . "Helping the Interstate Commerce Commission": *ICC Investigation*, 1:37, 692 (quotation); *New York Times*, May 14, 1914.

214 "his story of high finance . . . with wonderment": *New York Times*, May 15, 1914.

214 other directors thought . . . insisted the sale was legitimate: *ICC Investigation*, 1:509, 774, 776, 781, 986-989; Weller, *New Haven Railroad*, 140-142, 181-182.

214 In 1906 Mellen . . . agreed to take the idea: Harwood, *New York, Westchester*, 17, 19-26; Weller, *New Haven Railroad*, 99-103; Barron, *More They Told Barron*, 169-170.

215 J. P. Morgan immediately embraced . . . special committee: Weller, *New Haven Railroad*, 103; *ICC Investigation*, 1:744, 1006, 2:2008.

215 Frank Stetson . . . incorporated themselves: Weller, *New Haven Railroad*, 103-104; Harwood, *New York, Westchester*, 26; *ICC Investigation*, 1:4-5, 41, 51, 209-212, 742, 2:1341, 1343, 2008, 2019; Garrett, "Things That Were Mellen's," 106.

216 he did caution . . . might be money lost: *ICC Investigation*, 1:5, 2:1249.

216 Thorne and Perry spent $11 million . . . took over the Millbrook Company: *ICC Investigation*, 1:41-42, 2:2018-2021, 2221-2222; Garrett, "Things

That Were Mellen's," 106; Harwood, *New York, Westchester*, 26–27; Weller, *New Haven Railroad*, 103–104, 109–110.

216 **Panic of 1907 . . . Account No. 2 was closed out:** Chernow, *House of Morgan*, 124; Strouse, *Morgan*, 577–578; Weller, *New Haven Railroad*, 104–110; Barron, *More They Told Barron*, 171.

216 **"10 cents a pound":** *ICC Investigation*, 1:706. See also ibid., 1:4–7, 32, 224–225; Weller, *New Haven Railroad*, 110; Harwood, *New York, Westchester*, 28; Henry Lee Staples and Alpheus Thomas Mason, *The Fall of a Railroad Empire: Brandeis and the New Haven Merger Battle* (Syracuse, NY: Syracuse University Press, 1947), 166–168.

216 **on November 9 . . . directors were astonished:** Weller, *New Haven Railroad*, 110–112; Harwood, *New York, Westchester*, 27; *ICC Investigation*, 1:728–729, 733.

216 **"cowardice . . . when he disagreed with me":** *ICC Investigation*, 1:730.

217 **"Did not Mr. Stetson draw that vote? . . . than he does?":** *ICC Investigation*, 1:728 (quotations); see ibid., 1:727; *New York Times*, May 20, 1914.

217 **A group of the directors . . . incredulous:** *ICC Investigation*, 1:730–733.

217 **"Holy Caesarea Philippi . . . $11,000,000 of money?":** Ibid., 732 (quotation), 1014, 1070.

217 **"Not on your life":** Ibid., 730–732 (quotation), 1014, 1070.

217 **"I am sick and disgusted . . . the goat":** Ibid., 735.

217 **New Haven had spent $36 million . . . need to earn four and a half times:** Ibid., 292, 734, 737, 744, 977; Weller, *New Haven Railroad*, 115–116, 119.

217 **"an awful blunder . . . almost a crime at times":** *ICC Investigation*, 1:916.

218 **numerous irregularities . . . "Fourteenth Street":** Weller, *New Haven Railroad*, 114–115; Harwood, *New York, Westchester*, 31–32; *ICC Investigation*, 1:7–9, 214, 222, 699–703, 739–740; Staples and Mason, *Fall of a Railroad Empire*, 168.

218 **Thorne and Perry received . . . no claim it could enforce:** *ICC Investigation*, 1:8, 238–239, 742–746.

218 **"Mr. Stetson said . . . no use pursuing it":** Ibid., 746.

218 **Thorne and Perry also claimed $500,000 . . . Mellen felt they did not deserve:** Ibid., 8, 219–220, 743–748; Weller, *New Haven Railroad*, 113.

218 **"Mr. Stetson was a very high-class man . . . who he stood second for":** *ICC Investigation*, 1:746–747.

219 **Stetson submitted a statement . . . had their own lawyer:** *New-York Tribune*, July 15, 1914; *New York Times*, July 15, 1914. See also *ICC Investigation*, 2:2009, 1:1094.

219 **Millbrook Company had not supplied vouchers . . . burned all his books:** Weller, *New Haven Railroad*, 112–113; *ICC Investigation*, 1:215, 225–228.

219	"the most conspicuously wasteful . . . adventures": Weller, *New Haven Railroad*, 113, 119 (quotation).

220	Morgan had a bold vision . . . spend whatever it took: Ibid., 103; Harwood, *New York, Westchester*, 74–75.

220	Morgan had always looked to Stetson . . . legally what he wanted: Rousmaniere, 48, 99.

220	they could hardly justify . . . a virtual admission: Weller, *New Haven Railroad*, 117.

221	Cromwell simply jumped in . . . "one or two items": *ICC Investigation*, 1:999.

221	"business judgment rule" . . . a Michigan court case: Dodge v. Ford Motor Company, 204 Mich. 459 (1919). See also In re Caremark International Inc. Derivative Litigation, 698 A.2d 959 (Del. Ch. 1996); David Michael Israel, "The Business Judgment Rule and the Declaration of Corporate Dividends: A Reappraisal," *Hofstra Law Review* 4, no. 1 (1975): 73n2, 74n12; M. Todd Henderson, "Everything Old Is New Again: Lessons from Dodge v. Ford Motor Company," University of Chicago Law School, John M. Olin Program in Law and Economics Working Paper No. 373, 2007, https://chicagounbound.uchicago.edu/law_and_economics/198.

221	"really extravagant . . . damn fool family": *ICC Investigation*, 1:974 (first quotation), 975–978, 980 (second quotation).

221	relief of "congestion" . . . Grand Central service charge: Ibid., 1001–1002, 1007. See also ibid., 1:291, 1223–1226; Harwood, *New York, Westchester*, 57–60, 74–75.

222	"At that time the terminal charges . . . not any crazy scheme": *ICC Investigation*, 1:1001.

222	"You were buying . . . The foothold in the city?" "Yes": Ibid., 1002.

222	"Mr. Cromwell, I am not quite clear" . . . some other unnamed directors: Ibid.

223	"I want to enlighten" . . . "Yes": Ibid., 1005.

223	constant agitation . . . hampered the railroad's ability: Ibid., 1062–1064, 1069, 1072; *New York Times*, July 10, 1914.

223	Cromwell also had Skinner confirm . . . along with everyone else: *ICC Investigation*, 1:1064–1066.

223	"In all these years" . . . "Absolutely": Ibid., 1:1065.

224	"one of the most glaring . . . American railroading": Ibid., 2. See also *New York Times*, July 14, 1914.

224	"a story of the profligate waste of corporate funds": *ICC Investigation*, 1:4.

224	Brushing aside . . . no evidence it was discussed: Ibid., 8–9, 1007; Weller, *New Haven Railroad*, 116–117; Harwood, *New York, Westchester*, 75–76.

224	"The man who holds . . . anything he may do": *ICC Investigation*, 1:35.

224	directors criminally negligent . . . through civil suits: Ibid., 35–36, 38; *New York Times*, July 14, 1914.

224 Justice Department sued . . . entitled to the same immunity: Weller, *New Haven Railroad*, 187–189; *New York Times*, July 14, Nov. 3, 5, 1914.

224 Frank Stetson . . . was not sued. Nor was he among: *New York Times*, Nov. 3, 1914.

225 The criminal trials . . . but it never was: *New York Times*, Mar. 21, 1914, Jan. 10, 1916; Weller, *New Haven Railroad*, 187–192; Swaine, 2:158.

225 The Westchester did become . . . opened in 1913: Harwood, *New York, Westchester*, 61–68, 75–76, 105–106, 117–119.

225 The Clayton Act . . . were not much more specific: Ernest Gellhorn, William Kovacic, and Stephen Calkins, *Antitrust Law and Economics in a Nutshell* (1976; repr., St. Paul, MN: West Publishing, 2004), 34–39; Milton Handler et al., *Trade Regulation: Cases and Materials* (Mineola, NY: Foundation Press, 1975), 147–153, quoting Gerard C. Henderson, "The Federal Trade Commission: A Study in Administrative Law and Procedure" (1924); Kolko, *Triumph of Conservatism*, 261–268; Link, *Wilson and the Progressive Era*, 68–75. See also Gilbert H. Montague, "The Federal Trade Commission and the Clayton Act," in Stetson et al., *Some Legal Phases*, 275–326.

226 raging national debate . . . remains in place today: Mitchell, *Speculation Economy*, 209; Sklar, *Corporate Reconstruction*, 90, 173, 328–331; Bickel and Schmidt, *Supreme Court*, 143–144, 170; Freyer, *Regulation of Big Business*, 141, 166, 188, 194, 198, 208, 273, 326–327; Kolko, *Triumph of Conservatism*, 260 (Wilson quotation), 268 (Stetson quotation), 269–270; *New York Times*, Feb. 15, 1914 (Morawetz); August Heckscher, *Woodrow Wilson* (New York: Scribner, 1991), 324–325; Link, *Wilson and the Progressive Era*, 70–71; Gellhorn, Kovacic, and Calkins, *Antitrust Law*, 572–574.

227 William Hornblower became the first . . . honorary pallbearers: *New York Times*, June 17, 1900, Aug. 21, 22, 1913; June 17, 20, July 3, Dec. 29, 1914; *Verses of a Short Life: Poems and Political Quips of Lewis Woodruff Hornblower (1883–1913)*, ed. George S. Hornblower (New York: George H. Doran Co., 1914); George Sanford Hornblower, *Leisure* (New York: Duffield & Co., 1929).

228 Cravath suffered another setback . . . terraced music room: *New York Times*, Apr. 24, 1908, Apr. 15, 1914, July 2, 1940; Swaine, 1:676–677; Mateyunas, *Long Island's Gold Coast*, 16; Mackaye, "Public Man," 23–24; MacKay, Baker, and Traynor, *Long Island Country Houses*, 266–267.

228 Panama Canal opened . . . declared war on each other: Loizillon, *Bunau-Varilla Brothers*, 282.

Chapter 18: **Preparedness**

229 "must be impartial . . . in action": Berg, *Wilson*, 336–337.

229 Wall Street lawyers gave . . . charitable causes: *New York Times*, Sept. 3, 27,

Oct. 28, Nov. 11, 13, 1914, Feb. 17, Aug. 1, Oct. 24, 1915, Nov. 24, Dec. 24, 1916; *New-York Tribune*, Sept. 5, 1914; *New York Sun*, Jan. 5, 1915; *About the Daily Ardmoreite* (Ardmore, OK), Nov. 13, 1914; *Wilkes-Barre* (PA) *Times-Leader*, June 20, 1918; *Pueblo* (CO) *Chieftain*, Sept. 29, 1918.

229 Cromwell, semiretired . . . Legion's supreme award: Dean, 47, 156-157; *New York Times*, Dec. 9, 1935, July 20, 1948; Lisagor & Lipsius, 69-70; Piel and Moore, *Lamplighters*, 37-38; Francis Dickie, "New Wonders to Aid Blind," *Rotarian*, July 1928 (Clermont-Tonnerre mansion).

230 Cravaths raised money . . . Pablo Casals: *New York Times*, Nov. 29, 1914; *New-York Tribune*, Apr. 8, 1915.

230 "the principles of liberty . . . our profession to sustain": Cravath to Dwight W. Morrow, May 1, 1917, Morrow Papers, Amherst College, Series 1, box 16, folder 18, "Paul D. Cravath 1915-1919."

230 Preparedness Movement . . . other Morgan partners: John Patrick Finnegan, *Against the Specter of a Dragon: The Campaign for American Military Preparedness, 1914-1917* (Westport, CT: Greenwood Press, 1974); Russell F. Weigley, *History of the United States Army* (1967; repr., Bloomington: Indiana University Press, 1984), 342-345; Priscilla Roberts, "Paul D. Cravath, the First World War, and the Anglophile Internationalist Tradition," *Australian Journal of Politics and History* 51, no. 2 (2005): 195-201; Mark Davis, *Solicitor General Bullitt: The Life of William Marshall Bullitt* (Louisville, KY: Crescent Hill Books, 2011), 93-94; David F. Schmitz, *Henry L. Stimson: The First Wise Man* (Wilmington, DE: Scholarly Resources, 2001), 5-6, 37-39; James Brown Scott, *Robert Bacon: Life and Letters* (1923; repr., Pickle Partners, 2013), 214-215, 241-246; Chernow, *House of Morgan*, 186.

230 "Atlanticist" foreign policy establishment . . . "Anglophile internationalism": Roberts, "Paul D. Cravath," 194 (quotations), 195-200, 214-215; Davis, *Solicitor General Bullitt*, 93-94; Robert A. Divine, *Second Chance: The Triumph of Internationalism in America During World War II* (New York: Atheneum, 1967), 22-23. See also Priscilla Roberts, "The First World War and the Emergence of American Atlanticism, 1914-1920," *Diplomacy and Statecraft* 5, no. 3 (November 1994): 569-619.

230 "an epiphany . . . internationalist leanings": Roberts, "Paul D. Cravath," 197.

231 As a group they favored . . . military engineering: Scott, *Robert Bacon*, 243, 250-254, 259-260, 270-271; Jessup, 2:323; Weigley, *United States Army*, 343-345; Roberts, "Paul D. Cravath," 200; *New York Times*, Aug. 8, 9, 11, 12, 1915.

231 "the great disturber of peace in the world": Jessup, 2:310.

231 Friends pleaded . . . believed likewise: Ibid., 310-315, 318-321.

231 Hughes's position . . . privately criticized Wilson: Perkins, *Charles Evans Hughes*, 53, 56-58.

231 Hughes's son . . . Plattsburgh training camp: *New York Times*, June 7, 1916.

231 Henry Stimson . . . supported Wilson on neutrality: Schmitz, *Henry L. Stimson*, 38.

231 fighting for Western civilization: Ibid., 39.

232 Stetson was one of thirty signers . . . avoid pressing: *New York Times*, Mar. 1, 1915.

232 "I am a pacifist" . . . should be efficient: Stetson to Ralph M. Campbell, Mar. 17, 1915, Stetson Papers, Williams College, box 11, folder 19.

232 New York Peace Society . . . enforce the peace: *New York Times*, May 24, 1915.

232 Untermyer sympathized . . . ancestral homeland: Hawkins, "The 'Jewish Threat,'" 75-76.

232 "the most remarkable" . . . domestic industries: *New York Times*, Mar. 22, 1903.

232 When war broke out . . . safe passage home: *New York Times*, Aug. 6, 7, 1914; Hawkins, "The 'Jewish Threat,'" 79.

232 "there was no more ardent . . . than Germany": *New York Times*, Aug. 23, 1914.

232 More pro-German . . . anti-Jewish pogroms: Hawkins, "The 'Jewish Threat,'" 75-76.

232 Untermyer strongly supported American neutrality . . . honored guests: Hawkins, "The 'Jewish Threat,'" 81-83; Alva Johnston, "Little Giant 2," *New Yorker*, May 24, 1930, 25-26; *New York World*, Aug. 15, 16, 17, 1915; *New York Times*, Aug. 20, Nov. 29, 1915, Dec. 7, 1918; *New-York Tribune*, Aug. 18, 1915.

233 Root . . . believed the United States should have entered: Jessup, 2:323.

233 But Wilson . . . "too proud to fight": Berg, *Wilson*, 364-366 (quotation at 364).

234 Cravath's inclination . . . go ahead with the deals: Swaine, 2:204-206.

234 Cravath's client connections . . . "one of the deadliest of the 'war stocks'": *New Ulm* (MN) *Post*, Nov. 5, 1915. See also *New York Times*, Oct. 8, 1915.

234 The former governor . . . also attacked Cravath: *Watertown* (SD) *Saturday News*, Dec. 2, 1915.

234 La Follette . . . "dollar-scarred heroes": *The Commoner* (Lincoln, NE), Dec. 1, 1915.

234 "'Preparedness' fairly reeks . . . engines of death": *Labor World* (Duluth, MN), Nov. 27, 1915.

234 Illinois editorial writer called out Stetson . . . munitions sales: *Rock Island* (IL) *Argus*, Nov. 20, 1915.

234 Stetson's help in arranging . . . a Morgan partner: Stetson to Harry Garfield, Oct. 5, 1915, Stetson Papers, Williams College, box 12, folder 6; Chernow, *House of Morgan*, 197-198; Allen, *Lords of Creation*, 202-203; Rousmaniere, 76-77; Wardwell, *Reminiscences*, 63.

234 publicly opposed pro-German proposals . . . create their own: *New-York Tribune*, Sept. 6, 1915.

235 admitted fondness for England: *Washington* (DC) *Herald*, Dec. 23, 1916.

235 one critic alleged: *New York Sun*, Dec. 29, 1916.

235 Untermyer argued . . . heavily taxed: *New York Times*, Dec. 6, 1915.

235 Untermyer's wife . . . starving German babies: *New York Times*, Nov. 13, 1915; Hawkins, "The 'Jewish Threat,'" 93.

235 Anglo-French loan was plowed back . . . "as they fed the slaughter in Europe": Allen, *Lords of Creation*, 203.

235 "There isn't much doubt . . . wasn't created for their own interest": Wardwell, *Reminiscences*, 65.

235 Jack Morgan vetoed a proposal: Chernow, *House of Morgan*, 192; Dwight W. Morrow memorandum, Jan. 19, 1917, Morrow Papers, Amherst College, Series 1, box 16, folder 18, "Paul D. Cravath 1915-1919."

235 Wilson's secretary of state . . . resigned in protest: Berg, *Wilson*, 366-368; Chernow, *House of Morgan*, 186.

236 Robert Lansing . . . "credits": Berg, *Wilson*, 343-344; Chernow, *House of Morgan*, 186, 197-198.

236 John Foster Dulles to spearhead . . . Sorbonne: Ronald W. Pruessen, *John Foster Dulles: The Road to Power* (New York: Free Press, 1982), 2-12; Richard H. Immerman, *John Foster Dulles: Piety, Pragmatism, and Power in U.S. Foreign Policy* (Wilmington, DE: Scholarly Resources, 1999), 3-5; Piel and Moore, *Lamplighters*, 67-68; Stephen Kinzer, *Brothers: John Foster Dulles, Allen Dulles, and Their Secret World War* (New York: Times Books, 2013), 10-15.

237 "Christian lawyer" . . . $12.50 a week: Kinzer, *Brothers*, 15-17 (quotations); Lisagor & Lipsius, 61; Piel and Moore, *Lamplighters*, 67-68; Pruessen, *John Foster Dulles*, 10-11, 14-15.

237 Dulles found the everyday work . . . Holland America Line: Pruessen, *John Foster Dulles*, 17-19; Lisagor & Lipsius, 62-63; Kinzer, *Brothers*, 19.

238 "ruthless murdering . . . neutrals": Lisagor & Lipsius, 64.

238 took the life of a Sullivan & Cromwell client . . . Dulles's help: Lisagor & Lipsius, 65; *Los Angeles Herald*, May 10, 12, 1915; "Mrs. Albert Clay Bilicke (Gladys Huff)," The Lusitania Resource, 2003, http://www.rmslusitania.info /people/saloon/gladys-bilicke.

238 "It is hard . . . the war in Europe": Root to Stimson, Aug. 4, 1914, quoted in Jessup, 2:292.

238 Root presided . . . November referendum: Jessup, 2:291, 293, 296 (quotation), 305-306; Henry W. Taft, *Century and a Half*, 288.

239 "adverse to the true character . . . confess submission": Jessup, 1:178.

239 "not a natural right . . . needed reforms": *New York Times*, June 12, 1915.

239 George Wickersham, Frank Stetson . . . opposed the suffrage

amendment: *New York Sun*, Oct. 30, 1917. See also *New York Times*, May 19, 1912.

239 Stetson's wife, Elizabeth . . . Legal Aid Society: *New York Times*, Apr. 26, 1894, Apr. 17, 1896, Mar. 17, 1907, Sept. 23, 1913; Susan Goodier, *No Votes for Women: The New York State Anti-Suffrage Movement* (Urbana: University of Illinois Press, 2013), 31-33, 59.

239 Stetson favored giving Episcopal women . . . Columbia Law School: *New York Times*, Nov. 13, 14, 1913, Nov. 12, 1914, Nov. 11, 1915; *Richmond* (VA) *Times-Dispatch*, Jan. 10, 1915; *Miami Herald*, Mar. 25, 1917.

240 But Cromwell did contribute . . . the bulk of the estate: *New York Times*, Sept. 28, Oct. 8, 1914, May 2, 1915, Feb. 3, 1916; *Washington* (DC) *Times*, Dec. 13, 1914; *Topeka* (KS) *Daily State Journal*, Dec. 20, 1915; *New York Sun*, Jan. 26, 1917, Jan. 8, 1919; *Barre* (VT) *Daily Times*, Mar. 10, 1919; Lisagor & Lipsius, 94-95.

240 New York State voters . . . Mrs. Leslie's estate: Goodier, *No Votes for Women*, 115; Taft, *Century and a Half*, 288. Stetson, Stimson, and Wickersham all opposed the 1917 referendum as well. *New York Times*, Feb. 18, 1917; *New York Sun*, Sept. 28, 1917.

240 "reputation, character and professional career" . . . unfit to serve: *New York Times*, Mar. 15, 1916.

240 George Wickersham . . . had never forgiven Brandeis: A. L. Todd, *Justice on Trial: The Case of Louis D. Brandeis* (New York: McGraw Hill, 1964), 75-76, 128-132; Rebecca S. Shoemaker, *The White Court: Justices, Rulings, and Legacy* (Santa Barbara, CA: ABC-CLIO Supreme Court Handbooks, 2004), 27-28; *New York Times*, June 2, 1916.

240 "a muckraker . . . utterly unscrupulous": Quoted in David G. Dalin, *Jewish Justices of the Supreme Court: From Brandeis to Kagan* (Waltham, MA: Brandeis University Press, 2017), 46.

240 Personal animus . . . judicial philosophies: Dalin, *Jewish Justices*, 17-21, 49; Burton, *Taft, Holmes*, 128-129.

241 Root's reasons . . . had sparred with Brandeis: Melvin I. Irofsky, *Louis D. Brandeis: A Life* (New York: Schocken Books, 2009), 272; Leopold, *Root*, 80.

241 Root claimed . . . Brandeis lacked the moral standards: Jessup, 2:474.

241 *Wall Street Journal* . . . "preconceived and known opinions": Bickel and Schmidt, *Supreme Court*, 376; *New York Times*, Jan. 31, 1916 (quotation).

241 Wilson had wanted . . . refused to be photographed: Berg, *Wilson*, 264-265, 400-402; Kenneth Jost, *The Supreme Court from A to Z*, 5th ed. (Los Angeles: Sage/CQPress, 2012), 313. For more detailed accounts of the confirmation battle, see Paper, *Brandeis: An Intimate Biography*, chapter 16, and Bickel and Schmidt, *Supreme Court*, 375-392.

241 Hughes accepted . . . best candidate to unite: Perkins, *Charles Evans*

Hughes, 51–54; Hughes Notes, 178, 180–181; Bickel and Schmidt, *Supreme Court*, 392–396; *New York Times*, June 7, 11, 1916; Jessup, 2:334–352 (quotation at 347); *New York Sun*, May 11, 1916 (Wickersham statement).

242 **Hughes had compiled . . . National Labor Relations Act:** Perkins, *Charles Evans Hughes*, 35–37; Hughes Notes, 175, 312–313; Bickel and Schmidt, *Supreme Court*, 217–221, 254–264, 398–407; *New York Times*, June 10, 1914 (quotations); Minnesota Rate Cases, 230 U.S. 352 (1913); Houston E. & W. T. Ry. Co. v. United States, 234 U.S. 342 (1914).

242 **social welfare legislation . . . vertical resale price maintenance:** Perkins, *Charles Evans Hughes*, 38–42, 46–47; Hughes Notes, 174 and nn37, 39; Bickel and Schmidt, *Supreme Court*, 703–706, 856–874; Bailey v. Alabama, 219 U.S. 219 (1911) (peonage); Dr. Miles Medical Co. v. John D. Park & Sons Co., 220 U.S. 373 (1911) (antitrust).

243 **overruled in 2007:** Leegin Creative Leather Products, Inc. v. PSKS, Inc., 551 U.S. 877 (2007).

243 **"a leader . . . liberated intellect":** Bickel and Schmidt, *Supreme Court*, 367.

243 **"He kept us out of war" . . . Pancho Villa:** Berg, *Wilson*, 390–394, 405, 412 (quotation).

243 **Roosevelt was almost daily chiding . . . stinging letter:** Ibid., 395; *New York Times*, Mar. 5, 1916.

243 **Wilson gradually . . . Reserve Officers' Training Corps:** Berg, *Wilson*, 394.

243 **special patriotic exercises . . . "Americanism" and preparedness:** Ibid., 403; *New York Times*, May 31, 1916.

243 **Citizens' Preparedness Parade . . . Francis Lynde Stetson:** *New York Times*, May 14, 1916; *Los Angeles Herald*, May 13, 1916; New-York Historical Society, "Exhibitions: The Fourth of July, 1916," June 14, 2016, to Oct. 2, 2016, http://www.nyhistory.org/exhibitions/fourth-july-1916.

244 **In July he went . . . haunted looks:** *New York Times*, Feb. 11, 18, 1917.

Chapter 19: **Over There**

245 GERMANS FIRE AT PAUL CRAVATH . . . **"You have been under fire":** *New-York Tribune*, Oct. 2, 1916.

245 **The commandant then led . . .** AMERICAN AMBULANCE CORPS: *New-York Tribune*, Oct. 2, 1916; *Washington (DC) Evening Star*, Oct. 2, 1916. See also *New York Times*, Sept. 4, 1916; Swaine, 2:135.

246 **Cravath was back . . . imperiling its friendship:** *New York Times*, Sept. 15, 1916. For Cravath's account of his visit to the Somme front, see *New York Times*, Feb. 18, 25, 1917, and Paul D. Cravath, *Great Britain's Part* (New York: D. Appleton, 1917).

246 **"the Allies *must* win . . . salvation of Christendom":** Cravath, *Great Britain's Part*, 125 (emphasis in original).

246 Cravath led a lawyers' group . . . East Thirty-Ninth Street: *New-York Tribune*, Nov. 4, 1916; *New York Times*, Nov. 5, 1916.

246 "Brains have been . . . brakes": *New York Times*, Nov. 3, 1916.

246 "specifically and severely criticized . . . publish this letter": Stetson to Harry Garfield, Nov. 12, 1916, Stetson Papers, Williams College, box 12, folder 22. See also Harry Garfield to Stetson, Aug. 25, 1916, ibid., folder 20; Wardwell, *Reminiscences*, 66.

247 Wall Street oddsmakers . . . went to bed: *New York Times*, Nov. 3, 1916; Pusey, *Hughes*, 1:361. Pusey disputes the oft-repeated story that Hughes assumed he had won but concedes that Hughes believed his election probable when he retired for the evening.

247 "the president is asleep . . . no longer president": Gary A. Shuster, *From McKinley to the Monkey Trial: An Episodic History of America, 1900-1925* (Lulu.com, 2006), 169. See also Boller, *Presidential Campaigns*, 206. Pusey calls the story fiction. Pusey, *Hughes*, 1:361.

247 Hughes had run a disorganized . . . more for war than for Hughes: Perkins, *Charles Evans Hughes*, 54-61. See also Berg, *Wilson*, 410-412; Link, *Wilson and the Progressive Era*, 237-247; Lewis L. Gould, *The First Modern Clash over Federal Power: Wilson Versus Hughes in the Presidential Election of 1916* (Lawrence: University Press of Kansas, 2016), 79, 81-86, 101-102, 128; Boller, *Presidential Campaigns*, 202-206.

247 "human icicle": Pusey, *Hughes*, 1:174, 377.

247 Antoinette Carter . . . greatest asset: Ibid., 83-85; Gould, *First Modern Clash*, 76; Perkins, *Charles Evans Hughes*, 53; Boller, *Presidential Campaigns*, 207; *Washington* (DC) *Star*, July 2, Nov. 7, 1916.

248 Wilson was less sympathetic . . . endorsed by black rights groups: Gould, *First Modern Clash*, 5, 57, 112, 130; Perkins, *Charles Evans Hughes*, 42-43; *New York Times*, Sept. 16, 1916.

248 Hughes also supported a federal . . . "Hughesettes": Gould, *First Modern Clash*, 78-79, 108 (quotation); *New York Times*, Aug. 1, 2, 1916.

248 But of the twelve . . . peace issue: Gould, *First Modern Clash*, 129-130; Whitman College, Penrose Library, "Presidential Election 1916," Penrose Library Blog, Nov. 3, 2016, https://library.whitman.edu/blog/presidential-election-1916.

248 Hughes himself attributed . . . from the sidelines: Hughes Notes, 184-185.

248 "alive and happy . . . and War?": Link, *Wilson and the Progressive Era*, 244. See also Berg, *Wilson*, 412; Pusey, *Hughes*, 1:357, 369.

248 Hughes spoke . . . "he were somewhere else": *New York Times*, Jan. 23, 1917.

248 "embarrassment for future judges . . . public loss": *New York Times*, Jan. 23, 1917.

249 "unexpectedly firm and vigorous tone": Cravath to Nicholas Murray Butler,

Apr. 2, 1917, Butler Papers, Columbia University, "Arranged Correspondence," box 97.

249 "Wilson said to me . . . 'couldn't stand that'": Jessup conversation with Root, Sept. 17, 1931, Stewart Collection, LOC, box 2, folder "Post 1916." See also Jessup conversation with Root, Sept. 2, 1935, ibid., folder "Russian Mission."

249 Hughes . . . appointed a committee: *New York Times*, Mar. 9, 1917.

249 "virtually declared . . . ahead of the Government": Hughes Notes, 187 (quotation); *New York Times*, Mar. 17, 1917.

249 Root and Roosevelt had reconciled . . . bitterness still lingered: Scott, *Robert Bacon*, 278-279; Jessup, 2:203-204, 343-349; Leopold, *Root*, 182-183.

249 "Root spoke up . . . tension was relieved": Hughes Notes, 187. A similar version of the story appears in Jessup, 2:327.

250 "rejoicing in the triumph . . . sisterhood of free countries": *New York Times*, Mar. 26, 1917.

250 "We must have no criticism . . . as if every man there was a Republican": *New York Times*, Apr. 10, 1917.

250 "We're in it, thank God, we're in it!": Jessup, 2:323. See ibid., 327-331.

250 "we . . . can now stand up . . . complete defeat of Germany": Cravath to François Monod, Apr. 13, 1917, quoted in Swaine, 2:137-138.

250 Byrne . . . went to Italy: *Red Cross Bulletin* 2, no. 48 (Washington, DC: American Red Cross, Nov. 25, 1918): 8; *New York Times*, Nov. 5, 1942.

250 Henry Stimson . . . a lieutenant colonel: Schmitz, *Henry L. Stimson*, 37-41.

251 "nothing but how to kill Germans": Stimson to Root, Nov. 18, 1918, Root Papers, LOC, box 136.

251 Root traveled to Russia . . . mission a failure: Jessup, 2:353-371; Rousmaniere, 135; Leopold, *Root*, 116-120 (smallpox quotation at 119).

251 Hughes headed New York City's . . . speeding up the process: Hughes Notes, 188-191; *New York Times*, May 18, 1918.

252 George Wickersham served . . . use in Cuba: Hughes Notes, 188-189; *New York Times*, May 18, 1918, Jan. 26, 1936; *Pensacola* (FL) *Journal*, Sept. 18, 1917; Henry W. Taft, *Century and a Half*, 288-289.

252 Cravath, as chairman . . . up to fighting strength: *New York Times*, May 19, 1917.

252 wedding of his daughter: *New York Times*, Aug. 8, 1917.

252 He was named counsel . . . took the British side: Swaine, 2:210-216; Koegel, *Walter S. Carter*, 384; Roberts, "Paul D. Cravath," 201-204; *New York Times*, Nov. 18, 1917; *Grand Forks* (ND) *Herald*, Nov. 8, 1917; *Tulsa* (OK) *Daily World*, Nov. 30, 1917; *Augusta* (GA) *Chronicle*, Dec. 16, 1917; *Patriot* (Harrisburg, PA), Dec. 17, 1917.

252 "Our fortunes . . . advantage to do so": Cravath to Oscar T. Crosby, Apr. 24,

1918, Office Files of Paul D. Cravath, National Archives and Records Administration II, Record Group 56, box 3, folder "General Finance/2" ("Transfer of dollar credits from Italian and French to British Govt./purposes for which made").

252 "Our great standby . . . straightforward character": *The Collected Writings of John Maynard Keynes*, vol. 16, *Activities 1914-1919: The Treasury and Versailles*, ed. Elizabeth Johnson (London: Macmillan, 1971), 269. See Cravath to Keynes, Apr. 11, 15, 16, Nov. 7, 19, 25, 1918, Office Files of Paul D. Cravath, National Archives II, box 3, folder "General Finance/2" ("Transfer of dollar credits from Italian and French to British Govt./purposes for which made"); Keynes to Cravath, Apr. 12, 13, 20, 24, July 19, Nov. 5, 20, 1918, ibid.

253 "was indiscreet . . . too pro-British": Philip Mason Burnett, *Reparation at the Paris Peace Conference: From the Standpoint of the American Delegation* (New York: Columbia University Press, 1940), 1:436. The quoted official was Norman H. Davis, Wilson's assistant treasury secretary.

253 "with the least amount of illegality" . . . forgot to say "Your Majesty": Swaine, 2:212.

253 side trip to Italy . . . Italian king: Ibid., 217.

253 David Lloyd George . . . French marshal Foch: Roberts, "Paul D. Cravath," 203-204; Swaine, 2:214-215.

253 Russell C. Leffingwell . . . Liberty Loan program: Swaine, 2:17-18, 209-210; Chernow, *House of Morgan*, 203.

254 "ingeniously contrived . . . patriotic ballyhoo": Allen, *Lords of Creation*, 212.

254 deserved greater credit: *New York Times*, July 8, 1923.

254 Cromwell became an even more fervent . . . happy to be corrected: Piel and Moore, *Lamplighters*, 37-39; Lisagor & Lipsius, 69-70; Dean, 47; J. F. Dulles to Hjalmar H. Boyesen II, June 2, 1924, JFD Papers, Princeton, "H. H. Boyesen, 1924," box 6, reel 2 ("Cromwell Bureau").

254 "If you lived . . . the Allied cause": Piel and Moore, *Lamplighters*, 38.

255 Dulles was on leave . . . Cuba declared war on Germany: Pruessen, *John Foster Dulles*, 20-22; Kinzer, *Brothers*, 24; Lisagor & Lipsius, 66-67; J. F. Dulles, Memorandum of "Activities Relating to Cuban Affairs, Feb. 13th to Feb. 20th, 1917, inclusive," JFD Papers, Princeton, "Cuba, 1917," box 1, reel 1.

255 confidential mission to Central America . . . Nicaragua declared war: Pruessen, *John Foster Dulles*, 22; Kinzer, *Brothers*, 25; Lisagor & Lipsius, 65-66; J. F. Dulles to Chamorro, July 28, 1916, JFD Papers, Princeton, "Nicaragua, 1916," box 1, reel 1; Chamorro to J. F. Dulles, June 27, Sept. 4, Oct. 3, Nov. 27, 1916, ibid.; Robert Lansing to J. F. Dulles, July 29, 1916, ibid. (quotation); J. F. Dulles, "Notes on Nicaragua," May 23, 1917, ibid.

256 In Costa Rica . . . Wilson declined: Pruessen, *John Foster Dulles*, 22-23; Kinzer, *Brothers*, 25; J. F. Dulles, Confidential Memorandum to the Secretary

of State, "Political and Economic Conditions in Costa Rica, as Bearing on the Question of Recognizing the Government of General Tinoco," May 21, 1917, JFD Papers, Princeton, "Costa Rica, 1917," box 1, reel 1; J. F. Dulles, State Department Memorandum, "The Situation in Costa Rica," July 17, 1917, ibid.

256 **last stop was Panama . . . agreed to protect the canal:** Pruessen, *John Foster Dulles*, 23; Kinzer, *Brothers*, 25; Lisagor & Lipsius, 66; *New York Times*, Apr. 8, 1917.

256 **Dulles applied for admission . . . relations with Russia:** Pruessen, *John Foster Dulles*, 24–28.

256 **Dulles's brother, Allen . . . never heard from again:** Kinzer, *Brothers*, 22–24, 45; Leonard Mosley, *Dulles: A Biography of Eleanor, Allen, and John Foster Dulles and Their Family Network* (New York: Dial Press/James Wade, 1978), 46.

257 **Allen Wardwell . . . never had the same feeling again:** Wardwell, *Reminiscences*, 1–9, 12, 19, 26, 38, 45–47, 66–70; Rousmaniere, 131–133, 136; *New York Times*, Jan. 4, 1911, Dec. 29, 1916.

258 **"There is hardly . . . by any means":** Wardwell, *Reminiscences*, 109.

258 **Stetson's health . . . father expressed surprise:** Stetson to Franklin Carter, June 23, 1913, Stetson Papers, Williams College, box 9, folder 18; Stetson to Hamilton Mabie, June 25, 1913, ibid., folder 19; Stetson to John S. Sheppard, May 12, 1916, ibid., box 12, folder 17; Stetson to Edmund Seymour, Jan. 4, 1917, Stetson to Henry Harman, Jan. 8, 1917, ibid., box 13, folder 1; Stetson to John M. Thomas, Feb. 7, 1918, ibid., box 13, folder 18; Rousmaniere, 130; *New York Times*, Sept. 7, 1917; *New York Sun*, Sept. 7, 1917; *New-York Tribune*, Sept. 7, 1917; Miller, "The 1899 Francis Stetson House."

258 **"had been very fond of Miss Lee":** *New York Sun*, Sept. 7, 1917.

258 **"I now know . . . daughter can be":** Stetson to Franklin Carter, Mar. 4, 1918, Stetson Papers, Williams College, box 13, folder 18.

258 **During his year in Russia . . . Red Cross officials cordially:** Rousmaniere, 136–142; *Brewing and Liquor Interests and German and Bolshevik Propaganda: Report and Hearings of the Subcommittee on the Judiciary, United States Senate, Submitted Pursuant to S. Res. 307 and 439*, S. Doc. No. 62, 66th Cong., 1st Sess. (Washington, DC: Government Printing Office, 1919), 3:361, 375–376, 601, 848–849, 855, 924–927 (hereafter, *Bolshevik Propaganda Report*); Allen Wardwell, "Copies of Letters Home, July 31, Aug. 5, Sept. 6, 19, 1917," Allen Wardwell Papers, Columbia University Rare Book and Manuscript Library, box 2; Wardwell and Raymond Robins, Memorandum, Dec. 12/25, 1917, ibid., box 3, "Chronological File Sept.–Dec. 1917"; Robins to Wardwell, Apr. 19, 1918, ibid., box 1; Allen Wardwell diary entries for July 26–Aug. 7, Aug. 25, Sept. 2, 1917, Feb. 4, 6, May 10, 15, 24, 26, June 13, July 7, 1918, ibid., box 3, "excerpts from diary and letters," vol. 1, 1917, vol. 2, 1918.

259 **bankers and lawyers:** Anthony C. Sutton, *Wall Street and the Bolshevik*

Revolution: The Remarkable True Story of the American Capitalists Who Financed the Russian Communists (New York: Crown, 1974), 72-76.

259 "conservative lawyers . . . New York": *Bolshevik Propaganda Report*, 3:853-854.

259 Wardwell was escorted . . . Winter Palace: Rousmaniere, 141.

259 mission came to an end . . . was denied: Ibid., 142-145; Ann Hagedorn, *Savage Peace: Hope and Fear in America, 1919* (New York: Simon & Schuster, 2007), 4, 74, 80-90; Pritt Buttar, *Splintered Empires: The Eastern Front, 1917-21* (Oxford: Osprey Publishing, 2017), 351-352; Berg, *Wilson*, 498-500; Wardwell to Raymond Robins, Apr. 20, 27, 30, May 3, 1918; Robins to Wardwell, Apr. 9, 15, 19, Aug. 3, 1918; Wardwell to Georgy Chicherin, Sept. 8, 1918; Chicherin to Wardwell, Sept. 11, 1918, all in Allen Wardwell Papers, Columbia University Rare Book and Manuscript Library, box 1; Wardwell to William B. Webster, Aug. 5, 8, 1918; Wardwell to S. Possakhow, Aug. 20, 1918, ibid., box 2, "Chronological Files, Aug. 1-13, Aug. 14-31, 1918"; Allen Wardwell diary entries for Oct. 21, Nov. 15, 1918, ibid., box 3, "excerpts from diary and letters," vol. 2, 1918; *New York Times*, Oct. 23, Dec. 26, 1918.

260 Sauerkraut . . . in English: Berg, *Wilson*, 456; *New York Times*, Nov. 3, 1917, Jan. 4, 1918.

260 "strong considerations . . . point of view": Root to Lawrence A. Wilkins, May 22, 1918, Root Papers, LOC, box 136.

260 "one does not . . . can be avoided": Root to Richard J. Biggs, May 31, 1918, ibid.

260 "to be a strong . . . so essential": Root to Lawrence A. Wilkins, May 22, 1918, ibid.

260 "what the Country means . . . institutions mean": Root to Richard J. Biggs, Dec. 3, 1918, ibid.

260 Cravath had to defend . . . charges against de Gersdorff went nowhere: Swaine, 2:216n1; Cravath to William G. McAdoo, Aug. 24, 1918, Wilson Papers, LOC, Series 2, reel 99 (quotation).

261 Samuel Untermyer had . . . resented his spending: Hawkins, "The 'Jewish Threat,'" 83-92; Johnston, "Little Giant 2," 25; *New York Times*, Oct. 4, 5, 17, 1917.

261 "Untermyer's patriotism . . . necessity not conviction": Hawkins, "The 'Jewish Threat,'" 87.

261 "the enemy of freedom . . . oppressor of the Jews": *New York Times*, Nov. 3, 1917.

262 "There is just one way . . . by which it is maintained": *New York Times*, Sept. 18, 1918.

262 enemies remained unconvinced . . . he came to regret: Hawkins, "The 'Jewish Threat,'" 92-102; see ibid., 88. Untermyer's testimony in defense of his activities appears in *Bolshevik Propaganda Report*, 2:1835-1910.

262 Supreme Court adjourned . . . slap on the wrist: Bickel and Schmidt, *Supreme Court*, 155-160; Freyer, *Regulation of Big Business*, 168, 189; Swaine, 2:157-158; Chernow, *House of Morgan*, 149.

262 extraordinary level of collaboration . . . changed American attitudes: Freyer, *Regulation of Big Business*, 159-160, 164-165, 170; Bickel and Schmidt, *Supreme Court*, 516-517; Berg, *Wilson*, 443-446.

263 "the most interesting work . . . service to the government": Cravath to William G. McAdoo, Aug. 24, 1918, Wilson Papers, LOC, Series 2, reel 99.

263 "never had any experience . . . battlefronts in winter": Swaine, 2:213.

263 Cravath was in London . . . war's end: Ibid., 218.

263 "Though I have been hard at work . . . away from home": Cravath to Lord Reading (Rufus Isaacs), Feb. 25, 1919, Morrow Papers, Amherst College, Series 1, box 16, folder 18, "Paul D. Cravath 1915-1919."

263 "tall and beloved American friend": Colin Clifford, *The Asquiths* (London: John Murray, 2002), 463.

263 Distinguished Service Medal: *New-York Tribune*, Mar. 28, 1919.

263 special war cross . . . Legion of Honor: *New York Times*, Aug. 7, 1919; Swaine, 2:221; Mackaye, "Public Man," 24.

263 "a much more human person . . . founded by his father": Swaine, 2:256. See also Mackaye, "Public Man," 23.

Chapter 20: To End All Wars

265 Dulles attached himself . . . dinners at the Ritz Hotel: Kinzer, *Brothers*, 25-27; Berg, *Wilson*, 559; Lisagor & Lipsius, 70-72; Pruessen, *John Foster Dulles*, 29-30, 36.

265 cost him $110 . . . "worth it, don't you think?": Lisagor & Lipsius, 72.

266 Most of Dulles's time . . . small group meetings: Pruessen, *John Foster Dulles*, 31-32; Burnett, *Reparation*, 1:14n35; Immerman, *Dulles: Piety, Pragmatism*, 7; JFD Papers, Princeton, "Reparations and Reparations Commission, 1919," box 2, reel 1. The Reparations and Reparations Commission file in the Princeton collection contains voluminous pages of notes, memoranda, correspondence, and diary entries by Dulles and his wife detailing Dulles's activities in Paris in 1919. See, for example, Janet Dulles's diary entries for April 1, 2, 13, 22, and 29, 1919.

266 "caused more trouble . . . Treaty of Versailles": Thomas Lamont, "German Reparations," Feb. 25, 1921, JFD Papers, Princeton, "Reparations, 1921," box 4, reel 1.

266 "the critical financial situation of Europe": J. F. Dulles, June 3, 1919, memorandum, JFD Papers, Princeton, "Reparations, 1919," box 2, reel 1, reproduced in Burnett, *Reparation*, 2:107-109. See also Pruessen, *John Foster*

Dulles, 32-33, 45-50; Immerman, *Dulles: Piety, Pragmatism*, 7-8; Berg, *Wilson*, 566-567; Seligman, *Reminiscences*, 228-229.

266 "a valued customer . . . temporarily embarrassed": J. F. Dulles, undated memorandum to Senate Foreign Relations Committee, c. August 1919, JFD Papers, Princeton, "Reparations, 1919," box 2, reel 1; Pruessen, *John Foster Dulles*, 53.

266 "Our industries . . . and peoples": Quoted in Pruessen, *John Foster Dulles*, 51. See also Kinzer, *Brothers*, 32.

266 dread of bolshevism . . . just as Russia had: Pruessen, *John Foster Dulles*, 45-47; Berg, *Wilson*, 566; Kinzer, *Brothers*, 32-33.

267 "as to force . . . into revolution": Burnett, *Reparation*, 1:460.

267 err on the side of leniency . . . generation or more: Ibid., 467.

267 At a minimum . . . its solvency: Ibid., 460-462.

267 The British came . . . pressed for a time limit: Pruessen, *John Foster Dulles*, 33-34, 41; Lisagor & Lipsius, 72-73; Berg, *Wilson*, 560.

267 "war costs" . . . not at liberty to break: Pruessen, *John Foster Dulles*, 33-34; Immerman, *Dulles: Piety, Pragmatism*, 7-8; Berg, *Wilson*, 559-560; J. F. Dulles, foreword to Burnett, *Reparation*, 1:v-vii, xii; Burnett, *Reparation*, 1:16; J. F. Dulles memoranda, Feb. 13, 14, 19, 24, 1919, JFD Papers, Princeton, "Reparations, 1919," box 2, reel 1; Wilson to Robert Lansing, Feb. 23, 1919, ibid.

268 "scrap" with David Lloyd George: Janet Dulles diary entry for Apr. 5, 1919, JFD Papers, Princeton, "Reparations, 1919," box 2, reel 1.

268 "row with the French": Janet Dulles diary entry for Mar. 31, 1919, ibid.

268 To deflect . . . civilian population and property: Pruessen, *John Foster Dulles*, 34-35; Immerman, *Dulles: Piety, Pragmatism*, 8-9.

268 Americans ultimately won . . . "war guilt" clause: Pruessen, *John Foster Dulles*, 36-40; Immerman, *Dulles: Piety, Pragmatism*, 9; Berg, *Wilson*, 573; Burnett, *Reparation*, 1:66-70.

268 Dulles himself expressed regret: Immerman, *Dulles: Piety, Pragmatism*, 10. See also J. F. Dulles, foreword to Burnett, *Reparation*, 1:xi-xiv. Dulles wrote the foreword in 1938, when war was on the horizon.

268 "was both legally . . . a grotesque figure": J. F. Dulles, foreword to Burnett, *Reparation*, 1:v.

268 resisted a British proposal . . . "I am going to include pensions": Pruessen, *John Foster Dulles*, 39-41; J. F. Dulles memorandum, Apr. 1, 1919, JFD Papers, Princeton, "Reparations, 1919," box 2, reel 1; J. F. Dulles, foreword to Burnett, *Reparation*, 1:vii.

269 Nor did the Americans prevail . . . half in hard money: Immerman, *Dulles: Piety, Pragmatism*, 10; J. F. Dulles to Thomas Lamont, Feb. 15, 1921, JFD Papers, Princeton, "Reparations, 1921," box 4, reel 1; *New York Times*, Mar. 28, 1920; Burnett, *Reparation*, 1:15, 71-77; Berg, *Wilson*, 599.

269 "Carthaginian peace": Cravath to Edward T. Devine, Feb. 5, 1920, quoted in Swaine, 2:257n1.

269 "There are limits . . . slave and sacrifice": Cravath to Learned Hand, May 19, 1920, quoted in Swaine, 2:257n2.

269 recalcitrant Germany . . . only about 15 percent: Berg, *Wilson*, 599.

269 Historians continue to debate . . . lacked the political will: See, for example, Niall Ferguson, *The Pity of War: Explaining World War I* (1998; repr., New York: Basic Books, 1999); Gerald D. Feldman, *The Great Disorder: Politics, Economics, and Society in the German Inflation, 1914-1924* (New York: Oxford University Press, 1993); Sally Marks, "The Myths of Reparations," *Central European History* 11, no. 3 (September 1978): 231-255.

269 "not go quite yet . . . from the start": American Commissioners to Alfred Jaretzki Sr., May 30, 1919, JFD Papers, Princeton, "American Commission to Negotiate Peace and the War Trade Board, 1919," box 2, reel 1.

269 "You can assure him . . . by doing so": Jaretzki to Commissioners, June 2, 1919, ibid.

270 Dulles idolized the president: Kinzer, *Brothers*, 31; Pruessen, *John Foster Dulles*, 24.

270 "beg very earnestly . . . upon my own": Wilson to J. F. Dulles, June 27, 1919, JFD Papers, Princeton, "Woodrow Wilson, 1919," box 2, reel 1.

270 four US delegates . . . in Dulles's hands: Norman Davis et al. to American Peace Commissioners, June 28, 1919, JFD Papers, Princeton, "American Commission to Negotiate Peace and the War Trade Board, 1919," box 2, reel 1.

270 his portfolio expanded . . . Saint-Cloud course: See, for example, J. F. Dulles diary entries for July 9, 10, 11, 17, 21, 23-25, Aug. 5, 7, 11, 15, 18, 21, 23, 24, 1919, JFD Papers, Princeton, "Reparations, 1919," box 2, reel 1; Pruessen, *John Foster Dulles*, 53.

270 Dulles finally came home . . . promoted to a full partner: Pruessen, *John Foster Dulles*, 50, 53, 59-60; J. F. Dulles, undated memorandum to Senate Foreign Relations Committee, c. August 1919, JFD Papers, Princeton, "Reparations, 1919," box 2, reel 1; *Syracuse* (NY) *Standard*, Aug. 14, 1919; Lisagor & Lipsius, 77.

271 considered that a mistake . . . just another negotiator: Swaine, 2:219; Heckscher, *Woodrow Wilson*, 489-490; Kinzer, *Brothers*, 26-27; Jessup, 2:381.

271 George Wickersham even argued . . . Stetson publicly defended: *New York Times*, Nov. 28, 29, 1918.

271 "I am in favor . . . not an adverse critic of the President": Stetson to D. S. Henderson, Dec. 5, 1918, Stetson Papers, Williams College, box 13, folder 23.

272 Wilson also incurred .˙. . Republicans dismissed White: Heckscher, *Woodrow Wilson*, 492; Berg, *Wilson*, 517-518; Jessup, 2:379-380, 386; Perkins, *Charles Evans Hughes*, 74; Leopold, *Root*, 92-93, 124, 131-133, 189-190; Jes-

sup conversation with Root, Sept. 2, 1935, Stewart Collection, LOC, box 2, folder "Russian Mission" (quotations).

272 **Wilson further insisted . . . "irreconcilables":** Berg, *Wilson,* 549, 558, 612; Jessup, 2:381–384, 397, 399, 401–402; Leopold, *Root,* 123–127, 135–140; Root to Will Hays, Mar. 29, 1919, Root Papers, LOC, box 137; Root to Sen. Frank B. Kellogg, Aug. 19, 1919, ibid.; Kellogg to Root, Aug. 21, 1919, ibid.; Root to Sen. Walter E. Edge, Oct. 1, 1919, ibid.; Edge to Root, Oct. 3, 8, 1919, ibid.; Perkins, *Charles Evans Hughes,* 79; Hughes Notes, 210–214; Swaine, 2:139–140; Cravath to Dwight Morrow, Mar. 4, 1919, Morrow Papers, Amherst College, Series 2, box 2, folder 57, "Society of Free States, Correspondence 1919, A–H"; *New York Times,* Mar. 19, Aug. 17, 1919 (Wickersham), Mar. 31, 1919 (Root), Jan. 3, 1920 (Cravath). See also *New York Sun,* Mar. 14, 1919 (Union League).

273 **Cravath envisioned the League . . . power to enforce peace:** Roberts, "Paul D. Cravath," 206–209; see Cravath to William G. McAdoo, Nov. 7, 1918, Morrow Papers, Amherst College, Series 7, box 1, folder 2, "Allied Maritime Transport Council, Correspondence 1918." Cravath favored temporarily continuing the Inter-Allied Council and US aid to Europe after the war until the restoration of normal international relations. Ibid. See also Cravath to Russell C. Leffingwell and Albert Rathbone, Nov. 21, 1918, Office Files of Paul D. Cravath, National Archives II, Record Group 56, box 6, folder "General Finance 50" ("financial problems to be considered in view of armistice and peace—continuation of program committees, and other inter-allied organizations"); Cravath to Gordon Auchincloss, Nov. 30, 1918, ibid.

273 **Anglo-American guarantee:** Roberts, "Paul D. Cravath," 208; *New York Times,* Feb. 7, 1920.

273 **favored arbitration . . . at odds with the version:** Divine, *Second Chance,* 22; Jessup, 2:373–379, 383–384, 390–391, 418; Leopold, *Root,* 69, 124, 133–134; Swaine, 2:257, 259; Roberts, "Paul D. Cravath," 210; Perkins, *Charles Evans Hughes,* 76, 81; Hughes Notes, 195n35, 212, 222; *New York Times,* Jan. 19, 1919 (Guthrie); *New-York Tribune,* Apr. 13, 1919 (Wickersham).

273 **famous Article X . . . would usurp:** Perkins, *Charles Evans Hughes,* 75–77; Jessup, 2:383; Leopold, *Root,* 136–139; Heckscher, *Woodrow Wilson,* 588–589, Berg, *Wilson,* 653; Divine, *Second Chance,* 8; John Fischer Williams, "The League of Nations and Unanimity," *American Journal of International Law* 19, no. 3 (July 1925): 482–484.

274 **"not our business . . . in quarrels":** Guthrie to William E. Borah, Jan. 31, 1919, quoted in William G. Ross, *World War I and the American Constitution* (Cambridge: Cambridge University Press, 2017), 321. See also *New York Times,* Jan. 19, Mar. 14, 1919.

274 **Guthrie cautioned . . . American nationalism and independence:** *New York Times,* Jan. 19, 1919.

274 "Nothing can be worse . . . break them": Jessup, 2:378. See ibid., 2:417; Root to Sen. Le Baron B. Colt, Aug. 28, 1919, Root Papers, LOC, box 137.

274 As Hughes and Cravath argued . . . in the absence of Article X: Hughes Notes, 211; Cravath, "League of Nations in the Campaign, Notes by P.D.C., Preliminary Draft Sept. 10, 1920," at 13, Morrow Papers, Amherst College, Series 1, box 16, folder 19, "Paul D. Cravath 1920-1923."

274 would freeze the territorial status quo . . . dubious validity: Hughes Notes, 210-211, 216.

274 "arbitrary and irrational boundaries": Swaine, 2:140, quoting Cravath to (Lord) Stanley Buckmaster, Dec. 8, 1919.

274 Hughes said Article X unwisely . . . "It is in the teeth of experience": Hughes Notes, 210-211 (quotation).

275 "Change and growth . . . succeeding generations": Root to Will Hays, Mar. 29, 1919, Root Papers, LOC, box 137 (quotation); Jessup, 2:392-393.

275 Wilson, on the other hand . . . British and French imperialism: Heckscher, *Woodrow Wilson*, 630; Trygve Throntveit, *Power Without Victory: Woodrow Wilson and the American Internationalist Experiment* (Chicago: University of Chicago Press, 2017), 381n25.

275 Wall Street internationalists . . . gave little thought: Divine, *Second Chance*, 22; Roberts, "Paul D. Cravath," 204. See also Jessup, 2:391-392.

275 "benevolent, just and enlightened" . . . "to rule themselves": Paul D. Cravath, *Letters Home from India and Irak 1925* (New York: J. J. Little and Ives, 1925), 14, 79, 118-119, 122-123.

275 ignored the petition . . . Ho Chi Minh: Berg, *Wilson*, 528; Kinzer, *Brothers*, 29-30.

275 reservationists had other objections . . . right to withdraw: *New York Times*, Mar. 31, 1919 (Root); Root to Will Hays, Mar. 29, 1919, Root Papers, LOC, box 137; Cravath to Dwight Morrow, Mar. 4, 1919, Morrow Papers, Amherst College, Series 2, box 2, folder 57, "Society of Free States, Correspondence 1919, A-H"; Jessup, 2:391-392; Perkins, *Charles Evans Hughes*, 77; *New-York Tribune*, Apr. 13, 1919 (Wickersham).

276 Wilson returned to Paris . . . refused to compromise: Jessup, 2:397; Arthur S. Link, *Woodrow Wilson: Revolution, War, and Peace* (Arlington Heights, IL: Harlan Davidson, 1979), 106; Heckscher, *Woodrow Wilson*, 551-553, 588-589, 607.

276 "debating society": Berg, *Wilson*, 605.

276 "a plain need . . . injurious commitments": Hughes Notes, 210, 212 (quotations). See also *New York Times*, Aug. 5, 1919.

276 great opportunity . . . "mischievous": Root to Will Hays, Mar. 29, 1919, Root Papers, LOC, box 137 (quotation); Jessup, 2:388, 392, 400-401.

276 refrain from sending . . . against its will: Cravath to Dwight Morrow, Mar. 4, 1919, Morrow Papers, Amherst College, Series 2, box 2, folder 57, "Society

of Free States, Correspondence 1919, A-H"; Swaine, 2:140, quoting Cravath to (Lord) Stanley Buckmaster, Dec. 8, 1919.

277 **Henry Cabot Lodge . . . Wilson's folly:** Berg, *Wilson*, 608-609, 613, 652, 654; Jessup, 2:402, 405; Heckscher, *Woodrow Wilson*, 584.

277 **speaking tour . . . paralyzed the left side:** Heckscher, *Woodrow Wilson*, 585, 593-619.

277 **popular if exaggerated . . . de facto president:** Betty Boyd Caroli, *First Ladies: From Martha Washington to Michelle Obama*, 4th ed. (Oxford: Oxford University Press, 2010), 152-154; Berg, *Wilson*, 662, 674.

277 **Confined to his quarters . . . delusional:** John Milton Cooper Jr., *Woodrow Wilson: A Biography* (New York: Knopf, 2009), 7; Berg, *Wilson*, 662, 674.

277 **unwilling to accept a single . . . He instructed Senate Democrats:** Berg, *Wilson*, 654-656; Heckscher, *Woodrow Wilson*, 607-608, 618-619; Hughes Notes, 217-218.

277 **On November 19, 1919 . . . and was defeated:** Berg, *Wilson*, 657; *New York Times*, Nov. 19, 20, 1919; Root to Sen. Frank B. Kellogg, Nov. 12, 1919, Root Papers, LOC, box 137.

277 **"I am so irritated . . . join the party of Wilson":** Cravath to Lord Buckmaster, Dec. 8, 1919, quoted in Swaine, 2:139.

278 **Cravath . . . favored ratification, with or without reservations:** Cravath, "League of Nations in the Campaign, Notes by P.D.C., Preliminary Draft Sept. 10, 1920," Morrow Papers, Amherst College, Series 1, box 16, folder 19, "Paul D. Cravath 1920-1923."

278 **"I have never felt . . . that it created":** Cravath, "League of Nations," ibid.

278 **"a pathetic fate . . . American participation":** Cravath to Lord Buckmaster, Dec. 8, 1919, quoted in Swaine, 2:139-140, 140n1.

278 **Root, too, refused to give up . . . Lodge saw no reason:** Jessup, 2:407-408; Leopold, *Root*, 139-143; Root to George Gray, Dec. 1, 1919, Root Papers, LOC, box 137; Heckscher, *Woodrow Wilson*, 629-631; Berg, *Wilson*, 673-675.

278 **On a renewed vote . . . seven votes short:** Heckscher, *Woodrow Wilson*, 630-631; Berg, *Wilson*, 677.

279 **Great Britain had signaled . . . no objection:** Hughes Notes, 218.

279 **"the highest British authorities" . . . Wilson had forced Article X:** Cravath, "League of Nations in the Campaign, Notes by P.D.C., Preliminary Draft Sept. 10, 1920," at 10, Morrow Papers, Amherst College, Series 1, box 16, folder 19, "Paul D. Cravath 1920-1923." For a study of mixed British attitudes toward the League, see George W. Egerton, *Great Britain and the Creation of the League of Nations: Strategy, Politics, and International Organization, 1914-1919* (Chapel Hill: University of North Carolina Press, 1978).

279 **Hughes maintained . . . would have overwhelmingly passed:** Hughes Notes, 216-217.

279 **"the early opportunity . . . was lost":** Ibid., 214.

279 "willful self-sufficient pride": Jessup, 2:407.

279 stubbornness: *New-York Tribune*, Oct. 20, 1920.

279 Root himself later expressed ... using subterfuge: Jessup, 2:409–410. See also Leopold, *Root*, 149–150; Root to Sen. Frank B. Kellogg, Mar. 13, 1920, Root Papers, LOC, box 138.

279 Wilson also signed a separate treaty ... died a quiet death: Jessup, 2:401; Heckscher, *Woodrow Wilson*, 590.

279 "commit the folly ... like Senator Harding": Cravath to Lord Buckmaster, Feb. 14, 1920, quoted in Swaine, 2:140.

Chapter 21: Normalcy

280 passed an emergency measure: Bickel and Schmidt, *Supreme Court*, 531–532; Ruppert v. Caffey, 261 U.S. 264, 278–280 (1920).

280 hired Elihu Root and William Guthrie ... had some initial success: Bickel and Schmidt, *Supreme Court*, 531–532, 535n248; Jessup, 2:478–479; *New York Times*, Mar. 16, 18, 19, Apr. 25, May 24, 25, 27, Nov. 7, 16, 22, Dec. 16, 1919, Jan. 6, 1920; *New-York Tribune*, Mar. 19, Aug. 3, Oct. 28, 1919; *Philadelphia Inquirer*, Mar. 30, June 18, Oct. 16, 1919; *Idaho Daily Statesman* (Boise, ID), Apr. 24, May 24, 1919.

281 passed the Volstead Act ... banned regardless: *New York Times*, Aug. 3, Oct. 29, 31, 1919; Ruppert v. Caffey, 261 U.S. at 280–281; Bickel and Schmidt, *Supreme Court*, 532–536.

281 deep philosophical objections ... transferred to the federal government: Jessup, 2:476; Leopold, *Root*, 170; Daniel Okrent, *Last Call: The Rise and Fall of Prohibition* (New York: Scribner, 2010), 121; Root to Lewis L. Clarke, Dec. 20, 1919, Root Papers, LOC, box 137.

281 "Temperance ... through the law": Jessup, 2:476.

281 "takes away ... dull grey lives": Root to Everett P. Wheeler, Nov. 22, 1919, Root Papers, LOC, box 137 (quotations); Jessup, 2:477–478.

282 The Supreme Court considered ... upheld the ban on beer: Ruppert v. Caffey, 261 U.S. 264; Bickel and Schmidt, *Supreme Court*, 534–540; Jessup, 2:478.

282 The more important case ... "concurrent power": Bickel and Schmidt, *Supreme Court*, 540–543; Jessup, 2:479–480.

282 "While I thought ... if they saw fit": Hughes Notes, 192; see *New York Times*, Mar. 2, 1920; Pusey, *Hughes*, 1:386.

283 At the argument ... "sat upon your bench": Jessup, 2:479–480 (quotation).

283 Supreme Court soundly rejected: *New York Times*, June 8, 1920; National Prohibition Cases, 253 U.S. 350 (1920); Bickel and Schmidt, *Supreme Court*, 544–547.

283 obtain the return of two cases . . . finally released to Cromwell: Cromwell to J. F. Dulles, Jan. 22, 1922, JFD Papers, Princeton, "William Nelson Cromwell, 1922," box 4, reel 1 (quotation); Dulles to Cromwell, May 4, 1922, ibid.; *New York Times*, May 16, 1922; *New-York Tribune*, May 16, 1922; Lisagor & Lipsius, 80.

283 "This is a step in the right direction": Jessup, 2:481.

284 "Palmer Raids" . . . few Americans voiced: Heckscher, *Woodrow Wilson*, 619-620; Hagedorn, *Savage Peace*, 130-132, 218-220, 382-383, 399-402, 409, 419-422, 427-429; Regin Schmidt, *Red Scare: FBI and the Origins of Anticommunism in the United States, 1919-1943* (Copenhagen: Museum Tusculanum Press, University of Copenhagen, 2000), 72-82, 236, 313-314; R. G. Brown et al., *To the American People: Report upon the Illegal Practices of the United States Department of Justice* (Washington, DC: National Popular Government League, May 1920).

284 "ruthless and indiscriminate exercise of governmental power": Cravath to Oswald Garrison Villard, Jan. 9, 1920, quoted in Swaine, 2:263.

284 "I am a little afraid . . . deportation business": Frank Polk to John W. Davis, Jan. 17, 1920, Davis Papers, Yale, Series 2, box 10, folder 65.

284 Samuel Untermyer publicly criticized . . . had died down: *New York Times*, Jan. 23, 1920. Untermyer's criticisms of the postwar Palmer Raids were muted in comparison with his focus on Palmer's wartime seizures of German Americans' property and nonenforcement of the antitrust laws. Ibid. See also *New York Times*, Jan. 19, 21, 27, 1920.

284 Stetson was probably . . . dementia: *New-York Tribune*, Feb. 5, 1920; Frank Polk to John W. Davis, Apr. 6, 1920, Davis Papers, Yale, Series 2, box 10, folder 65; Allen Wardwell to John W. Davis, Jan. 25, 1920, ibid., folder 82.

285 "poisonous propaganda . . . unreasonable demands": *New York Times*, Feb. 20, 1920.

285 New York State Assembly . . . un-American: *New York Times*, Jan. 14, 15, 18, 20, 21, 1920; Perkins, *Charles Evans Hughes*, 68-69; Hughes Notes, 195; Pusey, *Hughes*, 1:391-392; Wardwell, *Reminiscences*, 113.

285 "The peaceful means . . . political opinion": *New York Times*, Jan. 21, 1920.

285 To the state bar association . . . dictatorship of the proletariat: *New York Times*, Jan. 18, 1920.

285 Guthrie argued . . . could not truthfully take the oath: *New York Times*, Jan. 15, 18, 1920.

285 which expelled . . . Even the Union League Club: Perkins, *Charles Evans Hughes*, 69-70; *New York Times*, Jan. 14, 20, 26, 27, Feb. 20, 21, Mar. 31, Apr. 2, 1920.

285 "nothing short of a calamity": *New York Times*, Apr. 2, 1920.

286 Hughes's eldest daughter . . . died: Hughes Notes, 196; *New York Times*, Apr. 19, 1920.

286 "violations of personal rights . . . even victoriously waged": *New York Times*, June 22, 1920.

286 The campaign continued . . . "normalcy": Boller, *Presidential Campaigns*, 212–213.

286 "don't give a darn . . . something to drink": Frank Polk to John W. Davis, May 7, 1920, Davis Papers, Yale, Series 2, box 10, folder 65.

287 Paul Cravath originally opposed . . . sake of party unity: Swaine, 2:251–253; Jessup, 2:410–414; Cravath, "League of Nations in the Campaign, Notes by P. D. C., Preliminary Draft Sept. 10, 1920," Morrow Papers, Amherst College, Series 1, box 16, folder 19, "Paul D. Cravath 1920–1923"; Cravath to Nicholas Murray Butler, Oct. 18, 26, 1920, Butler Papers, Columbia University, "Arranged Correspondence," box 97; Leopold, *Root*, 126–127, 143–147, 185; Randolph C. Downes, *The Rise of Warren Gamaliel Harding, 1865–1920* (Columbus: Ohio State University Press, 1970), 579, 589–592.

287 In a statement . . . hold them to it: *New York Times*, Oct. 15, 28, 1920, May 25, 1923; Cravath to Root, Oct. 11, 13, 1920, Root Papers, LOC, box 138; Cravath to Nicholas Murray Butler, Oct. 26, 1920, Butler Papers, Columbia University, "Arranged Correspondence," box 97 (quotation); Cravath to Butler, Oct. 14, 18, 1920, ibid.; Downes, *Harding*, 589–595; Swaine, 2:252; Jessup, 2:413–415; Leopold, *Root*, 147–149.

288 Harding abandoned . . . separate peace treaty with Germany: Jessup, 2:414, 416; Leopold, *Root*, 149–150, 151 (quotation), 152–158; Richard H. Dana to Root, Nov. 19, 1920, Root Papers, LOC, box 138; Swaine, 2:253–254, 317n3; Perkins, *Charles Evans Hughes*, 83–84; Hughes Notes, 213, 225.

288 Cravath visited Germany . . . under duress: Paul D. Cravath, "Impressions of the Financial and Industrial Conditions in Germany," *Annals of the American Academy of Political and Social Science* 92 (November 1920): 5–12; see *Springfield* (MA) *Republican*, Sept. 9, 1920.

289 "another power . . . military qualities": *New York Times*, Oct. 17, 1920.

Chapter 22: "The Last Great Epoch"

290 On December 5, 1920 . . . substantial trust fund: *New York Times*, Dec. 6, 8, 1920, May 4, 1921; *New-York Tribune*, Aug. 16, 1922.

290 US Steel had won . . . renewed merger wave: Bickel and Schmidt, *Supreme Court*, 155–170, 199; Freyer, *Regulation of Big Business*, 189; Gellhorn, Kovacic, and Calkins, *Antitrust Law*, 143–144; *New York Times*, Mar. 2, 1920; United States v. US Steel Corp., 251 U.S. 417, 439, 459 (1920).

291 Gone was the economy . . . heightened government oversight: These observations are further developed in Sklar, *Corporate Reconstruction*, 401–441 and passim; Freyer, *Regulation of Big Business*, 1 and passim; and Mitchell, *Speculation Economy*, 8–10, 216, and passim.

291 "If there was going to be a socialist world . . . have to be built up": Kelley, *Reminiscences*, 59.

292 "accept justice uncomplainingly": Cravath to T. Roosevelt, Nov. 7, 1906, TR Papers, LOC, reel 70.

292 academics, businessmen . . . before the federal government: See Walter Isaacson and Evan Thomas, *The Wise Men: Six Friends and the World They Made* (New York: Simon & Schuster, 1986); Joseph C. Goulden, *The Super-lawyers: The Small and Powerful World of the Great Washington Law Firms* (New York: Weybright and Talley, 1972). Of the influential public policy advisors profiled in these books, only one—John J. McCloy—was a Wall Street lawyer, and his career ended in the 1960s.

292 liberal Rockefeller wing: Rockefeller himself died in 1979. As members of the Eastern Establishment, Wall Street lawyers continued to hold positions of national influence in the 1970s and sporadically into the 1980s. Dewey protégé William P. Rogers, Eisenhower's attorney general, served as Richard Nixon's secretary of state from 1969 to 1973—the fifth in a line of Wall Street Republican lawyers, dating from Elihu Root, to serve as the nation's chief diplomat. However, Rogers was marginalized by a Harvard academic, National Security Advisor Henry Kissinger, who eventually succeeded him.

Lawrence Walsh, who had previously served as an assistant to both Dewey and Rogers, and who left the Davis Polk firm in 1981, was appointed independent counsel in 1986 to investigate the Iran-Contra affair during the Reagan administration. Noted trial lawyer Arthur Liman of Paul Weiss—a Democrat—was chief counsel for the Senate's investigation of Iran-Contra. Davis Polk lawyer Robert Fiske Jr. was the special prosecutor heading the Whitewater investigation during the Clinton administration until his replacement by Kenneth Starr as independent counsel. Onetime Cravath partner David Boies litigated the *Bush v. Gore* case for Al Gore in 2000.

Other examples may be cited, but the point remains that for quite some time now, Wall Street lawyers—Republican or Democrat—have not exerted nearly as much influence on national and international affairs as did their early-twentieth-century predecessors.

293 "We are living . . . will ever be participants": Piel and Moore, *Lamplighters*, 38.

Epilogue

294 He continued his iron rule . . . Council on Foreign Relations: Swaine, 2:256–259, 267, 318n3, 479–483; Koegel, *Walter S. Carter*, 386; Roberts, "Paul D. Cravath," 204–205; Mackaye, "Public Man," 23–24; *New York Times*, July 14, 1921, Feb. 18, Aug. 8, 1922, Sept. 30, 1924, Dec. 17, 1928, Nov. 26, 1930.

294 urged United States recognition of Soviet Russia . . . "fascinating experiment": Swaine, 2:262-263, 480 (quotation); Roberts, "Paul D. Cravath," 212.

294 "Is Big Business a Menace? . . . efficiency and volume": Swaine, 2:485. See also *New York Times*, May 1, 1929.

295 chairman of the Metropolitan Opera . . . music appreciation lessons: Mackaye, "Public Man," 21, 23; Swaine, 2:263n3, 483; Koegel, *Walter S. Carter*, 387.

295 "New York standpatters": Swaine, 2:452n4. See also ibid., 2:452n1, 453-454nn4, 5.

295 Cravath joined President Roosevelt . . . eliminate slums: *New York Times*, Apr. 18, 1934, Nov. 7, 1938.

295 favored American military support . . . barring some dramatic event: Swaine, 2:456n4, 457nn1, 3; ibid., 2:458n2; Roberts, "Paul D. Cravath," 213.

295 Cravath died . . . favorite selections: Swaine, 2:644-645; *New York Times*, July 2, 4, 1940.

295 "one of the last representatives . . . vast business corporations": *New York Times*, July 2, 1940.

296 "In recent years . . . older New York": *New-York Tribune*, July 2, 1940.

296 "Just when the efficient organization . . . useful life": *New York Times*, July 2, 1940.

296 1922 Washington Naval Conference . . . World Court: Hughes Notes, 222-225, 238-246; Perkins, *Charles Evans Hughes*, 90-92, 96-115, 281-283, 285-286, 290-291. See also Leopold, *Root*, 158-61.

297 Hughes the obvious choice . . . always denied this: Bernard Schwartz, "Supreme Court Superstars: The Ten Greatest Justices," *Tulsa Law Journal* 31, no. 1 (Fall 1995): 126; Hughes Notes, 291-295, 300-313; Perkins, *Charles Evans Hughes*, 141-144, 147-158, 172-180.

297 consistent enforcer . . . Alabama jury: Perkins, *Charles Evans Hughes*, 163-167, 170; Hughes Notes, 341-342.

297 Most scholars . . . constitutional revolution: Schwartz, "Supreme Court Superstars," 128-131; Kermit L. Hall, "The Warren Court in Historical Perspective," in *The Warren Court: A Retrospective*, ed. Bernard Schwartz (New York: Oxford University Press, 1996), 296.

298 ran a tight ship . . . "did virtually all the speaking": Schwartz, "Supreme Court Superstars," 127.

298 Hughes almost hugged him: Pusey, *Hughes*, 2:757.

298 cordial relations with Roosevelt . . . "a little monotonous!": Hughes Notes, 313.

298 Hughes retired . . . deeply affected: *New York Times*, Aug. 28, 1948.

298 Root drafted the blueprint . . . the greatest disappointment: Leopold, *Root*, 143-144, 161-168, 193; Jessup, 2:418-422, 428-434, 438-444.

299 scornful of Roosevelt's New Deal: Leopold, *Root*, 169; Jessup, 2:475; Jessup conversation with Root, Nov. 9, 1935, Stewart Collection, LOC, box 2, folder "New Deal."

299 "based upon a clear understanding . . . neglected to do": Jessup, 2:505.

299 could not prove . . . no fear of death: Ibid.

300 "a little more daring . . . able to contribute": Leopold, *Root*, 198. See also Jessup, 2:185–186.

300 If Root had a fondest dream . . . the lawbreaker: Jessup, 2:374. For more recent and divergent assessments of Root's legacy, see Charles N. Brower, Anne-Marie Slaughter, Anthony Carty, and Jonathan Zasloff, "Rereading Root," *Proceedings of the Annual Meeting (American Society of International Law)* 100 (2006): 203–216.

300 Guthrie gave a radio address . . . he predicted hordes: *New York State Bar Association Bulletin* 6, no. 4 (April 1934): 179–181; *New York Times*, Jan. 7, Dec. 9, 1935.

300 "William D. Guthrie . . . property relations": Upton Sinclair, *The Goose-Step: A Study of American Education* (Pasadena, CA: published by the author, 1923), 53.

301 warm, personal notes . . . landmark birthdays: Guthrie to Stetson, Apr. 21, 1916, Stetson Papers, Williams College, box 12, folder 16 (seventieth birthday); Guthrie to Root, c. Feb. 15, 1920, Root Papers, LOC, box 138 (seventy-fifth birthday).

301 successfully fought against proposals . . . foreign immigrant lawyers: Robertson, *Brethren and Sisters*, 80–87, 100n16; Martin, *Causes and Conflicts*, 220–223; Abrams, *Cross Purposes*, 114; Auerbach, *Unequal Justice*, 121–123.

301 "ultra-legalistic mind . . . stiff inflexibility": Martin, *Causes and Conflicts*, 220.

301 "man driven . . . tripped him up": Martin, *Causes and Conflicts*, 218.

301 Guthrie challenged an Oregon law . . . right of parents: Abrams, *Cross Purposes*, 98, 117–119; Pierce v. Society of Sisters of the Holy Names of Jesus, 268 U.S. 510 (1925); American Council for Private Education, "75th Anniversary of Pierce v. Society of Sisters," *Cape Outlook* 256 (June 2000): 1–4.

301 "The child is not the mere creature . . . additional obligations": *Pierce*, 268 U.S. at 535.

302 citing *Pierce* . . . same-sex marriage: Griswold v. Connecticut, 381 U.S. 479, 481 (1965); Roe v. Wade, 410 U.S. 113, 153 (1973); Lawrence v. Texas, 539 U.S. 558, 564 (2003); Obergefell v. Hodges, 135 S. Ct. 2584, 2600 (2015).

302 He died of a heart attack . . . Locust Valley Cemetery: *New York Times*, Dec. 9, 10, 1935.

302 Samuel Untermyer . . . auto magnate agreed to settle: *New York Times*, Mar. 17, 1940; Johnston, "Little Giant 1, 2"; Victoria Saker Woeste, *Henry*

Ford's War on Jews and the Legal Battle Against Hate Speech (Palo Alto, CA: Stanford University Press, 2012).

303 critic of Hitler's Nazi regime . . . predicted that Hitler: *New York Times*, Mar. 17, 1940; Richard A. Hawkins, "'Hitler's Bitterest Foe': Samuel Untermyer and the Boycott of Nazi Germany, 1933-1938," *American Jewish History* 93, no. 1 (March 2007): 21-50; *San Francisco Chronicle*, Feb. 14, 1934.

303 "big enemies keep him young": Johnston, "Little Giant 1," 29.

303 many notable friends . . . died in Palm Springs: *New York Times*, Mar. 17, 1940 (quotation); Hawkins, "Samuel Untermyer."

304 "Jewish law firm" . . . disappeared: Wald, "WASP and Jewish Law Firms," 1828-1832, 1852-1860.

304 Untermyer bequeathed: Hellman, "The Boutonnières of Mr. Untermyer," 54-64; "Greystone History," Untermyer Gardens Conservancy, http://www.untermyergardens.org/greystone-history.html.

304 after-dinner speaker: *New York Times*, Jan. 26, 1936. See also Wardwell, *Reminiscences*, 101; Henry W. Taft, *Century and a Half*, 282, 295-297.

304 "was never content . . . row or to steer": Henry W. Taft, *Century and a Half*, 294.

304 American Law Institute . . . Saint John the Divine: Ibid., 291-292, 294; *New York Times*, Jan. 26, 1936.

305 Wickersham was named . . . oversaw her $4,000: *New York Times*, Apr. 20, 1926, Feb. 21, 1933, July 26, 27, 1934, Jan. 13, 1935, Jan. 26, 1936; Gardner, *Cadwalader, Wickersham & Taft*, 17-18.

305 Wickersham Commission . . . more aggressive enforcement: Henry W. Taft, *Century and a Half*, 292-293; Robertson, *Brethren and Sisters*, 88-89; *New York Times*, Jan. 26, 1936; Mark E. Benbow, "The Wickersham Commission: The Wets Gather Support," Rustycans.com, 2017, http://www.rustycans.com/HISTORY/Wickersham.html.

305 Wickersham died . . . Century Club: *New York Times*, Jan. 26, 1936.

306 he was living in Paris . . . Museum of the Legion of Honor: Lisagor & Lipsius, 78-79; *New York Times*, July 20, 1948; Dean, 157; Chris Dickon, *The Foreign Burial of American War Dead: A History* (Jefferson, NC: McFarland, 2011), 78-79 (Lafayette Escadrille); Piel and Moore, *Lamplighters*, 38-39.

306 he objected violently . . . shipped back to New York: Cromwell to J. F. Dulles, Nov. 7, 1924, JFD Papers, Princeton, "William Nelson Cromwell, 1924," box 6, reel 2.

306 New York County Lawyers' Association . . . having survived: Dean, 159; Robertson, *Brethren and Sisters*, 82-87, 152-161, 173.

306 William Nelson Cromwell Foundation: Dean, 159.

306 Jennie Osgood . . . no children: *New York Times*, Mar. 29, 1931, July 20, 1948; Dean, 160; "Jane Osgood 'Jennie' Nichols Cromwell," Find a Grave, Feb. 12, 2016, https://www.findagrave.com/memorial/158085624.

307 **much younger mistress . . . equivocal at best:** Lisagor & Lipsius, 69, 162. The French-born Jane Renard was about nineteen, and Cromwell in his sixties, when she began serving as his secretary in Paris around the time of World War I and supposedly became his mistress. She also was Cromwell's secretary in New York from 1941 to 1948, when she was in her forties and he in his eighties. She never married, and in her wills (one of them French, the other made in New York) she left her estate to her adopted son and to a close female friend. Renard returned to France in 1971 and died there in 1978; in a later battle over the two wills, Sullivan & Cromwell, representing the executors, including Arthur Dean, defeated a challenge by the adopted son. Matter of Renard, 100 Misc.2d 347 (Surr. Ct. N.Y. Co.), *aff'd*, 71 A.D.2d 554 (App. Div. 1st Dep't 1979); Matter of Renard, 108 Misc.2d 31 (Surr. Ct. N.Y. Co. 1981); *aff'd*, 56 N.Y.2d 973 (1982).

    In his own will, disposing of an estate worth $19 million, Cromwell left Jane Renard $35,000, the same amount he left to another secretary. Various other Sullivan & Cromwell employees received small bequests as well. *New York Times*, July 27, 1948. Although the possibility of a closer relationship cannot be dismissed, it appears more likely that Jane Renard was simply a loyal longtime secretary to Cromwell and, like other Sullivan & Cromwell personnel, received a modest bequest in his will in appreciation of her service.

    The author attempted to contact Jane Renard's adopted son, Philip, who was listed as living in California at age eighty in 2017, to see if he might be able to shed light on the relationship. However, his last phone number was no longer in service and a letter to his last known address received no response.

307 **Cromwell died:** *New York Times*, July 20, 22, 1948.

307 **"He was a bright star . . . lawyers of that era":** I. Howard Lehman, in *Addresses, Memory of William Nelson Cromwell*, 7.

307 **estate valued at $19 million . . . Helen Keller:** *New York Times*, July 27, 1948; Dean, 158-162.

307 **"in an age . . . color and vigor":** Dean, 168.

307 **"He saw the need . . . impulses of his time":** J. F. Dulles, foreword to Dean, v.

307 **Dulles was anointed . . . his habit:** Piel and Moore, *Lamplighters*, 68; Seligman, *Reminiscences*, 223; Dean, 42, 75; Lisagor & Lipsius, 101-103, 106-111; Kinzer, *Brothers*, 42, 124.

308 **Dulles arranged billions . . . repudiated its obligations:** Pruessen, *John Foster Dulles*, 61-73, 93-96; 107-115; Piel and Moore, *Lamplighters*, 68; Dean, 74-75; Kinzer, *Overthrow*, 113-114; Kinzer, *Brothers*, 37-38, 41, 51-52; Lisagor & Lipsius, 90-95, 112, 119-123, 131, 134-136.

308 **"Heil Hitler!":** Lisagor & Lipsius, 132.

308 **partners back in New York . . . prevailed upon Foster:** Lisagor & Lipsius, 133-134; Kinzer, *Brothers*, 52-53.

309 Dulles always denied . . . successfully blocked: Pruessen, *John Foster Dulles*, 123-132; Lisagor & Lipsius, 124-127; Kinzer, *Brothers*, 49-51; Albert Norden, *Thus Wars Are Made* (Dresden, GDR: Verlag Zeit im Bild, 1970), 60-63.

309 He continued to visit Berlin: Pruessen, *John Foster Dulles*, 125-126.

309 "taken back her freedom of action": Lisagor & Lipsius, 132, quoting *Atlantic Monthly*, October 1935.

309 admiration for Hitler's rise: Peter Grose, *Gentleman Spy: The Life of Allen Dulles* (Boston: Houghton Mifflin, 1994), 125.

309 warmongers: Mosley, *Dulles*, 111.

309 "only hysteria": Grose, *Gentleman Spy*, 125; Lisagor & Lipsius, 140. See also *New York Times*, Mar. 23, 1939.

309 had his firm draw up . . . money to America First: Lisagor & Lipsius, 137-138; J. F. Dulles to Edwin S. Webster, Feb. 7, 1941, JFD Papers, Princeton, "America First, 1941," box 20, reel 4.

310 not an isolationist . . . memorandum admonishing him: J. F. Dulles to William R. Castle, Nov. 8, 1940, JFD Papers, Princeton, "America First, 1940," box 19, reel 4; Pruessen, *John Foster Dulles*, 182-184; Lisagor & Lipsius, 140-141, 339-340.

310 More than half of them . . . One forty-year-old partner: Lisagor & Lipsius, 141-142, 144-145, 155; *Princeton Alumni Weekly*, April 23, 1974, 13; Viscount Castlerosse, "An Appreciation of Rogers Lamont," from the *Sunday Express* (London), Oct. 27, 1940, JFD Papers, Princeton, "Rogers S. Lamont, 1940," box 19, reel 4.

310 critic of Roosevelt's New Deal . . . more palatable to Wall Street: Lisagor & Lipsius, 113-114, 173-182; Piel and Moore, *Lamplighters*, 99; Dean, 45-46; Dan Ernst, "Felix Frankfurter, Eustace Seligman, and the Securities Act of 1933," Legal History Blog, Dec. 14, 2009, http://legalhistoryblog.blogspot.com/2009/12/felix-frankfurter-eustace-seligman-and.html.

310 "with all your might" . . . created more business: Lisagor & Lipsius, 115-116.

311 drafting the preamble . . . lost a special election: Pruessen, *John Foster Dulles*, 261, 395, 398-403; 432, 436-437, and chapter 17; Piel and Moore, *Lamplighters*, 69; Seligman, *Reminiscences*, 219, 228; Dean, 43-44; 75; Neal Rosendorf, "John Foster Dulles' Nuclear Schizophrenia," in *Cold War Statesmen Confront the Bomb: Nuclear Diplomacy Since 1945*, ed. John Lewis Gaddis et al. (Oxford: Oxford University Press, 1999), 65-85; Kinzer, *Brothers*, 94-95.

311 deep religious convictions: See generally Mark G. Toulouse, *The Transformation of John Foster Dulles: From Prophet of Realism to Priest of Nationalism* (Macon, GA: Mercer University Press, 1985). Another author argues that Dulles's religious faith was more an idealized commitment to the betterment of humankind than a conscious acceptance of a transcendental reality or a belief

in the orthodox tenets of Christianity. Martin Erdmann, *Building the Kingdom of God on Earth: The Churches' Contribution to Marshal Public Support for World Order and Peace, 1919-1945* (Eugene, OR: Wipf and Stock, 2005), 119-122.

311 **his death . . . Arlington National Cemetery:** *New York Times,* May 25, 28, 1959.

311 **his controversial tenure . . . opinions differ:** *New York Times,* May 25, 1959. See generally Kinzer, *Brothers;* Immerman, *Dulles: Piety, Pragmatism;* Michael A. Guhin, *John Foster Dulles: A Statesman and His Times* (New York: Columbia University Press, 1972); Townsend Hoopes, *The Devil and John Foster Dulles* (Boston: Little, Brown, 1973); Piel and Moore, *Lamplighters,* 69; Jason Weixelbaum, "Who Is John Foster Dulles?," Jason Weixelbaum Publications and Research, Jan. 14, 2012, https://jasonweixelbaum.wordpress.com /2012/01/14/who-is-john-foster-dulles. For the fullest exposition of the view that Dulles's actions as secretary of state were largely shaped by his prior work as an international corporate lawyer, see Pruessen, *John Foster Dulles.*

SELECTED BIBLIOGRAPHY

MANUSCRIPT AND ARCHIVE COLLECTIONS

Bunau-Varilla, Philippe. Papers. Library of Congress, Manuscript Division.

Butler, Nicholas Murray. Papers. Columbia University Rare Book and Manuscript Library.

Cravath, Paul D. Office Files. National Archives and Records Administration II, Record Group 56.

Davis, John William. Papers. Yale University Library, Manuscripts and Archives.

——. *Reminiscences, 1954.* Columbia Center for Oral History Archives, Columbia University Rare Book and Manuscript Library.

Dulles, John Foster. Public Policy Papers. Department of Rare Books and Special Collections, Princeton University Library.

Garfield, James Rudolph. Papers. Library of Congress, Manuscript Division.

Kelley, Nicholas. *Reminiscences, 1953.* Columbia Center for Oral History Archives, Columbia University Rare Book and Manuscript Library.

Morgan, J. Pierpont. Papers. Morgan Library and Museum.

Morison, George S. Papers. Smithsonian National Museum of American History.

Morrow, Dwight W. Papers. Amherst College Archives and Special Collections.

Perkins, George W. Papers. Columbia University Rare Book and Manuscript Library.

Roosevelt, Theodore. Papers. Library of Congress, Manuscript Division.

Root, Elihu. Papers. Library of Congress, Manuscript Division.

Seligman, Eustace. *Reminiscences, 1975.* Columbia Center for Oral History Archives, Columbia University Rare Book and Manuscript Library.

Stetson, Francis Lynde. Papers. Williams College Archives and Special Collections.

Stewart, Emily A. Collection of Elihu Root Material. Library of Congress, Manuscript Division.

Taft, William Howard. Papers. Library of Congress, Manuscript Division.

Untermyer, Samuel. Papers. Jacob Rader Marcus Center of the American Jewish Archives.

Villard, Henry. Papers. Baker Library Historical Collections, Harvard Business School.

——. Papers, 1604–1948 (MS Am 1322). Houghton Library, Harvard University.

Wardwell, Allen. Papers. Columbia University Rare Book and Manuscript Library.

——. *Reminiscences, 1952.* Columbia Center for Oral History Archives, Columbia University Rare Book and Manuscript Library.

Wilson, Woodrow. Papers. Library of Congress, Manuscript Division.

BOOKS AND ARTICLES

Abrams, Paula. *Cross Purposes: Pierce v. Society of Sisters and the Struggle over Compulsory Public Education.* Ann Arbor: University of Michigan Press, 2009.

Addresses on the Occasion of a Meeting in Memory of William Nelson Cromwell. New York: Association of the Bar of the City of New York and New York County Lawyers' Association, Jan. 16, 1949.

Adler, Cyrus. *Jacob H. Schiff: His Life and Letters.* Vol. 1. New York: Doubleday, 1928.

Allen, Frederick Lewis. *The Great Pierpont Morgan: A Biography.* New York: Harper, 1949.

———. *The Lords of Creation.* New York: Harper, 1935.

Altman, James M. "Considering the A.B.A.'s 1908 Canons of Ethics." *Fordham Law Review* 71, no. 6 (2003): 2395-2508.

Ameringer, Charles D. "The Panama Canal Lobby of Philippe Bunau-Varilla and William Nelson Cromwell." *American Historical Review* 68, no. 2 (January 1963): 346-363.

Auerbach, Jerold S. *Unequal Justice: Lawyers and Social Change in Modern America.* London: Oxford University Press, 1976.

Ayala, César J. *American Sugar Kingdom: The Plantation Economy of the Spanish Caribbean, 1898-1934.* Chapel Hill: University of North Carolina Press, 1999.

Baker, Richard B., Carola Frydman, and Eric Hilt. "From Plutocracy to Progressivism? The Assassination of President McKinley as a Turning Point in American History." Boston University Working Paper, September 2014.

Barron, Clarence W. *More They Told Barron: Conversations and Revelations of an American Pepys in Wall Street,* edited by Arthur Pound and Samuel Taylor Moore. New York: Harper, 1931.

Beard, Patricia. *After the Ball: Gilded Age Secrets, Boardroom Betrayals, and the Party That Ignited the Great Wall Street Scandal of 1905.* New York: HarperCollins, 2003.

Berg, A. Scott. *Wilson.* New York: Simon & Schuster, 2013.

Bickel, Alexander M., and Benno C. Schmidt Jr. *History of the Supreme Court of the United States.* Vol. 9, *The Judiciary and Responsible Government, 1910-21.* New York: Macmillan, 1984.

Birchall, Frederick T. "William Nelson Cromwell: The Man Who Made the Panama Canal Possible." *Leslie's Monthly Magazine,* May 1904.

Boller, Paul F., Jr. *Presidential Campaigns.* New York: Oxford University Press, 1984.

Bradley, Robert L., Jr. *Edison to Enron: Energy Markets and Political Strategies.* New York: Scrivener/John Wiley, 2011.

Bunau-Varilla, Philippe. *Panama: The Creation, Destruction, and Resurrection.* 1913. Reprint, New York: McBride, Nast, 1914.

Burnett, Philip Mason. *Reparation at the Paris Peace Conference: From the Standpoint of the American Delegation.* 2 vols. New York: Columbia University Press, 1940.

Burrows, Edwin G., and Mike Wallace. *Gotham: A History of New York to 1898.* Oxford: Oxford University Press, 1999.

Burton, David Henry. *Taft, Holmes, and the 1920s Court: An Appraisal*. Madison, NJ: Fairleigh Dickinson University Press, 1998.

——. *Taft, Roosevelt, and the Limits of Friendship*. Madison, NJ: Fairleigh Dickinson University Press, 2005.

Carosso, Vincent P., and Rose C. Carosso. *The Morgans: Private International Bankers, 1854-1913*. Cambridge, MA: Harvard University Press, 1987.

Chandler, Alfred D., Jr. *The Visible Hand: The Managerial Revolution in American Business*. 1977. Reprint, Cambridge, MA: Belknap Press of Harvard University Press, 2002.

Chernow, Ron. *The House of Morgan: An American Banking Dynasty and the Rise of Modern Finance*. New York: Grove Press, 1990.

——. *Titan: The Life of John D. Rockefeller, Sr.* New York: Random House, 1998.

Cravath, Paul D. *Great Britain's Part*. New York: D. Appleton, 1917.

——. "Impressions of the Financial and Industrial Conditions in Germany." *Annals of the American Academy of Political and Social Science* 92 (November 1920): 5-12.

——. *Letters Home from India and Irak 1925*. New York: J. J. Little and Ives, 1925.

Croly, Herbert. *Marcus Alonzo Hanna: His Life and Work*. New York: Macmillan, 1912.

Curtis, William John. *Memoirs of William John Curtis*. Portland, ME: Mosher Press, 1928.

Dalin, David G. *Jewish Justices of the Supreme Court: From Brandeis to Kagan*. Waltham, MA: Brandeis University Press, 2017.

Davis, Mark. *Solicitor General Bullitt: The Life of William Marshall Bullitt*. Louisville, KY: Crescent Hill Books, 2011.

Davis Polk Wardwell Sunderland & Kiendl: A Background with Figures. New York: privately printed, 1965.

Dean, Arthur H. *William Nelson Cromwell 1854-1948: An American Pioneer in Corporation, Comparative and International Law*. New York: Ad Press, 1957.

Divine, Robert A. *Second Chance: The Triumph of Internationalism in America During World War II*. New York: Atheneum, 1967.

Downes, Randolph C. *The Rise of Warren Gamaliel Harding, 1865-1920*. Columbus: Ohio State University Press, 1970.

Eisner, Marc Allen. *Regulatory Politics in Transition*. 1993. Reprint, Baltimore: Johns Hopkins University Press, 2000.

Essig, Mark. *Edison & the Electric Chair: A Story of Life and Death*. New York: Walker Books, 2004.

Freyer, Tony. *Regulating Big Business: Antitrust in Great Britain and America, 1880-1990*. 1992. Reprint, Cambridge: Cambridge University Press, 2008.

Friedland, Martin L. *The Death of Old Man Rice: A True Story of Criminal Justice in America*. New York: NYU Press, 1996.

Friedman, Lawrence M. *A History of American Law*. 3rd ed. New York: Simon & Schuster, 2005.

Galambos, Louis. "The Emerging Organizational Synthesis in Modern American History." *Business History Review* 44, no. 3 (Autumn 1970): 279-290.

Galanter, Marc, and Thomas Palay. "The Transformation of the Big Law Firm." In *Lawyers' Ideals/Lawyers' Practices: Transformations in the American Legal Profession*, edited by Robert L. Nelson, David M. Trubek, and Rayman L. Solomon, 31-62. Ithaca, NY: Cornell University Press, 1992.

Gardner, Deborah S. *Cadwalader, Wickersham & Taft: A Bicentennial History, 1792-1992*. New York: Cadwalader, Wickersham & Taft, 1994.

Garner, James Wilford. "The Northern Securities Case." *Annals of the American Academy of Political and Social Science* 24 (July 1904): 125-147.

Garraty, John A. *Right-Hand Man: The Life of George W. Perkins*. New York: Harper, 1957.

Garrett, Garet. "Things That Were Mellen's and Things That Were Caesar's." *Everybody's Magazine*, July 1914.

Goodier, Susan. *No Votes for Women: The New York State Anti-Suffrage Movement*. Urbana: University of Illinois Press, 2013.

Goodwin, Doris Kearns. *The Bully Pulpit: Theodore Roosevelt, William Howard Taft, and the Golden Age of Journalism*. New York: Simon & Schuster, 2013.

Gordon, Robert W. "'The Ideal and the Actual in the Law': Fantasies and Practices of New York City Lawyers, 1870-1910." In *The New High Priests: Lawyers in Post-Civil War America*, edited by Gerard W. Gawalt, 51-74. Westport, CT: Greenwood Press, 1984.

——. "Legal Thought and Legal Practice in the Age of American Enterprise, 1870-1920." In *Professions and Professional Ideologies in America*, edited by Gerald L. Geison, 70-110. Chapel Hill: University of North Carolina Press, 1983.

Gould, Lewis L. *The First Modern Clash over Federal Power: Wilson Versus Hughes in the Presidential Election of 1916*. Lawrence: University Press of Kansas, 2016.

Grose, Peter. *Gentleman Spy: The Life of Allen Dulles*. Boston: Houghton Mifflin, 1994.

Hagedorn, Ann. *Savage Peace: Hope and Fear in America, 1919*. New York: Simon & Schuster, 2007.

Harwood, Herbert H., Jr. *The New York, Westchester & Boston Railway: J. P. Morgan's Magnificent Mistake*. Bloomington: Indiana University Press, 2008.

Hawkins, Richard A. "'Hitler's Bitterest Foe': Samuel Untermyer and the Boycott of Nazi Germany, 1933-1938." *American Jewish History* 93, no. 1 (March 2007): 21-50.

——. "The 'Jewish Threat' and the Origins of the American Surveillance State: A Case Study of the Untermyer Family." *Australian Journal of Jewish Studies* 24 (2010): 74-115.

——. "The Marketing of Legal Services in the United States, 1855-1912: A Case Study of Guggenheimer, Untermyer & Marshall of New York City and the Predecessor Partnerships." *American Journal of Legal History* 53 (April 2013): 239-264.

——. "Samuel Untermyer (1858-1940)." In Immigrant Entrepreneurship: German-American Business Biographies, 1720 to the Present, vol. 2, edited by William J. Hausman. German Historical Institute. Last modified Nov. 12, 2013. http://www.immigrantentrepreneurship.org/entry.php?rec=181.

Heckscher, August. *Woodrow Wilson*. New York: Scribner, 1991.

Hellman, Geoffrey T. "The Boutonnières of Mr. Untermyer." *New Yorker*, May 18, 1940.

Hendrick, Burton J. "The Battle Against the Sherman Law: How Capital and Labor Combine to Safeguard the Trust and Legalize the Boycott." *McClure's Magazine*, October 1908.

Hessen, Robert. "Charles M. Schwab, President of United States Steel, 1901-1904." *Pennsylvania Magazine of History and Biography* 96 (April 1972): 203-228.

———. *Steel Titan: The Life of Charles M. Schwab*. Pittsburgh: University of Pittsburgh Press, 1975.

Hobson, Wayne K. *The American Legal Profession and the Organizational Society, 1890-1930*. New York: Garland Publishing, 1986.

———. "Symbol of the New Profession: Emergence of the Large Law Firm, 1870-1915." In *The New High Priests: Lawyers in Post-Civil War America*, edited by Gerard W. Gawalt, 3-27. Westport, CT: Greenwood Press, 1984.

Hoffman, Paul. *Lions in the Street: The Inside Story of the Great Wall Street Law Firms*. New York: Saturday Review Press/E. P. Dutton, 1973.

———. *Lions of the Eighties: The Inside Story of the Powerhouse Law Firms*. Garden City, NY: Doubleday, 1982.

Hudson, Peter James. *Bankers and Empire: How Wall Street Colonized the Caribbean*. Chicago: University of Chicago Press, 2017.

Hughes, Charles Evans. *The Autobiographical Notes of Charles Evans Hughes*, edited by David J. Danelski and Joseph S. Tulchin. Cambridge, MA: Harvard University Press, 1973.

Hurst, James Willard. *The Growth of American Law: The Law Makers*. 1950. Reprint, Clark, NJ: Lawbook Exchange, 2004.

Immerman, Richard H. *John Foster Dulles: Piety, Pragmatism, and Power in U.S. Foreign Policy*. Wilmington, DE: Scholarly Resources, 1999.

Jessup, Philip C. *Elihu Root*. 2 vols. New York: Dodd, Mead, 1938.

Johnston, Alva. "Little Giant." 2 parts. *New Yorker*, May 17, 24, 1930.

Jonnes, Jill. *Empires of Light: Edison, Tesla, Westinghouse, and the Race to Electrify the World*. 2003. Reprint, New York: Random House, 2004.

Josephson, Matthew. *The Robber Barons: The Classic Account of the Influential Capitalists Who Transformed America's Future*. 1934. Reprint, San Diego: Harcourt Brace, 2008.

Keller, Morton. *The Life Insurance Enterprise, 1855-1910: A Study in the Limits of Corporate Power*. 1963. Reprint, Lincoln, NE: toExcel Press, 1999.

Kennan, George. *E. H. Harriman: A Biography*. Vol. 2. Boston: Houghton, Mifflin, 1922.

Kinzer, Stephen. *Brothers: John Foster Dulles, Allen Dulles, and Their Secret World War*. New York: Times Books, 2013.

———. *Overthrow: America's Century of Regime Change from Hawaii to Iraq*. 2006. Reprint, New York: Times Books, 2007.

Klein, Maury. *The Life and Legend of E. H. Harriman*. Chapel Hill: University of North Carolina Press, 2000.

———. *The Power Makers: Steam, Electricity, and the Men Who Invented Modern America*. New York: Bloomsbury, 2008.

——. *Union Pacific*. Vol. 2, *1894-1969*. 1989. Reprint, Minneapolis: University of Minnesota Press, 2006.

Knauth, Oswald W. "The Policy of the United States Towards Industrial Monopoly." In *Studies in History, Economics and Public Law* 56, no. 2, edited by the faculty of political science of Columbia University, 1-233. New York: Columbia University, 1914.

Koegel, Otto E. *Walter S. Carter: Collector of Young Masters, or the Progenitor of Many Law Firms*. New York: Round Table Press, 1953.

Kolko, Gabriel. *The Triumph of Conservatism: A Reinterpretation of American History, 1900-1916*. New York: Free Press, 1963.

Leopold, Richard W. *Elihu Root and the Conservative Tradition*, edited by Oscar Handlin. Boston: Little, Brown, 1954.

Levy, Beryl Harold. *Corporation Lawyer . . . Saint or Sinner?: The New Role of the Lawyer in Modern Society*. Philadelphia: Chilton Company, 1961.

Link, Arthur S. *Wilson*. Vol. 1, *The Road to the White House*. 1947. Reprint, Princeton University Press, 2015.

——. *Woodrow Wilson and the Progressive Era: 1910-1917*. New York: Harper, 1954.

——. *Woodrow Wilson: Revolution, War, and Peace*. Arlington Heights, IL: Harlan Davidson, 1979.

Lisagor, Nancy, and Frank Lipsius. *A Law unto Itself: The Untold Story of the Law Firm of Sullivan & Cromwell*. 1988. Reprint, New York: Paragon House, 1989.

Loízillon, Gabriel J. *The Bunau-Varilla Brothers and the Panama Canal*. 2008. Reprint, Panama: Lulu.com, 2016.

Lubben, Stephen J. "Railroad Receiverships and Modern Bankruptcy Theory." *Cornell Law Review* 89, no. 6 (September 2004): 1420-1475.

MacKay, Robert B., Anthony Baker, and Carol A. Traynor, eds. *Long Island Country Houses and Their Architects, 1860-1940*. New York: Society for the Preservation of Long Island Antiquities/W. W. Norton, 1997.

Mackaye, Milton. "Public Man." *New Yorker*, Jan. 2, 1932.

Martin, George Whitney. *Causes and Conflicts: The Centennial History of the Association of the Bar of the City of New York, 1870-1970*. New York: Fordham University Press, 1997.

Mason, Alpheus Thomas. *Brandeis: A Free Man's Life*. New York: Viking, 1956.

Mateyunas, Paul J. *Long Island's Gold Coast*. Charleston, SC: Arcadia, 2012.

McClure, Marc. "Victor Morawetz, Draftsman of Political-Economy: A Study in Constitutional Constraints and Solutions in the Era of Reform." Business and Economic History On-Line, vol. 13, 2015, 1-27. http://www.thebhc.org/sites/default/files/McClure_BEHO_Final%20Draft_0.pdf.

McCullough, David. *The Path Between the Seas: The Creation of the Panama Canal, 1870-1914*. New York: Simon & Schuster, 1977.

Mercer, Lloyd J. *E. H. Harriman: Master Railroader*. 1985. Reprint, Washington, DC: BeardBooks, 2003.

Meyer, Balthasar Henry. "A History of the Northern Securities Case." *Bulletin of the University of Wisconsin* 142 (July 1906): 216-349.

Miller, Tom. "The 1899 Francis Stetson House—No. 4 E. 74th Street." Daytonian in Manhattan: The Stories Behind the Buildings, Statues and Other Points of Interest That Make Manhattan Fascinating. Feb. 28, 2013. http://daytoninmanhattan .blogspot.com/2013/02/the-1899-francis-stetson-house-no-4-e.html.

Miner, Dwight Carroll. *The Fight for the Panama Route: The Story of the Spooner Act and the Hay-Herrán Treaty.* 1940. Reprint, New York: Octagon, 1966.

Mitchell, Lawrence E. *The Speculation Economy: How Finance Triumphed over Industry.* San Francisco: Berrett-Koehler, 2008.

Morris, Edmund. *Theodore Rex.* New York: Random House, 2001.

Mosley, Leonard. *Dulles: A Biography of Eleanor, Allen, and John Foster Dulles and Their Family Network.* New York: Dial Press/James Wade, 1978.

Mowry, George E. *The Era of Theodore Roosevelt: 1900-1912.* New York: Harper, 1958.

Mutch, Robert E. *Buying the Vote: A History of Campaign Finance Reform.* Oxford: Oxford University Press, 2014.

Novak, William J. "The Legal Origins of the Modern American State." In *Looking Back at Law's Century,* edited by Austin Sarat, Bryant Garth, and Robert A. Kagan, 249-283. Ithaca, NY: Cornell University Press, 2002.

Oller, John. *"One Firm": A Short History of Willkie Farr & Gallagher LLP, 1888-.* New York: Willkie Farr & Gallagher LLP, 2004.

Orbach, Barak, and Grace Campbell Rebling. "The Antitrust Curse of Bigness." *Southern California Law Review* 85, no. 3 (March 2012): 605-655.

Paper, Lewis J. *Brandeis: An Intimate Biography of Supreme Court Justice Louis D. Brandeis.* Englewood Cliffs, NJ: Prentice-Hall, 1983.

Perkins, Dexter. *Charles Evans Hughes and American Democratic Statesmanship,* edited by Oscar Handlin. Boston: Little, Brown, 1956.

Piel, William, Jr., and Martha Moore, compilers. *Lamplighters: The Sullivan & Cromwell Lawyers, April 2, 1879, to April 2, 1979.* New York: Sullivan & Cromwell, 1981.

Pringle, Henry F. *Theodore Roosevelt: A Biography.* New York: Harcourt, Brace, 1931.

Prout, Henry G. *A Life of George Westinghouse.* New York: Charles Scribner's, 1922.

Pruessen, Ronald W. *John Foster Dulles: The Road to Power.* New York: Free Press, 1982.

Roberts, Priscilla. "Paul D. Cravath, the First World War, and the Anglophile Internationalist Tradition." *Australian Journal of Politics and History* 51, no. 2 (2005): 194-215.

Robertson, Edwin David. *Brethren and Sisters of the Bar: A Centennial History of the New York County Lawyers' Association.* Bronx, NY: Fordham University Press, 2008.

Roche, John J. "No Par Value Stock." *Marquette Law Review* 7, no. 2 (1923): 76-80.

Roe, Mark J. "Foundations of Corporate Finance: The 1906 Pacification of the Insurance Industry." *Columbia Law Review* 93, no. 3 (April 1993): 651-684.

Roosevelt, Theodore. *The Letters of Theodore Roosevelt,* edited by Elting E. Morison. Vol. 3, *The Square Deal, 1901-1905.* Vol. 6, *The Big Stick, 1905-1909.* Vol. 8, *The Days of Armageddon, 1900-1914.* Cambridge, MA: Harvard University Press, 1951, 1952, 1954.

Root, Elihu. *Addresses on Government and Citizenship,* edited by Robert Bacon and James Brown Scott. Cambridge, MA: Harvard University Press, 1916.

Rosen, Jeffrey. *Louis D. Brandeis: American Prophet*. New Haven, CT: Yale University Press, 2016.

Rousmaniere, John. *Called in to Consultation: The History of an American Law Firm; Davis Polk & Wardwell, 1849-1993*. Stamford, CT: privately printed, 1999.

——. *The Life and Times of the Equitable*. New York: Equitable Companies, 1995.

Roy, William G. *Socializing Capital: The Rise of the Large Industrial Corporation in America*. Princeton, NJ: Princeton University Press, 1997.

Schmitz, David F. *Henry L. Stimson: The First Wise Man*. Wilmington, DE: Scholarly Resources, 2001.

Schwartz, Bernard. "Supreme Court Superstars: The Ten Greatest Justices." *Tulsa Law Journal* 31, no. 1 (Fall 1995): 93-157.

Scott, James Brown. *Robert Bacon: Life and Letters*. 1923. Reprint, Pickle Partners, 2013.

Skeel, David A., Jr. *Debt's Dominion: A History of Bankruptcy Law in America*. Princeton, NJ: Princeton University Press, 2001.

Sklar, Martin J. *The Corporate Reconstruction of American Capitalism, 1890-1916: The Market, the Law, and Politics*. 1988. Reprint, Cambridge: Cambridge University Press, 1993.

Skrabec, Quentin R., Jr. *George Westinghouse: Gentle Genius*. New York: Algora, 2007.

Smigel, Erwin O. *The Wall Street Lawyer: Professional Organization Man?* New York: Free Press of Glencoe, 1964.

Staples, Henry Lee, and Alpheus Thomas Mason. *The Fall of a Railroad Empire: Brandeis and the New Haven Merger Battle*. Syracuse, NY: Syracuse University Press, 1947.

Stetson, Francis Lynde. "The Government and the Corporations." *Atlantic Monthly*, July 1912.

——. "The Lawyer's Livelihood." *Green Bag* 21, no. 2 (February 1909): 45-57.

Stetson, Francis Lynde, James Byrne, Paul D. Cravath, George W. Wickersham, Gilbert H. Montague, George S. Coleman, and William D. Guthrie. *Some Legal Phases of Corporate Financing, Reorganization, and Regulation*. New York: Macmillan, 1917.

Stross, Randall E. *The Wizard of Menlo Park: How Thomas Alva Edison Invented the Modern World*. New York: Crown, 2007.

Strouse, Jean. *Morgan: American Financier*. 1999. Reprint, New York: Random House, 2014.

Sullivan, Mark. *Our Times, 1900-1925*. Vol. 1, *The Turn of the Century*. Vol. 2, *America Finding Itself*. Vol. 3, *Pre-War America*. New York: Charles Scribner's, 1926, 1928, 1930.

Swaine, Robert T. *The Cravath Firm and Its Predecessors, 1819-1947*. 3 vols. 1946-1948. Reprint, Clark, NJ: Lawbook Exchange, 2012.

Taft, Henry W. *A Century and a Half at the New York Bar*. New York: privately printed, 1938.

Taft, William Howard. *Essential Writings and Addresses*, edited with an introduction by David H. Burton. Madison, NJ: Fairleigh Dickinson University Press, 1998.

Taliaferro, John. *All the Great Prizes: The Life of John Hay, from Lincoln to Roosevelt.* New York: Simon & Schuster, 2013.

Urofsky, Melvin I. "Campaign Finance Reform Before 1971." *Albany Government Law Review* 1 (2008): 1–62.

Vanderlip, Frank A. *From Farm Boy to Financier.* In collaboration with Boyden Sparkes. New York: D. Appleton-Century, 1935.

Villard, Henry. *Memoirs of Henry Villard: Journalist and Financier.* Vol. 2, *1835–1900.* Boston: Houghton, Mifflin, 1904.

Wald, Eli. "The Rise and Fall of the WASP and Jewish Law Firms." *Stanford Law Review* 60, no. 6 (April 2008): 1803–1866.

Walker, James Blaine. *Fifty Years of Rapid Transit, 1864–1917.* New York: Law Printing, 1918.

Weigley, Russell F. *History of the United States Army.* 1967. Reprint, Bloomington: Indiana University Press, 1984.

Weixelbaum, Jason. "Harnessing the Growth of Corporate Capitalism: Sullivan & Cromwell and Its Influence on Late Nineteenth-Century American Business." Jason Weixelbaum Publications and Research. Dec. 25, 2010. https://jasonweixelbaum.wordpress.com/2010/12/25/harnessing-the-growth-of-corporate-capitalism-sullivan-cromwell-and-its-influence-on-late-nineteenth-century-american-business/#_ftn7.

——. "Who Is John Foster Dulles?" Jason Weixelbaum Publications and Research. Jan. 14, 2012. https://jasonweixelbaum.wordpress.com/2012/01/14/who-is-john-foster-dulles.

Weller, John L. *The New Haven Railroad: Its Rise and Fall.* New York: Hastings House, 1969.

Wickersham, George W. *The Changing Order: Essays on Government, Monopoly, and Education, Written During a Period of Readjustment.* New York: G. P. Putnam's, 1914.

Wiebe, Robert W. *The Search for Order, 1877–1920.* New York: Macmillan, 1967.

LEGISLATIVE MATERIALS

Bills and Debates in Congress Relating to Trusts, 1902–1913. 57th Cong., 2nd Sess. to 63rd Cong., 1st Sess., Inclusive, Dec. 1, 1902–Dec. 1, 1913. Washington, DC: Government Printing Office, 1914.

Brewing and Liquor Interests and German and Bolshevik Propaganda: Report and Hearings of the Subcommittee on the Judiciary, United States Senate, Submitted Pursuant to S. Res. 307 and 439. S. Doc. No. 62, 66th Cong., 1st Sess. Vols. 2, 3. Washington, DC: Government Printing Office, 1919.

Control of Corporations, Persons, and Firms Engaged in Interstate Commerce: Hearings Before the Committee on Interstate Commerce, United States Senate, 62nd Cong., pursuant to S. Res. 98, November 29, 1911. Washington, DC: Government Printing Office, 1911.

Diplomatic History of the Panama Canal. S. Doc. No. 474, 63rd Cong., 2nd Sess. Washington, DC: Government Printing Office, 1914.

Evidence Taken Before the Interstate Commerce Commission, Relative to the Financial Transactions of the New York, New Haven & Hartford Railroad Company, Together with the Report of the Commission Thereon. S. Doc. No. 543, 63rd Cong., 2nd Sess. 2 vols. Washington, DC: Government Printing Office, 1914.

Hearings Before the Committee on Interoceanic Canals of the United States Senate. Vols. 1, 2. Washington, DC: Government Printing Office, 1906.

Maintenance of a Lobby to Influence Legislation: Hearings Before a Subcommittee of the Committee on the Judiciary, United States Senate, June 13 to July 10, 1913. 63rd Cong., 1st Sess. Vol. 2. Washington, DC: Government Printing Office, 1913.

Money Trust Investigation: Investigation of Financial and Monetary Conditions in the United States Under House Resolutions nos. 429 and 504 Before a Subcommittee of the Committee on Banking and Currency. Parts 15, 21. Washington, DC: Government Printing Office, 1913.

Report of the Committee Appointed Pursuant to House Resolutions 429 and 504 to Investigate the Concentration of Control of Money and Credit. H. R. Rep. No. 1593, 62nd Cong., 3rd Sess. Washington, DC: Government Printing Office, 1913.

Report of the Isthmian Canal Commission, 1899-1901. S. Doc. No. 54, 57th Cong., 1st Sess. Washington, DC: Government Printing Office, 1901.

The Story of Panama: Hearings on the Rainey Resolution Before the Committee on Foreign Affairs of the House of Representatives. Washington, DC: Government Printing Office, 1913.

Testimony Taken Before the Joint Committee of the Senate and Assembly of the State of New York to Investigate and Examine into the Business of Life Insurance Companies Doing Business in the State of New York. Vols. 1, 2, 5, 6. Albany, NY: Brandon Printing, 1905.

ILLUSTRATION CREDITS

Except for the photograph of William Guthrie's Long Island estate on page 8 and the photograph of William Nelson Cromwell with Hellen Keller on page 16, all photos and illustrations are pre-1923 and in the public domain. Further acknowledgments are as follows:

Page 1
Photograph of Paul Cravath, c. 1899, from Robert T. Swaine, *The Cravath Firm and Its Predecessors, 1819–1947*

Illustration of John Feeks from Émile Desbeaux, *Physique Populaire*, 1891; drawing by D. Dumon

Photograph of William Guthrie, c. 1890, from the New York Public Library, Miriam and Ira D. Wallach Division of Art, Prints and Photographs

Page 2
Photograph of Francis Lynde Stetson, 1882, from the McCord Museum, Montreal, No. II-66344

Photograph of J. P. Morgan, 1902, from the Library of Congress

Page 3
Photograph of E. H. Harriman, 1908, from the Library of Congress

Cartoon of E. H. Harriman, 1906, from the Library of Congress

Cartoon of Theodore Roosevelt from Granger, NYC; cartoon by Rushneh, c. 1902

Page 4
Photograph of William Nelson Cromwell, c. 1920, from Alamy Inc.; photo by André Taponier

Photograph of Philippe Bunau-Varilla, c. 1900, from the Library of Congress

Photograph of Nicaragua postage stamp, c. 1902, from Philippe Bunau-Varilla, *Panama: The Creation, Destruction, and Resurrection*

Page 5
Photograph of painting of James Hazen Hyde from the New-York Historical Society; painting by Théobald Chartran, 1901

Photograph of the January 31, 1905, Hyde costume party from the Museum of the City of New York

Page 6
Photograph of front-page headline from the *New York American*, April 5, 1905

Photograph of Charles Evans Hughes, 1912, from the Library of Congress

Photograph of Hughes and his wife, Antoinette, 1916, from the Library of Congress

Page 7

Photograph of Thomas Fortune Ryan, 1910, from the Library of Congress

Photograph of Elihu Root, 1902, from the Library of Congress

Page 8

Photograph of William Howard Taft and Elihu Root, 1904, from the Library of Congress

Photograph of William Guthrie's Long Island estate, c. 1932–1934, from the DeGolyer Library, Southern Methodist University, Robert Yarnall Richie Photograph Collection

Page 9

Photograph of William Guthrie, c. 1910, from the author's collection

Photograph of Cravath's Long Island estate from *Town & Country*, November 30, 1907

Photograph of Cravath and August Belmont Jr., 1912, from the Library of Congress

Page 10

Photograph of the Francis Lynde Stetson home by the author, 2017

Photograph of Francis Lynde Stetson, c. 1910, from the author's collection; photo by Pach Brothers

Page 11

Photograph of George Wickersham, 1908, from the Library of Congress

Photograph of 1911 *Puck* magazine cover from the Library of Congress

Page 12

Photograph of front-page headline from the *New-York Tribune*, May 16, 1911

Photograph of William Hornblower, c. 1900, from Willkie Farr & Gallagher LLP

Page 13

Photograph of Samuel Untermyer, 1915, from the Library of Congress

Photograph of J. P. Morgan with friend, 1907, from the Library of Congress

Page 14

Photograph of David Lamar, 1913, from the Library of Congress

Photograph of Louis Brandeis, 1915, from the Library of Congress

Page 15

New Haven Railroad cartoon from the *New York World*, 1914; cartoon by Rollin Kirby

Photograph of Paul Cravath with others, in Reims, France, in 1917, from the Library of Congress

Page 16

Photograph of William Nelson Cromwell with Helen Keller and M. C. Migel, 1937, courtesy of the American Foundation for the Blind, Helen Keller Archive

Photograph of John Foster Dulles, c. 1919, from the author's collection

INDEX

Printed in the United States
by Baker & Taylor Publisher Services